Trading Environments

This volume examines dynamic interactions between the calculative and speculative practices of commerce and the fruitfulness, variability, materiality, liveliness, and risks of nature. It does so in diverse environments caught up in new trading relationships forged on and through frontiers for agriculture, forestry, and fishing. Historical resource frontiers are understood in terms of commercial knowledge systems organized as projects to transform landscapes and environments. The book asks: How were environments traded and with what environmental and landscape consequences? How have environments been engineered, standardized, and transformed within past trading systems? What have been the successes and failures of economic knowledge in dealing with resource production in complex environments? It considers cases from Northern Europe, North and South America, and New Zealand in the period between 1750 and 1990; and the contributors reflect on the effects of transnational commodity chains, competing economic knowledge systems, environmental ignorance and learning, and resource exploitation. In each case they identify tensions, blind spots, and environmental learning that plagued commercial projects on frontiers.

Gordon M. Winder is Professor of Economic Geography and an Affiliated Professor at the Rachel Carson Center for Environment and Society, LMU-Munich.

Andreas Dix is Professor of Historical Geography, Institute of Geography, Otto-Friedrich-Universität Bamberg.

Routledge Studies in Environment, Culture, and Society

Series editors: Bernhard Glaeser and Heike Egner

This series opens up a forum for advances in environmental studies relating to society and its social, cultural, and economic underpinnings. The underlying assumption guiding this series is that there is an important, and so far little-explored, interaction between societal as well as cultural givens and the ways in which societies both create and respond to environmental issues. As such, this series encourages the exploration of the links between prevalent practices, beliefs, and values, as differentially manifested in diverse societies, and the distinct ways in which those societies confront the environment.

Trading Environments

Frontiers, Commercial Knowledge, and
Environmental Transformation, 1750–1990

**Edited by Gordon M. Winder
and Andreas Dix**

Routledge
Taylor & Francis Group

LONDON AND NEW YORK

First published 2016 by Routledge

2 Park Square, Milton Park, Abingdon, Oxfordshire OX14 4RN

52 Vanderbilt Avenue, New York, NY 10017

Routledge is an imprint of the Taylor & Francis Group, an informa business

First issued in paperback 2020

Library of Congress Cataloging-in-Publication Data
Trading environments : frontiers, commercial knowledge, and environmental
    transformation, 1750–1990 / edited by Gordon M. Winder and Andreas Dix.
        volumes cm. — (Routledge studies in environment, culture, and society ; 4)
    Includes bibliographical references and index.
    1. Commerce—Environmental aspects—History.   2. Natural resources—
Social aspects—History.   3. Land use—History.   4. Environmental
sociology.   5. Cultural geography.   I. Winder, Gordon M.   II. Dix,
Andreas.
    HF497.T73 2016
    333.709'04—dc23   2015027607

ISBN: 978-1-138-93344-6 (hbk)
ISBN: 978-0-367-59750-4 (pbk)

Typeset in Sabon
by Apex CoVantage, LLC

Contents

PART V
Environmental Trading

Figures

Tables

Series Editor Foreword

The book series Routledge Studies in Environment, Culture, and Society offers a forum for advances in environmental studies relating to society and its social, cultural, and economic underpinnings. The underlying assumption guiding this series is that there is an important, and so far little-explored, interaction between societal as well as cultural givens and the ways in which societies both create and respond to environmental issues. As such, this series encourages the exploration of the links between prevalent practices, beliefs, and values, as differentially manifested in diverse societies, and the distinct ways in which those societies confront the environment.

The volume *Trading Environments*, edited by Gordon Winder and Andreas Dix, contributes to these aims in an excellent way. By combining business history with the questions of engineering, standardization, and transformation of landscapes and environments, the editors take an unusual and highly interesting environmental historian perspective. In general, when natural resources are exploited, the activity does not last and the companies pull out, leaving degraded environments in their wake, which are then subject to the analysis of environmental historians. The editors of *Trading Environments* stress that their collection of essays is not intended as a contribution to global environmental history. Instead, they compile studies on different environments affected by new trading relationships forged to and through frontiers. The contributions include case studies from Northern Europe, North and South America, New Zealand, and Japan, covering the period between 1750 and 1990 to examine spatial consequences of the politics of resource extractions in different resource economies with very different development outcomes: They show cases of short-term profits, of sustained growth, and even of (unintended) sustainable development. The editors and authors of this volume focus on two main themes: (a) frontier environments (with very different meanings of the term 'frontier') and (b) an understanding of nature, which perceives nature as 'hybrid socionatures,' acknowledging the social dimensions of nature—that is, its physical reconstitution through societies as well as the internalization of nature into social processes. The contributions show ways in which transnational commodity chains bind distant environments together and try to unearth the history of competing economic knowledge systems, illustrating how environmental learning took place, and revealing which environmental effects the resource exploitation on frontiers brought about.

It is an outstanding collection on an important topic with a fine selection of contributions and authors. We are delighted to include this publication in the series. We wish this volume a wide audience and hope that it will enjoy popularity soon.

Heike Egner (for the series editor)
Klagenfurt, June 2015

Acknowledgments

This volume is the result of a conference held in Munich in 2012. Entitled Trading Environments, the conference was held at and supported by the Rachel Carson Center for Environment and Society at the Ludwig-Maximilians University, Munich. For this support we thank Christof Mauch and Helmut Trischler. We are grateful for the stimulating presentations and discussions, including those of participants whose work is not directly published in this volume. Here we especially thank Corey Ross, Frank Uekötter and Christof Mauch. The Geography Departments at the Otto-Friedrich University of Bamberg and the Ludwig-Maximilians University Munich have supported the publication of this volume. Special thanks must go to Karolina Belza who helped to collate and format the manuscript. We would also like to thank the series editors, Heike Egner and Bernhard Glaeser for their interest in publishing this work and their foreword to the book, and the staff at Routledge for realizing our project. Above all we thank the authors of the chapters in this volume for their cooperation, enthusiasm, and dedication to this collection.

Gordon M. Winder and Andreas Dix
Munich and Bamberg, 2015

Part I

Introduction

Trading Environments

1 Commercial Knowledge and Environmental Transformation on and through Frontiers

Gordon M. Winder and Andreas Dix

Trading environments are the places and environments of trade. To illustrate, once Chicago's commodity exchange moved indoors in the 1870s, traders conducted their sometimes wild and frenzied business in the trading pits of the new Chicago Stock Exchange. There they were surrounded by support workers supplied by telegraph and later by telephone with notices of qualities, quantities, terms, prices, and delivery dates. Like its sister institution in New York, the Exchange was graced by symbols of bounteous harvests, honest toil, resource wealth, and human ingenuity (Figure 1.1).[1] The trading that occurred in these pits was distanced from the environments where timber was felled, iron and copper ore were mined, hogs were raised, or wheat and corn were harvested but was made possible by the communications infrastructure supplying letters, telegrams, newspapers, and telephone calls that linked them together. The Chicago Stock Exchange was a heavily coded place and therefore a classic example of an environment for trade, but even there trading was never completely separated from nature. This was exemplified by the reactions among brokers to news of hail or snow damage to crops in distant Nebraska. It was signified by the bear or bull, icons of the trading activities in these pits, and by the sculpture of Ceres, goddess of the harvest, that the traders passed each day. The traders understood many environments albeit through the distorted and rescaled lenses of their own calculative and imaginative practices. As they conducted their business, the markets that they framed and performed shaped the environments that were being conformed to the markets. Thus, to paraphrase economic geographers Christian Berndt and Marc Boeckler, their 'model of the world became the world of the model,' and their 'commercial knowledge of the environment became the environment of their commerce.'[2] But the wheat futures market, the prices and quantities traded, and the market's 'performance' remained outcomes of a complex trading environment.

The calculations of Chicago's wheat futures traders hinged upon knowledge of not only news of harvest gleanings but also of the stores of grain in elevators and mills, knowledge of the new standards and classes of grain products, and of prices in both grain production regions and grain markets. As the monoculture wheat crop spread out over the Great Plains and

Figure 1.1 **Facade of the New York Stock Exchange, 11 Wall Street, New York, USA.** Opened in 1903, the Exchange building features in its pediment sculptured figures designed by John Quincy Adams Ward. Entitled "Integrity Protecting the Works of Man" the group has 'Agriculture' and 'Mining' to one side of the winged figure of 'Integrity' and 'Science,' 'Industry' and 'Innovation' on the other.

Source: Gordon M. Winder, 2012.

Prairies, grain elevators lined the railroad tracks linking farm production environments with urban grain mills, portside elevators, and distant urban markets. Wheat farmers were empowered by this market-making infrastructure. The elevators and mills, erected by such 'grain barons' as Isaac

Friedlander, California's 'grain king,' or William W. Cargill and Frank H. Peavey who treated "the whole Midwest" as "a vast Monopoly board," buffered between markets and harvests.[3] Yet to become an international grain trader, even in the early 1900s, "it was not necessary to have huge amounts of capital, big grain depots, ships, and thousands of employees."[4] No, according to Dan Morgan, one needed only enough credit to cover margins and storage costs, a telephone, personal connections, and expertise, plus "charm, good instincts, luck, and audacity—the qualities of the gambler, salesman, and entrepreneur rolled into one."[5] When they made a market 'corner' or were lucky, traders and grain monopolists could extract spectacular profits, and this enraged wheat farmers, with one Granger newspaper of the 1870s railing against them: "Take the robber corporations and shake them all to Hell."[6] In fact, as Morgan argued, Americans had "no control over the price of wheat in the towns along the Mississippi River, or in Chicago" because wheat prices "were established in Liverpool, Buenos Aires, Karachi, Odessa, Antwerp, and Marseilles, not just in Chicago and New York."[7] As this vignette exemplifies, it turned out that the environments of trade comprised networks of production environments, trading environments, and consumption environments and that these networks had their own geography, history, and time space. They constituted a complicated trading environment, which was, in various ways, abstracted from the natural environments that framed them.

Thus *Trading Environments* moves beyond the idea of 'markets' to address the question how were environments traded and with what consequences? It focuses on the environmental and landscape consequences of trading networks and their associated practices and interdependencies. Particular attention is paid to spatial aspects of resource extraction and to the effects of environments on commercial practices. How have environments been engineered, standardized, and transformed within past trading systems? What have been the successes and failures of economic knowledge in dealing with resource production in complex environments? Environmental history has reasserted 'environment' into the histories of social and economic change, and, as part of this broad project, *Trading Environments* takes up the task of exploring a series of historical projects in order to identify and analyse the slippages, (mis)understandings, problems, and (mis)calculations inherent in the work of remaking environments. Where recent work in business history places the economic enterprises, business networks, entrepreneurs, or regional economies at the center of analysis, *Trading Environments* gives center stage to environments, to environmental knowledge, and to representations of nature in the business of making commodities and exploiting resources, especially when these are out of step with environments and nature. It therefore explores dynamic interactions between the calculative and speculative practices of commerce and the fruitfulness, variability, materiality, liveliness, and risks of nature.

This collection of essays is not intended as a contribution to global environmental history. Instead, the book's authors consider diverse environments caught up in new trading relationships forged on and through frontiers. The chapters deal with cases from northern Europe, North and South America, New Zealand, and the Pacific in the period between 1750 and 1990. They touch on agriculture, forestry, and fishing. The authors consider the ways in which transnational commodity chains bound distant environments together and reflect on the history of competing economic knowledge systems, on environmental learning, and on the environmental effects of resource exploitation on frontiers. In each case, they identify tensions, blind spots, and learning that plagued commercial and government frontier projects. This is achieved by focusing on two main themes and their interactions: frontiers and disconnections between first and second nature. 'Trading environments,' the places where environments are traded as well as the environments traded off against each other, serves as a shared framework and metaphor. 'Frontier,' referring to spatial, temporal, and economic projects, around which actors and environmental and economic outcomes assembled, is used to link the diverse case studies together. Each of these terms is introduced and discussed before the book's subsequent chapters are outlined.

TRADING ENVIRONMENTS

Historically, trading has been conducted both close to and far away from the sites of production or consumption, sometimes under strict regulations at other times under loose constraints, and with production environments included in some way or another in the transactions. Whether purchasing milk fresh from the cows stalled at the urban dairy or beer from the brewer across the street, some city dwellers made their purchases at the site of production and from a seller aware of the conditions and nature of production. Other urbanites purchased packaged goods assembled along long commodity chains with only graphic illustrations on the packaging to portray the idealized production or consumption environments.[8] In contrast, Christopher Kremmer found that the Kabul carpet merchant he met could not only hear the knots as he ran his thumbnail over the ridged back of the carpet, but he could establish the provenance of it by searching for it in its structure.[9] Note that the gulf in understanding between the connoisseur and the neophyte wine consumer may have diminished as they collected signs of quality, taste, and price from tasting sessions, recommendations, wine atlases, or signs on the bottles, but they may still have wondered about what was not revealed in these advertisements. Such transactions involved buyers or sellers who made calculations on supply, inventory, work, outgoings, and purchase price. Each also involved understandings and misunderstandings of impacts on environments whether local or distant, visible, or represented.

Trading environments bind commercial and environmental knowledge together. They are not only environments for trading, but they are also the environments that are traded. Indeed, trading environments require knowledge and practices such as normalized quality standards or certification that help to coordinate the commodity chain from the site of production and its environment, through numerous other environments associated with other links of the chain to the site of consumption and its environments, including imaginaries of the environments of production and consumption. These aspects of the metaphor are inspired by Actor Network Theory (ANT), which not only helps to make sense of science, its places of generation, centers of calculation, laboratories, field sites, immutable mobiles, networks, applications, and transferability but also business.[10] Thus a trading environment such as the Chicago Stock Exchange can be understood as a node in a network, and in this node immutable mobiles—grain futures contracts, quality standards, weather indicators, news—are brought together in a way that facilitates grain trade. Business is built upon sets of calculative practices that facilitate network building and functioning. This is perhaps most readily apparent in Bruno Latour's interpretation of pasteurization, where a finding in a laboratory facilitated the generation of a network that penetrated, organized, and regulated diverse environments and businesses; but Timothy Mitchell's *Colonizing Egypt* and Richard White's *Railroaded* also serve as inspiration for *Trading Environments*.[11]

Market, warehouse, and corporation are additional 'trading environments' where second natures are produced and networked, and there are many more places besides those already mentioned where environments are traded. These include the officers' cabins of ships trading on account, auction houses, as well as warehouses and retail shops. In these trading environments, commercial knowledge tends to dominate; but other rules and considerations mark out, for example, trade at fairs and exhibitions, where imagined environments of production and worlds of consumption are assembled and traded using displays, trade catalogues, tests, and competitions. In his Customs House, the customs officer calculates and levies the government's tariff and perhaps consigns some passengers and cargoes to the quarantine station as health and safety regulations are enforced. In the government's cabinet rooms, commercial knowledge and interests are weighed against other priorities, including defense, security and imperial expansion, national interests and treaty obligations, property rights, and ideas about nature. As NGOs, societies, trades unions, and lobby groups gathered in their halls to clamor and press for reforms or responses to new experiences of natural abundance or disaster, commercial knowledge was contested. All of these places are considered to be 'trading environments' in this volume.

Nature was traded in such places. In his effort to explicate Chicago's role as *Nature's Metropolis*, William Cronon sketched in both a dichotomy between first and second nature and a transformative geography of landscapes and environments associated with investment in second nature. He tended to conflate first nature with indigenous landscapes but was clearly self-aware. He warned that "Second nature, no less than nature itself, is necessarily an abstraction."[12] In his later work, Cronon elaborated this idea.[13] In an effort to remember that nature and environment are in states of transformation and therefore comprise tentative, evolving, disappearing, and hybrid forms, *Trading Environments* dispenses with first and second nature and instead refers to 'natures.' In this way it also builds upon the insights of Noel Castree and Bruce Braun's edited volume *Social Nature*.[14] They argue that societies physically reconstitute nature and at the same time internalize nature into social processes. Thus knowledge of nature reflects the biases of the knowers, while nature has more social dimensions than simply knowledge. This finding conforms to the idea of hybrid 'socio-natures,' and it is with various forms of these that *Trading Environments* works.

Cronon was largely interested in the effects of "new systems of value" that "determined the fate of entire ecosystems," or the ways in which "differential pricing of species produced dramatic shifts in far-flung regional landscapes."[15] While the effects simplified local ecosystems through the intensification and spread of monocultures, they also were explicitly framed as producing new geographies. He wrote of a "new market geography" envisaged in terms of the rings of land use around a market center modeled by Heinrich von Thünen in his *Isolated State*: "the economic imperatives of second nature—distance from the city, cost of transportation, supply and demand, price—played an ever more important role in determining the shape of the landscape."[16] These economic imperatives worked to separate production from consumption so that everything came together in Chicago: "The merging of first and second nature was thus a shift from local ecosystem to regional hinterland and global economy."[17]

Cronon's conceptualization has drawn critical reaction in that a number of prominent environmental historians have focused on the impossibility of separating nature and technology.[18] However, this leaves intact the problem of representation: How were nature and technology represented and with what effects? Representation is a special aspect of second nature. For example, landscape painting constituted an elite system of representation and one that commodified and celebrated social values and cultural ideals such as property, wealth, and class as well as related gender, race, and 'civilization' identities.[19] In such a representational system, commercial and noncommercial aspects of environments and natures were consolidated.

Various economic actors have legitimized landscape transformation using idealized environments portrayed in warehouses, bourses, fairs, advertisements, and trade catalogues. Fictive landscapes were generated by commercial interests to sell their products (Figure 1.2), so that trading systems developed their own landscape iconography and mobilized consumers and investors through ideals of frontier transformation and through reference to modernization discourses. The cornerstone of this development was the advent of a systematizing approach in the new natural sciences such as geology or botany. Scientists like Carl von Linné (1707–1778) established

Figure 1.2   **Signifying wine qualities.** Wine labels, such as these from vineyards near St. Emilion, Bordeaux, often use the images of an idealized, named wine region landscape along with other legitimating signifiers to communicate claims about wine quality, price, and class. The production and consumption environments are in this case entangled, for example, through wine tourism.

Source: Gordon M. Winder, 2015.

influential and successful typologies of natural organisms.[20] Within the development of these sciences, nature became known through a symbolic warehouse, where plants and animals, in all their single parts, were systematically stored according to their specific usability. The collection and publication of this knowledge itself started to be a big business within an exploding number of encyclopedias and encyclopedia projects.[21] Museums of natural history, zoological, and botanical gardens served as institutions for academic education and research, as vehicles for popularizing knowledge of nature among a wider audience, and as influences on the production of new commodities (Figure 1.3). Their qualities were matters of cultural production and consumption and that implied that entrepreneurs and innovators, taste makers and fashion setters could make new goods and new markets and establish consumption frontiers.[22]

'Trading environments' therefore carry a considerable weight of potential meanings in this volume. They can be places of sale, negotiation, planning, warehousing, display, or advertising—that is, they are environments for trade. They can be styles and processes of environmental transformation—that is, the environments that are traded. And each of these trading environments is assembled using images, prices, numbers, weights, certificates of quality and provenance, labels, and contracts. It is this nexus of possible roles and interactions and their meanings that the authors of this volume seek to explore.

Figure 1.3   **The Palm House, Royal Botanic Gardens, Kew, London, Great Britain.** Laid out between 1841 and 1849, the gardens constitute a fine example of a trading environment because of the entanglement of collection, display, science, and plant trading that they enabled.

Source: Andreas Dix, 2013.

FRONTIER AND COMMERCIAL KNOWLEDGE

Trading Environments develops 'frontiers' as an organizing framework for investigating interactions among commercial knowledge and environmental transformation. It explores frontiers and their environmental and commercial dynamics. This volume shows how some new frontiers were established, how 'valueless' and 'pristine' nature was investigated and separated into tradable pieces and goods, and how environments were revalued to create new frontiers for exploitation and transformation. In these circumstances, trade had effects on energy exchanges, biodiversity, environmental services, and natural processes, and it stimulated landscape transformation.

There are diverse strands to the literature on settlement frontiers, including the debates stimulated by Frederick Jackson Turner's proposition that US culture and society was made on the frontier or by the atomization thesis that emerged in the 1990s or as framed in environmental and gender terms within the New Environmental History. Alternatively, 'frontier' could be bound up in the more geographically interactive metropolitan-hinterland frameworks once proposed by the Canadians Harold Innis and James Careless or more recent scholars.[23] But all of these literatures assume that 'frontier' refers to a settlement frontier when 'frontier' has many other connotations and related literatures. There are resource frontiers with their projected resource economies, mining frontiers, fishery frontiers, cultivation or agricultural frontiers, urban frontiers or futures, and frontiers of technology, science, or knowledge including engineers' Cold War 'big solutions' or megaprojects, a digital frontier or outer space as a frontier. Today, business consultants write of a 'sustainability frontier', while scientists write of making the 'great transformation' so that society operates on a sustainable basis.[24] Each of these terms implies not only a spatial or settlement frontier but also an investment frontier. Investment should be directed toward internal and social targets, toward projects promoting labor, energy and material efficiency, waste saving, recycling and reuse, and reductions in harmful environmental effects. To some extent, the 'sustainability frontier' aims to develop sustainability and resilience through forms of autarky, even though such an approach clashes with the expectations and realities of a globalizing world.[25] Such 'frontiers' involve revaluing environments and projects to transform them. There are therefore many different types of frontiers, each of which has its own discourses, power relations, materialities, key actors, and calculative practices.

At its core, however, 'frontier' has four main attributes. 'Frontier' implies *newness*. That is, it is an empty, fresh, unfixed, unexplored space ready for calculation and opportunity, often associated with 'liberty' or, more precisely, different or relaxed rules. It is therefore a 'wild' place. At its worst it is a declaration by a powerful actor that some land constitutes a *terra nullius* with devastating implications for its inhabitants, fauna, flora, water, and soil. The 'frontier' is also a *margin*. It is a border, barrier, or zone, one that lies at the edge (of civilization or cultivation) or beyond it, and it is therefore marginal in the sense of being uncertain, unknown, risky, hazardous or suboptimal. It can also be positively interpreted as the opportunity for profit or efficiency from a new technology or activity: the investor's margin. A 'frontier' has an implied *unruly dynamic*. Frontiers are opened and closed, and they suffer cycles of boom, bust, and abandonment as they are worked over, transformed, or enrolled in civilizing projects. Finally, 'frontier' implies a *perspective*. It is a view from a center or core and involves a projection of values and identities onto a distant place, time, technology, or zone. It is therefore a term loaded with power asymmetries in unequal social and material relations. It is a term associated with diverse cultures of managing people, resources, and environments and various practices of storytelling associated with attempts at (de)legitimation. This last is important, since each of the resource frontiers studied here was embedded in formal or informal colonial power relations. Attention is therefore given to Cole Harris's outline of a critically informed historical geography of colonialism and to subsequent work on the roles of calculative practices in colonization.[26] But other literatures—such as those on contemporary land grabbing or accumulation by dispossession—could be equally relevant since they too engage with changing power relations.[27]

The commodification of nature was backed through the early stages of globalization, the colonial founding of many neo-European areas, colonization, and the new way of Physiocratic, economic thinking at the end of the eighteenth century, which, in many ways, mobilized the exploitation of nature all over the world as part of rationalizing projects. These literatures are marshaled to the tasks of theorizing 'frontiers' as a framework for understanding the linking of commercial projects and environments. The notion of changing frontiers is closely linked to the questions of core and periphery, of centers of commercial activities with their marketplaces for commodities and information, and the rather different circumstances for production, information, and environmental transformation in the marginal regions of the periphery.[28] Further, more or less, all of the case studies in this volume deal with capitalist economies, but 'capitalism' is not conceived of here in a narrow sense. Rather, capitalism is understood as referring to a broad variety of economic styles, each of which is culturally embedded. Various books written on this theme give fascinating insights into the plurality of economic worlds.[29]

In turn, this framework will help to answer the book's central question: What can we learn about environmental transformations, knowledge frontiers, and environmental learning by investigating the ways investors equipped with new forms of commercial exploitation, governments planning for commercial-imperial imperatives, and scientists working to improve limited environmental knowledge, encountered and revalued environments?

As international trade expanded during first the nineteenth and then the twentieth century, reference to diverse frontiers coordinated and coded commercial knowledge and environmental transformation. In particular, governments and companies assembled people, military, and capital around settlement, mining, forest, fishery, and agricultural frontiers so as to push through processes of exploration, conquest, land alienation, migration, colonization, settlement, and cultivation. Numerous and diverse institutions emerged to provide and interpret the commercial knowledge that enabled environments to be traded. The relations between natures, or between commerce and environment, are, in these and other ways, complicated.[30] This complexity has given rise to an array of concepts—including commodity chain, global production network, resource economy, and staples theory—each primarily focused on issues of political economy rather than environment but each offering rich insights for understanding interactions between commercial knowledge and environments.[31]

Throughout the 'long nineteenth century,' nature and natural resources were a major focus, as the emerging fields of natural sciences such as botany, geography, geology, and zoology more and more interpreted nature as a warehouse of natural goods.[32] Scientific expertise was used to exploit nature more effectively for economic purposes. The diverse ideas and ideologies of frontiers were linked to the search for natural resources and harnessed to colonial land markets. Colonial and mercantile power came to bear on diverse environments as these were articulated with markets and trade networks to produce new ecologies of trade between frontier and center.

The establishment of new frontiers had environmental effects. Once environments are articulated with markets or trade networks, the ecologies of trade that emerge develop their own dynamics. As we have already seen, environmental historian William Cronon argued that the very economic devices used to cope with natural diversity and variability produce a second nature whose distributions and rhythms are increasingly dictated by the needs of capital, and this is now a leitmotif in environmental history.[33] Further, efforts to manage exploitation for investors may meet with resistance and opposition as contending moral economies collide. Often when natural resources are exploited the activity does not last and the companies pull out leaving degraded environments in their wake. These issues have been taken up in North America, as environmental historians reconsider the role of environment in history.[34] They are aware of the many contending interpretive frameworks, including the 'Dutch disease,' the resource curse, the tragedies of the resource cycle or the staples trap, for diagnosing and understanding the economic problems that emerged as colonists, boosters, and tycoons swarmed over the country and now concentrate on the environmental transformations that emerged with these economic problems.[35] The authors of *Trading Environments* consider the politics of resource extraction in different resource economies as various actors worked to achieve what might later be called short-term profits as opposed to sustained growth or even sustainable development. They examine how the restructuring of trading networks generated new material exchanges and environmental relations with winners and losers, and they explicitly relate such economic interpretations of resource frontiers to environmental outcomes.

Trading Environments acknowledges that missing links have emerged between business history and environmental change and that new links need to be forged.[36] It seeks both to develop terms and concepts from business history, political economy, and geography within environmental history and to reassert environment and nature within these other disciplines. Recent work in environmental history investigates commercial empires and their environmental impacts, but generally a focus on economic and business institutions is rare.[37] The general trend is to write of imperialism, biological invasions, energy security, cultural imaginaries, or technology as the principal frameworks for conceptualizing human processes impacting on nature. For example, Richards's *The Unending Frontier* identifies settlement frontiers, biological invasions, commercial hunting of wildlife, and problems of energy security as the principal vectors for human-nature interactions in the Early Modern World.[38] In this way, ecological metaphors and processes tend to predominate in this literature, although this is not always the case. There are other scholars, such as Jason Moore, who are interpreting such Early Modern energetic and biological integration through the lenses of trade, investment, commerce, and imperialism.[39]

In contrast, neither 'environment' nor 'frontier' is a favored category in business history. For example, business practices, territorial expansion, and imperialism are more prominent in one recent history of mining tycoons than environment.[40] 'Frontier' is also not so prominent in these literatures. Environmental historians with history of science and technology interests, such as David Nye, or with geography interests, such as William Cronon or Gray Brechin, are much more likely to make connections between environment and business.[41] Even Michael Redclift's book *Frontier* defines the organizing concept broadly as boundaries, areas of settlement and commercial production, and cultural imaginaries.[42] Redclift conceptualizes market forces as bringing modernity to displaced people, an approach which is largely in step with that used in *Trading Environments*; however, this volume seeks to conceive of 'frontiers' in terms of modernizing commercial projects backed by cultural imaginaries and scientific, technical, and political calculations that are set to work in environments.

It is to be expected that the heroic tale of how economists and businessmen overcame the deficiencies of nature and thus reshaped the world through trade and better market management dominates the environmental attention of business and economic historians. After all, by promoting efficient markets and trade, economists have helped to increase resource availability for many, thus apparently erasing environmental and geographic differences.[43] But such a perspective cannot stand alone: trade and efficient markets must be related to the roles of economists, businesses, and states in legitimating and rationalizing, funding, organizing and promoting, regulating and policing diverse frontiers or projects, and to the environmental problems that they helped to produce. Further, the commercial knowledge that enables trade is not transparent or easily knowable. Quality and price, demand and supply, earnings ratio, and so on are artifacts of the private networks of business and so are only partly knowable to the public and then often through advertising. As environments and frontiers are commodified and marketized as various forms of property, public knowledge and commercial knowledge of the transactions involved are not the same but are the basis for unequal power. Further, the value frames used in these trades are never simply economic but also political, cultural, and social so that the efficacy of 'efficient markets' must be questioned from the start. Reconstructing the trading that takes place in trading environments and its implications is therefore a priority in political economy approaches, such as commodity chain research. The intent of the 'trading environments' metaphor is to focus attention on the reconstruction and interpretation of how environments are traded within the settings of the value frames at work in such trades.

The chapters in *Trading Environments* draw upon theorizations of business networks and their development under earlier forms of globalization, since innovations in institutional structure and business organization set important constraints on how environments can be traded and with what results.[44] Merchant adventuring, in which individual merchants sought to profit from one-time-only purchases and resales as they connected distant markets, involved an opportunistic approach to both markets and environments. In contrast, the plan spaces and capital resources of the giant corporation, not to mention the modern nation state, enabled systematic coordination of environments, production, and markets. Given the growing size and market power of multinational corporations during the period covered by this volume, such plan systems had dramatic environmental effects and constitute a significant component of the environmental transformations now attributed to the Anthropocene.[45] However, the authors of *Trading Environments* necessarily wrestle with diverse institutions, ranging from large corporate entities, through small- and medium-sized enterprises, government and nongovernment organizations, lobby groups, and state agencies to social institutions. As business historians come to terms with the business practices of what Naomi Lamoreaux and others call 'long-term relations,' as well as 'markets' and 'hierarchies,' the prospects for an expanded repertoire of business practices useful in environmental history will improve.[46] Loosely networked and coordinated webs of enterprise, articulated through such network organization as subcontracts, agencies, licenses, strategic alliances, joint ventures, agency management services, systematic buying, joint purse and leasing arrangements, and cartels facilitated coordination and control without direct ownership.[47] Such flexible organizational arrangements made sense in the context of imperial rivalries and nation state formation, but their environmental effects are underresearched. Government policies were crucial to the success or otherwise of such 'long-term relations' and *Trading*

Environments engages with these forms of business organization through the articulation of actors around frontiers. In this way, the volume develops links between business history and enviromental change.[48]

Political economists have tended to focus on regional economic performance and feature scholarship divided between pessimists and optimists on the question of escape from metropolitan control and exploitation through development of a diversified economy. In other words, the political economy and geography literatures focused on debate over whether expectations that rounded development through industrialization and urbanization would be followed through everywhere were realistic. The answer among geographers is unanimous: inequality, spatially differentiated, will persist. For example, within Canadian geography, a regional geography textbook inspired a generation of students with a heady mix of essays on industrialization and deindustrialization, metropolitan growth and stagnation, and shifting relations between Canada's regions and the competing metropoles London, New York, Montreal, and Toronto and politics of dependence and protest in the nation's resource hinterlands.[49] In this framework of centers and regions, heartlands and hinterlands 'frontiers' took on multiple, albeit conventional, meanings within changing geographies of regions. Subsequently, Canadian economic geographers propose 'resource economy' as an appropriate framework for analysis and theorizing.[50] This means an emphasis upon social and economic processes at work in diverse environments, but it is only recently that economic geographers have begun to propose a new 'environmental economic geography' that considers environmental and economic processes together.[51]

In fact, environment plays a disturbing dual role in these accounts: either as source of comparative (dis)advantage or as an object for transformation, with improved environments seen as necessary, logical, rational, and efficient outcomes of development. The effect is to privilege an economic and social geography over an environmental geography. There tends to be fewer discussions of degraded or improved environments than there are of degraded or improved social and economic landscapes. Built into some of the literature is the idea that wild or natural environments are not efficient enough in economic terms. This was clearly articulated by geographer Alex Clapp through his account of the resource cycle in forestry and fishing: He demonstrated that, according to economic logic, it is inevitable that wild resources will be devastated by commercial exploitation and perhaps eventually transformed into cultivated resources through agriculture, silviculture, or aquaculture.[52] In contrast, work in resource economics has tended to emphasize the resource curse: the debilitating effects on an economy from the emergence of one, resource-based sector with much higher economic rents than others.

In contrast, while environmental history parallels these themes, instead of focusing on economies, it highlights the outrageous attempts to build 'improved environments' to support expanded, apparently more 'efficient' production systems. Gail Hollander's *Raising Cane in the Glades* directly relates environmental transformation in Florida to the commercial and political calculations of the global sugar trade.[53] Where William Cronon developed the theme of symbiosis between Chicago and its hinterland, in *Imperial San Francisco*, Gray Brechin accentuated the "earthly ruin" that went with San Francisco's rise to metropolis.[54] Thus tensions have emerged between economic and environmental history over the environmental outcomes of commercial calculations: catastrophic or positive environmental effects?

There is much to learn from focusing on environments and environmental processes since this seriously complicates socioeconomic stories in several ways. First, nature involves risks, hazards, vulnerabilities, and opportunities. Environments have materiality and variability, not only in terms of regularity—as with the seasons following one another—but also in terms of liveliness and a lack of orderliness or reliability: Environments may frustrate economic expectations and clash with economic rationalities.[55] Indeed, environmental learning is crucial for effective economic systems as writers such as Richard H. Grove or Peter Holland have demonstrated in different contexts.[56] Second, ecosystem, watershed, and other units of 'environment' are not necessarily the same as those of the economy, they are thought of as having different sets of actors and processes, nor do they operate at the same scale. In many ways, environment and economy are at best only partially interrelated systems. Third, humans tend to modify environments by mixing components of different ecosystems, as seen, most famously in the Columbian Exchange, or by producing hybrid natures, such as feedlots or reworked coastal marshlands, such as the Everglades.[57] Such modified environments are controversial, not least because of the externality effects and issues of sustainability that envelope them. Finally, as the forbidden regions of the nuclear wastelands of Hanford, Chernobyl, or Fuskushima illustrate, it is the first time in history that nature can be 'destroyed' in such a radical way. The dimensions of such environmental hazards, whether conceived in terms of the longevity of the problems or the (spatial) scale of the damage, raise new questions regarding both 'sustainability' and the ecological footprint of our level of energy and material consumption.[58]

It is not just that the economy helps us to cope with unreliable nature through the provision of insurance, storage of reserves for times of dearth, or providing trade opportunities. Nor is it simply that environment is modifiable in order to promote economy through investments, mechanization, and innovation in production systems. In the Anthropocene it is readily apparent that markets and innovations make and unmake environments and that they can build resilience as well as increase vulnerability, but, in addition, it is also true that natural processes and environments act on and through economic systems. Perhaps this last will become even more apparent as climate change impacts upon our economies.

TRADING ENVIRONMENTS ON AND THROUGH FRONTIERS

The subsequent sections of *Trading Environments* each highlight a particular theme. The chapters in 'Frontier Environments' address environmental transformations at the edges of empire, whether geopolitical, technological, or commercial or in the metropolitan center's hinterland. In each case what is stressed is the asymmetric signaling between resource periphery and commercial metropolis. While knowledge of frontier environments and the environmental effects of integration in trading networks were often weak, the proximate hinterlands of some centers were dramatically transformed through combinations of changing consumer culture and energy systems that produced new natures. The constraints on and opportunities for commerce thrown up as commercial actors encountering environments a fresh are explored through contrasting examples, and the environmental impacts that accompanied them are here understood as either effects at the spatial margins of expanding commercial empires or as concomitant transformations near the imperial and commercial center resulting from new wealth, consumer culture, and energy availability.

Drawing on a range of examples, including viticulture and the trade in wine, Andreas Dix discusses the impact of consumer behavior, consumer needs, and consumer culture on the environment, a relatively neglected theme in environmental history.[59] When combined with the availability of new energy supplies, these forces transformed the European countryside (Figure 1.4). The chapter highlights the effects distant resource frontiers impacted on the local countrysides of metropolitan centers, making internal frontiers and, effectively, 'globalizing' the Central European countryside, in that this landscape was now increasingly interdependent with distant landscapes.

Stephen Bell discusses the making and exploiting of commercial frontiers and the intersections between merchant adventuring, natural resources, and science using three case studies of Northwest European mercantile enterprise in South America. These cases illustrate the roles of commercial intelligence, risk, political alliances, increasing capitalization, and different forms of environmental knowledge and ignorance in geographical and historical dynamics of commercial frontier development. South American environments were remade in the names of mercantile appraisals of European consumer demand and European technology.

Christian Lotz finds that information asymmetries emerged from the mid-nineteenth century onward as European demand for timber increased; conditions in the forest economy changed in the supply regions, Norway, Sweden, and Russia, including Finland and Poland; and conflicting expert opinion on the future for forestry in Europe emerged in discussions of measures to secure the future timber supply. Infrastructure development drove the 'timber frontier' further toward the North, but the warnings made by forestry experts of ecological consequences of timber harvesting in these

Figure 1.4   Small, artificial channel for the transport of fuel wood in the Palatinate Forest, Germany. Built in the early nineteenth century, this channel was rendered obsolete by changing energy systems, infrastructures, and demand.

Source: Andreas Dix, 2005.

distant supply regions failed to impress governments in London, Berlin, Oslo, Stockholm, or St. Petersburg.

In 'Valuing Environments,' authors take up the idea that environments are valued and undervalued in diverse ways through commercial activities and government projects. The chapters explore shifting frameworks for understanding and valuing environments within commerce and government: sometimes as opportunity, other times as hindrance. Gordon Winder considers the problems that the McCormick Harvesting Machinery Company encountered as they promoted their reapers and mowers in the diverse trading environments where they operated. Recent work in cultural geography interprets the representational system of this family enterprise in terms of the mechanization of the American environment and the fulfillment of the pastoral idea: this civilizing machine would aid cultivation and the USA's civilizing mission. Nevertheless, he argues that the McCormicks in fact remained conditioned by environment and nature in diverse ways. Their business simultaneously featured increasing engagement with nature in terms of both diverse forms of property and the conditioning effects of harvest season, physical distance, and the changing materiality of the machine on the enterprise. Winder argues that, despite their advertising, the McCormicks faced an expanding engagement with nature rather than a mastery over nature.

In the context of New Zealand's rapid transformation from a largely forested landscape to a largely pastoral one, Michael Roche discusses how surveyors divided Crown Land into various economic classes, how farming fared on some of the more marginal lands, how forest land was deemed to be of sufficient value to be reserved from settlement, and, finally, how scenic and scientific concerns were given expression in a way that enabled lands to be secured for these purposes. The chapter draws on research in three different districts to provide examples of a cartographic visioning of resource value, quantitative measures of the 'improvement' as forest was converted into farms, their financial nonviability as outliers among suppliers of meat and wool to Britain during the 1920s and 1930s, and, finally, of subjective measures of aesthetic and scientific value deployed to establish a network of parks and reserves. The chapter discusses the metrics developed to make commercial sense of modern land uses in a process of environmental learning.

Shawn Van Ausdal examines the failed attempt to expand the North Atlantic beef frontier into Colombia during the early twentieth century. He shows that dreams of cattle-led development based on ideas of tropical exuberance clashed with the material realities of ranching in the tropics, forcing a reassessment of local environmental conditions. Industry observers and government officials began to view the tropics as unruly and in need of domestication through the application of scientific principles. The new view contributed to a growing critique of the *latifundio* in Colombia and fueled a key debate of the 1930s ranching economy: Should the government promote or prevent the diffusion of zebu blood through the national cattle herd? By exploring the connections between trade (or its failure), environmental discourses, and material transformations, he reveals the circulation and mutation of ideas about tropical nature as they relate to cattle ranching in Colombia.

Esa Ruuskanen addresses the question of why different types of mires became part of a large-scale economic activity in the Nordic countries since the late eighteenth century. Mires, which were formerly valued and considered wasteland, became utilized in agriculture, forestry, peat production, and mining. The study disentangles how and on which basis different forms of land use were prioritized, how and why these practices changed, and how sciences, especially agricultural sciences, economics, forest sciences, and geology, promoted changes and to what extent there was continuity in the natural resource policies.

'Competing Modernist Logics' considers cases of environmental reappraisals and revaluations, as new 'frontier' projects are assembled or compete with older socioenvironmental regimes. Mathias Mutz explores the interconnection of industry and environment through the growth of the Saxon pulp and paper industry, which resulted in an industrialization of forests and an international trade system with far-reaching ecological effects. The new demand for fast growing small-dimensioned wood, especially spruce, altered the utilization strategies of state and private forest administrators, called for new regions in the supply chain and allowed for alternative supply strategies. He shows that wood as a raw material not only impacted the spatial structure of the pulp and paper industry but also, in regard to efforts to secure wood supply, influenced the strategic and organizational development of industrial enterprises. Natural preconditions never stood for themselves but were embedded into social organizations and managed by social actors, so that 'naturalizing industrialization' means to acknowledge the close and multilayered dependency between industrial enterprises, institutional arrangements, and environmental change.

Craig E. Colten explores the practices of revaluation as 'ruined' rural lands in the US South were designated as ripe for restoration. One ambitious New Deal project sought to wrest poor rural families from impoverished situations and resituate them to better circumstances. The object was to move them off forlorn farms and relief rolls and then to restore the vacated properties to more productive uses. While national in scope, the Resettlement Administration oversaw this effort and gave considerable attention to the American South. The process created a new geography of the land that had locked farm families into poverty, revalued the rural landscape, and reclassified the lands where farming was not a viable operation as 'submarginal.' Once defined as worthless, both places and people could be rehabilitated by the Resettlement Administration. Pressing a clear conservation agenda, federal authorities proclaimed that much of the exhausted land would be more productive as wildlife conservation tracts, federally managed forests or pasture, or recreation areas. As quickly as the land received a 'submarginal' classification, managers had to restore its value, and this time as worthy and productive in order to justify federal acquisition and conversion to other land uses. A sharp critique of social practices frowned upon by the New Dealers and of small farmers was inherent in this revaluation process and reinforced the view that the South writ large was a sprawling 'problem area.'

Carmel Finley explores the destruction of US fishing industries as the US government traded off domestic interests for strategic advantages during the Cold War. Transnational commodity chains, instituted for political reasons, tightly tied distant environments together, so much so, that the politics around a 1943 trade agreement between Iceland and the United States became the basis for the Japanese to increase the export of tuna into the United States. The American fishing industry sought protection from imported fish through tariffs but faced opposition from the State Department and the Department of Defense. The two agencies wanted to increase fish imports from Iceland to curry favor with Iceland as the two countries negotiated an agreement over the Keflavik air base, built by the Americans during the war. Additionally, the State Department wanted to strengthen the Japanese economy after World War II, and tuna was one of the few Japanese products with an unlimited market in the United State. These trade negotiations around Icelandic cod and Japanese tuna accelerated the decline of the New England fishing industry and set in motion the destruction of the Southern California tuna processing industry. Carmel Finley argues that fishing is always about more than just catching fish, and in this case, the US government's geostrategic priorities led to a reappraisal of US, Japanese, and Icelandic fishing industries and markets with dramatic implications.

In the book's final section, '*Environmental Trading*,' Gordon Winder and Andreas Dix discuss the effectiveness and effects of commercial calculative practices on environments, and, conversely, the implications of transformed or damaged environments on commercial activity are discussed in this concluding chapter in relation to environmental history, business history, and historical geography. Summarizing the findings of the earlier chapters, it identifies a series of practices that commonly emerge from the 'trading environments' metaphor and approach. It points to the shortcomings of historical commercial practice: a lack of attention to environmental remediation or to insurance and reliance on governments to revalue environments. Representations of environments as improvable and improved were regularly used in ways that obscured the damage done and to legitimize exploitation. At the same time, commercial exploitation was often designed to produce new environments that would facilitate long-term extraction of resources and profits. Thus the chapter is primarily concerned with what sustainability and resilience could mean in the context of historical frontiers. The chapter draws lessons from the (mis)alignment of natures and from the efforts to revalue environments in the case studies. Finally, the chapter identifies future research directions in commercial encounters with environment that emerge from the case studies explored in the book.

NOTES

1 D. Holdsworth and G. Tritch Roman, "From the pit to the globe: The reach of commodity exchanges." Paper presented at the special session The Urban Economy: Networks, Flows and Place, Twelfth International Conference on Urban History, Lisbon, Portugal, September 3–6, 2014. The 1885 structure featured four 11-meter-high allegorical figures two of which represented agriculture and industry. The 1930 art deco structure that replaced the earlier building featured an Egyptian with grain and a Native American holding corn positioned on each side of the clock facing LaSalle Street. Representations of bulls, a reference to bull markets, can be seen on the building's north and east sides. Atop the building stands an art deco statue of Ceres, the Roman goddess of grain, holding a sheaf of wheat and a bag of corn. Ceres also graced a three-story mural in the agricultural trading room. The six-story trading room featured raised octagonal trading 'pits' organized and named according to the commodities traded: corn, soybean or wheat. The individual pits are structures where open outcry trading occurs. Nearby desks were available for support workers, including first telegraph and then telephone operators.

2 William Cronon, *Nature's Metropolis: Chicago and the Great West* (New York and London: W.W. Norton, 1991): especially 120–132. On performativity and calculative practices see Christian Berndt and Marc Boeckler, "Geographies of circulation and exchange: Constructions of markets," *Progress in Human Geography* 33(4) (2009): 535–551, especially 543–544. They focus their outline of performativity and finance on the roles of academic economists, who "make the 'model of the world become the world of the model,'" and of economic practitioners, who "frame and perform markets" in the process paraphrasing and citing Michel Callon, Cécile Méadel, Vololona Rabeharisoa, "The economy of qualities," *Economy and Society* 31(2002): 194–217.

3 Dan Morgan, *Merchants of Grain* (Harmondsworth: Penguin: 1980), 75.

4 Morgan, *Merchants of Grain*, 102.

5 Morgan, *Merchants of Grain*, 102.

6 Morgan, *Merchants of Grain*, 75.

7 Morgan, *Merchants of Grain*, 77.

8 Mona Domosh, *American Commodities in an Age of Empire* (New York and London: Routledge, 2006); Anne McClintock, *Imperial Leather: Race, Gender and Sexuality in the Colonial Conquest* (New York: Routledge: 1995); Kristin Hogarson, "Cosmopolitan domesticity: Importing the American Dream, 1865–1921," *American Historical Review* 107(2002): 55–83.

9 Christopher Kremmer, *The Carpet Wars* (Sydney: HarperCollins Publishers, 2002), 4.

10 Recently, Michel Callon has begun to apply ANT to finance, business and economics. Callon, Méadel, Rabeharisoa, "The economy of qualities," 194–217. Koray Çalışkan and Michel Callon, "Economization, part 2: A research programme for the study of markets," *Economy and Society* 39(2010): 1–32. See also Berndt and Boeckler, "Geographies of circulation and exchange," 535–551, especially 543–544, and Gordon M. Winder, "Building trust and managing business over distance: A geography of reaper manufacturer D.S. Morgan's correspondence, 1867," *Economic Geography* 77(2) April (2001): 95–121.

11 Bruno Latour, *The Pasteurization of France* (Cambridge, MA: Harvard University Press, 1988). Timothy Mitchell, *Colonizing Egypt* (Berkeley, Los Angeles and London: University of California Press, 1991); Timothy Mitchell, *Rule*

of Experts: Egypt, Techno-politics, Modernity* (Berkeley, Los Angeles and London: University of California Press, 2003); Richard White, *Railroaded: The Transcontinentals and the Making of Modern America* (New York: W.W. Norton, 2011).

12   Cronon, *Nature's Metropolis*, 268.
13   William Cronon, "The trouble with wilderness or getting back to the wrong nature," *Environmental History Review* 1(1) (1996), 7–28.
14   Noel Castree and Bruce Braun (eds.), *Social Nature: Theory, Practice and Politics* (Malden, MA: Blackwell, 2001).
15   Cronon, *Nature's Metropolis*, 266–267.
16   Cronon, *Nature's Metropolis*, 267 and 268, referring to Johann Heinrich von Thünen, *Von Thünen's Isolated State*, translated by Carla M. Wartenberg, edited by Peter Hall (New York: Pergamon Press, 1966) first published 1826.
17   William Cronon, *Nature's Metropolis*, 267.
18   See for example Richard White, *The Organic Machine: The Remaking of the Columbia River* (New York: Hill and Wang, 1996) and David Nye, *America as Second Creation: Technology and Narratives of New Beginnings* (Cambridge, MA: MIT Press, 2003).
19   Stephen Daniels and Denis Cosgrove, "Iconography and landscape," in Denis Cosgrove and Stephen Daniels (eds.), *The Iconography of Landscape: Essays on the Symbolic Representation, Design and Use of Past Environments* (Cambridge, New York and Melbourne: Cambridge University Press, 1988): 1–10. James Duncan and Nancy Duncan, "(Re)reading the landscape," *Environment and Planning D: Society and Space* 6(1988): 117–126. Hugh Prince, "Art and agrarian change, 1710–1815," in Denis Cosgrove and Stephen Daniels (eds.), *The Iconography of Landscape* (Cambridge: Cambridge University Press, 1988): 98–118. Susanne Seymour, Stephen Daniels, and C. Watkins, "Estate and empire: Sir George Cornewall's management of Moccas, Herefordshire and La Taste, Grenada, 1771–1819," *Journal of Historical Geography* 24(3) (1988): 313–351. Susanne Seymour, "Historical geographies of landscape," in Brian Graham and Catherine Nash (eds.), *Modern Historical Geographies* (Harlow, England: Pearson Education, 2000), 193–217.
20   For Linné see the biography by Lisbet Koerner, *Linnaeus. Nature and Nation*, 3rd ed. (Cambridge, MA: Harvard University Press, 2001).
21   Robert Darnton gives an impression of this business in his classic work: Robert Darnton, *The Business of Enlightenment: A Publishing History of the Encyclopédie, 1775–1800*, (Cambridge, MA: Harvard University Press, 1979).
22   Arjun Appadurai, (ed.), *The Social Life of Things: Commodities in Cultural Perspective*, (Cambridge: Cambridge University Press, 1986); Callon, Méadel, and Rabeharisoa, "The economy of qualities," 194–217; Peter Jackson, "Commercial cultures: Transcending the cultural and the economic," *Progress in Human Geography* 26 (2002): 3–18.
23   Harold A. Innis, *Essays in Canadian Economic History* (Toronto: University of Toronto Press, 1956). James S. Careless, "Metropolis and region: The interplay between city and region in Canadian history," *Urban History Review* 78(3) (1979): 108–118, James S. Careless, *Frontier and Metropolis: Regions, Cities, and Identities in Canada Before 1914* (Toronto: University of Toronto Press, 1987); Mel Watkins, "A staple theory of economic growth," in W.T. Easterbrook and M. Watkins (eds.), *Approaches to Canadian Economic History* (Toronto: McClelland and Stewart, 1967): 49–60. Mel Watkins, "The staple theory revisited," *Journal of Canadian Studies* 12(5) (1977): 83–95. Mel Watkins, "The Innis tradition in Canadian political economy," *Canadian Journal of Political Science and Social Theory* 6(1–2) (1982): 12–34; Trevor Barnes, "External shocks: Regional implications of an open staple

economy," in John Britton (ed.), *Canada and the Global Economy: The Geography of Structural and Technological Change* (Montreal and Kingston: McGill-Queen's University Press, 1996): 48–68.

24 David Kiron, Nina Kruschwitz, et al., *Sustainability's Next Frontier: Walking the Talk on the Sustainability Issues that Matter Most*, MIT Sloan Management Review 2013 Sustainability and Innovation, Global Executive Study and Research Project with Boston Consulting Group (December 16, 2013). http://sloanreview.mit.edu/projects/sustainability_next_frontier. BSR, *The New Frontier in Sustainability: The Business Opportunity in Tackling Sustainable Consumption*, (2010) http://www.bsr.org/reports/BSR_New_Frontier_Sustainability.pdf. Wissenschaftlicher Beirat der Bundesregierung Globale Umweltveränderungen, *Welt im Wandel: Gesellschaftsvertrag für eine Große Transformation* Hauptgutachten (Berlin: WBGU, 2011).

25 In this volume, Mathias Mutz complicates this legitimization strategy of a sustainability frontier by showing that, in the context of an exploding demand for timber, von Carlowitz's eighteenth century 'sustainable forestry' practices quickly became functional only through a geographically expanding timber frontier—that is, sustainable forestry in urbanizing and industrializing Germany required (unsustainable) timber extraction elsewhere.

26 Cole Harris, "How did colonialism dispossess: Comments from an edge of empire," *Annals of the Association of American Geographers* 94(2004): 105–182. See also Cole Harris, *The Resettlement of British Columbia: Essays on Colonialism and Geographical Change* (Vancouver: University of British Columbia Press, 1997).

27 David Harvey, *The 'New' Imperialism: Accumulation by Dispossession* (Oxford: Oxford University Press, 2003). See also R. Brenner, "What is, and what is not, 'imperialism,' " *Historical Materialism* 14(4) (2004): 3–67; S.M. Borras Jr., R. Hall, I. Scoones, et al., "Towards a better understanding of global land grabbing: An editorial introduction," *Journal of Peasant Studies* 38(2) (2011): 209–216; and R. Bush, J. Bujra, and G. Littlejohn, "The accumulation of dispossession," *Review of African Political Economy* 38(128) special issue (2011): 187–192.

28 A concept of core and periphery was formulated in the classical work of Immanuel Wallerstein, *The Modern World-System* (New York: Academic Press, 1974). On the concept of 'frontier' see Michael Redclift, *Frontier: Histories of Civil Society and Nature* (Cambridge, MA: MIT Press, 2006).

29 See Peter A. Hall and David Soskice, *Varieties of Capitalism: The Institutional Foundations of Comparative Advantage* (Oxford: Oxford University Press, 2001); Bruno Amable, *The Diversity of Modern Capitalism* (Oxford: Oxford University Press, 2003); and Werner Abelshauser, David A. Gilgen and Andreas Leutzsch (eds.), *Kulturen der Weltwirtschaft*, (Göttingen: Vandenhoeck & Ruprecht, 2012).

30 Cronon, *Nature's Metropolis*, xvii.

31 Gary Gereffi and Miguel Korzeniewicz (eds.), *Commodity Chains and Global Capitalism* (Westport, CT: Greenwood Press, 1994). Roger Hayter, Trevor J. Barnes and Michael J. Bradshaw, "Relocating resource peripheries to the core of economic geography's theorizing: Rationale and agenda," *Area* 35(1) (2003): 15–23. Gary Gereffi, John Humphrey and Timothy Sturgeon, "The governance of global value chains," *Review of International Political Economy* 12(2005): 78–104, Peter Gibbon, Jennifer Bair and Stefano Ponte, "Governing global value chains: An introduction," *Economy and Society* 37(3) (2008): 315–338. Peter Gibbon and Stefano Ponte, "Global value chains: From governance to governmentality," *Economy and Society* 38(3) (2008): 385–392. M. Hassler, "Commodity chains," in R. Kitchin and N. Thrift (eds.), *International*

Encyclopaedia of Human Geography (Amsterdam: Elsevier, 2009): 202–208. L. van Grunsven, "Global commodity chains," in R. Kitchin and N. Thrift (eds.), *International Encyclopaedia of Human Geography* (Amsterdam: Elsevier, 2009): 539–547. Peter Dicken, Philip F. Kelly and Henry Wai-Chung Yeung, "Chains and networks, territories and scales," *Global Networks* 1(2010): 89–112. Among the pioneering works in staples theory were those of Canadian economist Harold A. Innis, *The Fur Trade in Canada: An Introduction to Canadian Economic History* (Revised edition Toronto: University of Toronto Press, 1956, First edition 1930). Harold A. Innis, *The Cod Fisheries: The History of an International Economy*, revised edition (Toronto: University of Toronto Press, 1954. First edition 1940) in which he aimed to understand the dynamics of interaction among international merchant enterprise and local communities and environments and to explore the limited onshore footprint that hundreds of years of fishery exploitation left on Newfoundland. See also Innis, *Essays in Canadian Economic History*. Subsequent development of the staples tradition has followed diverse paths. See Daniel Drache (ed.), *Staples, Markets, and Cultural Change: Selected Essays Harold Innis* (Montreal and Kingston: McGill-Queen's Universisity Press, 1995).

32 Jürgen Osterhammel, *Die Verwandlung der Welt. Eine Geschichte des 19. Jahrhunderts*, (München, 2009).

33 Cronon, *Nature's Metropolis*.

34 In environmental history see for example P.R. Mulvihill, D.C. Baker and W.R. Morrison, "A conceptual framework for the study of environmental history in the Canadian North," *Environmental History* 6(4) (2001): 611–626.

35 The problem of the Dutch disease was first diagnosed by W. Max Corden and J. Peter Neary, "Booming sector and deindustrialization in a small open economy," *The Economic Journal* 92(December 1982): 825–848. The resource curse or paradox of plenty was first theorized by Richard M. Auty, *Sustaining Development in Mineral Economies: The Resource Curse Thesis* (London: Routledge: 1993). On the tragedies of the resource cycle see Alex Clapp, "The resource cycle in forestry and fishing," *The Canadian Geographer/Le Geographe canadien* 42(2) (1988): 129–144. On the staples trap see Mel Watkins, "A staple theory of economic growth;" Mel Watkins, "The staple theory revisited;" and Mel Watkins, "The Innis tradition in Canadian political economy."

36 Hartmut Berghoff and Mathias Mutz, "Missing links. Business history and environmental change," *Jahrbuch für Wirtschaftsgeschichte* 2(2009), 9–21.

37 John F. Richards, *The Unending Frontier: Environmental Histories of the Early Modern World* (Berkeley: University of California Press, 2006). Sterling Evans, *Bound in Twine: The History and Ecology of the Hennequen-Wheat Complex for Mexico and the American and Canadian Plains, 1880–1950* (College Station, TX: Texas A and M University Press, 2007). Gail M. Hollander, *Raising Cane in the Glades: The Global Sugar Trade and the Transformation of Florida* (Chicago and London: The University of Chicago Press, 2008). Richard White, *Railroaded: The Transcontinentals and the Making of Modern America* (New York: W.W. Norton, 2011).

38 Richards, *The Unending Frontier*.

39 See for example Jason W. Moore, "Amsterdam is standing on Norway," Part I: "The alchemy of capital, empire and nature in the diaspora of silver, 1545–1648," *Journal of Agrarian Change* 10(2) (January 2010): 33–68 and Jason W. Moore, "Amsterdam is standing on Norway," Part II: "The global North Atlantic in the Ecological Revolution the long seventeenth century," *Journal of Agrarian Change* 10(2) (April 2010): 188–227.

40 Raymond E. Dumett (ed.), *Mining Tycoons in the Age of Empire, 1870–1945: Entrepreneurship, High Finance, Politics and Territorial Expansion* (Farnham: Ashgate Publishing, 2009).

41 David Nye, *America as Second Creation: Technology and Narratives of New Beginnings* (Cambridge, MA: MIT Press, 2003); Cronon, *Nature's Metropolis*; Gray Brechin, *Imperial San Francisco: Urban Power, Earthly Ruin* (Berkeley, Los Angeles, London: University of California Press, 1999).

42 Redclift, *Frontier.*

43 William J. Bernstein, *A Splendid Exchange: How Trade Shaped the World* (New York: Grove Press: 2008).

44 Naomi R. Lamoreaux, Daniel M.G. Raff, Peter Temin, "Beyond markets and hierarchies: Toward a new synthesis of American Business History," *The American Historical Review* 108(2) (2003): 421–435.

45 Simon L. Lewis and Mark A. Maslin, "Defining the Anthropocene," *Nature* 519 (12 March 2015): 171–180.

46 Lamoreaux et al. define 'long-term relations' as "transactions among otherwise independent economic actors in which the parties voluntarily choose to continue dealing with each other for significant periods of time." Lamoreaux, Raff, and Temin, "Beyond markets and hierarchies," 407.

47 See also Charles F. Sabel, Jonathan Zeitlin, "Historical alternatives to mass production: Politics, markets and technology in nineteenth century industrialization," *Past and Present* 108(1985): 133–176; Walter W. Powell; "Neither market nor hierarchy: Network forms of organization," *Research in Organizational Behavior* 12 (1990): 295–336; Peter Dicken, *Global Shift: Transforming the World Economy*, 3rd edition (New York: The Guilford Press, 1998); and Peter Dicken, "Geographers and 'globalisation:' (Yet) another missed boat?" *Transactions of the Institute of British Geographers* (NS) 29 (2004): 5–26. Gordon M. Winder, "Webs of enterprise 1850–1914: Applying a broad definition of FDI," *Annals of the Association of American Geographers* 96(4) (2006): 788–806. Timothy Guinnane, Ron Harris, Naomi R. Lamoreaux, Jean-Laurent Rosenthal, "Putting the corporation in its place," *Enterprise and Society* 8(3) (2007): 687–729.

48 Berghoff and Mutz, "Missing links."

49 Larry D. McCann (ed.), *Heartland and Hinterland: A Geography of Canada* (Scarborough: Prentice Hall, 1987). McCann and his coauthors drew upon and expanded the Harold Innis tradition in Canadian political economy.

50 Roger Hayter, Trevor J. Barnes, and Meric Gertler, "Harold Innis and the new industrial geography," *The Canadian Geographer/Le Géographe canadien* 37(1993): pp. 360–364. Hayter, Barnes, and Bradshaw, "Relocating resource peripheries to the core of economic geography's theorizing."

51 David Gibbs, "Prospects for an environmental economic geography: Linking modernization and regulationist approaches," *Economic Geography* 82(2006): 193–215. Roger Hayter, "Environmental economic geography," *Geography Compass* 2–3(2008): 831–850.

52 Clapp, "The resource cycle in forestry and fishing."

53 Hollander, *Raising Cane in the Glades.*

54 Brechin, *Imperial San Francisco.*

55 On the concept of 'nature' seen as chance or risk, see Peter Weichhart and Karl-Michael Höferl, "A place for space in risk research: The example of discourse analysis approaches," in Detlef Müller-Mahn (ed.), *The Spatial Dimension of Risk: How Geography Shapes the Emergence of Riskscapes* (New York: Routledge, 2013): 37–51 and Heike Egner and Andreas Pott, (eds.), *Geographische Risikoforschung: Zur Konstruktion verräumlichter Risiken und Sicherheiten* (Stuttgart: Franz Steiner Verlag: 2010).

56 See for example Richard H. Grove, "The origins of environmentalism," *Nature* 345 (3 May, 1990): 11–14; Richard H. Grove, *Green Imperialism: Colonial Expansion, Tropical Island Edens and the Origins of Environmentalism 1600–1860.* (Cambridge: Cambridge University Press: 1995); Richard H.

Grove, *Ecology, Climate and Empire: Colonialism and Global Environmental History, 1400–1940* (Cambridge: White Horse Press: 1997); Peter Holland, *Home in the Howling Wilderness: Settlers and the Environment in Southern New Zealand* (Auckland: Auckland University Press: 2013).

57 Alfred W. Crosby, *The Columbian Exchange: Biological and Cultural Consequences of 1492* (Westport, CT: Greenwood Press: 1972). See also Tom Brooking and Eric Pawson, *Seeds of Empire: The Environmental Transformation of New Zealand* (London and New York: L.B. Tauris: 2010). Michael Grunwald, *The Swamp: The Everglades, Florida, and the Politics of Paradise* (New York: Simon & Schuster, 2006).

58 See Michelle Gerber, *On the Home Front: The Cold War Legacy of the Hanford Nuclear Site* (Lincoln: University of Nebraska Press 2007).

59 But see Matthew W. Klingle, "Spaces of consumption in environmental history," *History and Theory* 42(4) (2003): 94–110.

2 Consumption History and Changing Environments

Andreas Dix

CONSUMPTION AS PERSPECTIVE

Consumption has become one of the major issues in recent debates on economic growth and its role in global change as scientists recognize, for example, that changing consumption patterns of the emerging middle classes in China or India have a new and crucial impact on the exploitation of the global natural environment. That is true in the case of growing consumption of meat, which causes land use changes, such as the conversion of huge areas of tropical rainforest for the production of soybean or palm oil. Also the severe air pollution in many mega cities can be linked with a higher demand for consumer goods produced by a large industrial complex. Consumption also had important influences on past environments, but this field seems to be a neglected one. In economic history, the advent and development of consumerism and a mass consumption society from early modern times onward is a well-introduced issue.[1] This is not the right place to recapitulate the debate around a proper definition and delimitation of mass consumption in general and of consumerism in detail. Looking back from a perspective that has the current situation in mind, the following text is focused on early modern and modern times, because the advent of a mass consumption society in a modern sense can be dated back to the eighteenth century.[2]

The main idea of this chapter is to discuss a conceptual framework that may be useful to combine changing demands and changing tastes with environmental change. Consumption in the sense of conspicuous consumption and the achievement of social distinction should be centered. That means to look on commodities mainly in their function as Veblen goods.[3] More precisely, commodities have to be analyzed with a focus on rareness and quality. Only few papers emphasize the ecological impact of consumer behavior, consumer needs, and a consumer culture in general.[4] With a virtual breakfast in Henry David Thoreau's famous lodge, Matthew Klingle tries to look on the material basis of consumption. He retraces the spatial history of coffee, paper, salmon, and bananas. As a result, it is clear that each of these commodities had its own sources, its own consumption patterns, and even its own time line of use in terms of broadening the use, popularity, or decline of use.

The historical reconstruction of commodity chains is one of the main ways to determine the relation of commodities to the changing demand. Combined with the analytical concept of social metabolism and its ecological footprint, it is possible to recognize major material flows and to connect them with distinct areas of production.[5] In one of his earlier publications, Krausmann reconstructed the changing flow of biomass in Austria using a cross section from the early stage of industrialization around 1830 and another in 1998.[6] With statistical data, it is possible to connect the energy consumption with biomass flows and production areas. In detail, he is able to prove that, at the end of the twentieth century, the energy consumption in Austria is six times as high as in the early nineteenth century, and 60 percent of this energy is from fossil fuels. Historical metabolism research has developed an impressive amount of data on a global scale.[7] The increasing demand of energy means a higher level of production and consumption, a broader range of consumer goods, and an unprecedented degree of freedom in choosing such goods. Nevertheless, it remains a complicated task to estimate influences of changing material flows on areas and landscapes on a regional or even a local scale.

That leads to the notion that consumption became an essential driving force for the global economy and global ecological change since the eighteenth century. Jürgen Osterhammel describes some concise examples of the advent of new consumer goods and of the development of national consumption patterns as a topic that was important for the development of an early global economy.[8] It was a self-increasing process: increasing opportunities have been causing increasing demands and especially demands of commodities with a higher quality and sourced from other and often more distant sources. In his chapter on the tropical beef frontier in Colombia, Shawn Van Ausdal describes such linkages and the intense discussions about the advantages of certain cattle breeds, tropical nature, and the beef quality.

In this paper, consumption and environmental change are analyzed in two broad contexts: first, quality, luxury, and mass consumption and the commodification of nature; and second, landscapes as arenas of consumption. Nature can be transformed through various types of exploitation, such as the extraction of raw materials or highly specialized agricultural systems. The change of consumer needs or taste often changed these natures dramatically. The development of markets for raw materials was often coupled with the ongoing search for higher qualities. The names of regions and landscapes were often used as symbols for certain qualities. The viticulture and the trade of wine is a typical example. The commodification of nature was backed through the early stages of globalization, the colonial founding of many neo-European landscapes, and the new way of physiocratic economical thinking at the end of the eighteenth century, which, in many ways, mobilized the exploitation of nature all over the world. The advent of the new natural sciences, such as botany, geology, and chemistry, enabled European scientists to file an inventory of the whole of nature from its stones and

Figure 2.1 View of the Vogelsaal in the Naturkunde-Museum of Bamberg, Germany. This Natural History Museum's 'Hall of the Birds' was completed in 1810.

Source: Andreas Dix, 2015.

minerals, to its plants and animals, each with an eye to possible economic usefulness. The modern system of naming plants and animals, also the periodic table and other ideas of establishing indexes for everything were based on this idea. Nature was seen as a warehouse of potential and useful goods for the need of humankind.[9] The results of collecting and categorizing were on display in the museums of natural history (Figure 2.1) or even in zoological or botanical gardens.[10]

However, in addition, nature itself, and the newly constructed or artificial natures, have been used as arenas of consumption. The more a society developed new ways of consumption, the more people needed new spaces of consumption in the sense of new areas and places for retail trade and recreation. Thus tourism can be seen as a form of consumption, and the search for distinctiveness, questions of taste, and the consumer needs of a growing leisure class changed the faces of many landscapes.

QUALITY, LUXURY, MASS CONSUMPTION, AND THE COMMODIFICATION OF NATURE

It was not only an increasing population but often an increasing demand for goods or for goods of a higher quality that generated forms of luxurious consumption. This phenomenon was always visible from earliest times but normally the development of a modern mass consumption society is limited to the early modern and modern period. It is evident that, especially in the European countries with colonial possessions, the contact with exotic commodities was more intensive. Britain, then, was the forerunner of countries where the consumption of a small privileged group turned early into a mass consumption society.[11] This process has had different driving forces, but the main idea was to get new exotic or rare objects such as porcelain, silk, or plants for display as symbols of social distinctiveness. While the introduction of new foodstuff, new raw materials and new commodities in general is a more or less well-established field of research, the search for better qualities, the differentiation of qualities, and their linkage with certain places or regions is a lesser-known area.

In probate inventories, the whole material culture has been preserved and gives us a good overview of and insight into the world of conspicuous consumption. With the help of an analysis of these registers, the original spatial context of the consumption of goods becomes visible.[12] In a colonial context, the presentation of goods imported from the mother country produced a sharp contrast to the life conditions of the autochthonous population.[13]

With his notion of a 'Columbian exchange,' Alfred W. Crosby introduced the idea that the exchange of plants and animals can be distinguished as the most powerful biological consequence of European expansion.[14] Within this context, new Europeanized countrysides were built through the export of species. These cultural landscapes can be distinguished as new production spaces. Their ecological settings enabled the producers not only to produce higher quantities but also to enhance the quality of raw materials. In this context, wool production is a good example to clarify the close connection of production expansion and a simultaneous enhancement of qualities.[15] In the middle of the nineteenth century, raw wool imported from the southern hemisphere replaced the domestic production within just a few decades and with far-reaching consequences for the land use patterns in Central Europe. In German highland regions, the typical heathlands, which arose mainly from extensive sheep farming, vanished almost completely. Bender analyzed this process in the Northern Franconian scarpland area by making a multi-temporal analysis of cadastral maps.[16] Over 90 percent of these regions were reforested or used in another way (Figure 2.2). Today the remaining open areas are highly appreciated by nature conservation authorities due to their biological diversity and have to be kept open. For centuries it had not been possible to produce wool of a finer quality. In the age of mercantilism many attempts were made to produce such types of wool. For this reason, sheep breeding was one of the main goals of agricultural innovation. In fact, the breeding of merinos was common in Spain since the late medieval times, and wool production there had a great value within the export economy. But it was not possible to duplicate this success in German regions. The massive import of high quantities of wool of a high quality from overseas stopped all these efforts.

Figure 2.2   Old open grassland areas near the town of Pottenstein in the Franconian scarpland, Germany. Reforestation proceeded when distant producers made sheep and wool production uncompetitive.

Source: Andreas Dix, 2008.

Dietary habits changed under the influence of globalized commodity chains. The more the network of an international economy grew during the nineteenth century, the more important was the question of quality of foodstuffs, especially within urban societies. The availability of a wide variety of food accompanied the rise of urban middle classes and supplied the want for social distinction. The consumption of luxurious goods and even rare, exotic, or expensive foodstuffs was intensively discussed and often criticized by contemporary intellectuals. The apparent affluence of foodstuffs, which was demonstrated at banquets, balls, and parties, seemed to be scandalous. Discussions and publications on this topic were especially numerous at the end of the nineteenth century in the case of the German empire under the rule of Wilhelm II.[17]

Not only a broader variety of exotic foods enriched the nutrition but also a growing variety of qualities within certain foodstuffs.[18] Wine consumption and its association with geographical areas might present a good example for this issue. Winegrowing as an old practice produced throughout the centuries a detailed knowledge of the link between production, taste, and quality in a broad sense. Even in early modern times, those areas with good conditions were commonly known. In her research on the development and geographical distribution of grape varieties in the German region of Württemberg, Christine Krämer could find plenty of evidence that the advent and the rising cultivation of certain grapes were not as much influenced by climate change as recent debates in climate history may suggest. Decisions were in fact much more consumption driven.[19] In the fifteenth and sixteenth centuries, people preferred sweet wines, such as the muscatel, or strong red wines, which were typically produced in Italy. That is a clear sign that underlines the importance of the trade exchange between South Germany and Upper Italy. In the eighteenth century, wine from France, such as champagne and red wine from Burgundy, were the favorite ones. In the nineteenth century, the white wines, such as the Riesling from the Rheingau and the tributaries of the Rhine, were served in upper class and aristocratic households. In the case of Württemberg, the changes and the reasons why certain types of grapes were favored can be reconstructed in some detail from archival sources. In the nineteenth century, the influence of the railway and introduced pests, such as mildew and phylloxera, caused the abandonment of many vineyards. This was a typical development in those wine-growing areas where the quality of the wine was traditionally a poorer one. Winegrowing now was increasingly concentrated in those areas where a production of good wine qualities was possible in most years. This process of spatial concentration was accompanied by the attempt of many early agronomists to collect and to systematize grape varieties, their advantages, disadvantages, and qualities.[20] This became commercially relevant for the international wine trade. In France at the same time, as a result of rising production and consumption of wine on the one side and the severe phylloxera crisis on the other, the whole process of winemaking was reorganized. In the eighteenth century, the Portuguese statesman Marquês de Pombal was the first who tried to circumscribe special wine regions as a part of the reorganization of the port wine trade. It was the interest of large estate owners to ensure the origin of their wines in order to realize better prices. Finally, in 1855, a classification of wines of the Bordeaux region was established and became the blueprint for various other classification systems.[21] This classification is closely linked with production places and regions and, in fact, describes a 'geography of quality.' This geography of quality was a basic knowledge for traders and constitutive for the formation of markets and marketplaces.[22]

Another example is the production, trade, and consumption of mineral water. The source of the small town of Niederselters in the Taunus Mountains near Frankfurt became a geographical synonym for table waters of high quality and was traded on a global scale as Selterswasser, Seltzer water or L'eau de Seltz.[23] In the seventeenth century, millions of steins were transported by ship in many countries and also overseas, which gives an idea of its overwhelming reputation. Many other table waters followed and, at the most fashionable places of the late nineteenth century, such as the luxurious steam liners or the grand hotels, many different table waters were served.[24] With this idea in mind, one can start a fascinating journey through the world of different geographies of qualities, which varied in space and time; but these geographies of qualities were often brought to the table where they helped to construct arenas of consumption.

LANDSCAPES AS ARENAS OF CONSUMPTION

Consumption needs, and always needed, landscapes as source areas for commodities but also as arenas of consumption. Even conspicuous consumption needs specific landscapes, areas, and arenas. Since early modern times, prestigious leisure activities within the landscape, such as hunting, development of landscape gardening, or a long vacation time in summer residences were reserved for a small group of the society: the nobility or rich bourgeois families from the city. These small groups invented new activities and staged them within landscapes. Since early modern times and more intensively in the eighteenth century, one obvious trend was that spending time in the nature as a leisure activity was more and more attractive.

Landscapes as arenas for leisure activities have had to be opened in a process of discovery and commodification. The opening process usually can be distinguished in two stages. In a first stage, adventurers or pioneering travelers discovered those areas, mostly landscapes with spectacular prospects. The popularization of these landscapes, which was fundamental for the commercial stage of the opening, depended from the mid-nineteenth century onward on early photographers. Those photographers, such as Francis Bedford (1816–1894) or Francis Frith (1822–1898), sold their photos in huge numbers.[25] Photography of landscapes, whether of ancient or exotic places, became a commodity in a society where the availability of financial resources to organize a growing leisure time caused a growing demand for information about those landscapes. A special sort of literature has accompanied the visual opening: guidebooks describing the regional geography of certain areas. This sort of literature started in the 1820s and 1830s in various countries. In Europe, one of the earliest was Karl Baedeker (1801–1859), a genuine bookseller from Coblenz. He published his first tourist guidebook on the Rhine Valley in 1838. Based on a forerunner published by John Murray, it was the cornerstone for his commercial success and rise as one of the most influential publishers of tourist guidebooks.[26] He invented a system of assessment of places. Stars indicated whether a place was more worthwhile to be visited than others. This system was redolent to similar systems of quality assessment for other commodities.

Artists formed another important group that has had a keen interest in picturesque landscapes. At the end of the eighteenth century, and parallel to early tourists, artists went first to remote places to find subjects for landscape paintings. These landscapes became very popular throughout the nineteenth century and constituted a very important part of the art market. Artists traveled through the countryside to find scenic places, villages, towns, and ruins.[27] Upper Bavaria with its royal art academy in Munich was one of the most important production and marketplaces for art with an international influence in the second half of the nineteenth century and the first half of the twentieth. That was the reason why so many artists discovered Upper Bavaria with its landscapes. Some of them settled in small villages and formed artists' colonies, the most famous one in Dachau near Munich. But this was not only a Bavarian specialty but a true phenomenon in Europe and European-influenced countries in the whole world. Colonies such as those in Barbizon in France or in Palenville, a small town at the foot of the Catskill Mountains in the State of New York, which was a place for painters of the Hudson River School, are only two famous examples.[28]

These few remarks may underline the growing impact and commercial importance of touristic information and communication. In Germany, the Middle Rhine Valley became one of the first touristic-influenced spaces. Within only a few decades, British travelers discovered the narrow and rocky valley of the Rhine between the towns of Bingen and Coblenz, and it was transformed into a tourist space.[29] Increasing attention to the scenic beauty of landscapes was one of the driving forces of the nature conservation movement.[30] The salvage of the ruins of the famous Drachenfels Castle in 1829 has had much to do with a romantic picture of landscape that was transported by early tourists (Figure 2.3). During the entire nineteenth century, nearly all the ruins of castles or churches in the Middle Rhine Valley were preserved and refurbished or reestablished as neo-Gothic buildings. It was just this development that gave the Middle Rhine Valley its romantic

Figure 2.3   **The ruins of the Drachenfels Castle, Germany.** Postcard picture in use around 1904.

Source: Andreas Dix.

Figure 2.4   **Bastei Bridge in the Saxonian Switzerland near Dresden, Germany.** Built in 1851, the bridge enhanced tourist access and transformed landscape perspectives.

Source: Andreas Dix, 2012.

attitude, which instantly was politically interpreted as a national landscape with a specific national identity. Also this perspective attracted many tourists and made this part of the Rhine into a blueprint for other river landscapes, such as the Hudson River.[31]

In a second step, mostly parallel or with a slight time lag, those landscapes have had to be opened with an infrastructure, that means railway lines, hotels, restaurants but also trails that enabled the development of a tourist gaze on landscapes (Figure 2.4).[32] Pioneers developed those areas, but the discovery and development of landscapes meant often a branding with a certain idea. The image of a 'whole region' changed when the French writer Stéphen Liégeard (1830–1925) published his book *Côte d'Azur* in 1887. Under this label, a whole seaside changed into a luxurious space. The small villages and scenic spots that he identified at the coast are now the areas with the most expensive real estate: they are arenas for luxurious consumption. This process can be seen as a commodification of landscapes. The branding of many areas in Germany as "Schweizen" (Little Switzerlands) or "Toskanen" (Little Tuscanies) can be interpreted as a sign for a commercial perspective on these landscapes as touristic spaces.

Landscape in general emerged as an arena for leisure activities initially for the upper class. The idea of a picturesque and bucolic landscape for riding, hunting, or walking around was widely acknowledged and part of literary discourses.[33] Early forms of modern sport developed out of these activities. Landscape was always an indispensable part as location but also as scenery. The early golf courses, for example, were established on those areas called "linkslands," which were normally useless either as arable land or as meadow.[34] These areas formed a sort of land reserve for leisure activities. Its distinguishing features, including shrub grass or sandy dunes, became popular in the nineteenth century as scenery for performing a sport as a social event. The growing diversity of outdoor leisure activities covered more or less the whole country already in the second half of the nineteenth century. In Germany, many hiking and rambling clubs and, in 1883, a national society of all these clubs, were founded. It was not a socially exclusive movement. Instead, it opened the landscape for a broader audience. Also ordinary people gained the opportunity to enjoy the nature outside the industrialized cities. The function of these clubs was not only to serve the members with an offer of guided hiking tours but also with the construction of hiking trails, the production and selling of hiking maps and guides. From the beginning it was not only the idea to promote leisure activities but also to support manifold activities for beautifying the countryside. As a result of these complex changes, landscapes seemed to be still dominated by agrarian land use, but in fact they were adopted gradually for the needs of tourism.

A last, but important, element needs to be added: different places specially dedicated to retailing and consumption emerged. This is well published in the case of the consumption cathedrals like early department stores and malls in the cities. Eating out became popular in early modern times, when restaurants and coffee houses opened. Even in the countryside picnic places and open spaces for recreation formed an important part of the touristic infrastructure. In Germany, a very significant example of such places is the so-called "Keller" or cellar in the Bavarian countryside: beer gardens installed on top of subterranean caves or arches in which the beer could be stored in a dry and cool place even in summertime.[35] Sometimes natural ice was needed to cool the barrels. For this purpose, ice was harvested in wintertime out of flat ponds, which were often designed for this special purpose. In other regions, the rising need for cooling foodstuffs converted ice into an important commodity. In the second half of the nineteenth century, the harvest and transport of ice in Norway and eastern parts of the United States caused a significant ecological impact because ice was not only excavated at the glaciers.[36]

From the eighteenth century onward and then with a clear peak in the nineteenth century, a specialized type of settlement, only for leisure and health activities, arose: the spa town or health resort.[37] They were situated on shorelines or at places with thermal springs or sources of mineral water. These towns were shaped by a noble architecture and palaces, grand hotels and public buildings such as fountains and bathhouses, galleries, ballrooms, casinos, race courses, and many other buildings and open spaces that were very well suitable for conspicuous consumption (Figure 2.5). A small group of what was a truly international elite of wealthy merchants, industrial entrepreneurs, and members of the high nobility with their families spent longer periods of the summer time in a certain number of internationally renowned and luxurious spa towns. Cities like Bath in England, Vichy in France, Spa in Belgium, Montecatini Terme in Italy, Baden-Baden and

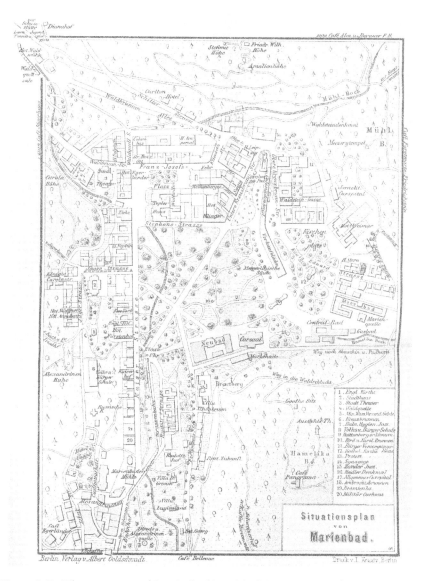

Figure 2.5 The town map of Marienbad/Mariánské Lázně, around 1912.

Source: Griebens Reiseführer, vol. 42, Marienbad und der Nachbarkurort Königswart nebst Umgebung. Praktisches Handbuch für Kurgäste und Touristen. Berlin: Grieben, 14th edition, 1907–1908.

Wiesbaden in Germany, or the Bohemian spa triangle with Franzensbad/
Františkovy Lázně, Marienbad/Mariánské Lázně, and Karlsbad/Karlovy
Vary became concourses of the social and political life of that period. In
this sense, nature, with its thermal springs but also with its natural beauty
and scenery, got a commercial value and was changed into a commodity, an
indispensable capital for those private and public companies running the
infrastructure. Ornamental gardens and the natural environment around
the cities were an integral part of this scenery. These spa towns were the
forerunners of a countless number of summer and winter resorts established
only for leisure activities and, at the end, for consumption purposes.

CONCLUSION

Consumption was introduced in this chapter as a key concept to get a
better understanding of the commodification of landscapes and nature in
general. Two main perspectives can be distinguished: the linkage of geographical patterns of production and consumption of goods and the function of landscapes as arenas for consumption. The chapter has illustrated
how the historical development of commodity chains linking producer and
consumer regions was accompanied and facilitated by the construction of
new geographies—geographies of qualities and arenas for consumption.
The regional and local landscape transformations that came with these new
geographies themselves drove ecosystem change, since the new landscapes
being produced were new 'socionatures.' These last, in turn, were associated
with realizing rents and increased land values from creating new motors of
production and consumption while destroying old ones. Thus with the help
of concepts of consumption studies, such as Veblen's theory of conspicuous
consumption, which points out that social mechanisms of a use of nature
are more intensive than necessary and useful, our consumption culture and
its ecological impact can be analyzed in more appropriate ways.

NOTES

1 For a brief overview of the development and current status see Frank Trentmann, "Beyond consumerism: New historical perspectives on consumption,"
   Journal of Contemporary History 39 (2004): 373–401; Frank Trentmann,
   "Consumption and globalization in history," *Journal of Consumer Culture* 9
   (2009): 187–220; and Frank Trentmann, "Introduction," in Frank Trentmann
   (ed.), *The Oxford Handbook of the History of Consumption* (Oxford: Oxford
   University Press, 2012), 1–19. For the earlier research on consumption history
   see Grant McCracken, "Culture and consumption. A theoretical account of the
   structure and movement of the cultural meaning of consumer goods," *Journal
   of Consumer Research* 13 (1986): 71–84 and Grant McCracken, "The history
   of consumption. A literature review and consumer guide," *Journal of Consumer Policy* 10 (1987): 139–166. For geographical perspectives see Jon Goss,

"Geography of consumption I," *Progress in Human Geography* 28 (2004): 369–380; Juliana Mansvelt, *Geographies of Consumption* (London: Sage, 2005); Jon Goss, "Geographies of consumption: The work of consumption," *Progress in Human Geography* 30 (2006): 237–249; Mark Jayne, "Cultural geography, consumption and the city," *Geography* 91 (2006): 34–42; Juliana Mansvelt, "Geographies of consumption: Citizenship, space and practice," *Progress in Human Geography* 32 (2008): 105–117; Juliana Mansvelt, "Geographies of consumption: The unmanageable consumer?" *Progress in Human Geography* 33 (2009): 264–274; and Juliana Mansvelt, "Geographies of consumption," *Progress in Human Geography* 34 (2010): 224–233. As a very inspiring perspective from historical sociology see Dominik Schrage, *Die Verfügbarkeit der Dinge. Eine historische Soziologie des Konsums* (Frankfurt am Main, New York: Campus, 2009); Dominik Schrage, "The availability of things. A short genealogy of consumption," *Krisis. Journal of Contemporary Philosophy* 1 (2012): 5–19.

2 On the problem of a chronological delimitation and periodization of consumption see Peter N. Stearns, "Stages of consumerism. Recent work on the issues of periodization," *Journal of Modern History* 69 (1997): 102–117 and Peter N. Stearns, *Consumerism in World History. The Global Transformation of Desire* (London, New York: Routledge, 2001). For the previous history see Ina Baghdiantz McCabe, *A History of Global Consumption 1500–1800* (London, New York: Routledge, 2015). For the beginnings of a mass consumption society see Timothy Hall Breen, "The meaning of things. Interpreting the consumer society in the eighteenth century," in John Brewer and Roy Porter (eds.), *Consumption and the World of Goods* (London, New York: Routledge, 1993): 249–260.

3 Thorstein Veblen, *The Theory of the Leisure Class. An Economic Study of Institutions* (New York: Macmillan, 1899).

4 Matthew W. Klingle, "Spaces of consumption in environmental history," *History and Theory* 42 (2003): 94–110.

5 Manuel González de Molina Navarro and Víctor Manuel Toledo, *The Social Metabolism. A Socio-Ecological Theory of Historical Change* (Cham: Springer, 2014) and Mathis Wackernagel and William Rees, *Unser ökologischer Fussabdruck. Wie der Mensch Einfluss auf die Umwelt nimmt* (Basel i.a.: Birkhäuser, 1997) [Updated version of: *Our Ecological Footprint: Reducing Human Impact on the Earth*, 1996].

6 Fridolin Krausmann, *Rekonstruktion der Entwicklung von Materialflüssen im Zuge der Industrialisierung: Veränderungen im sozioökonomischen Biomassenmetabolismus in Österreich 1830 bis 1998* (Stuttgart: Breuninger Foundation, 2001).

7 Fridolin Krausmann, "Global human appropriation of net primary production doubled in the 20th century," *Proceedings of the National Academy of Sciences* 110 (2013): 10324–10329.

8 Jürgen Osterhammel, *The Transformation of the World: A Global History of the Nineteenth Century*, (Princeton, NJ: Princeton University Press, 2014) [First German edition 2009].

9 See Günter Bayerl, "Prolegomenon der ‚Großen Industrie.'" Der technisch-ökonomische Blick auf die Natur im 18. Jahrhundert," in Werner Abelshauser (ed.), *Umweltgeschichte. Umweltverträgliches Wirtschaften in historischer Perspektive* (Göttingen: Vandenhoeck & Ruprecht, 1994): 29–56; Bayerl, Günter, "Die Natur als Warenhaus. Der technisch-ökonomische Blick auf die Natur in der Frühen Neuzeit," in Sylvia Hahn and Reinhold Reith (eds.), *Umwelt-Geschichte. Arbeitsfelder, Forschungsansätze, Perspektiven* (Wien, München: Verlag für Geschichte und Politik, 2001): 33–52.

10   On the linkage of zoological gardens and the exploitation of nature see Eric Baratay and Elisabeth Hardouin-Fugier, *ZOOS. Histoire des jardins zoologiques en Occident (XVIe-XXe siècle)* (Paris: Edition de la découverte, 1998).

11   For Britain see Maxine Berg, *Luxury and Pleasure in Eighteenth-Century Britain* (Oxford: Oxford University Press, 2005) and Colin Campbell, "Understanding traditional and modern patterns of consumption in eighteenth-century England: A character-action approach," in John Brewer and Roy Porter (eds.), *Consumption and the World of Goods* (London, New York: Routledge, 1993): 40–57. For France see the articles in Robert Fox and Anthony Turner (eds.), *Luxury Trades and Consumerism in Ancien Régime Paris. Studies in the History of the Skilled Workforce* (Aldershot, i.a.: Ashgate, 1998). For Germany see Michael North, *Material Delight and the Joy of Living: Cultural Consumption in the Age of Enlightenment in Germany* (Aldershot, i.a.: Ashgate, 2008) and Sheilagh Ogilvie, "Consumption, social capital, and the 'Industrious Revolution' " in early modern Germany," *Journal of Economic History* 70 (2010): 287–325.

12   Mark Overton, Jane Whittle, Darron Dean, and Andrew Hann, *Production and Consumption in English Households 1600–1750* (London, New York: Routledge, 2004). See 13–32 for a discussion of probate inventories as a source.

13   Examples of inventories of material cultures from Ireland and South Africa: David A. Whelan and Tadgh O'Keeffe, "The house of Ussher: Histories and heritages of improvement: Conspicious consumption and eviction on an early nineteenth-century Irish estate," *International Journal of Historical Archaeology* 18 (2014): 700–725 and Johan Fourie and Jolandi Uys, "Luxury product consumption in eighteenth-century Cape Colony households," *Tijdschrift voor Sociale en Economische Geschiedenis* 9 (2012): 29–60.

14   Alfred W. Crosby, *The Columbian Exchange: Biological and Cultural Consequences of 1492*, 2nd edition (Westport, CT: Greenwood, 1973); Alfred W. Crosby, *Ecological Imperialism: The Biological Expansion of Europe, 900–1900* (Cambridge: Cambridge University Press, 1986).

15   Andreas Dix, "Die ökologischen Folgen der modernen Weltwirtschaft des 19. Jahrhunderts in Deutschland," *Archiv für Sozialgeschichte* 43 (2003): 81–99.

16   Oliver Bender, *Analyse der Kulturlandschaftsentwicklung der Nördlichen Frankenalb anhand eines katasterbasierten Geoinformationssystems* (Leipzig: Deutsche Akademie für Landeskunde, 2007).

17   Warren G. Breckman, "Disciplining consumption: The debate about luxury in Wilhelmine Germany 1840–1914," *Journal of Social History* 24 (1991): 485–505. For a more theoretical perspective see Ulrich Witt, "Learning to consume: A theory of wants and the growth of demand," *Journal of Evolutionary Economics* 11 (2001): 23–36.

18   For a geography of food in general and the linkage to spatial patterns of origin see Ian Cook, "Geographies of food: Mixing," *Progress in Human Geography* 32 (2008): 821–833; Ian Cook and Philip Crang, "The world on a plate: Culinary culture, displacement and geographical knowledges," *Journal of Material Culture* 1 (1996): 131–153; and James Walvin, *Fruits of Empire: Exotic Produce and British Taste, 1660–1860* (Basingstoke, i.a.: Macmillan, 1997).

19   Christine Krämer, *Rebsorten in Württemberg. Herkunft, Einführung, Verbreitung und die Qualität der Weine vom Spätmittelalter bis ins 19. Jahrhundert* (Ostfildern: Thorbecke, 2006).

20   As an early example from Germany see Lambert von Babo, *Der Weinstock und seine Varietäten. Beschreibung und Synonymik der vorzüglichsten in Deutschland cultivirten Wein- und Tafeltrauben, mit Hinweisung auf die bekannteren Rebsorten anderer europäischer Weinländer* (Frankfurt am Main: Brönner, 1844).

21 Tim Unwin, *Wine and the Vine: An Historical Geography of Viticulture and the Wine Trade* (London, New York: Routledge, 1991), 278–283.

22 This could be an important aspect within modern perspectives of research on the formation of markets, see Patrick Aspers, *How are Markets Made?* (Cologne: Max Planck Institute for the Study of Societies, 2009).

23 Ulrich Eisenbach, *Wirtschafts- und Sozialgeschichte des Niederselterser Brunnenbetriebes bis zum Ende des Herzogtums Nassau* (Wiesbaden: Historische Kommission für Nassau, 1982).

24 A good overview about the most famous springs and their history see Philip E. LaMoreaux and Judy T. Tanner (eds.), *Springs and Bottled Water of the World: Ancient History, Source, Occurrence, Quality and Use*, (Berlin, i.a.: Springer, 2001). As an interesting case study of the ecological impact of (normal) water consumption see Enric Tello and Joan Ramos Ostos, "Water consumption in Barcelona and its regional environmental imprint: A long term history (1717–2008)," *Regional Environmental Change* 12 (2012): 347–361.

25 Stephanie Spencer and Francis Bedford, *Landscape Photography and Nineteenth-Century British Culture: The Artist as Entrepreneur* (Farnham, i.a.: Ashgate, 2011). Douglas Nickel, *Francis Frith in Egypt and Palestine: A Victorian Photographer Abroad* (Princeton, NJ: Princeton University Press, 2004).

26 Susanne Müller, *Die Welt des Baedeker. Eine Medienkulturgeschichte des Reiseführers 1830–1945* (Frankfurt am Main, New York: Campus 2012); Rudy Koshar, " 'What ought to be seen': Tourist's guidebooks and national identities in modern Germany and Europe," *Journal of Contemporary History* 33 (1998): 323–340. For the American example see Richard H. Gassan, "The first American tourist guidebooks: Authorship and the print culture of the 1820s," *Book History* 8 (2005): 51–74.

27 As a case study for the new kingdom of Bavaria in the nineteenth century see Karin Rhein, „Vom Erkundungsauftrag über Künstlerkolonie und touristische Pfade zu den stillen Winkeln—Bayern in Zeichnungen," in Sigrid Sylfide Bertuleit (ed.), *Künstler sehen Bayern. Bayern lässt staunen* (Schweinfurt: Museum Georg Schäfer, 2013), 147–153.

28 Michael Jacobs, *The Good and Simple Life: Artist Colonies in Europe and America* (Oxford: Phaidon, 1985); Nina Lübbren, *Rural Artists' Colonies in Europe 1870–1910* (Manchester: Manchester University Press, 2001); and Claus Pese, *Künstlerkolonien in Europa. Im Zeichen der Ebene und des Himmels* (Nürnberg: Germanisches Nationalmuseum, 2001).

29 Andreas Dix, "Das Mittelrheintal. Wahrnehmung und Veränderung einer symbolischen Landschaft des 19. Jahrhunderts," *Petermanns Geographische Mitteilungen* 146 (2002): 44–53.

30 On the examples of Great Britain and Germany, see David Evans, *A History of Nature Conservation in Britain*, 2nd edition (London, New York: Routledge, 1997) and Friedemann Schmoll, *Erinnerung an die Natur. Die Geschichte des Naturschutzes im deutschen Kaiserreich*, (Frankfurt am Main, New York: Campus, 2004).

31 Richard H. Gassan, *The Birth of American Tourism: New York, the Hudson Valley and American Culture, 1790–1935* (Amherst: University of Massachusetts Press, 2008).

32 See the basic publications of John Urry, such as John Urry, *The Tourist Gaze*, 2nd edition (London, i.a.: Sage, 2002); Urry, *Consuming Places*, 2nd edition (London, New York: Routledge, 2002).

33 Donna Landry, *The Invention of the Countryside: Hunting, Walking and Ecology in English Literature, 1671–1831* (Basingstocke, i.a.: Palgrave, 2001).

34 Kenneth I. Helphand, "Learning from linksland," *Landscape Journal* 14 (1995): 74–86.

35   For a good overview on the number and spatial distribution of those "Keller" see Thomas Gunzelmann, "Bierlandschaft Bayern: Keller als historische Orte des Konsums," *Siedlungsforschung. Archäologie—Geschichte—Geographie* 28 (2010): 7–53.

36   Gavin Weightman, *The Frozen Water Trade: How Ice From New England Kept the World Cool* (London: HarperCollins, 2003) and Bodil Bjerkvik Blain, *Melting Markets: The Rise and Decline of the Anglo-Norwegian Ice Trade 1850–1920* (London: London School of Economics, 2006).

37   John Towner, *An Historical Geography of Recreation and Tourism in the Western World 1540–1940* (Chichester, i.a.: Wiley, 1996), 53–95 and Volkmar Eidloth, "Europäische Kur- und Badestädte des 19. Jahrhunderts. Ein kon-sumorientierter Stadttyp," *Siedlungsforschung. Archäologie—Geschichte—Geographie* 28 (2010): 157–182.

Part II
Frontier Environments

3 New Frontiers and Natural Resources in Southern South America, c. 1820–1870

Examples from Northwest European Mercantile Enterprise

Stephen Bell

South American independence drew the natural resources of the region into a broader orbit. This moved in uneven stages. On the one hand, it reflected the degree of progress of the independence movement itself. The ports of Brazil opened to international commerce in 1808 and the first portion of Spanish America open to international trade was Buenos Aires, starting on 25 May 1810. An extraordinary bubble of commercial activity followed. All manner of European products, mainly British, headed for South America, some of them highly inappropriate for the local markets. For example, John Luccock, active as a general merchant at Rio de Janeiro after 1808, could not see any rationale for sending a consignment of pocketbooks and wallets to a country "where there was no paper money, and where the coin was so heavy that slaves were employed to carry it."[1] It was but one item from a long series of commercial absurdities. Once Northwest European merchants established themselves in South America, commercial intelligence grew. The geography of the mercantile presence focused heavily at first on the major ports, Rio de Janeiro, Montevideo, Buenos Aires, and Valparaíso. These ports became the bases for the examination of a series of trading peripheries and their environments.

This essay addresses intersections between mercantile adventuring, natural resources and science in Southern South America from the early national period through to the early history of the famous Liebig Extract of Meat Company at Fray Bentos, Uruguay, during the 1860s. In the Río de la Plata, a minority of Northwest European merchants was important from the1820s onward. As outsiders seeking wealth, their loyalties rarely to specific places, their lines of communication with Europe almost always present, European merchants maneuvered around political obstacles and sometimes over great geographical expanses in search of what Stanley and Barbara Stein once called 'privilege and preference.'[2] Such privileges carried environmental consequences.

Three examples of the development of regional peripheries are considered, beginning with the efforts from Buenos Aires of the Scottish merchants John and William Parish Robertson to open the Upper Plata as a resource frontier in the 1820s.[3] Their three-volume *Letters on South America*, published in 1843, takes as its main focus the investigation of natural resources along the Paraná River in what was often seen as the adventurous phase of commerce.[4] In their various books, rivers and the natural resources along them are key to understanding the Robertsons. The paper then turns to a consequence of civil wars in mainland South America and investigates how Samuel Fisher Lafone, a Montevideo-based merchant, managed to turn a large portion of the East Falklands (still identified as Lafonia on British maps) into a resource frontier during the 1840s under circumstances very different from those idealized by the British colonial government. Linkages are revealed between Lafone's economic exploitation of the Falklands (Malvinas) and his earlier patterns of economic activity within the South American mainland. The third case examined in this paper investigates various efforts to relay European science along yet another livestock resource periphery, the Uruguayan bank of the Uruguay River during the 1860s. With the traditional markets for salt-beef saturated following a generalized peace (a consequence of herd recovery following the disruptions of war), the low prevailing prices of this commodity provided an impetus for the development and use of new technology. Various new methods for preserving meat were tried within enclave enterprises in Western Uruguay, but the most important by far became the Liebig enterprise at Fray Bentos. The paper analyzes the threads that link Liebig's studies of the chemistry of food at Munich with the testing of his ideas in South America and the subsequent rapid development of an enterprise that quickly reached world renown.

TRADING UP: THE MERCHANT ADVENTURING OF THE ROBERTSON BROTHERS

Among the many striking descriptive passages in *Letters on South America*, there is a particularly compelling account given by the young William Parish Robertson of his transformation of a "wretched old hovel" into a "spruce little cottage" at Goya, a small river port located in a subtropical portion of Corrientes, within the Upper Plata.[5] William cannot have been much beyond the age of majority at the time, but he had already accumulated considerable experience of South American societies, including expulsion in 1815 from Paraguay by José Gaspar Rodríguez de Francia, its legendary dictator. Following the commercial trail opened by his elder brother John, the purpose of establishing a modest base at Goya was to gather ranch products from the interior of Corrientes then ship them more than a thousand kilometers down the river to Buenos Aires. Engagement with the riverine trade of the South American interior marked the Robertsons apart from the bulk of Buenos Aires–based, foreign-born merchants. The high profits gained in the early phase of their engagement with the interior added greatly to their capabilities in coastal environments.[6]

William Parish Robertson's temporary home in the interior of South America made a considerable local impact for its material culture. We read of an English yellow cane sofa and chairs, mahogany tables, the presence of a library, "smart wineglasses" on the sideboard:

> But what I prided myself on was my carpet. It was composed of magnificent tiger skins collected in the province, and it entirely covered my "sala," which was of a good size. I question whether our royal lady, Queen Victoria, has now in Buckingham-palace so splendid a carpet as was mine in Goya.[7]

One rancher who came on a livestock-selling visit supposedly could not forgive the economy of not adding an English carpet instead of a "parcel of common tiger skins rudely patched together."[8] Today we think back mainly on how the South American big cat (*Panthera onca*) had become more and more an object of trade. Hunted down for their skins by specialists using dogs, the jaguars of South America formed an exotic example of a more widespread incorporation of rural resources for trade. In less than a year's residence at Goya, William Parish Robertson, using a collecting network headed by Peter Campbell, an Irish-born adventurer who had assumed marked gaucho characteristics in his lifestyle and dress, shipped south 50,000 hides stripped from oxen, 100,000 taken from horses, and quantities of bales of wool and hair without count. The Robertsons were not alone in seeking to develop the trading possibilities of the Upper Plata. Even Alexander von Humboldt's former research companion, the French scientist Aimé Bonpland, spent much of the years 1820–1821 focused alongside a network of French merchant colleagues on trade in the region, with much of his emphasis on tropical hardwoods.[9] An essential feature of the famous Carrera del Paraguay during colonial Spanish America was the use of log booms and rafts for the river trade that could be broken apart once close to the market. Merchant adventurers had much to learn quickly about the hazards of navigation along the rivers. One aspect that made the Robertsons distinctive was the superior quality of their network of supply from regional ranchers. This concerned investment in credit to landowners, the provision of transportation, of storage, and of shipping facilities.[10] It was key for them in achieving high profits.

The Robertsons provide a fine example of the adventurous phase of South American commerce.[11] Not much is known for sure about their early circumstances in Scotland, but they evinced a superior level of general education. John Parish Robertson was born in 1792, his younger brother William two years later. John first came to the Río de la Plata in 1807. He was linked with political events at Montevideo in 1807 (the temporary British military occupation of the city) and at Rio de Janeiro in the following year. He formed part of the early international merchant community at Buenos Aires and was a resident there by 1810. By December 1811, John Parish

Robertson followed the ambitious course of following the great riverine system into the interior of South America, finding his way to Paraguay, a place then very little known in the broader world and sometimes compared with Tibet. It had an exotic reputation, stemming in part from the scale of the Jesuit mission system of the previous centuries and from the character of its politics. Paraguay would soon fall into the dictatorship of José Gaspar Rodríguez de Francia. John Parish Robertson's early contacts with this figure were highly successful. He left a fascinating account of his first chance meeting with him within the first volume of his *Letters on Paraguay*.[12] A young man not yet twenty, who had recently been engaged keeping books at Buenos Aires, saw remarkable profit margins on his trade goods, for example of twentyfold on salt brought north from the estuary.

The young John Parish Robinson's quick commercial success attracted his younger brother William out from Scotland in 1814. The two would then spend decades closely associated with Southern South American development, with John leaving the region for good in 1830 and William in 1834. Despite their strong attachment to a geographical region in a struggling stage of development, the brothers never spent much time together in one place. It was a clear commercial advantage to have a trusted correspondent who could cover an orbit greater than any individual alone.[13] We learn most of what we know about the Robertsons from their books published through subscription following their merchant careers, in efforts to make some money. The scoop, if there was one, was undoubtedly coverage of Paraguay and its singular dictator Francia. Their books, which warrant close reading from a variety of perspectives, are based on the retrospective method. They build from letters written often decades earlier. They vary considerably from the unembroidered commercial letters written by their somewhat younger employee and potential partner Charles Holland (born in 1799), who stayed much more directly on the trading environment, venting at times his frustrations to his father and uncle. Charles Holland, born into a family with deep roots in Lancashire, and later especially with the port of Liverpool, began to learn about a career in business at the age of thirteen, working from Malta.[14] From there, he arrived at Buenos Aires in 1819, quickly linking up with the Robertson brothers in their business.[15]

Whatever drama we glean from any reading of the Robertsons' books, and there is plenty of that, the image of the intrepid and youthful entrepreneurs needs also to admit the fact that their grandfather was one John Parish. Born in Leith, Scotland, John Parish became the founder of a great merchant banking house at Hamburg. And thus a Scottish family name became inscribed in the list of the Hanseatic merchant traders. In the later eighteenth century, and before Napoleonic disturbances that echoed widely, including across the Atlantic, especially visibly in Brazil, the 'Haus Parish' has been described as "the most important Hamburg merchant bank."[16] Although their grandfather had retired from business, in favor of a sybaritic retirement based in fashionable Bath, the commercial history he embodied and his commercial network were undoubtedly key in the expansion of the

Figure 3.1 Unsigned portrait of Charles Holland (1799–1870) as a young man.

Source: Reproduced from Holland, *Noticias de Buenos Aires*, frontispiece.

South American business run by the Robertsons. Charles Holland (Figure 3.1), desperate to emerge from the status of what he expressively described as an "adventurer quilldriver," also derived at least some moral benefit from having an uncle, Swinton Holland, who was a partner in Barings, which in the early nineteenth century was commonly viewed as the leading mercantile enterprise in the entire world.[17]

Eighteen letters and a fragment survive from a broader corpus of writing undertaken by Charles Holland from South America during the period 1820–1826. Only the first comes from Buenos Aires, written during the early stage of his involvement with the Robertsons in March 1820, when he argued trade stood very limited at Buenos Aires. Yet their involvement in the river trade—his employers still maintained an agent at Corrientes and kept two ships constantly engaged in this business—provided their business with sounder foundations than the other British merchant houses at Buenos Aires. An exaggerated sense of Paraguay's prosperity still prevailed in commercial intelligence, shown by Holland's comment that it was "by far the richest and most populous of the provinces which have thrown off the Spanish yoke."[18] At Buenos Aires itself, the activities of a merchant house bore many similarities with what Holland had known earlier in Malta. However, he reminded his uncle how much easier it was to account for the bulky consignments of colonial products that formed a large portion of Mediterranean trade "compared with the retail of a long Manchester invoice, and in these bad times we condescend to divide and retail the cases."[19] In addition, sales could only be affected by extending long credits, an understood pattern. Even then, business terms were far from easy to enforce. Whatever the challenges of the Río de la Plata, Charles Holland conveyed a strong sense of economic possibilities for his uncle, when compared with the immediate social and political challenges in Britain: "If we could but give the poor people with you the superfluous Beef that is wasted here it would be a most effectual physic for the Radicals."[20]

When William Parish Robertson later reflected on this period Holland described in his family letters to England, he saw it as constituting something of a golden age for business in Buenos Aires. While William remained in Buenos Aires, John set himself up in Liverpool. Their merchant house became a firmly founded one, corresponding with the leading houses in Europe, "importing German linens from Hamburg, shipping Spanish dollars for Bombay and Calcutta, freighting jerked beef for Havana."[21] Much of the foundation for this success in Buenos Aires came from the high profits drawn from the river trade with Corrientes and Paraguay. By 1820, the brothers had decided to extend their activities in several new areas. For one, they were interesting themselves in the expansion of trade along the west coast of South America. This explains why Charles Holland's later South American letters were written from Valparaíso and Santiago in Chile, and from Lima, Peru. The progress of trade there hinged to huge degree on the progress of the decolonization movement. The Robertson brothers also extended their commercial interests at Buenos Aires, not least in helping to arrange the commercial loans (government debt) assumed by Buenos Aires Province. In January 1824, they were a key part of the consortium established at Buenos Aires to negotiate a loan of £1,000,000 from London. In March of the same year, they signed an agreement for a colonization scheme.[22]

Charles Holland's letters from west coast South America laid bare his ambitions, his sense of his own strengths and weaknesses, and, above all, his perception of the difficulties for successfully conducting business in this newly independent region. By 1825, he was under consideration for a partnership, yet he confided to his uncle Swinton at Barings in London doubts that he could not meet the standards of his predecessor, who was about to go into retirement: "Impudence must carry me through as it does your friend Rothschild on some occasions."[23] In the same year, he drew a contrast for his father between his assistant's business skills at Lima and his own, praising the methods of the former (an individual trained within the Parish merchant house at Hamburg). As for Holland himself, he maintained he had learned within "the most unmethodical school possible say in South America."[24] Although still in his mid-twenties, the challenges of working from the west coast of South America seemed to be turning Holland into something of a curmudgeon, at least in the image of himself conveyed to relatives in England. He wrote of the "annoyances of being obliged to submit to the impertinencies of Manchester men in bad times, and to the rebukes of your Partners enjoying themselves over a fireside in England."[25] Any competing visions of the details of trade were hardly quickly exchanged. It took between four and six months to transport a letter from the west coast of South America to London. Sometimes they were conveyed over the Andes, then across the pampas to Buenos Aires; while based at Lima, Holland increasingly began to use the route through Panama. All of this placed considerable focus on the characters and business merits of those with whom Holland was involved. This was an area of enormous challenges: "You are compelled to trust important business to men who have no idea of regularity, in fact the patience of Job and the Ices from the neighbouring Cordillera are required to prevent your falling a victim to brain fever."[26] Even John Parish Robertson, the great pioneer of trade with Paraguay, perhaps showed difficulty keeping on track where commerce was concerned. As Holland informed his uncle from Santiago in February 1825

> Mr. J.P.R. studiously avoids the subject of the Loan finances, and indeed from the cavalier like way in which he treats us, giving us a few short lines occasionally when he condescends to leave Edinburgh & literary pursuits for business, I am inclined to think he feels no great relish now for trade.[27]

Only so much can be gleaned from a merchant correspondence where but one side is available for consultation. The Robertsons wrote books following their South American sojourns, based upon the letters they had exchanged earlier in their work. They profited from the fact that between 1810 and 1835 they "never contrived to spend altogether two years in each other's society" and this has resulted in remarkable printed sources for establishing many aspects of the historical geography of Southern South America during the first decades of the nineteenth century.[28] As with their early roots in Scotland, the details for the later lives of the Robertson brothers are sometimes sketchy and certainly uneven. Their South American business stood in liquidation by 1827. They had most probably overextended themselves, not least in their colony of Monte Grande, which attracted settlers from Scotland.[29] Although this was successful in some regards—it had attracted five hundred people by 1828—the project ultimately became a victim of politics. While their initial contract with the government at Buenos Aires provided for settlement on government land well to the south of Buenos Aires, the Robertsons opted instead to promote a colony design using the purchase of private land closer to the city. They invested heavily in this project, placing some £60,000 of their capital in it. Their key activities in connection with government loans at Buenos Aires and with colonization both brought obligations very difficult to meet after the general financial crash of 1825.

By 1830, John Parish Robertson had entered himself as a student at Corpus Christi College, Cambridge, perhaps bearing out an ambition Charles Holland had noted in him some years earlier. Leaving without a degree, he then turned to writing his books, produced in collaboration with his younger brother. He died at Calais in 1843. William Parish Robertson ultimately gained the longer involvement with South America. His roles following the demise of the house established with his elder brother included working as the head clerk of the important merchant house Antony Gibbs & Sons at London and serving there as the consul for Peru, then the consul-general for Ecuador.[30] There is some vagueness about the time and place of his death, possibly at Valparaíso in 1861. Neither of the Robertson brothers met the success of their grandfather John Parish in moving upward socially from engagement in trade. Based at Bath after 1807, he gave during the next sixteen years of his remaining life "579 dinners and 76 balls and suppers and disposed of 14,750 bottles of wine."[31]

Charles Holland withdrew from the politically challenged environment of the west coast of South America, returning eventually to the Río de la Plata and to Southern Brazil. In the case of the latter, his business was linked especially with Rio Grande do Sul, perhaps an obvious extension for his familiarity gained with trading ranch products from Buenos Aires. Unlike John Parish Robertson, Charles Holland stayed true to business throughout his life, working from a range of South American locations and trading up the urban hierarchy based on his profits made from detailed knowledge of commodities and their physical environmental bases. Ultimately, however, he was more attached to European circuits than to South American ones. The Hollands, kinsmen of the novelist Elizabeth Gaskell, played important merchant roles in the development of Liverpool during the eighteenth and nineteenth centuries.[32] In 1844, Charles Holland bought Liscard Vale House, an impressive estate on the Wirral Peninsula, opposite Liverpool, that became his domicile for the rest of his life. As a Unitarian, he seems to have been forward thinking on financial and social issues, especially in the Liverpool area. He chaired the Liverpool Chamber of Commerce, was active in the Finance Reform Association (providing testimony to the House of Commons on this subject), and he promoted public measures such as railways. Charles Holland died from yellow fever at Rome in 1870.[33] Whatever the misgivings about South American trading he expressed in his letters as a young man, working with commodities from this region had enabled him to trade up with marked success, since his assets upon death were valued at the considerable sum of £200,000.

THE DIVERSIFIED NETWORKS OF SAMUEL LAFONE

Liverpool was also the place of origin of the British merchant and investor Samuel Fisher Lafone (1805–1871), who by some accounts reached the status of the wealthiest Briton resident in South America around the middle decades of the nineteenth century, an impressive feat for somebody based most of the time in the small republic of Uruguay. Born in 1805, his family had links with the Liverpool leather trade reaching back into the eighteenth century. As with the Robertson brothers, Lafone enjoyed access to capital at some level within Britain itself. He began his South American career in the 1820s, working as a hide merchant from Buenos Aires. In 1832, he greatly complicated his life there by marrying into the regional creole elite. His marriage to María Quevedo y Alsina, undertaken in secret within a Protestant ceremony, led to considerable scandal in Argentina. It became a diplomatic incident with the government headed by Juan Manuel de Rosas (Argentina only recognized marriages conducted within the Roman Catholic rite), and it left Samuel Lafone an implacable enemy of the famous Argentine dictator. It was probably soon after this that Lafone moved across the estuary to Montevideo, where he developed the *saladero* (a salt-beef slaughtering plant) La Teja in the district of the same name (the toponym means 'clay tile,' perhaps reflecting the material used to roof the one-storey houses he built for his workers) on the outskirts of this city. By 1842, the district assumed a change of name to the Villa Victoria, in honor of the British sovereign, with its central square the Plaza Lafone. The profits drawn from the saladero business helped Lafone to accumulate quickly a very broad profile of commercial interests.

Lafone placed deep roots in Montevideo, and he used the city to influence politics across the broader region. A key piece of evidence for his commitment came in his buying of land for an Anglican church there. Founded in 1847, on the site where the Royal Navy had breached the city walls in an invasion forty years earlier, the iconography of both the site and the neoclassical architectural style of the building were telling. The formation of this Anglican church at Montevideo, the second oldest in Spanish-speaking South America, came in the midst of a civil war, the Guerra Grande of 1839–1851, which is in itself some testimony to Lafone's influence and power.

During the 1830s, Lafone's business involved his merchant house and the processing of ranch products. He also signed agreements with the Uruguayan government of the time to introduce agricultural colonists, with plans to draw these from the Canaries, Cape Verde and the Basque country, along with a portion of English artisans. Civil war across the Río de la Plata brought both challenges and opportunities for Lafone. By the early 1840s, he was a leading partner in a consortium that collected duties in the customhouse at Montevideo. The government there had mortgaged important public property to Lafone, who also held a long series of monopoly concessions, ranging from lucrative sea lion slaughter (for their pelts) on offshore islands to steam navigation on the Uruguay River.

In conjunction with his brother Alexander Ross Lafone, a figure who played key roles in the development of their business at both Buenos Aires and London, Samuel Lafone accomplished the most spectacular purchase of public lands in Uruguay. In 1843, they bought the whole of the Punta del Este peninsula near Maldonado for a truly modest sum, an Atlantic real estate transaction that has been compared (showing some degree of hyperbole) with the Dutch purchase of Manhattan in 1621.[34] In the motives for buying land there, geopolitics played a large role. The Royal Navy was looking for places along the South Atlantic mainland coast to establish a coaling depot for the provisioning of vessels that served the Falklands. The Lafones were working to foment ideas that a major new Atlantic port could be developed around Maldonado, to the north of Montevideo, which would provide a key to regional commerce. But in the shorter term, fishing, whaling, and sea lion slaughter provided plenty of revenue. Income from exploitation of natural resources provided support for broader scale speculations.

In 1843, the caudillo Manuel Oribe, an ally of Rosas and already in control of the territory of the rest of Uruguay, began his nine-year (and ultimately unsuccessful) siege of Montevideo. Samuel Lafone's response to the threat was in part to spread his risk, a good example of the theme of a 'web of enterprise.'[35] In 1844, he sent agents to the Falkland Islands in search of a land concession. Reports were prepared providing an attractive vision of what was possible in terms of colonization, the raising of sheep and of cattle, and the development of a station for catching whales. Alexander Ross Lafone moved to London in order to lobby the British government. The British colonial government had the idealistic design that the attraction of a single capitalist would lead to large-scale farming and thereby settlement of the Falklands (Malvinas). Alba Mariani has argued that the Lafones held a clear geopolitical vision of how to develop the area under their commercial control.[36] This vision centered on the Atlantic combined with the Río de la Plata. Their concession of the Punta del Este region on the Uruguayan mainland was projected to serve as the base for the connection of a series of ocean and river ports toward the south in the direction of the Falklands. A base in those islands was in turn valuable for trade links with the Pacific around Cape Horn, enabling business with Valparaíso. From Valparaíso, possibilities opened toward the north, with Callao, Guayaquil, and Panama, in an effort to impede the aggressive expansion of American commerce southward out of the port of San Francisco. Lafone bought the large portion of East Falkland that is still named after him and exclusive rights to the feral cattle, descendants of animals introduced by the French in the eighteenth century. The result of this investment was the erection of an extensive saladero at Hope Place and cattle slaughter unaccompanied by any herd management. In order to accomplish their relatively quick cull of the regional livestock resources, the Lafones imported gaucho labor from the South American mainland (Figure 3.2).

In 1851, the year of Oribe's defeat, Samuel Lafone sold his holding to the Falkland Islands Company, set up under royal charter for the express purpose of acquiring his interests in the islands. The long-term impact of this short-lived mercantile venture is inscribed in the toponymy of British maps of the Falklands.

The commercial adventuring undertaken by the Lafones in the Falklands may well show evidence of a geopolitical design on a broad scale within South America. But it was also about mobile access to resources during a

Figure 3.2 **Gauchos taking maté at Hope Place.** This is an extreme example of a rustic gaucho frontier environment underwritten by British capital.

Source: Watercolor by William Pownall Dale, c.1852, courtesy of the Historic Dockyard Museum, Falkland Islands.

long phase of political instability. By 1852, both Oribe and Rosas had been defeated. The return to a more generalized peace brought a deeper interest in technology in the labor-short Río de la Plata. For example, at Montevideo, Lafone reactivated and improved his large saladero La Teja. Successfully divesting himself of the cattle enterprise in East Falkland, he was quick to increase investment on the South American mainland.

The Lafones did not end their refocusing of strategy with a renewed emphasis on Montevideo, the leading traditional site of livestock slaughter in this country based so very heavily on a pastoral economy. A new direction of endeavor began following the freeing of the Paraná and Uruguay to international shipping. The Paraná was opened by the force of an Anglo-French naval effort in 1845, but freedom of navigation was not assured until after the fall of Rosas. The emergence of slaughtering plants along the rivers quickly followed the seesaw of politics. The largest plants in Entre Ríos, Argentina, clustered around Gualeguaychú, were owned by Justo José de Urquiza (1800–1870), the ambitious caudillo who controlled the province and played a major role in Rosas's downfall. In the period 1852–1856, while Urquiza was fully occupied with the business of the Argentine Confederation, the Montevideo capitalist Samuel Lafone also played a role in developing the resources of Entre Ríos by working the saladeros Santa Cándida (today the site of a major museum devoted to Urquiza's life and legacy), Constancia, and Concordia on Urquiza's behalf. Taken together, Urquiza and Lafone represented a remarkable concentration of political and economic power. Plants even emerged within the Upper Plata (in Corrientes) during the 1850s. By the early 1860s, Samuel Lafone's investment in saladeros had spread as far north as Goya on the Paraná. The decade of the 1850s also saw expansion along the east bank of the Uruguay River.

Samuel Lafone had been an important figure within the commerce of Uruguay before the civil wars that affected the Plata for so long. Despite the enormous risks entailed, he adjusted his investments during the wars, most visibly through his new venture in the Falklands, and emerged in the peace that followed to build on his role as the leading British investor in Uruguay with a diverse economic empire running from the South Atlantic islands to mines in the mountains of Catamarca, Argentina. The list of his economic activities is immense. He forms a very different case than the standard view of British merchants provided by D.C.M. Platt in his seminal study of Latin America and British trade, where most of these, ill acquainted with the politics, customs and characters of the peoples with whom they lived, gave up on South America in relatively short order.[37] By 1858, Samuel Lafone had built a personal fortune of £800,000, a massive sum for the era. Not surprisingly, he was sometimes dubbed the 'merchant prince' of Montevideo.[38]

Working on such an extensive geographical canvas, he clearly faced, like all other merchants and investors, issues of trust in the supervision and management of his enterprises. Peter Sims has undertaken immensely valuable research of late, showing how Samuel Lafone used his family network to advantage.[39] This began with family connections to firms in both Liverpool and London. Hides and cattle dealing were a key part of the family's commercial roots in England. Samuel's half brother Alfred (later in the nineteenth century a Conservative MP) married into a family well established in the hides trade with the Río de la Plata. Brothers and half brothers were used as managers and even as diplomats. For example, the agreement Samuel Lafone made with Queen Victoria regarding the East Falklands was completed by his younger brother Alexander Ross Lafone, acting as his attorney. John Pownall Dale, married to Samuel's sister Martha, managed at different times the model saladero La Teja and the Lafone colony in the Falklands, and he even acted as the temporary British consul at Montevideo during the early stages of the Guerra Grande. Juan Quevedo, the brother of Samuel's wife, came across the estuary from Buenos Aires as a young man and served his brother-in-law's business in numerous ways as an attorney. Research progress has certainly been made in recent years for documenting the huge scope of Samuel Lafone's business network. Yet even now, aspects of his enterprise are poorly understood. One indication of Lafone's recognized power at Montevideo can be seen in an 1840 request coming from the rebel government in southernmost Brazil (Rio Grande do Sul experienced civil war along the decade 1835–1845) asking him to assume the role of sole supplier of goods to the breakaway Riograndense Republic.[40] And while Lafone's linkages within the British community within South America are increasingly well established, there has thus far been little consideration of his ties to immigrants of other national origins in the broader business community, including with the Frenchman Benjamin Poucel, a figure of great importance in the development of Lafone's mining interests in Catamarca, Argentina.

A TECHNOLOGICAL FRONTIER: FRAY BENTOS AS THE 'KITCHEN OF THE WORLD'

The economies of Southern South America mainly hinged around the elaboration of ranch products. By the middle of the century, in response to expanding markets, little was being wasted in the ranching economies of Southern South America. Fat, bones, hair, and parts of cattle unsuitable for turning into salt-beef all found their specialized customers. Between metropolis and periphery stood the networks of merchant entrepreneurs who stimulated experiment. The historical geography of the international meat trade is an important theme connecting South America with Europe, but especially with Britain. Imports eventually provided a solution there to the problem of feeding a rapidly rising population and improving the amount of food available per head. Along with grains and sugar, meat played an important role in stoking the Industrial Revolution. The growing shortage of food in the face of a swelling population in Europe provided an impetus for the development and use of new technology.[41]

In the North Atlantic, refrigeration was the leading focus for experiment. In Britain, the number of patents taken out for meat refrigeration showed a sharp increase: 1850s (11), 1860s (30), and 1870–1874 (56).[42] Nevertheless, successful practical results lay only toward the end of the century. Nineteenth-century science also turned to the chemistry of meat, with the emphasis on preservation for nutrition. A wide variety of schemes were attempted, including the injection of preserving agents and the packing of meat under vacuum. The most distinguished work in this respect was conducted by Justus von Liebig (1803–1873), whose research contained explicitly humanitarian elements. Liebig was convinced of the nutritional importance of muscle juices, leading to the conclusion that it was important to eat meat along with its gravy or soup. Building on the findings of French chemists earlier in the century, in 1847 he developed 'extractum carnis' (extract of meat).[43] By the 1850s, Liebig's extract was much in demand at Munich, but it was in use there mainly as a remedy, something only the affluent could afford. The main obstacle to large-scale production of extract in Europe was the high cost of beef, the raw material. Although Liebig encouraged entrepreneurs to produce extract of meat in Buenos Aires and in Australia, the lapse between his theoretical findings and successful large-scale production was relatively long.

The scope for science in the periphery changed quite abruptly in the first half of the 1860s. In Europe, cattle diseases raised the price of meat almost beyond the reach of anyone but the most affluent. In Southern South America, the conclusion in 1852 of a lengthy series of wars was followed by recovery of the cattle herds. The recovery of these herds and the expansion of the slaughtering facilities led inexorably to temporary oversupply of the traditional markets for salt-beef in the plantation complex (Brazil and Cuba). The problem of oversupply of raw material was concentrated in Southern Brazil and especially in Uruguay, where the slaughter tally tripled. A 'crash' came in the early 1860s with a commercial depression, linked in large part to the American Civil War. As the prices for salt-beef fell, the scope for experimentation with more distant markets increased.[44] Some of this experimentation occurred around the established main places of slaughter, especially Buenos Aires and Montevideo, but much of it took place in the new saladeros opened by Northwest European entrepreneurs along the Uruguayan bank of the Uruguay River. The reasons why new saladeros appeared in this specific region were several. Issues of navigability were important, as was the wish of the entrepreneurs to avoid embroilment as much as feasible in Argentina's continuing metropolis-periphery struggle between Buenos Aires and the interior. These new plants were emphatically operations of the enclave type, only loosely related to the earlier economic geography of slaughter. In the western periphery of Uruguay, they showed only limited competition with the long-established Montevideo saladeros, and thus were able to pay very low prices for their raw material.

Most of the experiments tried in Western Uruguay were short lived, the bases of their technologies (the preservation of beef through forced infiltration with brine, or the use of bisulphite of lime, for example) eclipsed in the historical literature by the later massive success of refrigeration. But of all the efforts to relay European science along the ranching periphery of the Uruguay River, it was the Liebig Company at Fray Bentos that stood in relief. While around 1850 the economy there was still extremely narrow, based on little more than the exploitation of its timber resources to supply steamboats with fuel, this place was soon to become a household name, recognized around much of the globe well before the century's end. Of all the potential sites in the world for experiment, the historical and geographical contingencies in the selection of Fray Bentos are considerable. They involve a distinctive social network of ideas, linking Europe, South America, and Australia. What was to become a large-scale industrial enterprise, described by the Uruguayan historians José Pedro Barrán and Benjamín Nahum as "the first experience with world-scale capitalism" in their country, had its roots in a saladero established by the British merchant Richard Hughes.[45]

Hughes is probably remembered today mainly for his efforts in 1841 to open Paraguay to British commerce following Francia's death. His involvement in South American development ran deep and he constitutes a further excellent example of British merchants resident in South America prepared by background to scour a wide geographical area of frontier environments in search of wealth, what could be termed locational analysis by merchant adventure. As a young man, Hughes worked in mercantile houses in Santo Domingo (Dominican Republic) and in Rio de Janeiro (within the same firm, coincidentally, as Mauá, the great Brazilian entrepreneur of the nineteenth century). By the 1830s, he was in business for himself, trading hides from Montevideo. In 1855, Hughes opened a saladero at Corrientes in the Upper Plata, but this was advertised for sale as soon as 1858. It seems probable that Hughes made a conscious choice to invest capital in another location. Keen by the late 1850s to follow a familiar pattern of merchants investing in land, he seems to have weighed his options carefully. He rejected an offer of land in Buenos Aires province still exposed to Indian resistance, buying instead a large ranch in Western Uruguay around Fray Bentos, the best natural port on the whole of the Uruguay River. The saladero at Fray Bentos was constructed between 1859 and 1861 under Hughes's direction.

The next figure of key importance for the development of Fray Bentos was Georg Christian Giebert, a German railway engineer resident in Uruguay. Conversant with Liebig's writings on the chemistry of meat, Giebert thought that Fray Bentos could work as a site for testing Liebig's formula. Since it took about thirty kilograms of lean meat to produce one of extract, his formula was very exacting in its economic geography. It demanded inexpensive raw material. Giebert wrote to Liebig, subsequently visiting him at

Munich in 1862. A small factory, the Société de Fray Bentos Giebert & Cie., was set up alongside the saladero to manufacture extract through a sophisticated process of chopping, steaming, and evaporating. It is noteworthy that some of the technology involved, vacuum pan evaporation, borrowed from developments in the refining of sugar, another commodity of vast importance in the Americas.[46]

Giebert's enterprise was a commercial success. The project was rapidly expanded through the 1865 flotation in London of the Liebig Extract of Meat Company, a landmark in the South American search for new markets for cattle. This company was soon selling large quantities of extract of meat to the armies and the institutional poor of Europe. The product also played an important role in supporting colonial warfare and was extensively used by explorers, including Henry Morton Stanley on his journeys through Africa. Building its network on the knowledge base of the Antwerp hide merchants, the Liebig Company paid very serious attention to marketing. Within a few years, agencies for the sale of extract had been established in

Figure 3.3 **A section of the mural '*Con alma y vida*.'** This work by the artist Ricardo Ríos Cichero was dedicated in 2008 to the former workers of the Frigorífico Anglo at the Museo de la Revolución, Fray Bentos. The motifs within the mural provide an excellent example of how the technical transformation of ranch products within an enclave environment had global ramifications. Note how the artist has depicted not only the practical economy of products but also rich carnivalesque themes from the social life of Fray Bentos.

Source: Courtesy of Ricardo Ríos Cichero.

the United States, Mexico, Venezuela, Brazil, Chile, and the Dutch Asian colonies (Java), in addition to nearly every European country.[47] A sense of the scale of activity at Fray Bentos can be gained from the statistics on its waste and coal consumption. By the end of the 1860s, the plant was using around 6 thousand tonnes of coal per annum and dumping around 20 thousand tonnes of animal waste into the Uruguay River annually.

From the basis of extract of meat, the Liebig Company saw further technical developments along the remainder of the nineteenth century, widening its product base to include the famous corned beef. As the South American refrigerated meat industry spread beyond the environs of the major port cities in the early twentieth century, the Fray Bentos plant became increasingly marginal within Liebig's operations. The company sold its Fray Bentos plant in 1924, in favor of expanding its business within Argentina and a series of other world locations. But the market recognition of the name 'Fray Bentos' was so strong that the directors wisely reserved the legal rights to market their corned beef under that label. The number of people in the English-speaking world who not long ago imagined the words Fray Bentos conveying the idea of corned beef in Spanish, rather than a toponym, was probably high, testimony to the market visibility of the brightly colored paper wrappers around the distinctive trapezoidal cans used to package corned beef (Figure 3.3).

Any trip around the kitchen shelves will reveal other food products with strongly local place-based environmental associations, from Dr. Siegert's Angostura aromatic bitters, patented in 1824, through the remainder of much of the alphabet.

CONCLUSION

This study ultimately deals with only limited selections of Northwest European mercantile activity along roughly a half-century. These cases form part of broader patterns. The focus has been mainly with examples drawn from the British, who were the most numerous and powerful representatives within the South American commodity trade of the period under discussion, yet their hold on this was never exclusive.[48] There is much within the international history of mercantile activity in South America still worthy of investigation. The examples chosen here are perhaps more extreme than generally representative cases, but they do exemplify how adventuring merchant capital made its way into the Río de la Plata. It has been claimed of the Robertson brothers that they were "as enterprising a pair as ever made money in provincial Argentina."[49] They offer a fine example of how commodity trading bound distant places together. Enterprising these young men certainly were—there is some tradition that John Parish Robertson went across the Atlantic with only a guinea in his pocket—yet their family history hints strongly at links to capital back in Britain itself. At the peak of dependency theory's appeal for understanding the limited development of Latin

America, this during the 1970s, the Oxford historian D.C.M. Platt maintained some of his colleagues in Latin American history had greatly exaggerated the power and influence of British merchants in the region before 1860.[50] The second case considered in this paper deals with aspects of the commercial career of Samuel Fisher Lafone. Even within a brief treatment, a sense of a truly impressive network emerges. Curiously, Lafone's activities appear nowhere within Platt's often invaluable study of Latin America and British trade.[51] The British consular reports, heavily consulted as a source in Platt's work, were prepared from fixed locations. Whatever their richness on trade and investment, they offer little on the important subjects of mobility, networks, and the gaining of knowledge about interior environments. Lafone's career still begs for a truly in-depth scholarship, one that transcends individual national historiographies and ideally of an interdisciplinary kind. Finally, the third case reminds us of the increasing hold and importance of technology as the nineteenth century proceeded. Scientific findings in Germany would eventually see a small river port in distant South America become a famous supplier of food to Europe. European enterprises worked hard at market development, striving in numerous creative ways to stimulate consumption (see chapter two by Andreas Dix in this book). Liebig, for example, commissioned cookbooks for specialized markets, including one for the Austro-Hungarian Empire. The artistic trading cards prepared for Liebig as a marketing tool, sometimes the work of significant painters, are today often highly collectable objects. And the Art Deco Oxo Tower building on the south bank of the River Thames in London stands as a visual reminder of the market strength of Liebig's Oxo product division (not least the beef stock cubes first developed by them shortly before World War One, still in production today in numerous and modified forms across the world). By the early twentieth century, more than two hundred types of canned and processed food were produced in Fray Bentos. Different companies, products, and technologies were involved within the same enclave for a span of some 130 years, something bound to affect very deeply the local environment in its broadest sense.

The period under scrutiny here was marked by important political shifts. The Robertsons and Lafone worked in environments of at times extreme political instability and ones where infrequent and slow communications rendered impossible the thorough and regular checking of their trusted agents. The third case discussed begins to spill over into the era of steam and the telegraph. It represents a shift away from the exploitation of mobility to the concentration of resources on a scale new to the livestock economies of the interior. The perception of a higher level of political stability was of key importance for making investments involving expensive new technologies. The historical specifics of each case treated here are rich and distinctive, yet some common threads do emerge with implications for historiography. Themes to probe in future research include how merchants added to their limited stock of local knowledge. In each of the three cases, British residents in South America drew advantages from their European network connections. As these networks thickened, the levels of transience and risk generally diminished. During the first half of the nineteenth century, the mobility of investments is striking. The Robertsons worked to open resource frontiers from Buenos Aires with little thought for the future of local ecosystems; their trading of the commodities from the Upper Plata frontier zones had almost a quality of the short-term mining of resources. But at least this took place within an established livestock economy. Samuel Lafone, married to an Argentinean, had cut and run from Buenos Aires in favor of Montevideo. But having invested heavily there in the livestock-processing industry, he showed no rush to leave South America during the huge stresses of a long civil war, opting instead to substitute the feral livestock of the Falklands as the source of his raw material, leading to an intense, if relatively brief, environmental impact on the cattle there. Whenever politics stood in the way of access to resources, fluid investment patterns were often a way forward while the scale of fixed enterprises remained relatively modest. Fray Bentos also involved its own frontier adventuring. But it was much more about science and technology, a harbinger of things to come for the livestock economies of the Plata, the long-term intensification of ranching resources backed by a world of regular steamship and telegraphic connections. The plant came to have a major impact on the ranching environments of Western Uruguay, through such things as wire fencing and selective cattle breeding.

In closing, it is worthwhile reflecting for a moment on what has become of some of the particular places whose environments became much changed through commodity trade. Lafone developed La Teja on land which he bought at public auction and which had earlier belonged to the Jesuits, utopians of a very different kind. In the later nineteenth century, the district of La Teja became one of the more industrialized zones of Montevideo, although the saladero industry of salt-beef disappeared from there in the face of competition from the *frigoríficos* (packing plants) elsewhere in the city. Part of the former saladero site became the chosen location for Uruguay's state-run oil refinery, ANCAP, during the 1930s. La Teja subsequently gained a considerable history and a national reputation for labor militancy, its Plaza Lafone becoming "the site for countless labor rallies and demonstrations."[52] Hope Place in the East Falklands (most probably originally named from Lafonian memories of a once elite street of the same name in Georgian Central Liverpool), where gauchos from the South American mainland were busily employed during the 1840s killing all of the feral livestock at their disposal, is today devoid of human population. And the cattle are long gone, replaced by sheep flocks. Fray Bentos, a small town distinctive within Uruguay for its iconographic Victorian bandstand, is large on industrial archaeology, so it serves as a fitting site for this nation's Museo de la Revolución Industrial, housed in the somewhat ghostly remains of the once Liebig (then Frigorífico Anglo) dormant industrial plants. This landscape is distinctive enough that Uruguay currently has a project to see what is now termed the Paisaje Cultural Industrial de Fray Bentos recognized by UNESCO as part of the world's cultural patrimony. And on the outskirts of the town, towering above the river, shimmers a new testimony to ever-changing shifts in commodities and environments in the form of Uruguay's first, and highly controversial, mega-scale pulp and paper mill. This is a result of the Finnish company Botnia's recent massive investment of more than a billion US dollars in a cellulose factory producing bleached eucalyptus pulp. Their Fray Bentos plant constituted the Botnia Company's first major investment outside of Finland itself. Its scale is a quick reminder that the trading environments of interior Uruguay along the present century will no longer be a narrative mainly about the fortunes of ranching and commercial agriculture alone.

NOTES

1 Herbert Heaton, "A merchant adventurer in Brazil, 1808–18," *Journal of Economic History* 6 (1946): 14.
2 Stanley J. Stein and Barbara H. Stein, "D.C.M. Platt: The anatomy of 'autonomy'," *Latin American Research Review* 15(1980): 136.
3 Material for the comparative study of the environmental history of southern hemisphere resource frontiers is beginning to emerge. See, for example, Jim McAloon, "Resource frontiers, environment, and settler capitalism, 1769–1860," in Eric Pawson and Tom Brooking (eds.), *Environmental Histories of New Zealand* (Melbourne: Oxford University Press, 2002), 52–68.
4 John Parish Robertson and William Parish Robertson, *Letters on South America: Comprising Travels on the Banks of the Paraná and Rio de la Plata*, 3 vols. (London: John Murray, 1843).
5 Robertson and Robertson, *Letters on South America*, 1: 247.
6 Vera Blinn Reber, *British Mercantile Houses in Buenos Aires, 1810–1880* (Cambridge, MA: Harvard University Press, 1979), 95.
7 Robertson and Robertson, *Letters on South America*, 1: 249.
8 Robertson and Robertson, *Letters on South America*, 1: 250.
9 Stephen Bell, *A Life in Shadow: Aimé Bonpland in Southern South America, 1817–1858* (Stanford, CA: Stanford University Press, 2010), 45–50.
10 D.C.M. Platt, *Latin America and British Trade, 1806–1914* (New York: Barnes and Noble: 1973), 48–49.
11 Robert A. Humphreys, *Tradition and Revolt in Latin America and other Essays* (New York: Columbia University Press, 1969).
12 John Parish Robertson and William Parish Robertson, *Letters on Paraguay: Comprising an Account of Four Years' Residence in That Republic Under the Government of the Dictator Francia*, 3 vols. (London: John Murray, 1838–1839), 1: 330–336.
13 For a sophisticated analysis of correspondence for building trust in the conduct of business over long distances, see Gordon Winder's work on the reaper manufacturer D.S. Morgan: Gordon M. Winder, "Building trust and managing business over distance: A geography of reaper manufacturer D.S. Morgan's correspondence, 1867," *Economic Geography* 77 (2)(2001): 95–121.
14 Edgar Swinton Holland, *A History of the Family of Holland of Mobberley and Knutsford in the County of Cheshire* (Edinburgh: Privately printed at the Ballantyne Press, 1902).

15 Charles Holland, *Noticias de Buenos Aires, el Paraguay, Chile y el Peru: cartas del ciudadano inglés Charles Holland, 1820–1826*, presentation and introduction by Leon Tenenbaum; trans. Mabel Susana Godfrid de Tenenbaum and Leon Tenenbaum (Buenos Aires: Fundación Banco de Boston, 1990).
16 Michael North, "The great German banking houses and international merchants, sixteenth to nineteenth century," in Alice Teichova, Ginette Kurgan-van Hentenryk and Dieter Ziegler (eds.), *Banking, Trade and Industry: Europe, America and Asia from the Thirteenth to the Twentieth Century* (Cambridge: Cambridge University Press, 1997), 45.
17 Holland, *Noticias de Buenos Aires, el Paraguay, Chile y el Peru*, 32.
18 Ibid., 28.
19 Ibid., 25.
20 Ibid., 30.
21 Humphreys, *Tradition and Revolt in Latin America and other Essays*, 116.
22 Ibid.
23 Holland, *Noticias de Buenos Aires, el Paraguay, Chile y el Peru*, 44.
24 Ibid., 60.
25 Ibid., 43.
26 Ibid., 43.
27 Ibid., 42. It is unclear whether this comment refers to the Buenos Aires or the Peruvian loans. The Robertsons stood at the center of both as debt contractors. Neither had a happy history.
28 Robertson and Robertson, *Letters on South America*, 1: 2–3.
29 Cecilia Grierson, *Colonia de Monte Grande, Provincia de Buenos Aires: Primera y única colonia formada por escoceses en la Argentina* (Buenos Aires: Jacobo Peuser, 1925).
30 This merchant house had deep roots in trading with Spain, which formed the basis for opening a branch at Lima in newly independent Peru.
31 Humphreys, *Tradition and Revolt in Latin America and other Essays*, 116.
32 John Tiernan, "Mrs Gaskell—Liverpool, Wirral & the Holland family connection," meeting reports of the Liverpool History Society (talk given on 20 June 2010).
33 Holland, *A History of the Family of Holland of Mobberley and Knutsford in the County of Cheshire*.
34 Peter Winn, *El imperio informal británico en el Uruguay en el siglo XIX* (Montevideo: Ediciones de la Banda Oriental, 1975). Punta del Este is today, of course, a toponym associated with a very different kind of environment, the most expensive level of international tourism.
35 Gordon M. Winder, "Webs of enterprise 1850–1914: Applying a broad definition of FDI," *Annals of the Association of American Geographers* 96 (4) (2006): 788–806.
36 Alba Mariani, "La familia y las empresas de Samuel Fisher Lafone, 1805–1871," paper presented within the Asociación Uruguaya de Historia Económica, at the Sixth Jornadas de Investigación en Historia Económica, Montevideo (9–10 July 2009).
37 Platt, *Latin America and British Trade, 1806–1914*.
38 Winn, *El imperio informal británico en el Uruguay en el siglo XIX*.
39 Peter Sims, "Networks and the British community of Uruguay, 1830–1875: Outline and case studies," paper prepared for the Department of Economic History, London School of Economics and Political Science (October 2010).
40 Stephen Bell, "Early industrialization in the South Atlantic: Political influences on the *charqueadas* of Rio Grande do Sul before 1860," *Journal of Historical Geography* 19(4) (1993): 411.

41   Stephen Bell, "Social networks and innovation in the South American meat industry during the pre-refrigeration era: Southern Brazil and Uruguay in comparison," *Scripta Nova: Revista Electrónica de Geografía y Ciencias Sociales* (Universidad de Barcelona) 69 (84) (2000): 1–10.

42   Richard Perren, *The Meat Trade in Britain, 1840–1914* (London: Routledge & Kegan Paul, 1978), 82.

43   William H. Brock, *Justus von Liebig: The Chemical Gatekeeper* (Cambridge: Cambridge University Press, 1997).

44   Stephen Bell, *Campanha Gaúcha: A Brazilian Ranching System, 1850–1920* (Stanford, CA: Stanford University Press, 1998), 79–81.

45   José Pedro Barrán and Benjamín Nahum, *Historia rural del Uruguay moderno, 1851–1885* (Montevideo: Ediciones de la Banda Oriental, 1967): 1(1), 626.

46   Brock, *Justus von Liebig*.

47   J. Colin Crossley and Robert Greenhill, "The River Plate beef trade," in D.C.M. Platt (ed.), *Business Imperialism, 1840–1930: An Inquiry Based on British Experience in Latin America* (Oxford: Clarendon Press, 1977), 325–326.

48   The complex merchant profiles of Southern South America are reminiscent of other parts of the trading world, including the later example of Japan. But direct environmental knowledges acquired by merchants there, unlike in most of South America, were initially sharply confined to commercial adventuring within restricted concession zones. See Peter Ennals's interesting recent study *Opening a Window to the West: The Foreign Concession at Kōbe, Japan. 1868–1889* (Toronto, Buffalo, London: University of Toronto Press, 2014).

49   Platt, *Latin America and British Trade, 1806–1914*, 59.

50   D.C.M. Platt, "Dependency in nineteenth-century Latin America: An historian objects," *Latin American Research Review* 15(1980): 113–30.

51   Platt, *Latin America and British Trade, 1806–1914*.

52   Eduardo Canel, *Barrio Democracy in Latin America: Participatory Decentralization and Community Activism in Montevideo* (University Park, PA: The Pennsylvania University Press, 2010), 149.

4 Opening Up Untouched Woodlands

Forestry Experts Reflecting on and Driving the Timber Frontier in Northern Europe, 1880–1914

Christian Lotz

On May 21, 1907, forestry experts met at an International Congress of Agriculture in Vienna in order to discuss then-current issues of international cooperation. Among the numerous topics, participants debated the future supply of timber for (mainly Western and Central) European economies. They agreed on a resolution urging state forest authorities to afforest 'waste land' and "to open up those wooded areas in Northern and Eastern Europe that are still inaccessible for economic exploitation."[1]

This paper will take debates at international congresses and in forestry journals as examples to analyze how forestry experts and their knowledge influenced the timber frontier during the late nineteenth and early twentieth centuries and how, in turn, those changing economic and technological conditions have challenged forest management since the mid-nineteenth century.

Environmental historians usually refer to the opening up of 'untouched' woodlands as the *timber frontier*. During the nineteenth century, the timber frontier was mainly driven by the overall rising consumption of timber for building purposes, for mining (pit props), for the expanding railway network (sleepers), and so on. There is a broad range of historical study on the movement of the timber frontier and its ecological and economic consequences. In the 1970s, Sven Eric Åström published several articles regarding the timber trade in the Baltic Sea region.[2] Although he did not use the term 'timber frontier,' he succeeded in reconstructing a characteristic West–East movement of the main areas of commercial activity in the timber trade: Beginning in the eighteenth century in Western and Southern Norway, then slowly shifting to Southern Sweden and Northern Sweden, and later to Finland and the Baltic provinces of the Russian Empire. Also in the 1970s, Jozef Broda showed that state authorities in Galicia sold more and more forests to private owners during the nineteenth century, resulting in a continuous advancing deforestation of mountainous regions in that part of the Austro-Hungarian Empire.[3] Without referring to Åström or Broda, Francis Sejersted, in 1980, and Jörgen Björklund, in 1984, analyzed the way in which Swedish entrepreneurs moved eastward exporting their sawmill technologies to Finland and Russia during the nineteenth century. In his characterization of this eastward shift, Sejersted created the English-Norwegian term *'frontier'-bewegelse*, best translated as 'frontier-movement,' and referencing Frederick Jackson Turner's analysis of the role of the 'frontier' in North America.[4] Jörgen Björklund, evaluating statistical data on the main timber trade areas in Sweden, introduced the term *timmergränsen* (in Swedish) and later in English, 'timber frontier.'[5] Since then, environmental historians have been studying details of the timber frontier, in particular in Northern Europe and North America.[6] Marit Lie et al., for instance, analyzed the effects of selective logging in Norway.[7] Torbjörn Josefsson et al. investigated Northern Scandinavian forests, arguing that the forests there had not been pristine when the timber frontier arrived in the late nineteenth century, as the local population, although to a smaller extent, had been using these forests for centuries.[8]

Beyond that, since the 1990s, environmental historians have been studying the extension of trading networks and interregional entanglements, as well as the effects of increasing resource consumption. Richard H. Grove, for instance, showed in 1995 the efforts of scientists in British colonies to warn the government in London about the devastating effects of colonial timber consumption.[9]

However, the main supply of timber for the European economies came from Northern and Eastern Europe. Even Great Britain, the leading colonial power with enormous timber consumption, obtained its timber primarily from Scandinavia and Russia (including Finland and Poland). The period during and immediately after the Napoleonic Wars was an *exception*. During the wars, France tried to interrupt timber imports to Britain with a blockade, which showed effects in particular at North Sea and Baltic Sea ports. Great Britain in return imported a greater amount of Canadian timber and kept this policy after the Napoleonic wars, retarding imports from Northern Europe.[10]

This fact directs a spotlight of interest to *inter-European* entanglements: a great number of historical studies supply information about the European timber trade. Since the seventeenth century, the main trade routes have run from Scandinavia and the Baltic region to the Netherlands, Great Britain, Northern France, and, since the 1860s, to Germany.[11] Noting the increasing timber imports in Germany, Bernd-Stefan Grewe put forward the question as to whether forests in Germany survived industrialization due to the fact that, from the mid-nineteenth century onward, cheaper timber from abroad entered the German market to meet the rising demand.[12]

However, there are no studies so far investigating to what extent forestry experts did perceive those interregional entanglements of the economic use and the ecological function of wood and timber in Europe during the nineteenth century. How and why did these perceptions change? How did experts perceive and influence the movement of the timber frontier?

As the Baltic and North Sea regions were the economic core of the timber trade during the nineteenth century, this paper will put its focus there. It explores material from international congresses that took place from 1873 onward, as well as forestry journals that were published in the countries surrounding the North Sea and Baltic Sea.[13] On the basis of those texts, this chapter analyzes the changing concepts, vocabulary, and arguments regarding spatial aspects of forestry.

COEXISTENCE OF LOCAL SUSTAINABLE FORESTRY AND LONG-DISTANCE TIMBER TRADE DURING THE EIGHTEENTH AND EARLY NINETEENTH CENTURIES

Until the mid-nineteenth century, the manifold ways of forest management and the timber trade in the North Sea and Baltic Sea regions were structured by the topographical conditions of the different areas. Areas with rivers suitable for timber floating, as well as coastal areas with sea ports, participated in long-distance timber trade. By contrast, areas with no access to rivers suitable for floating timber, in particular mountainous regions in continental Europe, were not able to engage in timber trading due to the topography. As timber is a heavy commercial good, it could be transported only on waterways and only in one direction: that is, down river to the sea in a mono-directional timber trade. Therefore, areas with no access to waterways were forced to manage their forests in a sustainable manner. It was against this background that, especially in continental France and continental Germany, an increasing number of forestry experts devoted hundreds of articles and books to the question of how to run local forests in the most effective or sustainable (in German *nachhaltig*) way. Referring to a continuously increasing demand for timber, many authors saw a timber famine ahead.[14] Until today even, there has been an ongoing debate among historians as to whether these warnings applied to the real economic situation or whether they were just a means to push common people out of the woods and to raise profits from the sale of timber.[15] By mapping a woodland area, determining the number of trees it contained, estimating the trees' average age, and measuring their height and circumference, this new kind of scientific forestry aimed at calculating precisely the amount of timber loads that could be cut out of a woodland year by year without destroying it in order to ensure a continuous supply of timber.[16] Forestry experts in other European countries appreciated these efforts and tried to adopt German and French measurements of sustainable forestry in their own countries.[17]

However, the aim of this scientific, sustainable forest management was not only to provide timber for the local population and for local businesses. Experts also applied methods of sustainable forest management to regions with rivers capable of floating timber that were therefore able to export their timber. In particular in Central Europe, this export proved to be a profitable business, as markets in the Netherlands and in Great Britain offered good prices for commercial timber. The profitable prospect of timber exports and, at the same time, the continuous need of timber supply for local populations and businesses created massive tensions. As early as the eighteenth century, forestry experts put forward the question, how could state authorities moan about a coming timber shortage while advocating timber exports at the same time?[18] A number of conflicts regarding forest usage of various kinds that emerged in the period before the mid-nineteenth century have their origins in this tension between local supply and timber export.

While there were many publications during the eighteenth and early nineteenth centuries on the threat of a coming timber shortage, there were only a small number of texts ruminating about the effects of the long-distance timber trade on interregional entanglements between exporting and importing regions. Wilhelm Pfeil, for instance, one of the leading German forestry experts, reflected on the timber trade in his book *Grundsätze der Forst-wirthschaft* in 1822/1824. From his point of view, timber export characterized poor and backward countries, whereas wealthy countries were able to use their soil for more effective and beneficial aims.[19] When travelers, such as the Scottish writer Henry David Inglis, visited the south of Norway during the 1820s, they realized quickly that the region had had a successful past in the timber trade with Britain but that now—that is, in the years after the Napoleonic wars—the area suffered from British tariffs that prioritized Canadian over European timber.[20] Most of these texts from the eighteenth and early nineteenth centuries touching on timber trade reflect *commercial* aspects of interregional entanglement. By contrast, these authors reflected on ecological or social aspects, such as the destructive effects of clear-cutting or the alienation of usage rights for common people, only in passing.

RAILWAYS AND THE TIMBER FRONTIER: CHALLENGES FOR CLASSICAL FOREST MANAGEMENT SINCE THE MID-NINETEENTH CENTURY

Beginning in the 1880s, forestry experts from different countries—areas all facing ongoing increases in population and industrial growth—began to be aware of the changing economic and ecological parameters in forestry. In particular, they reflected upon three aspects that had already been changing the conditions of the timber trade and of local timber supply since the mid-nineteenth century, notably the increasing consumption of timber, the expanding railway network, and the advancing timber frontier.

The most obvious change was the enormous increase in timber trade and timber consumption. Imports to Great Britain rose from 3.5 million tonnes in 1874 to roughly 10 million tonnes in 1899. Germany, for centuries a country of timber exports, became an importing country; net imports to Germany rose from half a million tonnes in 1862 to 4.7 million tonnes in 1901.[21] This rapid increase prompted two opposing discourses from the 1880s onward: one pessimistic and one optimistic.

Among the pessimists was Peter Lund Simmonds, who addressed the new situation in 1884 at an International Forestry Exhibition in Edinburgh. Simmonds was a Danish economist, well known for several publications about economics and geography.[22] Great Britain, he argued, would face major economic problems, as the demand for timber was rising constantly and the future supply of timber was by no means secure. The "consumption of timber," he stated, "is out of all proportion to the natural upgrowth or even cultural renewal [. . .]. We are living on a capital which is vanishing rapidly, and we certainly look with inquietude upon the prospects of the future."[23]

Simmonds was not the only one pushing that argument. Already in 1879, a Norwegian forestry commission had published an alarming report. It said that even Norwegian forests were in danger, as the consumption of timber exceeded the annual regrowth of woodland areas in the country.[24] The alarmed voices culminated at the International Forestry Congress held in Paris in 1900. Here Albert Mélard, head of the French state forest administration, warned about a coming worldwide timber famine.[25]

At first glance, these warnings look like déjà-vu of the eighteenth century rumors regarding the threat of a coming timber shortage. However, those earlier warnings were widespread but had a local character. Now, around 1900, the warnings no longer had a local scope. Rather, forestry experts started to reflect European and even global entanglements of timber trade and reasoned about available and accessible woodland areas abroad.

This new scope of reflection was driven by the expanding railway network. Optimistic experts in particular based their arguments on this new timber transport situation caused by a growing railway network. The optimists, among them the Vienna forestry professor Adolf von Guttenberg, argued at an International Forestry Congress in 1890 that the railway enabled the transport of timber to every single edge of the world. Therefore, a balancing of the shortage and abundance of timber, even across countries and continents, was now possible. Guttenberg continued that the old concepts of sustainable forest management that experts had developed for small-scale and local forest economies should be questioned, because those old concepts were no longer necessary.[26] Other optimists argued that a shortage of timber was not very likely, as timber prices were constantly falling, especially on the British market.[27] Falling prices, they claimed, reflected an abundance of timber, not a coming shortage of timber.

The debate between pessimists and optimists saw no winner or loser. Instead, the debate continued over decades. In the course of the debate, experts reflected not only on increasing timber consumption and on the expanding railway network but on the advancing timber frontier, too. These reflections on the timber frontier cover manifold characteristics and they provide insight into the experts' different perspectives on the challenges to forest management in the late nineteenth and early twentieth centuries.

In an article about the International Forestry Congress in Paris in 1900, Marcus Bing Dahll of the Norwegian state forest authority first reported on the warnings of a timber shortage that Albert Mélard had presented to the audience and then reflected on the new conditions of forestry: In earlier times, he argued, woodland areas had their "certain sales area that decreased in relation of the distance to the sea and to the centres of consumption."[28] Advancing farther north in order to get timber was, in Dahll's opinion, no option as there was supposed to be no suitable timber in such severe climatic regions. Therefore, Dahll concluded, all expectations should be directed not in the northern but in the eastern direction (*østlig Retning*).[29] In Dahll's perspective, it was a question of bare necessity to drive the timber frontier farther east.

In a different way, Carl Metzger, a forestry expert with the German embassy in Helsinki, sketched the movement of the timber frontier in 1906. While evaluating data on forestry and the timber trade in Northern Europe, he realized that the sawmill industry was moving farther and farther north in order to seize suitable raw material, because southern woodlands were already exhausted of good timber. Metzger called it a 'natural process' (*natürlicher Prozess*) that sawmills were relocated to bring 'untouched' woodlands into the commercial circuit of production.[30]

Recognizing the rising consumption of timber, the participants of the International Congress of Agriculture that met in Vienna in 1907 took the same perspective. As quoted in the introduction of this paper, the participants urged the opening up of untouched woodlands, especially in Northern Europe and North America, in order to meet the rising demand for timber.[31] Such a congressional resolution obviously had a colonial dimension, as the raw material was supposed to come from the Northern European countries, whereas most of the congress participants saw Western and Central European economies as the proper consumers of this raw material. However, this colonial aspect of the Vienna congress in 1907 was only one perspective. Within the countries of Northern Europe, there was an ongoing debate on the question of foreign investments in the sawmill industry and on the question of how to earn as much as possible out of this lively timber trade with Western and Central European countries.[32]

In Britain, Herbert Maxwell, council member of the Scottish Arboricultural Society, took another point of view. In 1909, he stated that:

> Some of our [British] former sources of supply were already cut off. Thirty years ago we were drawing large supplies of timber from the German Empire. During that period the industrial expansion of Germany had been so great that, although the annual value of her forests was reckoned at twenty-two million sterling, she now required every stick of their yield for her own consumption. Not only so, but she had entered into competition with us as a purchaser, importing about 4,500,000 tons per annum of foreign timber, valued at £ 15,000,000. As with Germany, so with the United States and Canada, where the forests were long considered to be inexhaustible, and doubtless would have proved so but for reckless lumbering.[33]

Here Maxwell reflected on the effects of economic development: On the one hand, industrialized production was supposed to pave the way to prosperity and wealth. Therefore, many European governments strove for industrialization. On the other hand, it obviously caused a rising number of countries to consume more timber than the country itself was able to provide.

Dahll's, Metzger's, and Maxwell's reflections on the timber frontier, as well as the resolution of the International Forestry Congress in 1907 urging for an opening up of 'untouched woodlands,' can be seen as part of a broader debate about the human impact on the environment and on environmental learning in the late nineteenth and early twentieth centuries. Experts from several scientific disciplines such as botany, biology, geography, and geology thought about the effects of an increasing usage of resources. In 1901, the Russian meteorologist Aleksandr Ivanovič Voejkov, for instance, lamented the alarming increase in energy consumption and urged for intensifying solar energy usage.[34] Some years later, Ernst Friedrich, professor of geography at Leipzig University, even used the term *Raubwirtschaft* (in English perhaps 'plunder economy') to characterize human impact on the environment.[35]

It is interesting to see how environmental historians today refer to Voejkov, Friedrich, and other experts as part of a tradition of environmental concern.[36] However, looking closer into the geographers' argumentation at the end of the nineteenth century, their texts are less a part of a tradition useful to environmental historians. Instead, they provide insight into the intellectual framework of tackling environmental issues at the turn of the century. Friedrich, for instance, criticized European peoples who, having colonized large parts of the world, came to America and Africa, deprived the indigenous peoples of their resources, and brought hardship and death to them. "Our plunder economy," Friedrich reasoned, "is to be blamed for a large part of that [*ein gut Teil der Schuld daran hat unsere Raubwirtschaft*]."[37] At the same time, Friedrich called Raubwirtschaft a necessary step in order to overcome 'backwardness': "We will see," Friedrich concluded, "that this hardship caused by plunder economy finally leads to progress."[38]

Those ambivalent aspects of environmental concern were not only part of the geographers' general debate about resources and global economic entanglements, but they were part of the discussions about the timber frontier, too. The reports of Carl Metzger, the German forestry expert in Helsinki who has already been mentioned, were full of such ambivalences. In 1907, he set out on a three-month-long expedition to Northern Fennoscandinavia in order to calculate the economic potential of these northern regions to provide timber for Western and Central European markets.[39] In his expedition report, on the one hand, he appreciated Norwegian efforts to restrict timber export from Northern Norwegian provinces. He understood that these parts of Norway possessed only small portions of woodland and these small woodlands were needed to provide timber for local populations and businesses. On the other hand, Metzger viewed the Sami population using woodlands as pasture for herds of reindeer only with contempt. In his eyes, there was no need to protect this kind of Sami local woodland use. Instead, woodlands in the Sami regions should be opened up for commercial use, the timber frontier should be driven into Sami regions, and, in the long run, present local woodlands used as pasture should be converted into proper managed forests in order to provide timber for export.[40]

Generally, the advancing timber frontier as well as the growing railway network integrated more and more areas into an expanding timber market. It is important to realize that this kind of market integration caused different effects in different areas of the Baltic and North Sea regions. Sawmills at the edge of the advancing timber frontier in Northern and Eastern Europe brought more and more timber into commercial circuits. As a result, by the end of the nineteenth century, in Western and Central European marketplaces, there was a surplus of commercial timber and prices, for instance, at the London timber market, were falling although consumption was rising at the same time. In contrast, when the timber frontier reached remote areas in Northern and Eastern Europe, local populations were faced with rising prices, because the timber frontier included these regions in a larger market.[41] In many areas in Northern and Eastern Europe, the arrival of the timber frontier was the main trigger to transform traditional woodland use and forms of timber distribution as required into a 'modern' form of forest economy based on rational planning and on prices to be paid in hard currency and with alienation of existing users' rights.

The advancing timber frontier and, in particular, the expanding railway network not only changed local forest use but also led to a process that I call *rescaling sustainability*. European experts tried to adapt eighteenth century instruments and classical techniques of scientific, sustainable forestry for use in the new situation. This adaption faced enormous difficulties, as the conditions of forestry had changed fundamentally.[42] In the eighteenth and early nineteenth centuries, experts had developed the classical techniques in order to map forests and calculate a sustainable yield. These techniques, developed during the eighteenth century, worked with small-scale markets and with timber transport moving in only one direction. Around 1800, without railways or steamships, timber could only be transported on rivers suitable for floating logs due to their heavy weight. In Northern and Central Europe that meant timber trade was possible only in *one* direction—namely, from the mountains to the Baltic or North Seas. Therefore, the classical techniques applied to local conditions and were based on a *constant area* of reachable forests, as long-distance timber transport had been impossible in continental regions at the time.

In contrast, since the mid-nineteenth century and, in particular, since the rapid expansion of the railway network, available forest space and the possible accessible areas of 'untouched' woodland changed continuously. The more railways that were built, the greater and more entangled the area of forest management became. Therefore, the new situation included far more variables than the classical techniques could cope with. In the age of the railway, timber could (and still can) be transported in every direction via railway tracks. As a result, a classical forestry calculation that had predicted a certain income from timber sales in a small-scale woodland area in Central Europe proved to be useless as soon as railway tracks enabled the import of cheaper timber, from Russia or from Scandinavia, for instance. In other words, the new transport facilities and the fast-growing network of railway tracks overran classical forestry calculations, as the railways changed timber transport from mono-directional to multidirectional.

CONCLUSION

Based on examples from International Forestry Congresses, this paper analyses how concepts of forest management changed during the nineteenth century and how forestry experts perceived and influenced interregional entanglement, in particular, in the movement of the timber frontier in the Baltic and North Sea regions.

The period of the eighteenth and early nineteenth centuries was characterized by a coexistence of local sustainable forest management and the long-distance timber trade. This coexistence was determined by the topographical conditions of the respective areas. Continental areas with no access to rivers suitable for floating timber were forced to manage their forests in a sustainable manner, because timber is a heavy commercial good and could be transported only down river on waterways to the sea. By contrast, areas with access to rivers or sea ports were able to run a lively timber trade. Forestry experts of the time were well aware of the economic effects of this kind of interregional entanglement through the timber trade. However, ecological aspects, such as the clear-cutting of areas in the exporting countries, did not play any significant role in forestry publications at that time.

The conditions of forest management and of the timber trade changed fundamentally beginning in the mid-nineteenth century. At International Forestry Congresses, starting in Vienna in 1873, forestry experts, mainly from European countries, debated the future prospects of forestry and about changes in general. In particular, they focused on three major challenges to the existing concepts of forest management and their interrelated effects: the rapidly increasing consumption of timber, caused by rising demand particularly for building purposes and for mining; the expanding railway network; and the advancing timber frontier. Two opposing arguments can be discerned in the debates over these issues. On the one hand, pessimistic experts argued that the rising consumption would lead to a timber shortage. On the other hand, optimistic experts believed falling timber prices in Western European markets along with a growing railway network meant that a balance would be enabled between areas with a shortage and areas with an abundance of timber. The reason for the paradoxical situation of increasing consumption and falling prices was the specific spatial situation of the timber trade. The timber frontier in Northern Europe advanced more quickly and brought more timber to the markets in Western and Central Europe than these markets could consume at the time.

From the 1880s onward, the debates about the effects of an expanding railway network and of an advancing timber frontier led to a process of rescaling sustainability. Experts tried to adopt traditional, local techniques of forest measurement and calculation to the new situation. Before the age of the railway, timber could be transported in only one direction: down the river, from the mountainous regions to the sea. With the growing railway network, this mono-directional traffic changed to multidirectional traffic. Now timber could be transported in every direction and to every region with the arrival of railway tracks. Therefore, experts tried to continuously gather data and include in their calculations newly available data about those forests in Northern and Eastern Europe that were to be 'opened up' by the timber frontier and about those markets that could be reached with new railway tracks. However, at the same time, the expanding railway network and the advancing timber frontier steadily changed the spatial framework of these calculations. Therefore, the process of rescaling sustainability evoked a tension between the gathering of new data about the available woodland area in order to get reliable information for future forest management planning on the one hand and, on the other hand, the continuously changing spatial dimension due to an expanding railway network and an advancing timber frontier.

NOTES

1 Ferdinand Lobkowitz (ed.), *Achter (VIII.) Internationaler landwirtschaftlicher Kongreß, Wien 21. 25. Mai 1907*, Vol. 1 (Wien, 1907), 481.
2 Sven-Erik Åström, "English timber imports from Northern Europe in the eighteenth century," *The Scandinavian Economic History Review* 18 (1970): 12–32; Sven-Erik Åström, "Northeastern Europe's timber trade between the Napoleonic and Crimean wars. A preliminary survey," *The Scandinavian Economic History Review* 35 (1987): 170–177.
3 Józef Broda, "Gospodarka leśna (od połowy XIX w. do I Wojny Światowej)," in Stanisław Arnold (ed.), *Zarys historii gospodarstwa wiejskiego w Polsce*, Vol. 3, (Warszawa, 1970), 607–657, here 619.
4 Francis Sejersted, "Veien mot øst," in: Sievert Langholm and Francis Sejersted (eds.), *Vandringer* (Oslo: Aschehoug, 1980), 163–204, here 164.
5 Jörgen Björklund, "From the gulf of Bothnia to the White Sea. Swedish direct investments in the sawmill industry of Tsarist Russia," *Scandinavian Economic History Review* 32 (1984): 17–39; Jörgen Björklund, *Den nordeuropeiska timmergränsen i Sverige och Ryssland* (Umeå: Umeå Universitet, 1998).
6 See for example Lars Östlund, "Logging the virgin forest. Northern Sweden in the early-nineteenth century," *Forest and Conservation History* 39 (1995): 160–171; Ismo Björn, "Takeover. The Environmental History of the Coniferous Forest," *Scandinavian Journal of History*, 25 (2000): 281–296; Torbjörn Josefsson and Lars Östlund, "Increased production and depletion. The impact of forestry on Northern Sweden's forest landscape," in H. Antonsson and

U. Jansson (eds.), *Agriculture and Forestry in Sweden since 1900: Geographical and Historical Studies* (Stockholm: The Royal Swedish Academy of Agriculture and Forestry, 2011), 338–353; and Ken Olaf Storaunet, Jørund Rolstad and Rune Groven, "Reconstructing 100–150 years of logging history in coastal spruce forest (Picea abies) with special conservation values in central Norway," *Scandinavian Journal of Forest Research* 15 (2000): 591–604.

7 Marit H. Lie, Torbjörn Josefsson, Ken Olaf Storaunet and Mikael Ohlson, "A refined view on the 'Green lie': Forest structure and composition succeeding early twentieth century selective logging in South East Norway," *Scandinavian Journal of Forest Research*, 27 (2012): 270–284.

8 Torbjörn Josefsson, Björn Gunnarson, Lars Liedgren, Ingela Bergman and Lars Östlund, "Historical human influence on forest composition and structure in boreal Fennoscandia," *Canadian Journal of Forest Research* 40 (2010): 872–884.

9 Richard H. Grove, *Green Imperialism. Colonial Expansion, Tropical Island Edens and the Origins of Environmentalism 1600–1860* (Cambridge: Cambridge University Press, 1995).

10 Sven-Erik Åström, "English timber imports from Northern Europe in the eighteenth century," *The Scandinavian Economic History Review* 18 (1970): 12–32. William Schlich, *Schlich's Manual of Forestry, Vol. 1: The Utility of Forests and Fundamental Principles of Sylviculture* (London: Bradbury, Agnew, 1889), 62.

11 Dietrich Ebeling, *Der Holländerholzhandel in den Rheinlanden. Zu den Handelsbeziehungen zwischen den Niederlanden und dem westlichen Deutschland im 17. und 18. Jahrhundert* (Stuttgart: Steiner, 1992); Sven-Erik Åström, "Northeastern Europe's timber trade between the Napoleonic and Crimean wars. A preliminary survey," *The Scandinavian Economic History Review* 35 (1987): 170–177; Arnvid Lillehammer, "The Scottish-Norwegian timber trade in the Stavanger area in the sixteenth and seventeenth centuries," in Thomas Christopher Smout (ed.): *Scotland and Europe 1200–1850* (Edinburgh: John Donald Publishers, 1986), 97–111.

12 Bernd-Stefan Grewe, "Das Ende der Nachhaltigkeit? Wald und Industrialisierung im 19. Jahrhundert," *Archiv für Sozialgeschichte* 43 (2003): 61–79.

13 *Allgemeine Forst- und Jagdzeitung* (Frankfurt am Main), *Zeitschrift für Forst- und Jagdwesen* (Eberswalde), *Centralblatt für das gesammte Forstwesen* (Wien), *Den norske Forstforenings Aarbog* (Christiania), *Forstligt Tidsskrift* (Christiania), *Tidsskrift for Skovbrug* (Christiania), *Transactions of the Scottish Arboricultural Society* (Edinburgh), *Sylwan* (Warszawa/ Lwów), *Lesnoj Žurnal'* (St. Petersburg).

14 Richard Hölzl, "Historicizing sustainability: German scientific forestry in the eighteenth and nineteenth centuries," *Science as Culture* 24 (2010): 431–460; Bernd-Stefan Grewe, "Shortage of wood? Towards a new approach in forest history. The Palatinate in the 19th century," in Mauro Agnoletti and Steven Anderson (ed.), *Forest History. International Studies on Socioeconomic and Forest Ecosystem Change* (Wallingford: CABI, 2000), 143–152.

15 Joachim Radkau, "Zur angeblichen Energiekrise im 18. Jahrhundert. Revisionistische Betrachtungen über die Holznot," *Vierteljahrschrift für Sozial- und Wirtschaftsgeschichte* 73 (1986): 1–37; Frank Uekötter, *Umweltgeschichte im 19. und 20. Jahrhundert* (München: Oldenbourg Verlag, 2007), 44–46.

16 See Richard Hölzl, *Umkämpfte Wälder. Die Geschichte einer ökologischen Reform in Deutschland 1760–1860* (Frankfurt am Main/New York: Campus-Verl., 2010), 105–166. For historical examples see for instance Georg Ludwig Hartig, *Anweisung zur Taxation und Beschreibung der Forste*, 2., ganz umgearbeitete und stark vermehrte Auflage (Gießen/Darmstadt,

80   *Christian Lotz*

1804) and Heinrich Cotta, *Systematische Anleitung zur Taxation der Waldungen* (Berlin, 1804).

17 Antoni Żabko-Potopowicz, "Wpływ zachodnioeuropejskiego piśmiennictwa i idei ekonomicznych na rozwój wczesnokapitalistycznego gospodarstwa leśnego w Królestwie Polskim,"*Studia z Dziejów Gospodarstwa Wiejskiego* 8(1966): 311–320; Ian G. Simmons, *An Environmental History of Great Britain. From 10,000 Years Ago to the Present* (Edinburgh: Edinburgh University Press, 2001), here 153; Mark L. Anderson and Charles J. Taylor, *A History of Scottish Forestry* vol. II (London/Edinburgh: Nelson, 1967), 324 and 396; Torgeir Fryjordet, *Skogadministrasjonen i Norge gjennom tidene*, vol. 2 (Oslo: departementet, 1962), 103–109, 595–597.

18 See Joachim Radkau, *Holz. Wie ein Naturstoff Geschichte schreibt* (München: Oekom-Verlag, 2007), 140–142.

19 Wilhelm Pfeil, *Grundsätze der Forstwirthschaft in Bezug auf die Nationalökonomie und die Staatsfinanzwissenschaft*, vol. 1 (Züllichau und Freistadt, 1822/1824), 137–147.

20 Henry David Inglis (pseudonym: Derwent Conway), *A Personal Narrative of a Journey through Norway, Part of Sweden, and the Islands and States of Denmark* (Edinburgh, 1829), here 127 and 158.

21 Brian R. Mitchel, (ed.), *European Historical Statistics 1750–1975* (London/ Basingstoke: Macmillan, 1975).

22 Peter Lund Simmonds, *A Dictionary of Trade Products, Commercial, Manufacturing, and Technical Terms. With a Definition of the Moneys, Weights, and Measures of all Countries, Reduced to the British Standard* (new edition, rev. and enlarged) (London, 1863); Peter Lund Simmonds, *Waste Products and Undeveloped Substances: A Synopsis of Progress Made in Their Economic Utilisation during the Last Quarter of a Century at Home and Abroad* (London: R. Hardwicke, 1873).

23 Peter Lund Simmonds, "Past, present and future sources of the timber supplies of Great Britain," *Journal of the Society of Arts* 19(1884): 102–121; here 104.

24 Riksarkiv Oslo, S-1600/ Dc/ L 2287, Skovkommission: Motiver til Skovkommissionens foreløbige Udkast til Lov om Forstvæsenet, Arendal, Mai 1879.

25 M. Daubrée (ed.), *Congrès international de sylviculture, tenu à Paris du 4 au 7 juin 1900* (Paris, 1900); Bernhard Danckelmann, "Forstkongreß auf der Weltausstellung des Jahres 1900 in Paris,"*Zeitschrift für Forst- und Jagdwesen* (1900): 104–116 and 605–615; Maryan Małaczyński, "Z wystawy paryskiej," *Sylwan* (1900): 356–359 (część I), and 392–394 (część II); James S. Gamble, "The International Congress of Sylviculture,"*Transactions of the Royal Scottish Arboricultural Society* (1901): 262–274.

26 Adolf von Guttenberg, "Inwieweit ist bei dem heutigen Stande der Wirthschaft und der durch dieselbe bestimmten Forsteinrichtungs-Praxis die Forderung strengster Nachhaltigkeit der Nutzungen überhaupt noch aufrecht zu erhalten?,"*Centralblatt für das gesammte Forstwesen* (1890): 364–372.

27 For example, Dietrich Brandis, "Forstliche Ausstellung in Edinburgh, Teil I," *Allgemeine Forst- und Jagdzeitung* (1885): 97–106 and 242–248, here 247.

28 Marcus Bing Dahll, "Fra den internationale Forstkongres i Paris 1900," *Tidsskrift for Skovbrug* (1901): 13–18, here 13.

29 Marcus Bing Dahll, "Fra den internationale Forstkongres i Paris 1900," *Tidsskrift for Skovbrug* (1901): 13–18, here 17 ["I ethvert Fald har Europa ikke meget at vente sig herfra, da Fremdriften kun vil være mulig, naar den gaar i østlig Retning."]

30 BArch, R 901/ 14480, Carl Metzger: "Holzhandel und Waldbenutzung in Nordeuropa 1905/06," undated [March 1907].

31 Ferdinand Lobkowitz (ed.), *Achter (VIII.) internationaler landwirtschaftlicher Kongreß, Wien 21.-25. Mai 1907*, vol. 1 (Wien, 4 vol., 1907): 481. The

congress was broadly received in Europe's forestry journals. See Fritz Jentsch, "Der VIII. internationale landwirtschaftliche Kongreß in Wien, 21. bis 25. Mai 1907," *Zeitschrift für Forst- und Jagdwesen* 39 (1907): 603–617, 680–690, and 745–755; Josef Friedrich, "Der VIII. internationale landwirtschaftliche Kongreß in Wien 1907," *Centralblatt für das gesamte Forstwesen* 33 (1907): 378–389, 434–440, and 475–484; Stanisław Sokołowski, "Międzynarodowy kongres rolniczy w Wiedniu 1907," *Sylwan* 25 (1907): 219f and 269–275; and Anonym, "Congrès international d'agriculture de Vienne,"*Revue des eaux et forêts* 46 (1907): 343f.; Anonym, "Der VIII. Internationale landwirtschaftliche Kongress in Wien vom 20. bis 25. Mai 1907," *Allgemeine Forst- und Jagdzeitung* 83 (1907): 435–437.

32 See for example Jörgen Björklund, "Exploiting the last phase of the north European timber frontier for the international market 1890–1914. An economic-historical approach," in Mauro Agnoletti and Steven Anderson (eds.), *Forest History. International Studies on Socioeconomic and Forest Ecosystem Change* (Wallingford: CABI, 2000), 171–184; Torgeir Fryjordet, *Skogadministrasjonen i Norge gjennom tidene*, vol. 2 (Oslo: Landbruksdepartementet, 1962), 46–50.

33 Herbert Maxwell, "The forest resources of the United Kingdom," *Transactions of the Scottish Arboricultural Society* XXII (1909): 1–7, here 4–5.

34 Alexandre Ivanovitch Woeikof [Александр Иванович Воейков]: "De l'influence de l'homme sur la terre," *Annales de Géographie* 10 (1901): 97–114.

35 Ernst Friedrich, "Wesen und geographische Verbreitung der 'Raubwirtschaft'," *Petermanns Geographische Mitteilungen* 50 (1904): 68–79 and 92–95.

36 See for example Michael Williams, *Deforesting the Earth. From Prehistory to Global Crisis*, (Chicago: University of Chicago Press, 2003), 384.

37 Ernst Friedrich, "Wesen und geographische Verbreitung der 'Raubwirtschaft'," *Petermanns Geographische Mitteilungen* 50 (1904): 68–79 and 92–95 here 93.

38 Ibid., here 70.

39 See in detail on Metzgers expeditions Christian Lotz, "Expanding the space for future resource management. Explorations of the timber frontier in Northern Europe and the rescaling of sustainability during the 19th century," *Environment and History* 21 (2015): 257–279.

40 Barch Berlin, R 109/ 14480, Carl Metzger: Bericht über eine durch Finmarken und finnländisch Lappland ausgeführte Reise, ohne Datum [März 1907].

41 See for example Antoni Żabko-Potopowicz, "Wpływ zachodnioeuropejskiego piśmiennictwa i idei ekonomicznych na rozwój wczesnokapitalistycznego gospodarstwa leśnego w Królestwie Polskim," *Studia z Dziejów Gospodarstwa Wiejskiego* 8 (1966): 311–320, here 313.

42 See for example the debate on the economic potential of Northern Europe's forests: Albert Mélard, "Insuffisance de la production des bois d'œuvre dans le monde," *Revue des eaux et forêts* 39 (1900): 402–408 and 417–432; Max Endres, "Über die Unzulänglichkeit der Nutzholzerzeugung auf der Erde. Bemerkungen zu dem Vortrage des Forstinspektors Mélard-Paris," *Forstwissenschaftliches Centralblatt* 22(1900): 611–623; Max Endres, "Über die Unzulänglichkeit der Nutzholzerzeugung der Erde. Erwiderung [auf den Artikel von William Schlich, C.L.] von Universitätsprofessor Dr. Endres," *Forstwissenschaftliches Centralblatt* 23 (1901): 621f.; Fritz Jentsch, "Holzproduktion und Holzhandel im Lichte der Pariser Weltausstellung von 1900," *Mündener forstliche Hefte* 10 (1901): 13–27; Èduard È. Kern, "S Parižskoj vsemirnoj vystavki 1900 g. [Teil 1]," *Izvestiâ S.-Peterburgskogo Lesnogo Instituta* 7 (1901): 25–62; sowie Èduard È. Kern, "S Parižskoj vsemirnoj vystavki 1900 g. [Teil 2]," *Izvestiâ S.-Peterburgskogo Lesnogo Instituta* 8 (1902): 61–107; Anonym, "Fra den internationale Forstkongres i Paris

1900," *Tidsskrift for Skovbrug* 9 (1901): 13–18; and William Schlich, "Über die Unzulänglichkeit der Nutzholzerzeugung der Erde," *Forstwissenschaftliches Centralblatt*, 23 (1901): 289–297; William Schlich, "The Outlook of the World's Timber Supply," *Transactions of the Scottish Arboricultural Society* XVI (1901): 355–383.

Part III
Valuing Environments

5 Problems with Nature in the Trading Environments of the McCormick Reaper, 1850–1902

Gordon M. Winder

Over the course of the nineteenth century, Cyrus Hall McCormick and his family sold an enormous number of harvesting machines to farmers. Theirs was a growing transnational business focused on the mechanical harvesting of wheat, rye, barley, timothy, and grass using horsepower.[1] Their machinery simultaneously epitomized the mechanization of the American environment, abundance and a perpetual harvest, and the achievement of the technological sublime, outcomes that buttressed the superiority of settled cultivation, which constituted a key claim within settler nation building. The reaper was marketed as an adjunct to the pastoral ideal and was systematically combined both with images and stories of modernization related to the railroad, steamship, and telegraph and with depictions of 'others' using an Orientalist lens designed to produce narratives of a march toward civilization and cultivation. Cultural geographer Mona Domosh has shown how, from the beginning of the 1880s, the McCormick catalogues turned this story of the 'civilizing machine' into a narrative of America's 'civilizing mission.' To achieve this, the catalogues featured both the 'flexible racism' embedded in this imperialist project and the rhetoric of a 'civilizing commerce': the machines of US manufacturers were sent out to conquer the world, bringing peace and plenty and eradicating savagery, as part of a US business mission.[2] In that rhetoric, Cyrus Hall McCormick and his machines were central actors claiming to reshape the world.

This interpretation of the McCormick representational system speaks to environmental history in two main ways. First it abandons the exploration of tensions and ambivalences in Leo Marx's 'machine in the garden' problematic to instead analyze and interpret the rhetoric of harvesting machinery advertising. US environmental history has highlighted contending approaches to the 'machine in the garden' problematic. Scholars have emphasized either that machines can create gardens, consume them, or destroy them or that they have transformative power through the technological sublime or that there has been no time when the human and the natural were disentangled. However, such efforts to address tensions between machines and nature are rendered of secondary importance when subordinated to civilization discourse.[3] Second, if environmental history is to take up the challenge presented by the cultural geographers, then it needs to engage with the trading environment of the McCormick reaper, in terms of both the rhetoric of environmental transformation bound to the reaper in company advertising and in terms of the ambiguities and tensions inherent in the trading environments of the reaper. That entails an inquiry into, for example, both the natures related to harvesting machinery and the calculative, business practices of the manufacturing company.

Harvesting machines have not received much attention in US environmental history. The singular exception is William Cronon, who dedicated part of one chapter of *Nature's Metropolis* to McCormick's reaper. Nevertheless, in the ensemble of machines, ideas, practices, and environments that made 'nature's metropolis,' Cronon prioritized the railroad over the reaper.[4] Cronon interpreted the McCormicks' success to first waterborne and later railroad transport, development of his own dealer network, elaborate advertising, and the settlement of the Great West.[5] For him, the reaper was an example of how country and city were linked.[6] In contrast, analysis of the advertising rhetoric of the 'civilizing machine' prioritizes harvesting machinery as agent of civilization and cultivation over the railroad and sees the claims made for the machines' effects pitched at multiple scales, including the global, rather than at the scale of metropolis-hinterland relations.

William Cronon's interest in the railroad as environmental transformer and trading environment stems from the insight that the railroad linked farm, forest, and mine to town, suburb, factory, and city, in the process unifying a regional field of activity, even though, for Cronon, the engine's unifying and harmonizing power were not the same everywhere. At the same time that it intensified, specialized, and spread agriculture, it spawned industrial plants, disgorged tourists at resorts in the wilderness, and obliterated existing towns, farms, and forests. Railroad companies built networks of main trunk, feeder, and competitor lines; sidings and halts associated with stations and yards; grain elevators; hotels and workers' housing; car factories; steel mills; and coal fields. They produced hierarchies of passengers, drivers, service crews, and construction gangs, including armies of immigrant navies. Its effects were industrial, hierarchical, and exploitative, as well as empowering. A new geography of railroad hazards emerged, including fires, crossing fatalities, and train wrecks. The railroad fostered economic growth through private ownership and foreign investment but in the context of controversies over public subsidies, monopoly rents, robber barons, syndicates, and trusts.[7] Above all, the railroad had the effects of massing, specializing, and intensifying human activity in diverse environments. The railroad was a monstrous, disturbing, and unnatural force in America's environment. In these ways, the railroad was not only effective but also contested, and, like the reaper, we can expect it to be embedded in trading environment relations that feature problems articulating natures, problems that cannot simply be read off the rhetoric of its advertising.

It is this aspect of the trading environments of the McCormick enterprise that this chapter addresses: What were the problems that the McCormicks encountered as they promoted their 'civilizing machine,' and how can we use them to understand the contradictions and tensions bound up in the reaper as transformative agent? The paper argues that the family enterprise was confronted with five sets of issues in the diverse trading environments where they operated, each of which was hidden in the firm's advertising and has received scant attention in the environmental or business history literature.

First, the McCormicks chose well in relocating from rural Virginia to Chicago but in 'nature's metropolis' they faced a relentless problem: environmental constraints on production. Chicago was a 'busy hive' where labor and materials were readily available, but this did not mean that the firm's owners did not have to scour the United States for the most suitable materials, supplies, and machine tools and decide on the most reliable ways to access them: should they purchase them from other firms or purchase the supplier to ensure control over the products? Into the 1880s, the production schedule at the works ran to the beat of rural seasonality in a way that really did make Chicago into *nature's* metropolis. Railroad development transformed but did not end the environmental constraints on the McCormicks' factory production.

Second, the performance of the reaper depended on the transformation of environments. In addition to the building of Chicago and its related railroad lines, the reaper required a dramatic increase in the national horse herd and thus an expansion of the area devoted to fodder crops. It also required mining, timber felling, steel production, and timber milling. As the machines multiplied, they also came to rely on fiber production, since twine was used to bind the cut grain into sheaves ready for threshing. The reaper was thus a hybrid machine and its materiality had environmental effects, ones that, so far, have been only partially explored.[8]

Third, while railroads made distribution feasible, distribution presented special challenges for harvesting machinery manufacturers.[9] The McCormicks were constantly looking to better coordinate and manage their expanding distribution network, farmer defaults on machinery payments, and postponed revenue streams. Again the rhythms of Chicago's countryside and the geography of access to it conditioned the commercial knowledge and the trading environment generated at head office.

Fourth, the machine itself was developed and improved: It was a very different machine in 1880 than it had been in 1850, and, increasingly, it was contested at agricultural fairs, in expositions and field trials, in museums, and in patent courts by a growing number of rival machines and their owners.[10] The original claim made for Cyrus Hall McCormick's 'Virginia Reaper'—saving farm labor—was not contested, but competitors mounted stern challenges so that his machines were put to the test in field trials and patent courts all over the world, all of which required the close attention of the McCormicks.

Fifth, around the family-owned McCormick Harvesting Machine Company the McCormicks developed and managed a growing amount of property. This ranged from patent rights and licenses, through forests, farms, mines, land, and houses to diverse contracts, bonds, and railroad stocks. Through this property, the McCormicks enjoyed enormous rewards, including personal and social mobility, as well as a high standard of living; but they were themselves increasingly abstracted from nature and had to find ways to cope with the demands of their property empire. This property was mediated by a growing web of contracts, property rights, legal affairs, calculative practices, and modern institutions. Not evident in the company catalogues, these property interests trapped the family into the calculative practices of modernizing institutions in banking, finance, and law.

Together these issues meant that the McCormicks faced an expanding engagement with nature. This, however, had two aspects: Increasingly the enterprise became engaged with nature as property through contracts, catalogues, and statistics, with institutions standardizing relations and natures, and with management at a distance; simultaneously, the enterprise remained conditioned by first nature, and especially by harvest season, by physical distance, and by the materiality of the machine.

This chapter investigates the McCormick enterprise in terms of the relations between the trading environments and the environments traded so as to reveal that the abstraction of the firm from nature was at best apparent. It first interprets the rhetoric of the new hybrid nature that the company's product was claimed to make within the civilization discourse that dominated its advertising. Then it considers the problems that emerged for the firm as it strove to more efficiently manage nature. Each of the five sets of issues noted earlier is discussed in turn, with each keyed to a representation of the firm and its product drawn from the company's advertising.[11] In this way, the tensions between rhetoric and business practice can be better understood. I argue that, as the McCormicks confronted the challenges of massing production, transforming environments, as well as managing distribution, innovation, and property they themselves were 'civilized' by their 'civilizing machine.'

THE CIVILIZING MACHINE AND ITS DISCONTENTS

Well before 1900, the firm boasted advertising and sales efforts that required the services of advertising agencies and printers, an international dealer network featuring warehouses and showrooms, and representation at numerous agricultural and trade fairs. In this trading environment, McCormick promised that his reaper was an original invention and a reliable and constantly improved machine, one celebrated in the world's fairs as a model modern machine. It was a product of a vast industrial complex that assembled and used enormous quantities of raw materials. This was a civilizing machine that would produce a moral and domesticated environment. It made a natural team: Men drove horses to pull the machine through the crops, thus easing farm labor without disturbing the seasons.[12] As an aid to cultivation and settlement the reaper would help to build the nation. By buying a McCormick, a farmer promoted a better environment. His purchase would help to produce an improved and prosperous countryside that would be filled with so many harmonious, industrious, and well-off farm families. Simultaneously, his investment would create an urban society in which bread was cheap and manufacturing work abundant. City and countryside would be linked together by a civilizing commerce best exemplified by the transnational activities of the McCormick enterprise. Mr. McCormick would, with the help of the railroad, send out his modern machine to mechanize, improve, and civilize environment and society.

McCormick's catalogues invoked the idea of a perpetual harvest: It is always harvest time with the McCormick: "while the American farmer relaxes by his winter fire, the McCormick reaper is at work under the summer sun of the Antipodes."[13] The reaper had an autumn harvest season, but the railroad and the steamship (civilization) helped to make these separate

Figure 5.1 **The Sunrise of Agricultural Prosperity**—Original pen and ink drawing of an illustration for a McCormick Company advertising catalog. It features a drawing of men holding grain cradles in a wheat field, and looking over a series of hills at a "sunrise" over a mountain on top of which is a McCormick grain binder. McCormick Harvesting Machine Company, 1890 ca., McCormick-International Harvester Collection, Image ID: 86965, Wisconsin State Historical Society, Madison, Wisconsin, Viewed online at https://www.wisconsinhistory.org/.

Figure 5.2 **McCormick Harvesting Machine Company annual catalog cover**—This cover features an illustration of a woman carrying a sheaf of wheat. Below the text reads: "Harvesting Machine Co. Chicago, ILL U.S.A. The Maiden Reaper and the only one that ante-dates the McCormick." McCormick Harvesting Machine Company, 1886, McCormick-International Harvester Collection, Image ID: 1886, Wisconsin State Historical Society, Madison, Wisconsin, Viewed online at https://www.wisconsinhistory.org/.

harvests into a perpetual global harvest: an abundant crop to feed the populations of so many cities. As Jackson Lears argues in his book on early American advertising, abundance is what is sold by such commercials.[14] The scythe, long associated with Goddesses of the harvest, is 'mechanized' in the catalogues, and the new mechanical reaper promised a 'Golden Harvest' (Figure 5.1). So cornucopia, horns of plenty, wild roses, flowers from the fields, and wheat sheaves adorn the pages of the catalogues, while spiders weave their webs on the abandoned reaping hooks (Figure 5.2). Beginning in the mid-1870s, McCormick tended to portray his machines at work in modern harvest scenes. These were invariably flooded with sunlight so that the golden sea of wheat could be neatly conveyed using the latest color lithographic techniques. Battalions of horse-drawn machines worked these monoculture wheat fields. To emphasize abundance further, the catalogues were replete with images of wheat sheaves, with children playing and chickens foraging among the farm buildings, and, in one image, a farmer giving his children a geography lesson.[15] These images emphasized the ordering of the environment, with proper seasons, bountiful harvests, disciplined household economies, happy homes, and education rather than leisure. Civilized nature was productive on a grand scale and involved not only grain, grass, and humans but many domesticated animals.[16]

Harvesting machinery companies proclaimed their grim machine as a heavenly 'chariot of progress' illuminating an ordered and prosperous nature—a bringer of plenty to all those farms it passed.[17] In its catalogues, the firm constituted the farm family as a bourgeois rural ideal. Compared with deplorably dark and dismal foresters, America's mechanized farmers were productive embodiments of Jeffersonian citizenship ideals.[18] The reaper was an emancipating force. It freed peasants from arduous labor in the fields and made education feasible. It produced the modern rural woman. When McCormick celebrated 59 years of business, his catalogue featured a man with a walking stick and a woman with a parasol in repose under a tree, while a farmer operated a horse-drawn grain binder in a farm field and an inset illustration showed a man cutting wheat with a cradle while a woman gathered bundles of grain over the text '1830.' Indeed they had come a long way.[19] The mechanical reaper also civilized men: As he rested by the fire in his hovel, stubborn Pat's wife pressured him, "Come now, Pat, you *must* buy the McCormick binder," to lift his household out of penury.[20] At another level, the reaper built the nation by supporting the productivity of its propertied citizens. For example, in the McCormick catalogue of 1876, the reaper was associated with the founding of the US Republic and echoed the theme of that year's world's fair in Philadelphia.[21] This last contrasted strongly with the positioning of Black Americans: Where White American farm families were represented as actively engaged in the civilization narrative, Black Americans were only ever portrayed as onlookers to the advance of the machine. Thus, as Mona

Domosh argued, Orientalism was a feature of McCormick's advertising: Various more primitive others were used as foils to promote the identities and associations that McCormick sought to foster. Representation was one aspect of this strategy but omission was another.[22] The catalogues contrasted the pastoral landscape to the (vanishing) wild landscapes of the Great West and answered the question "grass or grain?"[23] The eradication of the uncivilized was both active (they were portrayed as powerless and unknowing onlookers) and comprehensive (they were missing from the pages). At first absent, the pastoral landscape ideal became increasingly evident, along with ideas about the role of farmers in national political economy, the civilizing of the Great West, and the United States' Manifest Destiny.

Harvesting machinery manufacturers drew their rhetoric from civilization discourse. This tied the reaper to urban settings, to international awards, to nation states as the agents of modernization, to evolutionary theory, to competition, improvement and progress, to hierarchies of races, to useful and improvable animals, to abundance, to consuming farm families with their gendered divisions of labor, and to railroads and steam ships and the new connectivity they produced. Harvesting machines linked the abundant harvest to the 'Busy Hive' of industry, to the possibilities of large-scale factory production, and to a potentially inclusive internationalism. Reapers were associated with pastoral landscapes as well as the rhetoric of ideal machines, engineering expertise, and correct business practice. Harvesting machinery was declared to be a powerful agent reshaping environments.

Figure 5.3 **McCormick Reaper Works**—Illustration of the McCormick Reaper Works (factory) from an advertising folder. Printed by Gies and Company, Buffalo. McCormick Harvesting Machine Company, 1887, McCormick-International Harvester Collection, Image ID: 39554, Wisconsin State Historical Society, Madison, Wisconsin, Viewed online at https://www.wisconsinhistory.org/.

ECONOMIZING FACTORY PRODUCTION

Like all of his competitors, McCormick declared the modernity and size of his factory (Figure 5.3). He did this through images of the factory showing the yards of stockpiled timber and the smoke billowing from the foundry chimneys, bolstered by a combination of output figures and descriptions of the productive effort and practices to convey a sense of the grand and growing scale of manufacture. Factory activity was signaled by the arrivals and departures of locomotives, canal boats, wagons, and men, each bearing loads of materials; and this confirmed the links between city and countryside. However, behind the factory and production rhetoric of company advertising lay issues that had to be confronted by the McCormick enterprise. The production system needed to be expanded to meet the growing demand, but it had to remain efficient and profitable, and its expansion remained hedged in by environmental constraints.

The McCormicks' blacksmith shop at Walnut Grove Farm, Virginia, never produced more than two hundred machines a year in the period 1841–1847, and so McCormick licensed experienced factory owners to ensure a larger total output and to spread production to other regions.[24] The move to Chicago in 1848 dramatically altered this situation, even though it was not until 1851 that the McCormicks secured 100 percent ownership of the plant. The factory was doubled in size in 1849 so that in 1850 the plant's 120 workers made 1,603 machines at a rate of 13 reapers each. Forty percent of the $56,775 worth of supplies was sourced in Chicago, with New York (23.9 percent), Massachusetts (13.8), and Connecticut (6.2) suppliers also prominent.[25] The next year the enterprise received $72 per machine, a much better return than the $30 royalty they had been receiving for production of a machine in the Chicago plant just a few years earlier.[26] In 1858, after further expansion of the works, production cost per machine was $43 and the sale price $245; and in 1859, three hundred workers produced five thousand machines at the rate of 17 each.[27] The 1860 census reports McCormick's establishment, with two hundred workers, having a gross output per worker of $2,070, gross output per dollar spent on wages of $7.53, and net output per dollar spent on wages of $5.78.[28] This placed McCormick among the largest and most efficient works in the United States: The Chicago investment was paying off, but fires that ravaged the works in 1851 and 1856 obstructed these plans and efforts.

During the 1860s, however, production costs rose and rates of return on machines fell, and this occurred despite the urbanization and agglomeration economies that were clearly emerging through Chicago's spectacular urban growth. In 1872, a McCormick machine sold for $186 and had a production cost of $121.[29] In fact, the urban plant remained a creature of rural seasonality: Its annual activity was aimed at a short sales season before the fall harvest. In harvesting machinery establishments located in the United States' and Canada's small towns, the production season began in the early winter, using idle farm labor, and orders were filled before midsummer.[30] Thus, even in the McCormick works of the 1860s, work began each August on the next year's models, with the works running through the winter with ten-hour days. It took the McCormicks some time to reduce the annual shutdown for inventory and repairs: In 1868, this was down to just three weeks.[31] But even in the early 1880s, the number of employees at the works doubled each year from 700 in the early autumn to the height of the busy season. In1884, the peak was 1,800 men.[32] This fact highlights the problems that the official statistics of the McCormick establishment presented: How efficient was the establishment if we have only a rough idea of the number of workers at the plant and the number of diverse 'machines' produced when the census officer visited and not a total number of hours worked for the year? Other key factors contributing to the cost increases were the increasing use of iron parts as the machines became larger and more complicated with additional functions, such as raking the reaped grain and binding it, and the presence of a local of the Iron Molders International Union (IMIU) in the works from 1860, not to mention the Civil War or the fire of 1872 that once again devastated the works.

Nevertheless, in a concerted campaign, the McCormicks drove their costs down during the late 1870s and into the 1880s. To a large extent, the improved economic figures related to the accounting of binders for wrapping twine around bundles of cut grain and the much larger harvesting machines to which they were attached as separate machines. By 1879, 650 workers produced 29 machines (including binders counted as separate machines) each, with a production cost per machine of just $38.[33] Lewis Wilkinson, trained at the Springfield Armory, replaced Leander McCormick as factory superintendent in 1880.[34] Aided by substitution of steel for iron in harvesting machine manufacture, the new superintendent got the average cost per machine down to $15.00 in the early 1880s with a profit per machine of $40.00.[35]

Cyrus Hall McCormick "tolerated unions but not strike action and insisted on an open shop."[36] The Haymarket Riot of 1866, which shaped subsequent American Federation of Labor strategies, took place in the square not far from the McCormick's Chicago plant and in the context of a protracted lockout of unionized iron workers at the McCormick factory.[37] That year management broke the IMIU local and banned trade unions from their plant, in the process introducing molding machines that ended the role and power of the skilled molders in the works.

After each fire, the McCormicks rebuilt and on a grander scale than before. Nevertheless, throughout the period under consideration in this chapter, the McCormick enterprise was under challenge from other US manufacturers who matched or surpassed the enterprise's output of harvesting machines. In 1855 and 1857, John H. Manny of Baltimore, Maryland, turned out 2,893 and 4,565 machines respectively to McCormick's 2,534 and 4,091. In 1875, the Champion Company of Springfield, Ohio, manufactured

30,000 machines to McCormick's 11,500. In 1897, William Deering of Chicago claimed an output of 238,000 machines, while McCormick produced 150,000.[38] As the McCormicks responded to these challenges, they set about systematically rescaling their production, economizing their plant operations, and substituting materials, and they were keen to drive wages lower and to reset labor conditions. Nevertheless, it took decades to seemingly break the hold of the seasonality of production and sales seasons, the need for skilled factory labor, or the need for extra labor during the busy season at the works. In these ways, production remained subject to nature.

ENVIRONMENTAL EFFECTS

As the scale of production rocketed during the 1880s, the Chicago works exerted transformative effects on diverse environments. The pressure ranged from the need for growing numbers of horses where the machines were used, through increasing purchases of steel and coal, heavy use of railroad freight cars, the construction of boarding houses near the works, or purchases of sawmills and forests in Missouri and Arkansas, to imports of fiber with consequent environmental and social impacts in the Philippines and Mexico.[39] For the purposes of this chapter, the growing on-farm horse herd and the increasing weight of fiber landing at the docks are illustrative.

Horsepower was vital to this 'mechanization' of the harvest. Horses are omnipresent in company catalogues, even when, as was McCormick policy, they are not the focal point of the advertising images. Increased use of harvesting machinery meant increasing use of horses. As the numbers of harvesting machines increased, so the horse herd multiplied, and the acres of grasses and clovers, the harvests of hay, barley, timothy, and rye also increased. In 1880, the US census authorities counted $406.5 million worth of implements and machinery on farms and 10.3 million horses on farms. Twenty years later, the inventory was $761.2 million of machines and 18.3 million horses.[40] Gasoline powered vehicles had dramatic impacts on both the national horse herd and the land area devoted to fodder crops, but largely after 1920.[41]

However, the effects of the machines on farm activities, farm layout and size are not mentioned in the advertising brochures. Neither the remnants of the wild prairie (the so-called back-40 acres on each section that were not yet cleared, plowed, or sown), nor the acres of grasses are mentioned or shown. The wheat farmer provided food for humans rather than fodder for animals and grass was played down in the catalogues. The lawn (associated with recreation) and the paddock (associated with fodder for livestock) did not feature prominently in advertising, even though the grass-cutting mower also sold strongly. Nevertheless, the catalogues presented a natural ensemble: Sun, soil, plants, animals, humans, and machines all working together. This natural team was on show at field trials, but, in company advertising,

the grain harvest was emphasized. The reaper was associated with the production of bread, the staff of life, and the American farmer was envisaged as
the provider of food for an urban society—for civilization.[42]

In *Bound in Twine*, Sterling Evans envisioned the "henequen-wheat complex" straddling the Canadian prairies, the Great Plains, and Yucatán, as he
elaborated the continental business interconnections and the local environmental transformations that, by the 1890s, came with the use of Mexican
fiber as binder twine.[43] McCormick launched his twine binder in mid-1880.[44]
Since the harvest of one acre of wheat required 0.9 to 2.7 kg of twine, annual
US imports of fiber rapidly grew to around two hundred thousand tonnes.[45]
As early as 1879, McCormick prepared for the demand for the new material
by buying manila twine from the Elizabethport Steam Cordage Co., New
Jersey. In 1883, the firm switched to a manila and sisal combination, and
by 1991, the McCormicks had stitched up a cartel arrangement controlling
Yucatán fiber production through its agreements with the trading house of
Henry W. Peabody and Co., of Boston. Evans analyses the environmental
and social transformations in the Yucatán that came with this new combination and highlights the controversies and reactions that emerged in the
United States from both the cartel conspiracy and dependence on Mexican
fiber, which was especially an issue during the Mexican Revolution, and in
Mexico from the environmental transformation of the Yucatán.

In these ways, the production and sale of the McCormick reaper transformed environments and produced new interdependencies. The reaper
was in fact not separate from nature but a hybrid: A human-operated,
horse-powered mechanism built from iron, steel, wood, and fiber and
requiring maintenance, replacement parts, and, eventually, replacement. Its
performance required the transformation of environments, and these were
celebrated in the rhetoric of the company catalogues when they fitted with
the ideals of cultivation, civilization, modernization, and improvement.

THE MODEL MODERN MACHINE

The McCormick Harvesting Machine Company promised farmers a reliable and constantly improved machine, one that was part of a natural
team—men drove horses to pull the machine through the crops—and one
celebrated in agricultural fairs, field trials, and the world's fairs as a progressive and civilizing force, as a model modern machine. Harvester companies
informed farmers that their reaper was, as it were, the first machine in the
garden: the progenitor of a multiplying family of useful machines, whose
functionality was being constantly perfected. Reaper manufacturers made
their products the objects of a steady public gaze: These machines were
on permanent trial. There was a close relationship between performance
at world's fairs and sales of harvesting machinery, because the McCormick
reaper became a creature of world's fairs.[46] In order to expedite domestic

sales manufacturers had to trial their machines against others on local and international stages. They had to be seen to be competitive at trial and, in turn, competition results became advertising claims.

At first, and for over two decades, Cyrus Hall McCormick advertised his reaper as a reliable machine. His early circulars and order forms described to would-be purchasers the reaper's parts and gave directions on how to assemble the machine (Figure 5.4). He proclaimed that the 1850 'Virginia Reaper' had been improved on the earlier, 1848 model, but he also located this improved machine in a proper business contract. The circulars of the 1850s were order forms not illustrated catalogues and most attention was

Figure 5.4 **McCormick's Patent Virginia Reaper, 1849.** Handbill advertising McCormick's Patent Virginia Reaper, manufactured by the company then known as McCormick, Ogden & Co., features a small drawing of the reaper in use. This early model required a person to ride on the machine and rake the grain off the platform by hand. The 1849 price was $115 cash or $120 on a payment plan. McCormick, Ogden & Co., 1849, McCormick—International Harvester Collection, Image ID: 40413, Wisconsin State Historical Society, Madison, Wisconsin. Viewed online at https://www.wisconsinhistory.org/.

given to the conditions of purchase. Both a payment schedule and reasonable performance of the machine were defined. A fair trial of the machine was expected, but McCormick included a return policy. In addition, the firm printed lists of approved dealers and testimonials from farmers to indicate their machines could be trusted: They had withstood the test of farm use. Sales of this expensive, durable producer good were conceived of as long-term, binding contracts between manufacturer and purchaser.

The image used in these pamphlets was of two men working the horse-drawn machine (Figure 5.4). In what became a regular feature of McCormick advertising, the horses are placed away from the focal point of the graphic, thus already making them of secondary importance to the machine. The machine, its parts, and their operation are the center of attention. One man drives the horses, while a second sweeps the cut wheat stalks from the reaper table. The third man, the one who gathers the wheat stalks into sheaves for transport to threshing, is not shown. While there is wheat on the machine there is no wheat field. Neither is there any sign of a house or of the improved farm landscape. These elements appear for the first time in the engraving used for the next year's harvest circular, but for the remainder of the 1850s, the order form, the contract, and the image of a machine, horses, workers, and wheat, with little more than a sketch of a farm landscape in the background, remained largely unchanged. Thus the 'Virginia Reaper' was imagined as a reliable machine. Its place was in the harvest, but it merely made the work of the harvest easier: At this stage it did not produce a new environment, nor did it complete the farm.

In fact, the reaper was represented as a model modern machine. While the reaper was invented in the McCormicks' barn, its subsequent development testified to technical and engineering expertise.[47] Early advertising emphasized the machines themselves. These were cunning arrangements of specially produced parts, which could be constantly improved by extending their functionality, transforming their assembly, and by introducing new materials. During the 1850s, the McCormicks changed virtually every part of the reaper from year to year.[48] The company catalogues often presented the reaper as an improvement on hand tools for cutting grain and grass; and in one catalogue image dating from 1883, this development was specifically wrapped in the rhetoric of evolution.[49] The reaper was also represented as the first of a growing family of machines. First the industry produced a reaper, then a mower in addition, then a combined reaper-mower, and then a harvester-binder, with first wire and then twine binding apparatus. By 1900, the reaper was being advertised with 'full-lines' of agricultural equipment, including plows, rakes, harrows, hay tedders, manure spreaders, lawn mowers, cream separators, windmills, threshers, separators, stationary gas engines, and traction engines.[50] In a sense, harvester companies informed farmers that their reaper was the progenitor of a multiplying family of useful machines, whose functionality was being constantly perfected. As the century closed, farmer testimonials gave way to engineering comment, reflecting the emergence of in-house engineering departments in place of the teams of skilled mechanics who had previously dominated innovation.[51] In 1901, the annual catalogue claimed that the McCormick was the only machine that could stand up to a 'technical search light.'[52] Cuts revealed some of the fitting points of the machines and were still a regular feature of the catalogues.

While harvesting machinery was celebrated in McCormick's catalogues as evidence of the power of modern technical expertise through annual design changes, innovations and technical progress, the experts, scientists, engineers, and skilled workers were not mentioned. Instead, Cyrus Hall McCormick was celebrated as a much decorated heroic inventor, 'the man who made bread cheap.'[53] Pivotal in this representation was the painting *Men of Progress*, which hangs in the National Portrait Gallery, Washington, DC. Painted by Christian Schussele, it features the bearded Cyrus Hall McCormick standing next to a patent office model of his Virginia Reaper and in front of Samuel Colt, inventor of the Colt revolver, in an arranged visualization of the United States' nineteenth-century inventors. *Men of Progress* never featured in the company's catalogues, but the engraving of the same scene by John Surtain circulated widely, and the company made use of the image, for example in 1868, when a copy of this engraving was given to Emperor Napoleon III along with a mowing machine on the occasion of McCormick's receipt of prizes at the Paris Exposition.[54] Rhetorically, the heroic inventor took the place of the teams of skilled workers who were busy improving the reaper 'offstage' in numerous workshops and field tests.

Harvesting machinery manufacturers made their products the objects of a public gaze when they displayed them at agricultural and world's fairs.[55] McCormick's triumph before the judges at the 1851 Crystal Palace Exposition was a central feature of company advertising. McCormick's success at field trial earned him the award, and the UK press justified the victory by announcing the machine's efficiency. By harvesting 15 acres (6 ha) in 10 hours at a cost of 9 s per acre, the machine offered farmers a saving of 4 pounds, 7 seconds, and 6 days on manual harvesting, so that "This machine is worth to the farmers of England the whole cost of the exhibition."[56] Such a success was vital to future sales, and McCormick endeavored to repeat this remarkable triumph at subsequent fairs, trials, and exhibitions. With his machines on permanent trial, McCormick filled his catalogues with references to competitions, awards, and honors. Triumphs were reported from fields at home and abroad. Testimonials from farmers and experts were featured in the pages of company catalogues. Reaper inventors were celebrated as modern heroes, so their honors and prizes were also proclaimed. Such imagery bolstered the advertising claim that the reaper was an ideal modern machine. In McCormick's catalogues, his machine was at first a reliable and economizing machine, then it was an improved one, then world beating, with "world renowned" added to the company logo in 1880 and a globe added in 1881.[57] The 1882 catalogue announced that McCormick's machines "are the Best in the World."[58] The escalating rhetoric was backed by international successes.

Nevertheless, the machine encountered opposition. Especially in the 1870s, the Grange campaigned against this and other companies and their cartel and pricing policies. In the 1880s, they established cooperative factories to manufacture harvesting machines. Farmers threatened antitrust action against the captains of the industry when a cartel to be called the American Harvester Corporation was suggested in 1890. Subsequently, nationalist actions against foreign corporations followed the McCormick machines, notably in Russia.[59] The idea that invention should not be rewarded by long-term monopoly rights united this diverse opposition, especially since McCormick was rumored to be making fantastic profits on his expensive machines.

Behind the rhetoric lay interfirm competition and contested rights to innovation. The field trials and exhibitions that were initially so important to Cyrus Hall McCormick's claims and success quickly became threats to his business as rival machines and enterprises, some particularly innovative, vied for the honors.[60] McCormick became locked into a growing international program of fairs, expositions, and field trials. In 1878, his machines showed at 27 separate events in the UK, France, New Zealand, and Australia, as well as one in the United States.[61] Each show required elaborate preparations, including advanced planning, appointment of special agents and staff, keeping track of commissioners and jury members, gifts of machines, and preparation of not only special display and performance machines but also memorandum books, pamphlets, catalogues, souvenir albums, model machines, and displays.[62] This soon required advertising departments and contracts to lithographic artists, printers, and advertising firms. Each manufacturer planned to outdo the others.

McCormick had an enviable record of successes, but, especially in the 1860s and 1870s, his machines did not always carry away the prizes and were instead outcompeted by rival machines made by manufacturers in New York state and Ohio.[63] Such competition came to a head at the 1893 Columbian World's Fair held in Chicago, where controversy swirled around the awarding of prizes in the agricultural machinery hall and the staging of the field trial and again at the 1900 Paris Exposition.[64] Tactics became dirty as competition intensified among Canadian and American harvesting machinery manufacturers during the depression of the 1890s. The introduction of tests of draft weight using dynamometers did not reduce the potential for success through rigging juries or excluding machines, but the prizes constituted important capital for advertising, as the frequent representations of medals and honors presented in the McCormick trade catalogues attest.

The root problem was that, while he was acknowledged as inventor of the first successful reaping machine, McCormick's claims to subsequent innovations were hotly contested by other innovators. Initially, McCormick managed to extend his patent rights, as with his 1845 raker seat patent, which was extended in 1847 with expanded claims, but his rivals were also active in securing patents.[65] In 1847, Obed Hussey patented open-backed guard fingers, a major improvement for the industry. The two leading protagonists, Hussey and McCormick locked in struggle as each sought to extend the life of their existing patent rights in 1848–1849. The US Patent Extension Board ultimately denied any extension, and Congress, lobbied by farmers who sought an end to patent extensions and who complained about the magnitude of McCormick's profits—at their expense—confirmed the result.[66]

In 1848, in the middle of this patent contest, the McCormicks decided to relocate to Chicago, buy out a licensed manufacturer, and resume the property rights war against their rivals and other former licensees from there. Their successes were at first limited, however. McCormick launched an infringement suit against former licensee Seymour and Morgan in 1850 and won $9,354 in 1857; but in his much more important patent war with rivals Obed Hussey and John H. Manny, McCormick was defeated.[67] During the 1860s, contestation increased, as did the sums of money involved, and the McCormick enterprise was found to be lagging rivals in the improvement of machines. For example, between 1860 and 1871, the hinged-bar mower pool, which controlled new patents related to a light mower, excluded McCormick from access to the new technical system. Charging royalties of $7.50 to $10.00 per machine, the pool had, by 1868, collected $530,000 in license fees from 25 or more manufacturers that had together produced over 120,000 machines.[68] The McCormick enterprise was playing catch up throughout this period as it strove to acquire innovations in mowers and then automatic binders, first wire and later twine.

It was not until mid-1880, when McCormick launched a twine binder, that the Chicago enterprise was again in the forefront of the patent wars.[69] Having settled for $225,000 in 1884 with the Gordon brothers, who had important binder patents, and then with some other claimants, the McCormicks established control of binder patents through the McCormick-Gorham Binder Ring in 1886. They then sold shop rights to 16 manufacturers covering production rights for May 1883 to July 1886 for $271,000.[70] This action highlights not only McCormick's attention to patent rights and innovation but the extent of competition. In order to remain competitive, McCormick had to retain patent lawyers who would be active in Washington, DC, Pennsylvania, Ohio, and New York, as well as Illinois, Canada, and the United Kingdom. He had to employ agents to seek out, assess, and, where possible and wise, purchase inventions and patents. Indeed, all of the other manufacturers of harvesting machinery were similarly preoccupied.[71]

The firm's rhetoric of the model modern machine, announced in the 1850s, came with a price attached: an escalating engagement with patent lawyers and courts, patents, licenses, and infringements suits, research obligations, and eventually engineering teams. Patent infringement suits and court action and efforts to discredit the improvements claimed by rivals were common in this industry. As sales competition heated up in the 1890s, manufacturers resorted to price cutting, influencing the decisions of the juries at field trials and shows, accusing other manufacturers of illegal copying, and even destroying their machines in 'tug of war' competitions. Dirty practices infiltrated what Mona Domosh has called the rhetoric of 'civilized commerce' that pervaded McCormick's advertising.[72] More importantly, Cyrus Hall McCormick became increasingly abstracted from his machines and their improvement, as well as from innovation in harvesting machines generally. Instead, he became a manager of patents, work teams, and innovation. This was evidenced as early as 1880 by the removal of the head office from the works to the McCormick Block, corner of Dearborn and Randolph Streets, Chicago. Subsequently, both head office and the works' innovation team expanded inexorably, both before the merger of the firm into International Harvester Corporation in 1902 and after.[73]

PYRAMIDS OF SALES

In 1889, McCormick's catalogue celebrated "Our Pyramid of Sales: The Wonder of the Age" and the shift in scale from 50 machines sold in 1844 to over 60,000 in 1887 was certainly an impressive achievement.[74] Further, the image confirms the idea that the reaper, the steamship, and the railroad were inextricably linked in company advertising, since departing trains en route to "Europe," "Australia," and other destinations are shown under the pyramid of sales. Trains of finished machines were dispatched to rural agents, with traveling agents and set-up men accompanying them. Steamships carried reaper freight to distant lands.[75] The telegraph wires that flanked the railway carried the bulletins announcing quantities, orders, and prices. Freight rates were signaled in the contracts that farmers signed. Steamships and submarine cables extended this system overseas so that this interconnectivity linked gigantic industrial concerns to farms in the Americas, Africa, Asia, Australasia, and Europe. In the process, companies emphasized the growing scale of their production and their seamless and efficient connectivity with markets. The railroad gave mass to the economy and linked farm, mine, forest, factory, and city, so that the reaper was understood as a creature of the railroad mega-machine.

However, the McCormick enterprise faced enormous challenges in selling and distributing machines. To begin with, these challenges were in large part geographic: Where should the firm concentrate its sales effort for best effect? So, in 1850, McCormick sold $36,890 worth of machines with his 19 agents in Illinois making 67 percent of the sales, but the rest of his sales were made over an extensive territory. Agents in Iowa, Missouri, and Wisconsin altogether accounted for 16.7 percent of sales. Indiana, Louisiana, Ohio, and other unknown states comprised a further 16.6 percent, while an agent in Buffalo, who was responsible for the Canada territory, made another 4.6 percent of sales.[76] Having established depots in Baltimore, Philadelphia, and Rochester in 1854 to facilitate sales in eastern US states, McCormick abandoned eastern markets in the 1860s and 1870s in the face of stiff competition from New York and Ohio manufacturers.[77] In any case, he was able to continue to increase sales, for example, receiving $89,016 in 1858, by concentrating on Midwest markets: That year 84 percent of those sales were made in Illinois.[78] As late as 1872, the enterprise's chief sales territory comprised six states flanking the Mississippi River from Kentucky and Missouri to the Canadian border.[79] Again, the location of the works in Chicago paid off: The McCormicks rode the farm settlement frontier as it flowed through the Midwest.

While there were enormous profits to be made on each sale—for example, production cost per machine in 1858 was $43 but the sales price was $245—there were also significant costs attached to distribution. For one thing, that year 84 percent of the sales were in unpaid notes.[80] Machines were expensive and sold on credit, so that collection agents were a necessity. Often the McCormicks sold out their production but were rewarded with a long-term stream of receivables rather than cash. In this context, it was important to find skilled and reliable agents, and this meant offering commissions on sales, sometimes up to 20 percent of the sale price, although different manufacturers adopted different contracts and pricing strategies. Setting agents up with a suitable warehouse, advertising, and stock added further costs.

Since farmers first sowed their land and then went to town to compare harvesting machines at the state fairs, an annual calendar of fair displays and field trials had to be prepared for. Then the sales season was short and intense, but farmers would be disappointed if the machinery they purchased was not on hand and ready to perform when the harvest needed to be made. Consequently, manufacturers not only dispatched knocked-down reapers packed in crates and loaded in railroad cars to their agents in time for the harvest rush but also trained set-up men to ensure that the harvesters were ready for action in the fields. During the winter, rural areas were canvassed to ascertain the scale of likely demand in the next season. Again, as with factory production, distribution marched to the drum of rural seasonality.[81]

Each territory presented separate transport costs and arrangements, local harvest conditions, competitors, and language of sale. In the 1870s, McCormick machines sold for cash from Ohio to East Kansas, but for credit in Minnesota, the Dakotas, and Nebraska, where, in what was "a new, one-crop country" with exemption laws, "the solvency of every prospective buyer had to be studied with special diligence" and agents worked for salary and not commissions.[82] Transport costs and capacity in the United States and Canada varied among railroad companies, by line, and direction of route. Exports of machines faced similar capacity and cost issues. Manufacturers in Atlantic coast states had transport advantages over those located in the US interior, in Transatlantic, and even in US Pacific coast markets. In contrast, as railroad companies introduced preferential freight rates around 1872 for freight traveling in empty grain cars returning west, new cost advantages accrued to manufacturers in Chicago.[83] Thus the civilizing machine was not available everywhere at the same price or the same quantities, and reaper sales were unevenly distributed over the maps being produced in head office.

The reorganizing of the McCormick Harvesting Machinery Company's distribution system from 1881–1884 illustrates the scale, organization, and technical aspects of making farm machinery sales.[84] After a period when each agent made his own transport arrangements, this logistics exercise was centralized to head office, which had been separated from the works in 1880 and was now equipped with telephones and typewriters and staffed by female as well as male clerks. In 1880, 50 general agents coordinated local sales forces. For the 1883 harvest, they were backed by a force of 140 field experts and an army of salesmen and collectors, so that McCormick had more workers engaged in sales and distribution than in manufacturing. Display machines and scale models filled the sales rooms. Annually, the firm published eight hundred thousand catalogs, eight thousand show cards, plus repair catalogues, and in addition paid for advertisements in newspapers. A new policy of allowing variations from the previously fixed terms was adopted: Agents were allowed to discount from official spring price lists to a minimum price.

Despite this reorganization, the enterprise anticipated that 30 percent of the sales price was required to cover the cost of selling and collecting.[85] In the 1890s, as competition mounted and depression gripped the country, distribution expenses became more and more a matter of concern. Cyrus McCormick Jr. claimed companies selling good machines needed $150 in property and stocks for every $100 of annual business to offset the costs of field trials, exhibitions, advertising, and delayed earnings associated with the distribution system.[86] Efforts to end the cutthroat competition through cartel agreements, such as the 1883 negotiations in Chicago and Niagara Falls that aimed to set the retail price for harvesters, the wholesale price of binder twine, agents' commissions, and the production quota for machines for each manufacturer, were made annually but no agreement was reached. Instead, the industry faced repeated years of overproduction and price-cutting, with even a case of dumping unsold machines in the Canadian Prairies market.[87] McCormick struggled to cope with the organizational demands of distributing his machines over an ever wider territory and spreading his returns over future seasons.

PROPERTY

In the course of his activities as an inventor and manufacturer, Cyrus Hall McCormick accumulated property. Since in 1880 the firm's profit was

$1,192,733 on 22,000 sales, up from $722,326 on 18,700 sales the year before, this was hardly surprising, but the extent and character of this property empire and its implications deserve attention.[88] As early as 1872, the firm of Lord, Day & Lord of New York City managed $350,000 of stocks and bonds, including stocks in 7 railroad and 18 other companies for Cyrus Hall McCormick.[89] More than a decade later, upon the death of the famous inventor in 1884, an inventory of the McCormick estate was compiled.[90] It reported a total value of $10,796,810 in assets, including $7,554,800 in company stock. In addition to the $1,875,000 of shares that Cyrus Hall McCormick personally held in the McCormick Harvesting Machinery Company, he owned a further $593,423 worth of shares in diverse, but mostly railroad, companies, bonds worth $436,393, and land in Chicago valued at $2,053,996. Further land property in Illinois, Indiana, Iowa, Missouri, Nebraska, and Wisconsin filled a three-page list. Not only would the inventor have made it onto the Forbes list of his time, but his property list indicates his transition from inventor and manufacturer to regional- then national-scale entrepreneur.[91] Moreover, his accumulated property helps to reveal several aspects of his broader trading environment.

McCormick's property investments reveal a diversification strategy around his manufacturing activities. This was still not a strategy of integration backward into materials production—this had to wait for his son's investments in forests and sawmills, steel mills, and foundries in the late 1880s and 1890s—but already forward into distribution. He could make good and reliable returns on bonds and stocks while his returns on investments in railroad companies proved erratic. However, his railroad stocks secured for McCormick seats on some boards and insider commercial knowledge and advantageous deals on freight rates. His investments here were strategic as well as prudent, since the railroads "were a never-ending source of aggravation on account of their erratic tariffs and the "public-be-damned" attitude of their officials."[92] Investments in Chicago businesses placed him on the boards of several leading businesses and made him a more prominent member of the city's inner circle. Thus his son was a member of the Columbian World's Fair committee as well as a member of the Chicago Stock Exchange. Investments in land provided a cushion against delayed earnings from machinery sales. Through defaulting farmers and strategic investments, McCormick accumulated a land bank whose assets would continue to grow as the farm settlement frontier progressed. Investments in Chicago property could be subsequently realized through office or factory construction and contributed a steady stream of rentals. Landed property constituted a reserve fund. Of course, these investments meant that the inventor and manufacturer in fact built a commercial empire, and to manage this he needed the assistance of lawyers, accountants, agents, and advisers. McCormick became a man at the center of a growing web of businesses where he enjoyed structural autonomy.[93] The conversion of the McCormick Harvesting Machinery Company into a part of International

Harvester Corporation (IHC) through merger in 1902 altered this structural autonomy. Where the manufacturing company was concerned, Cyrus
McCormick was entitled to a seat on the board and was a major share-
holder, but he no longer ran the enterprise. However, through the diversification of the family enterprise into other property, Cyrus McCormick
remained wealthy, influential, and autonomous.

Cyrus Hall McCormick's collection of houses offers one indicator of his
personal mobility. McCormick was peripatetic for most of his career, and
hotels were his normal habitat. Nevertheless, for a time he owned houses
in Philadelphia and a cottage in Washington, DC, which he used to be close
to the patent courts. His lavish Rush Street, Chicago, residence was a base
for his interactions with the factory, where his brothers and son were the
active partners. His residence on Lower Fifth Avenue, New York, facilitated
his engagements with New York bankers, brokers, and lawyers, as well as
his work overseeing sales, distribution, and world's fair representation in
Europe. His house in Richfield Springs, New York, anchored summer recreation and a round of church-related activities. Late in his career he made
regular annual sojourns to Paris, and, as his health deteriorated, he took the
cures in numerous US resorts.

The extent to which the inventor lived out ideals of cultivation and civilization rather than a newfound environmental awareness can also be gauged
through aspects of the property that he accumulated. There are no records
that I have discovered of Cyrus Hall McCormick identifying with conservation, national parks, or wilderness. During his lifetime it was, if anything,
too early for these ideas to register. His brother, W.S. McCormick, "enjoyed
annual hunting and fishing trips to northern Wisconsin or Minnesota."[94]
But other ideas, related to the making of improved middle landscapes, featured. For example, in 1871, Cyrus Hall McCormick purchased land at
Richfield Springs, Otsego County, New York, which was a regular summer
haunt, with the intention of building a summerhouse, which was eventually
erected in 1882. Designed by McKim, Mead, and White, 'Clayton Lodge'
enjoyed a panoramic view and was set on six acres, first planted with an
orchard and shrubs and later landscaped under the supervision of Frederick
Olmstead. Here McCormick spent the summers of 1882 and 1883 "enjoying his roses," "happy" to "be back upon the land" and, as he had done
for many years, meeting with other "prominent Presbyterians," a group of
whom met regularly at Richfield Springs in the summer.[95] In 1882, the family farm at Walnut Grove, Virginia, was acquired as a memorial and thus
invested with heritage values. Subsequently, McCormick had its 518 acres
surveyed, drained, and fenced; the house refurbished; and the property ten-
anted.[96] This was a man who insisted on being surrounded by flowers and
music and whose Chicago house was reported in family correspondence as a
menagerie.[97] There are photographs in the McCormick archives of the family on vacation at the lake and cottage, images that testify to the importance
of the last chapter of William Cronon's *Nature's Metropolis*, but these date

from around 1900 and not earlier.[98] McCormick invested in improved and cultivated nature, not just at the Columbian World's Fair but also at the cottage and by the lake. His son, Cyrus McCormick, continued with this ideal when he owned a house called 'Walden,' in Lake Forest, Illinois, indicating both his embrace of Emerson's romanticism and, given its design and layout, of a parkland setting for his grand house (Figure 5.5).

The McCormicks engaged with a wide array of experts as they accumulated and administered their property. It has long been acknowledged that professional engineers, accountants, advertising men, and lawyers were recruited in larger numbers as some US companies were transformed into corporations and, in the process, professionalized many of their management functions.[99] The McCormick Harvesting Machinery Company was no exception: Its reaper was produced in the context of proliferating and modernizing state institutions, such as departments of agriculture, the patent office, agricultural fairs, industrial exhibitions, or the census. In addition, however, the diversifying property interests of the McCormick family called for further professionals. Stockbrokers and bond agents, insurance agents and bankers, patent lawyers and railroad experts were consulted,

Figure 5.5   Aerial view of "Walden," the estate of Cyrus McCormick, Jr., Lake Forest, Illinois. Chicago Aerial Survey Company, McCormick - International Harvester Collection **Image ID: 3617**, Wisconsin State Historical Society, Madison, Wisconsin, Viewed online at https://www.wisconsinhistory.org/.

contracted, or retained. In addition, architects, property lawyers, and land-scape gardeners provided professional services related to rural and urban property. The young Cyrus McCormick was sent to university, unlike his father. Thus the burgeoning wealth and property of the family intensified interactions with modern institutions, simultaneously distancing the family members from the daily grind of work with nature on the farm or in the factory and intensifying their familiarity with standards, statistics, forecasts, plans, and other constructions produced by the calculative practices of desk professionals.

CONCLUSION: MCCORMICK'S TRADING ENVIRONMENTS

The modern mechanizing farm illustrated in the McCormick catalogues was not separated from nature but involved more machines in a natural team to produce abundance. Harvesting machinery companies presented the reaper as a force mechanizing, civilizing, and improving environments. This was a 'chariot of progress' comprising a 'natural team': a modern hybrid of men, horses, crops, and machines. It was an agent of Manifest Destiny, part of a 'civilizing commerce,' a social agent that would extend and reward produc-tive and disciplined masculinities and would provide abundance through a 'perpetual harvest,' and so make bread cheap and end famine. In this rheto-ric, companies promised to farmers a moral machine that would produce a moral environment.

In fundamental ways, then, the rhetoric of the reaper disturbs the central-ity afforded in environmental history to either the pastoral ideal or to the railroad. While the reaper produced the pastoral landscape, it was, above all, portrayed as an agent of civilization. The nature-machine relationships expressed in company advertising did not cast the pastoral landscape of modernized and mechanized agriculture as unnatural nor did it treat them as an example of the technological sublime. What was on offer to farmers was the ideal of cultivation, mechanized as part of grand narratives of civili-zation that linked farms to cities, and, at the world scale, linked to abundance and to various primitive 'others' constructed in order to accentuate the attri-butes ascribed to this civilizing machine.

Behind the rhetoric, indeed, obscured by it, the McCormick enterprise and its reaper encountered diverse problems in its trading environments. Despite the advantages—urbanization and agglomeration economies—of locating their factory in Chicago, the owners encountered ongoing environ-mental constraints as they strove to increase production and contain costs. Into the 1880s, the production schedule at the works ran to the beat of rural seasons, so that, in surprising ways, railroad development transformed but did not end the environmental constraints on the McCormicks' factory production. Successive factories were wrecked by fires or subject to trade union action. As the wooden reaper morphed into a steel harvester-binder, they scoured the United States for the most suitable materials, supplies, and machine tools. The performance of the reaper depended on the transformation of environments. As the output of machines increased, more railroad lines and a different Chicago built environment were needed. Increasing demand for coal, iron, steel, fiber, and lumber transformed environments not only in Chicago's immediate regional hinterland but much further away, including Mexico and the Philippines. Farm use of the reaper required a dramatic increase in the national horse herd and thus an expansion of the area devoted to fodder crops. Ironically, while a transformed first nature legitimized commercial expansion in company rhetoric, the closing of the US farm settlement frontier around 1890 and shifts from wheat to hay and then maize production across the Midwest coincided with intensifying industrial competition: The very success of environmental transformation threatened the firm's markets and survival.

Railroads facilitated distribution and the McCormick enterprise first rode on a wave of frontier settlement and then the capture of export markets, but organizational problems in distribution and innovation remained persistent challenges, especially in terms of costs. Again the rhythms of Chicago's countryside; the geography of access to it; and the geography of farm type, productivity, and enterprise complicated machinery sales. The firm's sales force and distribution costs were, by 1880, larger than the factory workforce and production costs. Farmer defaults on machinery payments, which were often the result of poor harvests or poor farm account management, combined with sales on credit to postpone revenue streams for manufacturers. They had to set aside extra assets to cope with the financial stress of not knowing when their sales would be realized. Further, their modern machine had to be developed and improved, and it was constantly on show, its performance contested at agricultural fairs, in expositions, and field trials and in patent courts by a growing number of rival machines. Any attempt to monopolize the rights to such a useful invention incurred farmer outrage, but any lack of diligence with regard to innovation would be a costly mistake. Thus the modern machine became hedged around by a proliferating set of modern trading environments in which its attributes were contested or legitimated.

The McCormicks accumulated vast amounts of property, which they managed by becoming more mobile and extensible and by learning and acquiring the calculative practices of modernizing institutions in banking, finance, and law. Ultimately, through the formation of IHC in 1902, the family ended up as property managers and capitalists, distanced from not only their famous machine, factory, and invention practices but from the nature that their machine was transforming.

Company advertising was only one of this machine's trading environments: others included legal offices and courts, board rooms, warehouses and displays, factory work rooms, railroad cars, agricultural fairs and farms, even, eventually, the New York Stock Exchange. In turn, the ensemble of machines and trading environments were constrained by materials, seasonality, distance, and the dynamics of environmental transformations bound up in a tangled web of property rights and enrolled in advertising claims. In this tangled web it is well to remember that, while the McCormick company trumpeted a civilizing mission over and above the environmental transformations wrought by the inventor and his machine, they and their Chicago remained subject to and constrained by nature as they became creatures of the 'civilization' they were said to represent.

NOTES

1 Gordon M. Winder, *The American Reaper: Harvesting Networks and Technology, 1830–1910* (Farnham, Surrey and Burlington, VT: Ashgate Publishing, 2012). See also Siegfried Giedion, *Mechanization Takes Command: A Contribution to Anonymous History* (New York and London: W.W. Norton and Company, 1969) (first published 1948): 130–168, who argued, citing the effects of the McCormick reaper on Ralph Waldo Emerson's "man with the hoe," (131) that through mechanization "The farmer, symbol of continuity, has been drawn into flux" (130) and that mechanization induced "the structural transformation of the farmer from self-sufficiency to specialization" (132).

2 Mona Domosh notes the framing of the reaper within a dynamic hierarchy of civilization, grounded not only in 'commodity racism' and a 'cosmopolitan domesticity,' terms offered by Anne McClintock and Kristen Hogarson, but in what Mona Domosh calls 'flexible racism.' That is, race was not a fixed category: all peoples were on the road to civilization and were potentially 'white,' but their character and their choice of technology set them on different rungs of the ladder of progress. By choosing American technology, a higher state of civilization could be achieved. Nevertheless, some peoples represented in the catalogue pages were demonstrably "not able to participate in the community of commodities." Mona Domosh, *American Commodities in an Age of Empire*, (New York and London: Routledge, 2006: 101–126, and 181–192), citing Anne McClintock, *Imperial Leather: Race, Gender and Sexuality in the Colonial Conquest* (New York: Routledge, 1995) and Kristin Hogarson, "Cosmopolitan domesticity: Importing the American dream, 1865–1921," *American Historical Review* 107 (2002): 55–83. See also Michael Adas, *Dominance by Design: Technological Imperatives and America's Civilizing Mission* (Cambridge, MA: Harvard University Press, 2006); Mona Domosh, "A 'civilized' commerce: Gender, 'race', and empire at the 1893 Chicago Exposition," *Cultural Geographies* 9 (2002): 181–201; Kay Anderson, "White natures: Sydney's Royal Agricultural Show in post-humanist perspective," *Transactions of the Institute of British Geographers* 28(4) (2003): 423; Jackson Lears, *Fables of Abundance: A Cultural History of Advertising in America* (New York: Basic Books, 1994); Stuart Ewen, *Captains of Consciousness: Advertising and the Social Roots of the Consumer Culture* (New York: McGraw-Hill, 1976); Richard Wightman Fox and T. J. Jackson Lears (eds.), *The Culture of Consumption: Critical Essays in American History, 1880–1980* (New York: Pantheon, 1983); and William Leach, *Land of Desire: Merchants, Power and the Rise of a New American Culture* (New York: Pantheon, 1993).

3 Leo Marx's intent was to identify the technological sublime—the naturalization of the machine in the garden—and the anxious uncertainty that went

with this combination of a dehumanizing and polluting technology and the organic, life-affirming garden. Leo Marx, *The Machine in the Garden: Technology and the Pastoral Ideal in America* (New York: Oxford University Press, 1964); Roderick Nash, *Wilderness and the American Mind* (New Haven, CT: Yale University Press, 1982, first published 1967); Ruth Swartz Cowan, *A Social History of American Technology* (New York: Oxford University Press, 1977); Leo Marx, "Afterword: The machine in the garden," *Massachusetts Review* 40(4) (1999): 483–496; Yi-Fu Tuan, *Topophilia: A Study of Environmental Perception, Attitudes and Values* (Englewood Cliffs, NJ: Prentice-Hall, 1974); John F. Kasson, *Civilizing the Machine: Technology and Republican Values in America, 1776–1900* (New York: Grossman Publishers, 1976); Susan Danby and Leo Marx (eds.), *The Railroad in American Art: Representations of Technological Change* (Cambridge, MA: MIT Press, 1988); David Nye, *American Technological Sublime* (Cambridge, MA: MIT Press, 1994); Joel Pfister, "A garden in the machine: Reading a mid-nineteenth-century two-cylinder parlor stove as cultural text," *Technology and Society* 13(3) (1991): 327–343; David E. Nye, "Technologies of landscape," in David Nye (ed.), *Technologies of Landscape: From Reaping to Recycling* (Amherst, MA: University of Massachussetts Press, 1999), 3–17; Richard White, *The Organic Machine: The Remaking of the Columbia River* (New York: Hill and Wang, 1995); Carroll W. Purcell, *The Machine in America: A Social History of Technology* (Baltimore: Johns Hopkins University Press, 1995); William Cronon, "The trouble with wilderness or getting back to the wrong nature," *Environmental History Review* 1(1) (1996): 7–28; L. Nash, "The changing experience of nature: Historical encounters with a northwest river," *The Journal of American History* 86(4) (2000): 1600–1629; Peter F. Cannavò, "American contradictions and pastoral visions: An appraisal of Leo Marx, *The Machine in the Garden*," *Organization and Environment* 14(1) (2001): 74–92; Jeffrey L. Meikle, "Leo Marx's 'The machine in the garden," *Technology and Culture* 44(1) (2003): 150; Benjamin R. Cohen, "Escaping the false binary of nature and culture through connection: Richard White's *The Organic Machine: The Remaking of the Columbia River*," *Organization and Environment* 18(4) (2005): 445–457.

4 William Cronon, *Nature's Metropolis: Chicago and the Great West* (New York and London: W.W. Norton, 1991).
5 William Cronon, "The Busy Hive," chapter 7 in Cronon, *Nature's Metropolis*: 310–318.
6 McCormick's "advertising campaigns became a tool for educating members of a broad rural public about the wondrous new technology spewing forth from the firm's Chicago factory." And "By 1860, farmers had apparently decided that the machine from McCormick's urban factory had become almost a necessity of rural life." Cronon, "Busy Hive," p. 314 and p. 318.
7 Richard D. White, *Railroaded: The Transcontinentals and the Making of Modern America* (New York: W.W. Norton, 2011).
8 Sterling Evans, *Bound in Twine: The History and Ecology of the Henequen-Wheat Complex for Mexico and the American and Canadian Plains, 1880–1950* (College Station, TX: Texas A. and M. University Press, 2007).
9 Alfred D. Chandler Jr., *Strategy and Structure: Chapters in the History of Industrial Enterprise* (Cambridge, MA: MIT Press, 1962).
10 Gordon Winder, "A trans-national machine on the world stage: Representing McCormick's reaper through world fairs, 1851–1902," *Journal of Historical Geography* 33(2007): 352–376.
11 The company archives located at the State Historical Society of Wisconsin, Madison, contain a complete collection of the firm's annual trade catalogues and a large collection of pamphlets, trade cards, and other advertising material.

12   While mechanical harvests are contrasted with the arduous labor in traditional harvests, the reaper involved only limited relief from labor or nature. The machine was a work in progress: mechanization was not yet automation. Farm work still involved riding the uncomfortable reaper seat and hiring extra men as rakers, threshers, and so on. This was a machine that required disciplined, hardworking, and competent farmers with capital. It actually intensified horse labor: If the machine had a heavy draft then it was called a horse killer.

13   'It's always harvest time with the McCormick,' *McCormick Catalogue*, 1890 (McCormick Collection, SHS Wisconsin, Madison, Company, Advertising, McC Mss 5X Box 2).

14   Lears, *Fables of Abundance*. See also Ewen, *Captains of Consciousness*; Fox and Lears (eds.), *The Culture of Consumption*; and Leach, *Land of Desire*.

15   McCormick Catalogue Art: A lithograph illustration for the back cover of the McCormick Harvesting Machine Company catalogue shows a gentleman sitting in a Victorian parlor pointing to a globe for a boy and girl. His didactic purpose is captured by the caption: "Teaching object lessons: my children on this globe you see the harvest fields of the earth where the McCormick is ever king." McCormick Harvesting Machine Company, McCormick—International Harvester Collection, 1890, Image ID: 4413, State Historical Society of Wisconsin, Madison, Wisconsin.

16   Catherine Johnston, "Beyond the clearing: Towards a dwelt animal geography," *Progress in Human Geography* 32(5) (2008): 633–649; Clare Palmer, "Taming the wild profusion of existing things"? A study of Foucault, power, and human/ animal relationships" *Environmental Ethics* 23(4) (2001): pp. 339–358; Sarah A. Radcliffe, Elisabeth E. Watson, Ian Simmons, Felipe Fernández-Armesto, Andrew Sluyter, "Environmentalist thinking and/in geography," *Progress in Human Geography* 34(1) (2010): 98–116.

17   Other harvesting machinery companies proclaimed their grim machines as 'Chariots of Progress.' What was portrayed was the spirit of the reaper. Lighting the way across the heavens and heralded by angels and 'Prosperity' or a 'goddess of summer,' the airborne reaper promised to bring plenty to all those farms it passed. See D.S. Morgan and Co., Brockport, New York, *1877. The Triumph Reapers and Mowers Manufactured by D.S. Morgan and Co., Brockport, New York* (Chicago: Staats-Zeitung Job Printing Co., 1877), D. S. Morgan Collection, Drake Memorial Library, SUNY, Brockport, New York. Curiously, Morgan's machine flew at night so that the torchlight from the angels accompanying it lit up a bucolic landscape with no railroad, but this was an ordered pastoral landscape with ample signs of abundance. See also Aultman, Miller & Co. catalogue cover, which features a chromolithograph illustration of a 'goddess of summer' guiding a horse-drawn binder through the sky with the earth visible far below. The caption reads: "Summer and the Buckeye go round the world together." Aultman, Miller & Co., Akron, Ohio, 1895, McCormick—International Harvester Collection, Image ID: 11914, Wisconsin State Historical Society, Madison, Wisconsin.

18   Graeme Wynn, '"Deplorably dark and demoralized lumberers?" Rhetoric and reality in early nineteenth-century New Brunswick," *Journal of Forest History* 24(4) (1980): 168–187.

19   McCormick Harvesting Machine Co., *Catalogue* 1890, Wisconsin State Historical Society, Madison, Wisconsin, McCormick—International Harvester Collection, Image ID: 86968.

20   McComick Harvesting Machine Co., *Catalogue* 1883, Wisconsin State Historical Society, Madison, Wisconsin, Company, Advertising, McC Mss 5X Box 2.

21   The company catalogue featured two images portraying the colonists as republican revolutionaries and as heroic farmers. The presence of these images in the

catalogue associated the reaper with Jeffersonian political economy and with the production of the armed, propertied farmer, backbone of the nation. The color lithograph illustration on the back cover of the McCormick Harvesting Machine Company catalogue shows an American Revolutionary War battle scene. It also includes an inset illustration of a farmer-soldier with a plow and rifle and the text: "'76 The Call to Arms" and "Honor to Whom Honor is Due." There is a further text: "Here once the embattled farmer stood, And fired the shot heard 'round the world." 'McCormick Catalogue Art,' McCormick Harvesting Machine Company, 1894, McCormick—International Harvester Collection, Image ID: 4416, Wisconsin State Historical Society, Madison, Wisconsin.

22 Black Americans were not referred to in the catalogues as part of the 'civilization' that was brought by the harvesting machines. There are very few representations of Black or Native Americans in the McCormick catalogues until the 1890s. The major exception is the lithograph published in 1883 to commemorate the invention of the reaper at McCormick's farm in 1831. This lithograph portrays the first field trial of the Virginia Reaper at Steele's Tavern and represents Black Americans as idle witnesses. Native Americans were also at first portrayed as onlookers with no future in Manifest Destiny, but later they became part of the representation system associated with corn harvesters. 'Testing the First Reaping Machine,' 1883, Wisconsin Historical Society Image ID 2497, Wisconsin State Historical Society, Madison, Wisconsin.

23 See David Lulka, "Grass or grain? Assessing the nature of the US bison industry," *Sociologia Ruralis* 46(3) (2006): 173–191. The McCormick catalogue of 1889 was unequivocal. The back cover illustration labels a buffalo as "the last of his race," and the plains on which he gazes "what was only a few years ago the grazing ground of the buffalo is now the home of the McCormick." 'McCormick Catalog Art,' McCormick Harvesting Machine Company, 1889, Wisconsin Historical Society, Image ID 4398, Wisconsin State Historical Society, Madison, Wisconsin.

24 Winder, *The American Reaper*, 44–45.

25 Ibid., 81 and 84.

26 Ibid., 45.

27 Ibid., 81–82.

28 Ibid., 72.

29 Ibid., 82.

30 Ibid., 80.

31 Robert Ozanne, *A Century of Labor-Management Relations at McCormick and International Harvester* (Madison, WI: University of Wisconsin Press, 1967), 4 and William E. Hutchinson, *Cyrus Hall McCormick*, 2 vol. (New York and London: The Century Company, 1930 and 1935), 486.

32 Hutchinson, *Cyrus Hall McCormick*, II, 696.

33 Winder, *The American Reaper*, 82.

34 David Hounshell, *From the American System to Mass Production: The Development of Manufacturing Technology in the United States, 1850–1920* (Baltimore: Johns Hopkins University Press, 1984), 159.

35 Robert Ozanne, *Wages in Practice and Theory: McCormick and International Harvester 1860–1960* (Madison, WI: University of Wisconsin Press, 1968), Table 26.

36 Hutchinson, *Cyrus Hall McCormick*, II, 695.

37 Carville Earle, "The last great chance for an American working class: Spatial lessons of the General Strike and the Haymarket riot of early May 1886," in C. Earle, *Geographical Inquiry and American Historical Problems* (Stanford, CA: Stanford University Press, 1992), 378–399.

38 Winder, *The American Reaper*, 19–20.

39 Ibid., 82.
40 Every state except Washington, DC, recorded an increase in herd, and several new states were formed. In increasingly mechanized grain states such as Illinois, Kansas, Minnesota, and Nebraska, the number of horses per 100 acres of improved land and per farm increased between 1880 and 1900. In both New York and Vermont, where transitions from grain into mixed farming and livestock farming were already occurring, there were nevertheless increases in the number of horses. Similarly, in both California and Texas, each with rather different agricultural specializations and average farm size, the horse herd increased.
41 Fred Shannon, *The Farmers' Last Frontier: Agriculture 1860–1897* (New York: Farrar and Rinehart, 1945).
42 This was an important theme in advertizing, especially as the machines were associated with world's fair medals, and the inventor of the reaper was often named 'the man who made bread cheap.' See Winder, "A trans-national machine," 352–376. See also Cyrus McCormick, *The Century of the Reaper* (Boston and New York: Houghton Mifflin Company, 1931), 4 and 16: "If the rest of civilization could have suddenly become modern while agriculture remained in the slough of inefficiency, the economic results would have been disastrous" and "That was a day when famine was ordered from the land and the drudgery of old agriculture was banished."
43 Evans, *Bound in Twine*.
44 Hutchinson, *Cyrus Hall McCormick*, II, 555–572.
45 Evans, *Bound in Twine*, 16.
46 Winder, "A trans-national machine," 352–376.
47 John Nader, "The rise of an inventive profession: Learning effects in the Midwestern harvester industry, 1850–1890," *Journal of Economic History* 54(1994): 397–408.
48 Hounshell, *From the American System to Mass Production*, 159.
49 'The Evolution of the Reaper: Survival of the Fittest' (*McCormick Catalogue*, 1883, McCormick Collection, SHS Wisconsin, Madison) shows three, progressively more complicated and efficient, McCormick machines, and, behind the last of these, the pigs that had broken into the wheat field in the first cartoon hang on hooks to cure. This image clearly communicated ideas of competitive innovation using farmyard analogies. Cyrus Hall McCormick was a devote Christian, and the rhetoric in his company's catalogues can be read as embracing Christian virtues of discipline, toil, and prudence, as well as holding out the promise of God's bountiful harvest, but they did not trumpet these ideas using Biblical verses. There are no direct quotes from the Bible and no references to the parables of the harvest. Mona Domosh explains that the Christian millenarian vision—all are on the path to civilization—embraced Darwinian evolution and economic development and simultaneously legitimized commercial expansion. Domosh, *American Commodities*, 185–186.
50 For descriptions of these separate lines of development and for discussions of the implications of these eventually interrelated machinery types see R.L. Ardrey, *American Agricultural Implements* (Chicago: R.L. Ardrey, 1894, facsimile by University Microfilms, Ann Arbor, Michigan, 1968); L. Rogin, *The Introduction of Farm Machinery in its Relation to the Productivity of Labor in the Agriculture of the United States During the Nineteenth Century* (New York: Johnson Reprint Company, 1931, reprinted 1966); Gordon M. Winder, "Before the corporation and mass production? The licensing regime in the manufacture of North American harvesting machinery, 1830–1910," *Annals of the Association of American Geographers* 85/3(1995): 521–552; and Gordon M. Winder, "Following America into the second industrial revolution: New

rules for competition and Ontario's farm machinery industry, 1850–1930," *The Canadian Geographer* 46/4(2002): 292–309.

51 Nader, "The rise of an inventive profession."
52 McComick Harvesting Machine Co., Catalogue 1901 (Wisconsin State Historical Society, Madison, Wisconsin, Company, Advertising, McC Mss 5X Box 2).
53 This was especially so in the company catalogue of 1894. It celebrated Cyrus Hall McCormick among a pantheon of other great Americans. Quotations from each of these were supplied. At least two of these were directly associated with the pastoral ideal, the Great West, and Jefferson's political economy rhetoric: George Washington is quoted and Horace Greeley advises young Americans to 'Go West'!
54 But McCormick, also advertised as a US patriot, was 'the inventor of the reaper,' who helped to make bread cheap and thus advanced civilization everywhere. 'The shot heard around the world', *McCormick Catalogue* (1876), (Wisconsin Historical Society, Madison, Wisconsin, Company, Advertising, McC Mss 5X Box 2).
55 McCormick, *The Century of the Reaper*, 81; Hutchinson, *Cyrus Hall McCormick* II, 362 and 435–436. *Men of Progress* John Surtain/Christian Schussele, Object Number NPG.67.88 National Portrait Gallery, Washington D.C.
56 Winder, "A trans-national machine," 352–376.
57 London 1851 Exposition, 'Views of McCormick's American reaper and McCormick from the Crystal Palace and its contents' (London, 1852), (Wisconsin Historical Society, Madison, Wisconsin, Company, Exhibitions 1851, McC Mss 6X Box 1). See Winder, *The American Reaper*, 160.
58 Domosh, *American Commodities*, 101.
59 McCormick Harvesting Machine Company, *McCormick Harvesting Machine Co., 1882* (1882) (Company, Advertising, McC Mss 5X Box 2).
60 Mona Domosh, "Uncovering the friction of globalization: American commercial embeddedness and landscape in revolutionary-era Russia," *Annals of the Association of American Geographers* 100(2) (2010): 427–443; Fred V. Carstensen, *American Enterprise in Foreign Markets: Studies of Singer and International Harvester in Imperial Russia* (Durham, NC: Duke University Press, 1984).
61 See Winder, "A trans-national machine," 352–376.
62 McCormick Harvesting Machine Co., 'List of prizes awarded at exhibitions and competitive field trials 1851–1880,' (Wisconsin Historical Society, Madison, Wisconsin, Company, Exhibitions 1851, American and Foreign, McC Mss 6X Box 1, ME576).
63 Winder, *The American Reaper*, 161–166.
64 Winder, "Before the corporation and mass production," 530–532.
65 Winder, "A trans-national machine," 371–374.
66 Winder, *The American Reaper*, 45.
67 Ibid., 11.
68 The January 1856 verdict in *McCormick v. Manny* was upheld in 1858, with McCormick losing on all counts and the following action against Hussey also failed. Winder, *The American Reaper*, 45.
69 Winder, *The American Reaper*, 55, citing Hutchnson, *Cyrus Hall McCormick* II, 373.
70 Winder, *The American Reaper*, 129, citing Hutchinson, *Cyrus Hall McCormick* II, 555–572.
71 Winder, *The American Reaper*, 61–62.
72 See Winder, *The American Reaper*; Hutchinson, *Cyrus Hall McCormick*; and Gordon M. Winder, "Building trust and managing business over distance: A geography of reaper manufacturer D.S. Morgan's correspondence, 1867," *Economic Geography* 77/2(2001), 95–121.

73 Mona Domosh, "A "civilized" commerce," *Cultural Geographies* 9(2002): 181–201.
74 Hutchinson, *Cyrus Hall McCormick*, II, 692.
75 McCormick Harvesting Machine Company, *McCormick Harvesting Machine Co.,1887* (1887) (Wisconsin Historical Society, Madison, Wisconsin, Company, Advertising, McC Mss 5X Box 2).
76 McCormick also used the image of a 'Ship of Progress' in his 1897 catalogue to evoke the company's 'civilizing mission.' The ship would sail to foreign lands with its cargo of reaper freight, which was destined to mechanize agriculture the world over. This color lithograph cover illustration for the McCormick Harvesting Machine Company catalogue shows a steam powered sailing ship named *Progress* with a McCormick grain binder on the bow. The cover includes the text "The ship of progress; hail, mighty ship, where'er you dip the billows roll with life anew, as with your weight of reaper freight, you plow the waters through, forevermore, each wave-kissed shore a welcome holds for thee, and all the years shall ring with cheers—the land unto the sea." McCormick Catalogue Cover, McCormick Harvesting Machine Company, 1897, Image ID: 4419
McCormick—International Harvester Collection, State Historical Society of Wisconsin, Madison, Wisconsin. See Domosh *American Commodities in an Age of Empire*.
77 Winder, *The American Reaper*, 81, 83, footnote 48, 84.
78 Winder, *The American Reaper*, 46.
79 Ibid., 82.
80 Hutchinson, *Cyrus Hall McCormick*, II, 463.
81 Winder, *The American Reaper*, 82, citing Hutchinson, *Cyrus Hall McCormick*, II, 475 and 607.
82 Hutchinson, *Cyrus Hall McCormick*, II, 709–714.
83 Ibid., 704–705.
84 Winder, *The American Reaper*, 103; Hutchinson, *Cyrus Hall McCormick*, II, 319–324.
85 Winder, *The American Reaper*, 120–121.
86 Hutchinson, *Cyrus Hall McCormick*, 708.
87 Winder, *The American Reaper*, 121.
88 Winder, *The American Reaper*, 125–126.
89 Hutchinson, *Cyrus Hall McCormick*, II, 690.
90 Winder, *The American Reaper*, 88.
91 Ibid., 118.
92 Gordon M. Winder, "Webs of enterprise 1850–1914: Applying a broad definition of FDI," *Annals of the Association of American Geographers* 96(4) (2006): 788–806.
93 Hutchinson, *Cyrus Hall McCormick*, II, 593. See especially chapter V, and pp. 89–92, 148–149,333–334, 452–460, 579–580, 593–595, 714–716.
94 Ronald S. Burt, *Structural Holes: The Social Structure of Competition* (Cambridge, MA: Harvard University Press, 1992); Walter W. Powell and Laurel Smith-Doerr, "Networks and economic life," in Neil J. Smelser and Richard Swedberg (eds.), *The Handbook of Economic Sociology* (Princeton, NJ: Princeton University Press, 1994), 368–402.
95 Hutchinson, *Cyrus Hall McCormick*, II, 101.
96 Ibid., 765–766.
97 Ibid., 734–735.
98 Family correspondence was filled with notes on cats and on horses and riding. Hutchinson, *Cyrus Hall McCormick*, II, 762.

99 See for example, 'McCormick family at Island Lake Camp,' 1888. A McCormick family group photo at Island Lake Camp in Northwestern Wisconsin, owned by Dr. William C. Gray (editor of *The Interior*) and the McCormicks. McCormick—International Harvester Collection, Image ID: 8376, State Historical Society of Wisconsin, Madison, Wisconsin.

100 David F. Noble, *America by Design: Science, Technology and the Rise of Corporate Capitalism* (New York: Knopf, 1977).

6   Valuing Wetlands and Peatlands
Mires in the Natural Resource and Land Use Policies in the Nordic Countries from the Late Eighteenth Century to the Present Day

Esa Ruuskanen

Fennoscandia was and still is one of the most mire-rich regions of the world calculated in relation to the land surface.[1] However, as a consequence of peatland drainages in the eighteenth, nineteenth, and twentieth centuries over 50, circa 30 and circa 25 percent, of the peatlands in natural condition in Finland, Sweden, and Norway respectively were damaged or destroyed.[2] Beginning in the nineteenth century, human-mire relationships were revalued and they continue to be subject to debate, new policies, and changing priorities. The goal of this article is to offer a historical explanation of why different types of peatlands became part of large-scale economic activities in Sweden and Finland[3] since the early eighteenth century. Particularly, this study seeks to disentangle how and on which basis different forms of land use were prioritized, how and why these practices changed, and how sciences and environmental knowledge promoted changes. The main research focus is on the developments in Sweden and Finland, although they are compared in relation to the countries from which they sought models and practices on the reclamation and utilization of bogs and mires.

Little historical research has been done on human relationships with peatlands in Northern Europe. However, this can be regarded as an important research topic as such due to the high proportion of peatlands in the region. Globally, the topic becomes ever more important, because the drainage of peatlands have had implications on climate change, biodiversity loss, and degradation of aquatic ecosystems, among others.[4] Overall, natural scientists have dominated studies of peatlands, specifically botanists, chemists, climate change scientists, ecologists, forestry scientists, geologists, and hydrologists. This paper aims at providing a humanistic approach to this theme, contemplating cultural, political, and societal aspects regarding human interventions in nature.

Theoretically the aforementioned issues are intertwined in academic discussions on 'frontiers,' 'environmental knowledge,' 'commercial knowledge,' and 'environmental learning' in a broad sense.[5] This paper takes part in that debate by asking how peripheral areas, in this case, peatlands, became objects of the ambition to transform them into territories that are seen as being 'made valuable' by the intervention of local people, states, and companies. Moreover, these 'frontiers' can be analyzed in terms of knowledge and technological systems and how they bear upon the altered ecologies of Nordic peatlands in the 'Anthropocene epoch.' In a sense, peatlands epitomize historical 'resource frontiers,' comprising both horizontally extensive 'frontiers,' such as land for agricultural and forestry activities, as well as 'frontiers' that extend vertically downward in terms of resources of extractive activities.

The research is based on the methods of comparative and contextual analysis. The long-term perspective employed in this study makes it possible to cast light on manifold knowledge transfer processes, ways of using and selecting environmental knowledge, and the ways in which values, ideals, and practices change or may even become institutionalized. As sources, white papers and other printed sources are used. Overall, this article does not attempt to be a comprehensive study on the developments of the Swedish and Finnish land use practices of peatlands from the early eighteenth century to the present day. Rather than concentrating on details, I wish to elucidate the general developments in these matters.

The term 'peatland' is quite new and still a matter for discussion and debate among natural scientists worldwide. Besides, in earlier times these areas were termed by different names. When it comes to recent global definitions, Wetlands International defines peatlands as "wetlands with a thick water-logged organic soil layer (peat) made up of dead and decaying plant material. Peatlands include moors, bogs, mires, peat swamp forests and permafrost tundra." International Peat Society, in turn, suggests that "peatlands or mires are wetland ecosystems that are characterized by the accumulation of organic matter." On the whole, it is good to note that various types of peatlands have been identified solely in the boreal and temperate zones. In many respects, these classifications can be seen as agreements and abstractions that may alter.

THE DIVISION BETWEEN VALUABLE AND WORTHLESS NATURE

In his dissertation defended at the Academy of Åbo (*Kungliga Akademien i Åbo*) in 1757, Adolph Backman (1734–1760) and his *praeses* Pehr Kalm (1716–1779) discussed how mires in the eastern part of the Swedish realm could be utilized profitably. By this they meant economic benefits to the realm and prosperity to all royal subjects. Actually, mires in the provinces of the eastern and northern part of Sweden remained still almost completely untapped and epitomized the farthest wilderness of the realm. For Backman and Kalm, that kind of situation represented a pure waste of resources.[6]

Conventionally, Swedish and Finnish peasants, as well as noble landowners, had considered peatlands as almost impossible and at least too laborious to convert into arable land.[7] In addition, peasants usually somewhat feared these rough and watery areas, although they also resourcefully utilized best offerings of surrounding bogs, fens, and mires by, for example, using fen meadows as natural pastures; by taking advantage of bogs and mires as hunting places for bean goose, duck, elk, and grouse; by digging peat by hand for heating and roof material, especially in sparsely wooded areas; by harvesting herbs for medicinal and dyestuff purposes; and by picking cloudberries and cranberries.[8] These attitudes and practices became thoroughly challenged in mid-eighteenth century Scandinavia.

The ideas and visions of Adolph Backman and Pehr Kalm were by no means unique but were rather very current in those days when mercantilist and cameralist perspectives on nature gathered momentum throughout Northern, Central, and East-Central Europe.[9] In many respects, Swedish scholars both emulated and developed originally Dutch, French, or German mire cultivation or peat extraction practices to meet the Nordic conditions. This connotes how fundamentally knowledge transfer networks among participants in the eighteenth century Republic of Letters affected the ways in which various approved reclamation and amelioration examples diffused northward and eastward and in a sense bound quite distant and distinct environments together when it comes to the appraisal of nature. In a similar vein, it was regarded almost as a truism that it was the literati's duty to set and explicate a value for the physical world and, consequently, appraise nature as an object of mobilization resting on human will, needs, and preferences. This way of thinking called forth utilitarian values toward nature, promulgating a way of thinking that nature exists only for the welfare of humankind.[10]

It was between the 1740s and 1780s when scientific debate on the 'hidden potential' of wetlands and peatlands was at its height in Sweden and the Baltic provinces of Russia as well. In Sweden the discussion took place mainly at the then Academies of Uppsala and Åbo, and at the Royal Swedish Academy of Sciences, established in 1739. Major research results were presented in dissertations, popularized farming guides written by the leading scholars in the field in question, and in *Transactions of the Royal Swedish Academy of Science (Kungliga Svenska Vetenskapsakademiens Handlingar)*, a journal that was founded in 1739 by the Academy of Sciences. The principal scientific language in Sweden was Latin in the seventeenth century, whereas the scholars of the 1730s and beyond began to publish their dissertations and scientific journal articles mainly in Swedish. This furthered and enabled the dissemination of knowledge outside the scientific community within the realm.

Overall, the studies on the utilization of pristine peatlands were characterized by strong optimism between the 1740s and 1780s.[11] The aforementioned Adolph Backman and Pehr Kalm even suggested in 1757 that a Dutch-style canal system could be adopted in some parts of Sweden, including windmills and mechanical pumps to promote the water flow, with carp farming in the canals, and the use of peat as a heating fuel.[12] There were also those who were slightly less optimistic about converting all peatlands into arable land, for instance, Vicar Jacob Stenius (1704–1766) from Pielisjärvi parish in the eastern part of the realm, but their notices mostly escaped the majority's attention. Stenius, however, wished that more drainages would come true but only on mires where it was realizable and lucrative.[13]

The Swedish literati's call for large-scale drainages and reclamation of peatlands rested upon interrelated arguments and premises. First, it was thought to be certainly a sensible move to convert 'worthless nature' into 'valuable property.' This would benefit the realm in many ways, not only by increasing the area of arable and pasture land but also by indirectly accelerating population growth and increasing tax revenues.[14] From cameralistic and mercantilistic points of view, population growth was a key factor when a nation armed itself for escalating struggle for natural resources and 'resource frontiers.'

Second, it was believed that the reclamation of peatlands would be both valuable and profitable. Swedish scholars commonly referred to Dutch practices and how they "had raised that country from a marshy area to one of the greatest powers in Europe."[15] Dutch examples, they stated, would also help the realm to save its valuable timber forests from excessive logging for heating, construction, or tar manufacture purposes and from expanding slash-and-burn cultivation, which was found to degrade the soil and damage economically essential spruce forests.[16] Whereas forests, especially those in Ostrobothnia, where tar and pitch burning and shipbuilding thrived due to increasing demand for these products in Western Europe, became framed within the concept of nascent scarcity, bogs and mires in turn were labeled within the concept of undesirable abundance.

That undesirableness mostly arose from two premises. For centuries, bogs and mires had been conceived as unhealthy areas from where many diseases, disease-spreading mosquitoes, and rotten water originate—a notion which sprang from the miasmatic theory.[17] In eighteenth century Sweden, bogs and mires were no longer judged as being the seedbed of all diseases, although their impact on the spread of livestock diseases and spoilage of fresh water resources was still esteemed as considerable. This was thought to hinder animal husbandry and also settlement of the wilderness in both the east and north.[18] Furthermore, peatlands set obstacles to the progress of agriculture in another way too. Eighteenth century literati throughout Western, Central, and Northern Europe generally believed that bogs, fens, and mires, as well as dense forests, caused the cold climates of the region and induced summer frosts. Deducing from these notions, they believed that drainages would lead to warming the climate and dissipation of disastrous frosts during growing seasons. Climate change was desirable and, as leading scholars stated, already observable in France, Germany, and Holland where winters were shorter and more temperate compared to those of the previous century.[19] As it is now known, this was an insupportable conclusion based on the fact that eighteenth century scholars observed weather rather than climate in a modern sense of a long-term statistical definition. However, being convinced of, for example, Comte de Buffon's (1707–1788) climatic theories, Pehr Kalm and Adolph Magnus Foeder (1751–1817) envisioned that "as a consequence of increasing settlement, climate can be converted so that it becomes temperate."[20] Kalm and Esaias Wegelius (1744–1821) in turn judged that "our useless mires are a considerable cause of our short summers and long and cold winters."[21]

Those who envisaged taming pristine peatlands and making them more pleasing for humans naturally needed influential supporters so that their visions would be transferred into practice. Among the most well-known supporters of the reclamation of peatlands were Professor Anders Berch (1711–1774), entrepreneur Carl Fredrik Nordenskiöld (1702–1779), Inspector of Survey Administration Jacob Faggot (1699–1777), Bishop (later Archbishop) Carl Fredrik Mennander (1712–1786), and governor of the Province of Åbo and Björneborg, Christoffer Johan Rappe (1719–1776). Mennader, one of the most optimistic proponents of large-scale drainages, stated that there was almost no bog or mire in Sweden that could not be converted into arable land. Berch, professor of *Oeconomie* at the University of Uppsala and one of the most powerful supporters of cameralistic ideas in Sweden, came to the conclusion that if all the land in Sweden, including wetlands and peatlands, were tapped into the growth of agriculture, the population of the realm would exceed 26 million instead of the then 3 million. In addition, Jacob Faggot and his colleague Ephraim Otto Runeberg (1722–1770) estimated that the only profitable way to increase the amount of arable land in the eastern part of the realm was full-scale drainages of bogs and mires, as well as lake lowering projects.[22] No exact surveys of the land area covered by bogs, fens, and mires were available at that time, but the overall area was estimated to be very large, perhaps even a third of the land mass.[23]

At the regional and local levels, royal bureaucracy and clergy finally introduced the visions describer earlier. Pastors played important roles in knowledge transfer and persuasion because, at the beginning, peasants usually looked askance at these ideas. Pastors had educated themselves at the then academies of Lund, Uppsala, or Åbo and had realigned their thinking with Berch's, Gadd's, Kalm's, and Carl von Linné's (1707–1778) cameralistic and natural theology-influenced visions of taming nature for the benefit of humans.

Despite prevalent optimism for the reclamation of mires and bogs in Sweden among the literati, the results appeared quite modest. Just to name some of the barriers to drainages, most of the peasants were reluctant to enter into the work and the task itself proved to be quite difficult after all. The main reason for the peasants' lack of interest was the concern over financial burden that would fall on them as an obligation to work or to send their tenant farmers or farmhands to work on the projects.[24] In general, drainages should be executed during summer, which was already the busiest working season.

Furthermore, to commit to a drainage project, landowners expected instant benefits, which were practically not possible to obtain for several reasons. First, the drainage of a bog, fen, or mire is a slow and multistep process, and it takes years or even more than a decade before the drainage area is ready for big crops. Second, little was known about which crops were suitable and profitable for cultivation in peat-rich soils, leading to quite frequent failures. Finally, little was known about the real challenges of the drainage of Boreal peatlands. Dutch, English, or French drainage practices did not always suit the Nordic environment.

In the eastern part of the realm, only a few drainage projects, for instance, Lattomeri near the city of Björneborg in Southwestern Finland between the 1760s and 1770s and Röjsjö in the parish of Pernå in Southern Finland in the 1790s, were completed by the turn of the century. The experience and results gained in Lattomeri raised hopes to follow its example in Alajoki, a wide area of open bogs and mires along the River Kyrönjoki in Ostrobothnia in Western Finland. The work, which started in the early 1790s, reflected very well peasants' fluctuating expectations and stances toward the land-use policy planned by the literati and royal bureaucracy. The landowners were at first unwilling to take part in the project, became by and by enthusiastic as a consequence of the news from Lattomeri, and, finally, completely tired of the task as the outcomes were not seen immediately following a few years' hard work. Eventually the result of the artificial drainage was the increase in spring floods in the low-lying fields on the banks of the River Kyrönjoki. The bogs and mires around Alajoki were not converted into arable land until the mid-nineteenth century when the rockiest rapids on the River Kyrönjoki and its tributaries were dredged.[25]

Environmental learning, a multifaceted process that was closely interfaced with the aforementioned extractive and anthropocentric activities, in this case, usually proceeded as learning-from-mistakes and was confronted with existing knowledge that quite often consisted of inaccuracies or even erroneous assumptions as it was later witnessed. Characteristic of that knowledge was its general unawareness of problems human interventions in nature may cause indirectly or afterward. Environmental learning became thus a process characterized by interest in practical details, utilitarian values, and the ambition to develop suitable technologies and engineering to drain the water from marshy areas.

Regardless of setbacks in drainage projects in the late eighteenth century, the ideas of the possibilities to 'refine' peatlands to arable land became gradually more common as a consequence of science-policy interaction. This began to affect the notions as to the economic appraisal of nature. In the case of peatlands, the value was set in the sense that they could be valuable if they only were drained, commercialized, and, hence, bound together with the realm's prosperity. Indirectly, this led to an assumption that wetlands and peatlands in natural condition did not have any value at all. Indeed, it was even economically harmful to follow old practices and judge wetlands, peatlands, or any other untamed and outermost parts of nature as if they were wages of sin.

Particularly, natural history, which in the eighteenth century was a concoction of botanical, mineralogical, and zoological inquiries, as well as *Oeconomie*, an entirely new discipline in the then Swedish universities, participated in this knowledge transfer process in which certain areas were seen as being 'made valuable.' At the same time, more thorough plant species inventories, land surveys in the eastern and northern provinces of the realm, and expeditions to Lapland were completed.[26] Consequently, nature became framed in an ever more far-reaching manner. A clear vision of what was desired and how even the most remote wilderness of the realm could be settled and thus tamed began to diffuse and, step by step, impact on all societal levels.

THE DREAMS BEGIN TO COME TRUE

The visions of large-scale drainage of bogs and mires began to come true after the early nineteenth century. Generally, the same paths were followed both in Sweden and Finland, whose societal development became influenced by substantial population growth and increasing land hunger.[27] Projects that aimed at lake lowering, river dredging, or artificial drainage of wetlands and peatlands gained more attention and, most importantly, were no longer just the elite's visions but also peasants were more vigorously committed to these schemes through new civil organizations.[28] Through these organizations, the knowledge transfer process accelerated. Yet in the early nineteenth century, it was still based mainly on top-down approaches, and bottom-up approaches only became common at the end of the century when several nongovernmental agricultural organizations were established in the Swedish and Finnish countryside.[29]

Consequently, in Sweden 1,482,600 acres (around 600,000 hectares) of peatlands were converted into arable land before 1900. Solely between the 1870s and 1900s 370,659 acres (circa 150,000 hectares) of new fields were cleared as a result of drainage and lake lowering projects.[30] In the mid-nineteenth century, the state began to contribute more strongly to the drainage projects by allocating funds for them, particularly in Scania in Southern Sweden and Södermanland in Central Sweden. Knowledge on peat chemistry, cultivation of peatlands, and suitable crop and root vegetable species accumulated, and new agricultural research institutions were established on the basis of English and German models.[31] Swedish *mosskultur*, a combination of various reclamation and utilization practices, techniques, and visions emerged and began to tighten up existing frames for the economic appraisal of nature. Although Swedish *mosskultur* was, in many ways, an imitation of German *Moorkultur*, particularly in its initial stage, plenty of original and complementary practices and techniques were developed. Swedish *mosskultur* even became emulated in Finland and the Baltic provinces of Russia along with German, Dutch, and English bog, fen, and mire reclamation practices. Common for these practices was their unswerving faith in progress, whether it applied to the economy, science, technology, or even 'civilization' seen from a wider viewpoint.

In Finland, 351,880 and 18,864 acres (circa 142,401 and 7,634 hectares) of mires and marshland, respectively, were converted into agricultural land between 1817 and 1900. Although the amount of arable land increased quite significantly as a result of these projects, qualitatively the outcomes varied widely. The majority of the mire drainages took place between the 1860s and 1890s, whereas most of the marshland drainages were already completed by the mid-nineteenth century. Even if Berch, Gadd, Kalm, von Linné, and other eighteenth century scholars encouraged landowners and the state to initiate drainage projects in Lapland, such work did not materialize in the 1800s. Geographically most of the drainage projects were located in Satakunta in Southwestern Finland and Ostrobothnia in Western Finland, whose role as the breadbaskets of the grand duchy was thus further strengthened.[32] In the 1850s and 1860s, the senate opted to finance a growing number of drainage projects in Karelia and Central and Northern Ostrobothnia. The largest of them was the drainage of Pelso mires (42,007 acres or 17,000 ha), which was carried out not only for agricultural purposes but also for the benefit of forestry.[33]

Especially in the 1860s, as a result of the famines of 1857, 1862, and 1865–1868, drainage projects were executed vigorously in Finland.[34] The outcomes of these state-funded projects were found to be encouraging for both agriculture and forestry.[35] Between the 1870s and 1890s, a decline in the reclamation of bogs and mires occurred due to the senate's changed land-use policy, which canceled state aid and instead introduced low-interest state loans.[36]

Overall, nineteenth century drainage visions intertwined with conventional notions concerning the causes of the cold northern climate, which burdened the peasants with summer frosts and long winters. The elite still tirelessly carried on convincing the peasants of the necessity of the drainage projects as a struggle against frost risks. A poem "Bonden Pavo" (*"Saarijärven Paavo"*), written by the Finnish poet Johan Ludwig Runeberg (1804–1877), whose verses were commonly quoted in Swedish and Finnish elementary school textbooks between the 1850s and 1930s, epitomizes that settler ethos very well. The poem illustrates how Bonden Pavo, when he was afflicted by summer frosts, didn't give up, but dug ditches two times larger than the previous ones, baked *pettu bread* (a surrogate of bread made using the inner layer of pine tree bark), and trusted in the Lord. The poem in a sense reflects the mid-nineteenth century Nordic elite's ideals of good imperial subjects—diligence, modesty, and devotion to God and the Lutheran church.

For its part, that poem also shows how the ideas about 'worthless pristine bogs and mires' and 'valuable tamed and refined bogs and mires' became institutionalized in many ways in the Nordic countries during the nineteenth century. This took place at different arenas, spanning from science, politics, administration, nongovernmental organizations' objectives, and the organization of vocational education to literature and fine arts. Through this institutionalization, the ideas began to be taken as natural and obvious. Framed and labeled as wastelands, bogs and mires had far-reaching effects on political and economic approaches in the late nineteenth century and into the twentieth century.

Moreover, another land use priority, already introduced in Sweden in the eighteenth century, also began to change attitudes toward bogs and mires from the mid-nineteenth century onward. This related to the utilization of peat as a fuel or in animal husbandry as litter. The use of peat as a fuel was already a centuries-old practice and quite commonly in use in England, France, Friesland, and Holland since the seventeenth century, but now its pull grew as a consequence of novel technologies with which peat was extracted and processed mechanically.[37] These innovations made peat products more affordable than those produced by hand and, due to the breakthrough of railways, ever easier to transport. Consequently, first peat fuel and litter peat companies capitalizing on mechanical peat extraction and pressing machines were incorporated in Sweden and Finland, as well as in the Baltic provinces of Russia between the 1870s and 1890s. Initially they employed German machines, but by the end of the century, Swedish machines were already strong competitors to those from Berlin and Hamburg particularly in the Nordic countries and Russia. Peat fuel produced by the companies mentioned earlier was used locally in railway engines, as well as in ironworks and textile factories.[38]

As a matter of fact, a bubble of optimism prevailed at the beginning of the twentieth century among those entrepreneurs who had great faith in the breakthrough of peat as a versatile raw material for almost whatever was invented, starting from litter products for cowsheds and public conveniences, through peat briquettes for heating or even electricity generation, to peat coke for kilns and foundries, lubricants for motors, and so on. Industrialization had finally gathered momentum in the Nordic countries and energy appetite grew significantly, increasingly fed by imported British or German coal. These peat companies, however, didn't succeed in establishing themselves in a larger scale or in challenging the strengthening place of coal in fuel markets.[39] The same happened also in the Baltic provinces of Russia, where especially Baltic Germans tried to push the breakthrough of peat fuel production between the 1880s and 1910s.

Despite noticeable zigzag movements in the peat fuel and litter peat business, the need to mechanically and more scientifically exploit the cheap natural resources from the new 'frontiers' turned out a new page in the history of the utilization of Nordic peatlands. The concept of the 'commodity frontier,' which applies neatly to peatlands, became broadened by a series of new knowledges and technologies that repeatedly pushed the frontier into various layers of strata. Most importantly, making pristine peatlands valuable was no longer only to convert them into arable land: Now extractive activities began to set priorities to land-use policies in certain areas, particularly near the cores of industrial activities in which the demand for affordable fuels rose significantly.

NEW PRIORITIES, CONTRADICTORY AMBITIONS

In late nineteenth century Sweden and Finland, the economic importance of the forest industry increased considerably due to technological innovations related to the timber blank board, pulp and paper production, and growing demand for these products in Central and Western Europe.[40] That resulted in major economic and societal changes in the Nordic countries. The industrialization spurred the transition to a monetary economy in the Swedish and Finnish countryside and also completely changed the peasants' attitudes to the value of forests. Geographically expanding 'commodity frontiers' set new priorities, which reflected local and national urges to prosper, foreign needs to ensure the security of commodity supply, and even British and German geopolitical interests.

Schemes to convert sparsely wooded or bald peatlands into productive forestlands emerged quite simultaneously in both of the countries. This, however, was not an entirely new practice in Europe, for the drainages of mires for forestry were put into practice in Bavaria in the beginning of the nineteenth century and in France and Russia in the mid-nineteenth century.[41] In Scandinavia, the most advanced country in this area was Sweden, where some owners of large forest holdings implemented experimental drainage projects already in the 1830s in order to improve forest growth. In Germany and Sweden as well, the most common difficulties with relation to the silvaculture in former bogs and mires were fairly well known in the late nineteenth century. Nevertheless, having been convinced by optimistic forest scientists, the state in Sweden estimated in the 1880s and 1890s that these projects were in any case worthy of support and initiated drainages on state-owned mires and cofinanced the projects carried out by private forest owners.[42]

Spurred on by concern over further paludification—the natural process of peatland formation—in Boreal conifer forests, Swedish and Finnish forest scientists began to develop scientifically-based techniques to address the problem and worked to convince state bureaucrats of the need to promote and finance drainage and forest ditching projects for the benefit of forestry. The aim was to increase the area of new forest land and to ameliorate the quality of old forest holdings.[43]

The concern about the impending paludification of valuable timber forests can be seen in light of contemporary debates on 'degeneration' in its broad sense. In late nineteenth and early twentieth century contexts, the concern over degeneration appeared in many levels in Europe and North America, especially in the fields of eugenics and social control.[44] Although it was already known at the turn of the century that paludification was a natural process, the downright fear toward the effects of that process was striking. That illustrates how profoundly peatlands had become conceived not only as worthless but also as major barriers to 'progress.' At that time in the Nordic countries, economic progress was believed to rest increasingly on the success of the forest industry. Simultaneously, forest sciences became institutionalized and knowledge on how to improve forest growth on former bogs and mires accumulated. Interventions in nature became ever more scientifically grounded regardless of their goals. This statement holds as true for forestry as for the ways in which 'resource/commodity frontiers' could be utilized more efficiently and profitably compared to the times when knowledge on soil chemistry was on a narrower base.

Drainages for forestry peaked in Sweden first in the beginning of the twentieth century, again between the 1920s and 1930s, and then again between the 1950s and 1980s. Consequently, 3,706,599 acres (around 1.5 million hectares) of former peatlands were converted into forestland since the mid-nineteenth century. It has been estimated that 20 percent of these new forests or 'commodity frontiers' are nowadays classified as 'wasteland' (*impediment*) under the taxation on forests, indicating that in these cases the end in demand was never realized.[45] Moreover, these drainages have been criticized for unbalancing the natural water cycle and producing washout of soil to waterways.[46]

Once again, until the 1960s, these developments were characterized by a general unawareness and sometimes even disregard of problems human interventions in nature may cause afterward or indirectly. Forests as such had been incorporated into debates on human activities that may burden nature and therefore also cause loss of income since the eighteenth century, and from the end of the nineteenth century that debate became influenced by Haeckelian-style reasoning about the economy of nature and the role forests play within it.[47] Pristine peatlands, in turn, were almost completely ruled out of these preecological debates, leading to assumptions that they actually do not have any particular functions in nature's equilibrium. Nor were they valued aesthetically to the same degree as conifer forests, oak groves, ridges, tree-covered hills, or lakes, which became integral parts in framing national landscapes and outlining future national conservation areas in Sweden and Finland in the late nineteenth century.

In early twentieth century Sweden, mire drainages were reasoned to bring a double gain by both mitigating frosts during the growing season and inhibiting the paludification of valuable conifer forests. Convinced by forest scientists and biologists, the state began to allocate funds for that purpose, targeted mostly at the amelioration of forest growth in Norrland in Northern Sweden. While the benefits of the 'frost preventing drainages' became questioned by, for example, geologist Arvid Högbom (1857–1940), key authorities' attitudes altered and eventually the state ceased financing these projects in the 1920s. Forest drainages, however, were still backed up by the state to prevent 'the threat of paludification' and also to tackle the burning mass unemployment question in the early 1930s. Nevertheless, after World War II, drainages were 'rationalized,' by replacing costly manpower—commonly a few dozen men working with hoes and shovels—with more affordable explosives and machines.[48]

In Finland, drainages of bogs and mires for forestry began a bit later than in Sweden. In this case, important milestones were the establishments of the state's forest manager posts in the 1910s and 1920s, a state-backed loan system for the private forest owners in the early 1920s, the enactment of the Forest Improvement Law (*Metsänparannuslaki*) in 1928, and the establishment of the Department of Mire Drainages (*Suonkuivausosasto*) within the Finnish National Board of Forests (*Metsähallitus*) in 1930.[49] As in Sweden, those mires where only stunted trees existed became objects of the ambition to transform these areas into territories seen as being 'made valuable' by the intervention of local people, the state, and forest companies.

As a result of the drainages for forestry, 1,865,600 acres (circa 755,000 hectares) of bogs and mires were converted into forestlands in Finland by the 1950s. A peak in these activities took place in the 1930s when local forest societies began to utilize state loans and commercialize previously untapped 'resource frontiers.' However, this was just the eve of immense forest drainages, which peaked between the 1960s and 1970s when several million hectares of former bogs and mires were drained.[50] Overall, Finland holds the unofficial world record when it comes to peatland drainages for forestry in the postwar era.[51] In the long term, unpleasant indirect effects of these activities on waterways have been much the same as in Sweden.[52]

As peatland drainages for forestry proceeded, older land-use practices were implemented. Peatlands were still converted into arable land, especially in Finland in the 1920s when land reform was finally implemented and again in the late 1940s when over four hundred thousand Karelian evacuees and those who had served in the military during the war were resettled. Consequently, 'resource frontier' still referred to Finland's until then unsettled wilderness. In addition to these human interventions in pristine peatlands, peat fuel production continued, albeit fluctuations marked that business, which was quite reliant on financial and fiscal backing from the state.[53] However, that extractive activity along with litter peat and garden peat production which developed quite in parallel also affected the ways in which new 'commodity frontiers' were mapped and tapped.

The most intense phase of peatland drainages was nearing an end in the early 1970s. Drainages for agriculture ceased in the late 1950s when the viability of smallholdings was challenged. The expansion of the forestry-propelled 'commodity frontier' on peatlands, in turn, ended only at the turn of the 1970s and 1980s and since then the ambition was rather in ditch network maintenance operations. Since the 1970s the most effective interventions in peatlands were fulfilled by extractive activities by companies producing horticultural, litter, milled or sod peat, or corporations starting mining underneath northern bogs and mires.

Interventions in peatlands when agriculture, forestry, or peat extraction and processing were the issue did not yet pose any hard choices to those responsible for decisions about land use policy. All of these projects could coexist without any irreconcilable collisions of interests. Even the need to earmark certain bogs and mires for recreational use between the 1960s and 1990s did not interfere with economic priorities. Completely different situations arose since the late 1960s when conservationism and other ecologically grounded ambitions became an issue. Fitting technologies and the measurable success of drainages were no longer the focal case within 'environmental learning,' which became touched by cumulative 'environmental knowledge' on the unpleasant effects of drainages and the use of peat as a fuel, as well as on the vitalness of bogs and mires as natural and more often endangered habitat as well. It was almost self-evident that difficulties lay ahead in order that rules of the land use of peatlands could be negotiated in entirely mutual understanding between more economy-oriented quarters, often including the key ministries in this matter, and more ecologically oriented quarters, which from the mid-1980s also included newly established environmental ministries in both countries. More often conventional economic ambitions collided with incoming ambitions aiming at confirming the role of aesthetical, ecological, existential, and recreational aspects in current discussions on the future of peatlands. It became more obvious that by following earlier perceptions of 'resources' and 'resource frontiers' it may be complicated to meet the challenges of the twenty-first century. One such challenge is to create new conservation areas and corridors for endangered animal species to help them adapt to global warming and also help humans to prevent still ongoing biodiversity loss.

CONCLUSION

Human interventions in pristine European, as well as Nordic peatlands, have a centuries-old history, but it was only between the eighteenth and twenty-first centuries that these interventions irrevocably altered the specific ecologies of these environments over wide areas. Peatlands have been converted into agricultural land, forestlands, or peat extraction sites, they have been drained to alleviate flood risks, and they have been covered by reservoirs and artificial lakes. Now it is known that these activities not only boosted economic growth as it was aspired but also caused unpleasant indirect effects in the long term, including the loss of carbon sinks and biodiversity and of important recreational areas for communities as well, increased flood and wildfire risks and the washout of soil to waterways. These interventions in nature have multifaceted cultural, historical, and spatial roots and they, in a sense, reflect quite common ambitions to tame and refine nature in the 'Anthropocene epoch.'

In the eighteenth century Nordic scientific and political climate, human-mire relationships were completely revalued by literati in a manner which emphasized the inadequateness of conventional notions and urged the promotion of projects that would transform peatlands into territories that are seen as being 'made valuable.' Pristine peatlands as such were labeled as 'worthless' and even 'harmful' but, importantly, these areas could be 'valuable' when being drained, converted into 'valuable property,' and thus tamed. Besides, as eighteenth century literati generally accepted, converting damp and mosquito-infested bogs, fens, and mires into arable land or peat extraction sites would result in both regional warming and dissipation of many livestock diseases. Conceiving mires as one of the ultimate causes of cold and damp in the northern climate, as well as of frosts during the growing season became important rhetoric in efforts to tempt disinclined and hesitant peasants to involve themselves in the plans of literati. Although plans became reality very slowly in the late nineteenth century, visions to encroach on new horizontally extensive 'frontiers' were, however, gradually implanted into the minds of ever more royal subjects. Basically, priests and newly established weeklies disseminated knowledge.

The earlier mentioned visions began to be partly realized in the nineteenth century when they became backed up by the government and newly established agricultural civic organizations. The priority of drainages in the Nordic countries was for agriculture in the nineteenth century, but new goals emerged. The more society grew reliant on coal and the more coal prices fluctuated, the more ambitions to produce peat fuel by new mechanical technologies gained attention. That business, however, was marked by great supply and demand swings, as well as by its dependency on state backing from the outset. Between the 1860s and 1930s, new technologies and accumulating knowledge on peatland geology and chemistry generated colorful ideas to utilize these 'frontiers' that extended vertically downward and gave rise to firms producing litter peat, peat briquettes, peat coke, or peat lubricants. Litter peat and, since the 1950s, the horticultural peat business proved to be rather lucrative in the long term, whereas oil and coal products put peat coke and peat lubricants completely in the shade apart from wartimes when fuel imports were ceased.

As Sweden and Finland began the twentieth century, the focus of peatland drainages turned and from then on mostly propelled by the calls of thriving and increasingly influential forestry. In addition to the demands of that prospering industry, drainages were given a reason for being de rigueur for curtailing the dreaded expansion of paludification and thus the degeneration of 'commodity frontiers-to-be.' That trend thoroughly altered the ecologies of untapped peatlands over a remarkably wide area, particularly between the 1920s and 1930s and the 1950s and 1970s, even though the first peatland forest ditchings had already been made in the mid-nineteenth century. As much as several million hectares of former bogs and mires became converted into conifer forests solely between the 1950s and 1980s, which in many cases measured up to the expectations of land owners, firms, and the states but quite often also misfired in the long term and caused undesired indirect effects by, for instance, speeding up the washout of soil to waterways.

As a result of peatland drainages for both agriculture and forestry, peatland ecologies began to tilt toward monoculture. Natural and rarely diverse peatland flora, including numerous mosses, vascular plants, *Ericaceae* and *Cyperaceae*, as well as dwarf birch, were replaced by plant species humans valued most both economically and often also aesthetically. In turn, bogs and mires as such were hardly ever conceived as aesthetically valuable and inspirational in the ways that conifer forests and pastoral landscapes were in nineteenth and early twentieth century cultural contexts. Quite to the contrary, they were regarded as forbidding and disturbing places. Farmers tried to win their new fields blooming with rye, wheat, barley, potato or timothy grass. Owners of steam sawmills and pulp and paper mills hungrily acquired the conifers tried out on former marshy wilderness by private forest owners, forest companies, and the state. Consequently, many bird and insect species became endangered due to the fragmentation and even complete destruction of their natural habitat. That endangeredness was not observed until the 1960s. In step with that trend toward 'monoculturization' and the establishment of 'conifer plantations,' drainages contributed to the expansion of 'resource and commodity frontiers' in northward and northeasterly directions. Especially in nineteenth century Sweden and Finland, 'mire clearances' announced the then current settler ethos bolstered by elites, priests, and 'enlightened' landowners. Although forestry and extractive activities took the place of agriculture as the engines of that expansion of 'commodity frontier' since the 1920s and 1930s, the ethos remained quite the same until the end of the twentieth century. Despite ecological calls to see alternative possibilities for and appraisal of peatlands, their value was mainly weighed on the strength of their potential for economic exploitation. Nevertheless, that convention has been challenged since the 1970s and, importantly, in some cases, and particularly in the long term, it may prove to be even more lucrative to leave pristine peatlands untapped so that they can provide vital services to society.

NOTES

1 See, e.g., http://www.peatsociety.org/peatlands-and-peat/global-peat-resources-country (last accessed August 15, 2014) and http://www.wetlands.org/Desktop Modules/QuickImageRepository/image.ashx?forceDownload=0&fileId= 5987 (last August 15, 2014).
2 Kaisu Aapala, Tapio Lindholm, and Raimo Heikkilä, "Protected mires in Finland," in Asbjørn Moen and Richard Binns (eds.), *Regional Variation and*

Conservation of Mire Ecosystems (Trondheim: Universitetet i Trondheim and Vitenskaapsmuseet, 1994), 205–221; Ingerid Angell-Petersen, "Conservation and management of mires in Norway," in Asbjørn Moen and Richard Binns (eds.), Regional Variation and Conservation of Mire Ecosystems (Trondheim: Universitetet i Trondheim and Vitenskaapsmuseet, 1994): 389–404.

3 In the eighteenth century, the eastern part of Sweden, today known as Finland, consisted of a number of provinces that had belonged to the Swedish realm since the medieval times. In 1809, as a consequence of the Napoleonic Wars, the provinces were formed into an autonomous grand duchy within the Russian Empire. Finland gained its independence from Russia in 1917.

4 On this issue, see, e.g., http://www.ipcc.ch/ipccreports/tar/wg2/index.php?idp=274 (last accessed June 15, 2014) and http://www.worldwildlife.org/climate/WWF Binaryitem11334.pdf (last accessed June 15, 2014).

5 On these theoretical aspects, see, e.g., Michael R. Redclift, *Frontier: Histories of Civil Society and Nature* (Cambridge, MA: MIT Press, 2006); John F. Richards, *The Unending Frontier: Environmental Histories of the Early Modern World.* (Berkeley: University of California Press, 2006); John R. McNeill and Verena Winiwarter, "Soils, soil knowledge and environmental history," in John R. McNeill and Verena Winiwarter (eds.), *Soils and Societies: Perspectives from Environmental History* (Isle of Harris: White Horse Press, 2006), 1–6; Jürgen Osterhammel, *Die Verwandlung der Welt. Eine Geschichte des 19. Jahrhuderts* (Munich: C.H. Beck, 2009); and Edward B. Barbier, *Scarcity and Frontiers: How Economies Have Developed Through Natural Resource Exploitation* (Cambridge: Cambridge University Press, 2011).

6 Pehr Kalm (præses) and Adolph Backman (respondent), *Huru sådana kjärr kunna gjöras nyttiga, hvarifrån vatnet ej kan ledas med diken* (Åbo: Frenckell, 1757). [in Swedish].

7 It can be argued that the broad lines of the state's politics in Sweden from the beginning of the 1600s to the 1710s were defined by expansionism, including the conquest of fertile lands of the Baltic region, Scania, and Pomerania. When the visions of the Northern superpower foundered as a result of the losses of the Swedish army personally led by King Karl XII in the beginning of the eighteenth century, the elite had to rediscover the resources of the remaining areas.

8 On the values and notions regarding mires and bogs in Scandinavia in the early modern period, see, e.g., Brauner 1755; Anders Berch (præses) and Carl Fjellström (respondent), *Tankar om upodlings möjlighet i Lappmarkerna* (Stockholm: Salvius, 1760) [in Swedish]; Fischerström 1761; and Gösta H. Sjöberg, "Våtmarkerna i människans tjänst," in Rune Engström, Sigfried Leander and Birgitta von Malmborg (eds.), *Myrmarker: En bok om bruket av våtmarkerna förr och nu* (Stockholm: Riksförbundet för hembygdsvård, 1976).

9 See, e.g., Clarence J. Glacken, *Traces on the Rhodian Shore: Nature and Culture in Western Thought from Ancient Times to the End of the Eighteenth Century* (Berkeley: University of California Press, 1967), 655–705 and Lisbet Koerner, *Linnaeus: Nature and Nation* (Cambridge, MA: Harvard University Press, 1999), 95–139.

10 Pietarinen, "The principal attitudes of humanity towards nature," in H. Odera Oruka (ed.), *Philosophy, Humanity, and Ecology: Philosophy of Nature and Environmental Ethics* (Nairobi: Proceedings of the World Conference of Philosophy, 1992), 290.

11 Kalm and Backman, *Huru sådana kjärr kunna gjöras nyttiga*; Carl Fredrik Nordenskiöld, *Tal on nyttan af ofverflödig: vattens uttappande utur insjöar, kärr och måssar i Finland*; hållit för Kungl. Vetenskaps Academien, vid praesidii nedläggande den 20 augusti, år 1758 (Stockholm: Salvius, 1758); Pehr

Adrian Gadd (præses) and Jacob Foenander (respondent), *Chemisk och Oeconomisk Uthandling om Bränne-Torf* (Åbo: Frenckell, 1759); *Svar på frågan om bästa sättet: at upodla mosslupna ängar*; hvilken fråga, af Kongl. Vetenskaps Academien blef upgifven (Stockholm: Salvius, 1761); Pehr Kalm (præses) and Esaias Wegelius (respondent), *Tankar om Nödvändigheten at Utdika och Upodla Kärr och Mossar i Finland* (Åbo: Frenckell, 1763).

12 Kalm and Backman, *Huru sådana kjärr kunna gjöras nyttiga.*

13 Jacob Stenius, *Kort underrättelse om kiärr och mossar samt deras nyttiande, efter flere åhrs giorde försök* (Stockholm: Merckell, 1749).

14 Jacob Faggot, "Tankar om Fäderneslandets Känning oh Beskrifwande" *Kungliga Svenska Vetenskapsakademiens Handlingar* (1741): 6–29; Jacob Faggot, "Afhandling om svedjande samt utväg til Hushållning med Skogar," *Kungliga Svenska Vetenskapsakademiens Handlingar* (1750): 138–150; Henrik Hassel (præses) and Johan Welin (respondent), *Velmente Tankar om landthushållningens Förbättrande i Finland* (Åbo: Frenckell, 1751); Pehr Adrian Gadd, (præses) and Johan Heinrich Hallenberg (respondent), *Finska Ängskötselens Hinder och Hjelp* (Åbo: Jacob Merckell, 1757); Pehr Kalm (præses) and Esaias Wegelius (respondent), *Tankar om Nödvändigheten at Utdika och Upodla Kärr och Mossar i Finland* (Åbo: Frenckell, 1763); Pehr Kalm (præses) and Salomon Kreander (respondent), *Om Möjeligheten, Sättet och Nyttan at Utan Ängar Sköta Landbruket* (Åbo: Frenckell, 1775).

15 Kalm and Kreander, *Om Möjeligheten, Sättet och Nyttan at Utan Ängar Sköta Landbruket.*—Original Swedish text, translated by Esa Ruuskanen: "Har icke Holland ifrån et sumpigt trask höjt sig en af de största magter i Europa?"

16 Hassel and Welin, *Velmente Tankar om landthushållningens Förbättrande i Finland*; Pehr Adrian Gadd (præses) and Anders Agricola (respondent), *Ovälduge Tankar om Jordens Svedande och Kyttande i Finland* (Åbo: Jacob Merckell, 1753); Pehr Adrian Gadd (præses) and Fredrik Sjöstedt (respondent), *Academisk Afhandling om Medel at Underhålla och öka Skogväxten i Finland.* (Åbo: Frenckellska Boktryckeriet, 1792).

17 Frank Egerton, *Roots of Ecology: Antiquity to Haeckel* (Berkeley: University of California Press, 2012), 2 and 11; Paul Reiter, "From Shakespeare to Defoe: Malaria in England in the Little Ice Age," *Emerging Infectious Diseases* 6(1) (2000): 1–11.

18 Pehr Adrian Gadd, "Om ursprunget, beskaffenheten och nyttan af kärr, mossar och moras i Sverige," *Kungliga Svenska Vetenskapsakademiens Handlingar* (1776): 97–115; Johan Haartman (præses) and Johan Christian Florin (respondent), *Om Skärgårds Febren Omkring Åbo* (Åbo: Frenckell, 1781).

19 Glacken, *Traces on the Rhodian Shore*, 658–679.

20 Pehr Kalm (præses) and Adolph Magnus Foeder (respondent), *Tanckar om den Wärkan Som Et Lands Upodling har på des Climat* (Åbo: Frenckell, 1778).

21 Pehr Kalm (præses) and Esaias Wegelius (respondent), *Tankar om Nödvändigheten at Utdika och Upodla Kärr och Mossar i Finland* (Åbo: Frenckell, 1763).

22 Jacob Faggot, "Beskrifning öfver Pernå Socken i Nyland" *Kungliga Svenska Vetenskapsakademiens Handlingar* (1754): 182–188; Ilmari L. Palmén, "Suonkuivaustyöt Suomessa XIX vuosisadalla: Historiallinen tutkimus," in *Suomen Suonviljelysyhdistyksen vuosikirja 1903* (Helsinki: Suomen Suonviljelysyhdistys, 1903), 191–194; Leif Runefelt, "Svensk mosskultur som överhetsprojekt före 1886," in Leif Runefelt (ed.), *Svensk mosskultur: odling, torvanvändning och landskapets förändring 1750–2000* (Stockholm: Kungliga Skogs- och lantbruksakademien, 2008), 28–30.

23 Pehr Adrian Gadd, "Om ursprunget, beskaffenheten och nyttan af kärr, mossar och moras i Sverige," *Kungliga Svenska Vetenskapsakademiens Handlingar* (1776): 97–115.
24 Palmén, "Suonkuivaustyöt Suomessa XIX vuosisadalla: Historiallinen tutkimus," 192–195 and 207–212; Runefelt, "Svensk mosskultur som överhetsprojekt före 1886," 43–46.
25 Palmén, "Suonkuivaustyöt Suomessa XIX vuosisadalla: Historiallinen tutkimus," 192–194.
26 The most well-known Swedish scientist in this area was Professor Carl von Linné (1707–1778), the father of modern botanical nomenclature. In his expeditions to Lapland, he was convinced that even the most remote north could be tamed and converted into arable land.
27 Finland's population tripled and Sweden's population doubled in the nineteenth century.
28 In Sweden in the first half of the nineteenth century, the major civil organizations that were focusing on the agricultural development schemes were the Royal Swedish Patriotic Society (*Kungliga Patriotiska Sällskapet*, Est. 1772) and the Swedish Rural Economy and Agricultural Societies (*Hushållningssällskapet*, established in the beginning of the nineteenth century) and its local branches. An influential scientific community in this area was formed within the Royal Swedish Academy of Agriculture and Forestry (*Kungliga Skogs- och Landbruksakademien*, Est. 1811). The Finnish counterpart of the Swedish Rural Economy and Agricultural Societies was the Finnish Rural Economy and Agricultural Societies (*Suomen Talousseura*, Est. 1797).
29 The most well-known of these were local level agricultural societies and agricultural cooperatives. Olof Brandesten, *Lantbrukarnas organisationer: Agrart och kooperativt 1830–1930*. Skogs- och lantbrukshistoriska meddelanden nr 35. Eskilstuna (2005); Markku Kuisma, et al., *Kansan talous: Pellervo ja yhteisen yrittämisen idea 1899–1999* (Helsinki: Pellervo-seura, 1999); Veikko Anttila, *Järvenlaskuyhtiöt Suomessa: kansatieteellinen tutkimus* mit Deutsches Referat (Helsinki: Suomen Muinaismuistoyhdistys, 1967).
30 Leif Runefelt, "Svenska Mosskulturföreningen 1886–1939," in Leif Runefelt (ed.), *Svensk mosskultur: odling, torvanvändning och landskapets förändring 1750–2000* (Stockholm: Kungliga Skogs- och lantbruksakademien, 2008), 87.
31 Hugo Osvald, *Myrar och myrodling* (Uppsala: Landbrukshögskolan, 1937), 233–264; Runefelt, "Svensk mosskultur som överhetsprojekt före 1886," 39–43.
32 In the end of the nineteenth century, the peasants of these areas shifted from cereal growing to dairy farming, leading to increasing imports of grain from Russia. Dairy farming offered more prosperity for the peasants, but at the same time the grand duchy's security of food supply was weakened, which finally resulted in a broad social inequality during the First World War when the earlier mentioned imports were hamstrung by the wartime chaos.
33 Palmén, "Suonkuivaustyöt Suomessa XIX vuosisadalla: Historiallinen tutkimus," 197–205 and 240–254.
34 Around 8 percent of the population died in Finland during the great famine of 1865–1868.
35 O.J. Lukkala, *Nälkävuosien suonkuivausten tuloksia* (Helsinki: Metsätieteellinen tutkimuslaitos, 1937).
36 Palmén, "Suonkuivaustyöt Suomessa XIX vuosisadalla: Historiallinen tutkimus," 245–246.
37 K.H. Göttlich, K-H. Richard, H. Kuntze, R. Eggelsmann, J. Günther, D., Eichelsdörfer and G. Briemle, "Mire utilisation," in A.L. Heathwaite and K.H.

136   Esa Ruuskanen

Göttlich (eds.), *Mires: Process, Exploitation and Conservation* (Chichester: Wiley, 1993), 325–329 and 375–377; M.A.W. Gerding, *Vier eeuwen turfwinning: De verveningen in Groningen, Friesland, Drenthe en Overijssel tussen 1550 en 1950* (Wageningen: Landbouwuniversiteit Wageningen, 1995).

38 Runefelt, "Svenska Mosskulturföreningen 1886–1939," 70–72; Esa Ruuskanen, *Suosta voimaa ja lämpöä: Turve Suomen energiapolitiikassa 1940–2010* [Power and Heat from Peat: Peat in Finnish Energy Policy] with English summaries (Jyväskylä: WS Bookwell Oy, 2010).

39 Leif Runefelt, "Torvbubblan 1900–1925," in Leif Runefelt (ed.), *Svensk mosskultur: odling, torvanvändning och landskapets förändring 1750–2000* (Stockholm: Kungliga Skogs- och lantbruksakademien, 2008), 329–352; Ruuskanen, *Suosta voimaa ja lämpöä*, 34–35.

40 Susanna Fellman, "Growth and investment: Finnish capitalism, 1850s–2005," in Susanna Fellman, Martin Jes Iversen, Hans Sjögren and Lars Thue (eds.), *Creating Nordic Capitalism: The Business History of a Competitive Periphery* (Basingstoke: Palgrave Macmillan, 2008), 142–153; Hans Sjögren, "Welfare capitalism: The Swedish economy, 1850–2005," in Susanna Fellman, Martin Jes Iversen, Hans Sjögren and Lars Thue (eds.), *Creating Nordic Capitalism: The Business History of a Competitive Periphery* (Basingstoke: Palgrave Macmillan, 2008), 24–39.

41 Wilhelm Graf zu Leiningen, *Die Waldvegetation praealpiner bayerischen Moore, inbesondere der südlichen Chiemseemoore* (München: 1907), 64–66; Antti Tanttu, *Tutkimuksia ojitettujen soiden metsittymisestä* (Helsinki: Suomen Keisarillisen Aleksanterin Yliopisto, 1915), 1 and 12.

42 Tanttu, *Tutkimuksia ojitettujen soiden metsittymisestä*, 12–15.

43 Tanttu, *Tutkimuksia ojitettujen soiden metsittymisestä*, 1–16; Lauri Ilvessalo, "Ehdotus Suomen metsätieteellisen tutkimustoiminnan kehittämiseksi" with English summary, *Silva Fennica* 7(1927): 1–18, 2–6; O.O.J. Tirkkonen, "Suomen metsäojitus 1900-luvun alkupuoliskolla," with English summary, *Silva Fennica* (1952): 7–12; Per Eliasson, "Skogsdikning och skogsväxt under 1900-talet," in Leif Runefelt (ed.), *Svensk mosskultur: odling, torvanvändning och landskapets förändring 1750–2000* (Stockholm: Kungliga Skogs- och lantbruksakademien, 2008), 185–188.

44 Wendy Kline, *Building a Better Race: Gender, Sexuality, and Eugenics from the Turn of the Century to the Baby Boom* (Berkeley: University of California Press, 2005), 8–16.

45 Björn Hånell, "Effektiv skogsskötsel på torvmarker," in M. Strömgren (ed.), *Växthuseffekt och skogsproduktion: hur ska vi hantera våra dikade skogsmarker* (SLU, Rapporter i skogsekologi och skoglig marklära 90, 2006).

46 Emelie Gunnarsson, *Diken i skogsmark. Bedömning av produktionsnyttan i ett avrinningsområde i Västergötland* (Världsnaturfonden WWF, 2009), 21–22; Michael Löfroth, *Våtmarkerna och deras betydelse*, Rapport 3824 (Solna: Naturvårdsverket, 1991).

47 Jacob Faggot, "Afhandling om svedjande samt utväg til Hushållning med Skogar" *Kungliga Svenska Vetenskapsakademiens Handlingar* (1750): 138–150; Kalm and Wegelius, *Tankar om Nödvändigheten at Utdika och Upodla Kärr och Mossar i Finland*; P.W. Hannikainen, *Wähäsen Metsistä* (Helsinki: Kansanvalistuseura, 1888); A.G. Blomqvist, "Skoghushållningens nationalekonomi och synpunkter i forstpolitii" (Helsingfors: G.W. Edlunds Förlag: 1893).

48 Eliasson, "Skogsdikning och skogsväxt under 1900-talet," 182–190.

49 *Komiteanmietintö 1900:5*. Komitealta, joka asetettu antamaan lausuntoa niistä periaatteista, joihin valtion metsätalouden tulisi perustua (Helsinki:

1900); Lauri Ilvessalo, "Ehdotus Suomen metsätieteellisen tutkimustoiminnan kehittämiseksi" with English summary, *Silva Fennica* 7(1927): 4–6; Lukkala, *Nälkävuosien suonkuivausten tuloksia*, 4–12; Suonkuivausmetsänhoitajien vuosikertomukset 1915–1930, Hcb: 1–2, KA [The National Archives of Finland]; O.O.J. Tirkkonen, "Suomen metsäojitus 1900-luvun alkupuoliskolla," 18–36.

50 Metsätilastolliset vuosikirjat 1955–2005 (Statistical Yearbook of Forestry).
51 See, http://agl.cc.jyu.fi/visu/index.php?id=546 (Last accessed November 19, 2014).
52 Marketta Ahtiainen and Pertti Huttunen, "Long-term effects of forestry management on water quality and loading in brooks," *Boreal Environment Research* 4 (1999): 101–114.
53 Ronnie Liljegren, "Pluddetorv, tramptorv och maskintorv: Om torvtäkt och torvanvändning I Sverige 1800–1950," in Leif Runefelt (ed.), *Svensk mosskultur: odling, torvanvändning och landskapets förändring 1750–2000* (Stockholm: Kungliga Skogs- och lantbruksakademien, 2008), 313–324; Ruuskanen, *Suosta voimaa ja lämpöä*, 111–115.

7   Lands for Settlement, Forests, and Scenic Reserves
Nature and Value in New Zealand, 1890s to 1920s

Michael Roche

INTRODUCTION: CONSIDERING 'TRADING ENVIRONMENTS'

New Zealand disproportionately captured the attention of US environmental historian Alfred Crosby in his book *Ecological Imperialism*.[1] He was not the first nor is he likely the last to see the country as an isolated island group of recent settlement that provides a fascinating case study of environmental transformation. This chapter in part continues this intervention though, in this instance, it is an insider viewpoint that is presented. Intersecting the theme of recent European settlement in New Zealand with the intellectual space opened up by the term 'trading environments,' conjures up at least three distinct and rich conceptual possibilities for the latter, concerned with 'translation,' 'transformation,' and 'enterprise,' which are elaborated on next. Thereafter these three separate but related imaginaries of 'trading environments' are explored in more detail through New Zealand examples but also by recourse to a discussion about 'improvement,' which was a powerful force in Western colonial settlement narratives. Albeit at somewhat different scales, these imaginaries consider, first, the rapid nineteenth century transformation of largely forested New Zealand into a farm landscape oriented, from the 1890s, toward supplying the British market with a limited range of meat and dairy produce; second, the simultaneous moves to reassess the land in terms of 'natural value' by protecting some limited areas for scenic purposes; and lastly, the relentless expansion of the settlement frontier that eventually produced regional episodes of land deterioration and disrupted the dominant settler discourse of progress and improvement. Collectively these three vignettes reveal how 'trading environments' offers a means of readdressing older debates about the course of rural land use in New Zealand, as well as posing new questions about how to understand key moments in the course of its European settlement and its aftermath in the late nineteenth and early twentieth centuries.

Trading Environments as Translation

For New Zealand, which was incorporated into the British Empire in 1840 and when by 1858 the settler population had just overtaken the Maori population at over 58,000 apiece, 'trading environments' can be applied to the overseas expansion and relocation of a largely British population during the nineteenth century to create a settler colony where the early expectation was that it would become self-governing, albeit as part of the Empire. For the advocates of 'systematic colonization' in the 1840s and 1850s, New Zealand was to become a transplanted but more socially mobile vertical slice of a vanishing English rural society. For later settlers in the 1890s, they were building a better 'South Britain.' This point can be pushed a little further, however, in that, being a temperate southern hemisphere archipelago, New Zealand had a milder version of British weather and climate, although there were many overblown claims about the salubrity of local conditions and a need for new environmental learning.[2] It was comparatively easy to envisage the replication of familiar British agricultural systems in a new and distant land. The execution of these desires was not, however, achieved without all manner of environmental impacts, intended and unintended, as Ken Cumberland, a British geographer and one of the first university appointments in the discipline, noted in 1941, three years after his arrival.

> What in Europe took twenty centuries, and in North America four, has been accomplished in New Zealand within a single century—in little more than one full lifetime. Although extensive and achieved with remarkable speed, this accomplishment can scarcely be regarded as permanent. Destruction of natural vegetation, animal life, and soil properties has been widespread, and nature's revenge is already in evidence-and at an ever accelerating rate. The decimation of the natural vegetation has been the most obvious manifestation of this 'victory over environment.' The ousting of the indigenous plant cover and the partial establishment of an exotic (mainly European) vegetation in its place is at one and the same time the essential theme of the history of New Zealand and the foundation of the regional differentiation of its area.[3]

The particularly noteworthy dimensions of this translation were its scale and speed: much of this environmental change taking place as late as the 1890s to 1910s. As Eric Pawson has observed, Cumberland's first sentence has been often quoted but the second that "the accomplishment can scarcely be regarded as permanent" is typically overlooked, although it was prescient and is returned to later in the chapter.[4] Trading environments as 'translation' is also shorthand for establishing a new settlement frontier. A significant dimension of trading environments as 'translation' was actually the degree of 'mistranslation' based on false or misleading information and colonial boosterism.[5] Indeed, trading environments as 'translation' intersects in a causal manner with aspects of Beattie's identification of environmental anxiety in colonial New Zealand.[6] A further layer of 'mistranslation' was produced by acclimatization of a wide range of species for hunting and fishing, many of which, such as rabbits, later caused considerable damage to colonial pastoral farming endeavors.[7]

Trading Environments as Transformation

The attempt to introduce British farming systems in New Zealand leads on readily to "trading environments as transformation" as a subset of processes encapsulated by Crosby's 'ecological imperialism,' while acknowledging caveats and modifiers to his ideas in the New Zealand setting.[8] "Trading environments as transformation" further unfolds in three ways. First, in a predominantly forested environment, British settlers after 1840, rather unlike earlier sojourning sealers, whalers, or flax and spar gatherers, endeavored to recreate the mixed faming landscapes of their homeland. These efforts were exemplified by the activities of the New Zealand Company and its derivatives, which were inspired by E.G. Wakefield's theories of systematic colonization, particularly the idea of the 'sufficient price' of land. Wakefield sought to avoid the free land grants and dissipation of capital and population of the North American and Australian colonies by keeping land prices high and settlement contained. Another important feature in a 'trading environments' context is that the New Zealand Company envisioned the reproduction of a British mixed-farming landscape but paid little attention to an export economy and in so far as this was considered, wheat was the favored commodity. This was not unrealistic given the distances involved, in excess of 18,000 km and around 100 days by sailing ship from New Zealand to Great Britain, along with the problems of transporting agricultural produce across the equator, wheat was one of the few commodities that was sufficiently durable enough not to spoil on the voyage. Nevertheless, wheat production proved marginal or unworkable in many, especially North Island, districts.

Second, British farming models did not translate in their entirety, in some cases because they did not need to in more temperate conditions where year around stocking was possible; in other instances, it was because local plants could be exploited for grazing and also introduced species that were more familiar from the settlers' home environments. Almost simultaneously, however, other possibilities were recognized. In the adjacent Australian colonies, a form of extensive pastoralism had developed based on Merino sheep producing wool for export. Some Australian graziers, prompted by droughts, moved to occupy the tussock grasslands particularly of the South Island in the 1850s and to develop a distinctive form of large-scale sheep farming for wool based on extensive leasehold property rights under environmental conditions that were much less harsh than in Australia. To complicate this picture, elements of British upland sheep rearing and Scottish shepherding traditions were also introduced, and this is an area of some historiographical revisionism at present, particularly regarding the 'burning off' of the indigenous tussock grasslands.[9] Pastoralism did, however, actually add sizable quantities of wool to the small list of exports otherwise still dominated by timber and other produce of a 'quarry economy era.'[10]

Third, the major transformation of the forest lands of the North Island waited until the 1890s and came about as a consequence of the interplay of political, economic, and technological interventions. The economic context was one in which industrializing Britain had been dependent on meat imports since the 1870s. Experiments in the South Island with canning sheep meat for export proved uneconomic, but by the 1880s, refrigeration equipment that was reliable enough for the seaborne journey had been developed and gave New Zealand farmers access to the British market. Land monopoly was a legacy of extensive pastoralism, and, in 1890, 422 landowners (or less than 1 percent) still controlled eight million acres [3.2 million ha] or 64 percent of freehold land in the colony.[11] The Liberal government elected in 1890 marked the end of faction politics and the beginnings of a modern party system. Its support base rested on town workers and rural laborers and would-be farmers. This situation eventually gave rise to political reform whereby in the early 1890s the Liberals' compulsorily acquired and subdivided some large freehold estates and repurchased others voluntarily for subdivision as part of a policy of closer land settlement. As well as orchestrating the breakup of some of the great estates in the South Island, in the North Island, and this is less appreciated, they purchased large amounts of Maori land for closer land settlement.[12] Having saved the Bank of New Zealand from bankruptcy in 1891, through it the government acquired a large number of some very large North Island properties mortgaged to the bank; these were also sold as part of the closer land settlement program.[13] Temperate conditions, particularly a reliable rainfall of 600 to 1600 mm, across much of the country meant that grass grew well over a long growing season and this was ultimately to lie at the heart of New Zealand farmers' capacity to efficiently convert it to meat, butter, and cheese and thence still profitably ship produce halfway around the world. These connections were not necessarily made smoothly or without difficulty, there were boom-bust cycles involving immigration, overseas borrowing, infrastructure development, and collapse before more enduring and economically viable linkages were forged around meat and dairy produce in the 1890s. Closer land settlement meant the clearance of the forest of the North Island hill country, much of it recent purchases of Maori land. By 1900, the forest area of the country had been reduced to about 25 percent, down from 53 percent in 1840 and much of it was felled from the 1890s. These pioneer farmers who eventually developed mixed sheep and beef farms had their viability undergirded by refrigeration, which provided access to the British market. Significant export dairy industries emerged in the North Island's Taranaki and Waikato regions at this same time. The population of New Zealand itself did not exceed one million until 1910 and so was a weak engine for domestic economic growth. Instead, agricultural exports, principally to the UK market, were the mainspring of national economic development.

Trading Environments as Enterprise

Within the two previous sorts of 'trading environments,' resided a third type, termed here 'trading environments as enterprise.' This third type signals that the translation and transformation outlined earlier took place within a market-based economy, albeit one where the settler state actively intervened through regulation, especially from the 1890s, for instance, through use of the Babcock test for butter fat in the dairy industry, as a player in the economy via the State Insurance Company, and by acting as banker under the Advances for Settlers Act. A distinction can be made between the large-scale, estate-based farming of the 1850s to 1880s exporting wool and later briefly wheat and the small farms of the 1890s onward reliant on meat (and wool) and or butter/cheese. The agricultural history of the South Island especially of the large pastoral estates and their survival in the High Country, have been comparatively well studied as have some of the large land holdings and their subdivision in the North Island.[14] Rather than rehearse these narratives, this chapter takes up the challenge implicit in Cumberland's comment about 'victory over environment' and concentrates instead on some of the legacies of closer land settlement in the hill country of the North Island with respect to small farmers. The North Island hill country was also in many respects the final expansive pulse of the settlement frontier, which arguably extended well beyond World War II into the 1960s when a further round of intensification was made possible through subsidies and aerial top dressing.[15] I remain uneasy about 'enterprise' as a label, not only because 'enterprise' ought not to be equated with success but also because it does not quite fully capture the entirety of this third type of 'trading environment.' Trading environments as enterprise also helpfully overlaps substantially with the notion of 'commercial knowledge' as a subcategory of second nature (See Winder and Dix this volume).

New Zealand's emergence as one of Britain's imperial farms was cemented in place by the use of refrigeration technology. A set of commodity chains emerged with a distinct geography. For frozen meat, the chains emanated from Argentina, Australia, and New Zealand and terminated in the United Kingdom with New Zealand farm producers tending to specialize in lamb and Argentina in beef. The dairy commodity chain from New Zealand was similarly concentrated on the United Kingdom. Into the 1890s, large-scale South Island estate production of lamb exports were significant, but moving into the twentieth century, production from the smaller farms from both main islands began to dominate production. From their inception, the meat and dairy commodity chains had significant differences: Both were dependent on refrigeration technology but had different ownership and organizational configurations at the processing level.

The freezing works which slaughtered and froze the stock were owned by a combination of local merchants and overseas, largely British, firms with only a few controlled by local farmer shareholders. The typical form was as private or public companies, with only a minority cooperatively owned before 1945.[16] Until as late as the 1980s, the emphasis was very much on maximizing carcass production for consignment. In contrast, the dairy commodity chain, constructed around the more perishable product milk, initially featured local processing organized at the local scale and on a cooperative model. Cooperatives prevailed over proprietary ownership with successive mergers over time producing a decreasing number of larger cooperatives. For both of these commodity chains, shipping space was a vulnerable part in the system. Government intervention appeared early along the commodity chain in terms of inspection and grading standards. In the early 1920s, after the cessation of the WWI bulk purchases agreements between the New Zealand and British governments, known as the 'commandeer,' and amid concerns about US meat trust companies seeking to enter New Zealand, producer board legislation was enacted. This in turn enabled, especially in the United Kingdom, more coordinated marketing of New Zealand brands of meat and dairy produce. Thus, in terms of 'trading environments as enterprise,' New Zealand producers were oriented toward UK markets half a world way and were sometimes severely impacted by fluctuations in primary produce prices in these markets, a problematic feature of these specific second nature relations, which in turn shaped local farming practices, for instance, in terms of preferred carcass weights and meat grading standards.

Against this broader backdrop and these possible ways of thinking about 'trading environments,' the remainder of the chapter will, using three case studies, further explore at some key moments and at differing scales ideas about how 'value' resided in some land in the North Island.

1. The first of the case studies will consider 'trading environments as transformation and enterprise' by examining ideas about land value and improvement in the context of the Pohangina Valley in the late 1890s and early 1900s. The Pohangina situated in the Manawatu in the southern part of the North Island is thus a case study of pioneer settlement in a defined localized region.
2. The second case study probes 'trading environments as transformation' by going against the grain and looking at resistance to the dominant land development ethos manifest in the emergence of a national system of protected natural areas focusing on scenic reserves in the early 1900s. Scenic reserves as a class of lands reserved from settlement were scattered across the country but typically at the margins of settlement, along major transport routes, and, more infrequently, at the margins of town and cities. This case study thus also considers questions around valuing nature.

3. The third case study hones in on 'trading environments as enterprise' but again reads against the dominant settler narrative of progress and improvement by considering a regional example of failure situated on the settlement frontier, associated with what Cumberland termed 'victory over environment' in the West Taupo and Whanganui hill country of the North Island during the 1920s and 1930s.

IMPROVEMENT

Cumberland, a mere three years after his arrival in New Zealand, insightfully drew attention to the rate and scale of environmental transformation and likely future problems, but he said little about the social forces driving these changes.[17] Important among these, especially in the nineteenth century, was the idea of 'improvement.' John Weaver, in a comparative study of 'the land rushes' that characterized European settlement in many parts of the 'New World' from 1650 to 1900, observed that, "in an embedded cultural sense, improvements meant humankind's duty to tame wilderness, rescue wasteland—even more to deliver itself from want and indolence."[18] This observation held true for settler society in nineteenth century New Zealand and still applied well into the twentieth century.

Weaver tracked 'improvement' back to Locke's theories about property rights. Linked to ideas of improvement were those about the 'value' of land. It tends to be overlooked that Les Heathcote's seminal study on land appraisal in outback Australia that compared and contrasted early official and popular 'appraisal of the plains' was grounded firmly in the context of related debates in early nineteenth century European political economy.[19] Rev. Thomas Malthus and others advanced the idea of 'the natural value of land' based on its inherent physical characteristics, the 'gifts of nature,' but there were countervailing viewpoints, such as 'acquired value' produced by an investment of labor and capital, though as Heathcote noted, the idea of 'natural value' lingered on in Australia to the mid-twentieth century. A Commission of Inquiry into the valuation of land in New Zealand in 1915 was prompted by concerns over excessive valuations, particularly of the 'unimproved value' of land, since landowners paid rates, a form of tax, on the value of their land holdings. Much of its focus is not pertinent here, but the commissioners' noting of settler complaints that the soil was being valued "as it exists to-day, irrespective of the money and labor expended in bringing it to its present condition" resonates with Heathcote's comments, while perhaps suggesting that there are also important Australian and New Zealand divergences.[20]

Many New World colonial governments depended on land sales as one of their few sources of revenue but, nonetheless, in their desire to promote land settlement, opted for a 'natural value' approach by setting nominal prices for land, though less so in New Zealand than in many earlier colonial outposts in part because colonization occurred later than in Australia or North America. By the early twentieth century, with land valuation becoming more dependent on the 'market value' of land, older distinctions between natural and acquired value had been overtaken. Elements of improvement, natural value, and acquired value are evident in the manner in which the settler state in New Zealand orchestrated land sales and monitored the progress of settlement in the Pohangina Valley.

The acquisition of the first scenic reserves, in contrast, was based on their productive value, in the negative sense, that these were lands that were of no value for settlement. Simultaneously, the 'scenery' thereon was acknowledged as having other less tangible values particularly as part of the newly established overseas tourist circuit. Land values in natural or acquired terms were not immutable; the biophysical qualities of the land could be enhanced or degraded through human use and the latter ran counter to the settler discourse of 'improvement.' Yet as the third case study will reveal, closer land settlement in some regions triggered what Cumberland termed 'nature's revenge' with an attendant loss of capital and unimproved land value.

TRADING ENVIRONMENTS AS TRANSFORMATION AND ENTERPRISE: LAND SETTLEMENT IN THE POHANGINA VALLEY

> *the idea of organising a landscape so that nature might better serve human needs was long embedded in Western thought.* [21]

Land settlement in the Pohangina Valley provides an entry point into the dominant discourse of settler agriculture as progress and improvement. The area under consideration is a valley on the western side of the Ruahine Ranges running north of the Manawatu Gorge in the North Island. The farming frontier reached the upper Pohangina Valley comparatively late, in the mid-1890s, but shares many features with other areas of closer land settlement in the North Island, where a heavily forested landscape was rapidly cleared for pastoral farming. That the valley from 1895 was a separate county, the smallest unit of local government until their abolition in 1989, means that selected statistics can also be used to trace the course of settlement in the district, but the main focus here is on the cartography of progress and improvement as recorded by minor government officials in the field in the form of the Crown Lands Rangers.

The predominant view of settler efforts in converting forest to farm throughout the nineteenth century and beyond was summed up by Thomas Kelly, a Taranaki newspaper proprietor and member of Parliament, who was emphatic in 1877 that, "bush felling is a noble work; there the effort of colonisation is more palpably displayed than perhaps in any other mode of utilising waste lands. It is literally carving a home in the wilderness."[22] The state, for much of the nineteenth century the sole authorized purchaser of Maori land, which was then on sold more expensively to land hungry settlers, played a major role in this process. These land purchases accelerated again under the Liberals in the 1890s and 1900s as part of their vision for a densely settled rural landscape.

One of the Liberal government's major legislative efforts, the Land Act, 1892 specified conditions under which Crown Land could be acquired for settlement. It laid down maximum size limits on land suited to different types of farming, as well as minimum auction prices for its sale. Crown Land for sale was classified as Town, Suburban, or Rural Land, with the latter being further divided into First Class, Second Class, and Third Class lands. These were to be given over to a graduation from intensive through to more extensive land uses. A minimum capital value was prescribed for the sale of Crown land; with rural land, First class land could not be auctioned for less than £1 per acre, second class for less than 10/- per acre and Third Class land for less than 2/6d per acre.[23] The Liberal government, which was as opposed to land aggregation as it was determined to break up large private estates, placed limits on the maximum amounts of Crown Land that a person could occupy. Consequently, no individual could purchase or lease from the Crown more than 640 acres [one square mile or 259 ha] of First Class Rural Land. Where the land was a mixture of First and Second Class, the maximum area was 2000 acres [809 ha] of which no more than 640 acres (32 percent) could be First Class land. Pastoral lands were of necessity considerably larger up to 5000 acres [2023 ha] for a First Class small grazing run and 20,000 acres [8090 ha] for a Second Class small grazing run. Extensive stock rearing on leasehold only Pastoral Runs were calculated not on area but on a carrying capacity basis of up to 20,000 sheep or 4000 cattle with individuals limited to a single run.

Ideas about land value in New Zealand by the 1890s combined ideas of the natural and acquired value of land. Indeed there had been vigorous debate about the idea of the 'unearned increment' at a time when comparatively few owned much of the freehold land in the country and the crusading single tax remedy of Henry George as well as the more idealistic vision of Henry Bellamy gained expression in Liberal Party policy via their commitment to use the tax system to encourage the breakup of the great estates and to move to promote a range of leasehold tenures (including lease-in-perpetuity). Pragmatism was also afoot in that leasehold tenure on Crown Land enabled new farmers to sink more of their capital into farming operations expanding the settlement frontier rather than on (excessively priced) existing farms on freehold land.

The Land Act, 1892, its complex leasehold tenurial arrangements notwithstanding, continued to endorse ideas of progress and improvement.

"Substantial improvements" it defined as those of permanent character which included, reclamation from swamps, clearing of bush, gorse,
broom, sweet briar, or scrub, cultivation, planting with trees or live
hedges, the laying out and cultivating of gardens, fencing, draining,
making roads, sinking wells or water-tanks, constructing water-races,
sheep dips, making embankments or protective works of any kind, in
any way improving the character or fertility of the soil, or the erection
of any building.[24]

The range of 'improvements' was intended to cover the spectrum of horticultural, agricultural, and pastoral activity that existed across the country.
Cultivation itself was similarly defined as including "drainage, the felling
of the bush, or the clearing of land for cropping, or clearing and ploughing
for laying down with artificial grasses."[25] Thus pioneer farmers not only
had a moral obligation but also an economic imperative to 'improve' the
land. This can be understood at the farm level in cartographic terms by
examination of the Crown Lands Rangers' notebooks for the Pohangina
Valley. At an operational level, this volume and associated files record the
Crown Lands Rangers' visits to the new farmers in the Pohangina Valley
to check that they were complying with the terms of their occupation of
the land. The farm is typically drawn as a simple line sketch besides which
some critical data is recorded. As an exercise in the cartography of colonial
land settlement it is instructive. The spread of the rectilinear survey for the
disposal of land, though not of the scale nor geometric precision of the US
survey and subdivision, generally won out over topography, though there
were exceptions to this to allow for watercourses and roadways, especially
over hilly terrain.[26]

The ranger's sketch is very much a symbolic empty space on which
improvement may be recorded. The forest is minimally identified, just a
bush margin, even when it covered virtually the entire farm. Instead attention is given to the recording of improvements. A careful reading of the
successive sketch plans produced as the ranger returned on periodic visits shows that he used a set of simple symbols to portray the felling of the
bush, the building of boundary fences, the erection of a house and farm
dwellings, the presence of internal tracks and fencing. To this the ranger
recorded other quantitative information about bush felled, area in grass,
chains (20m) of fencing, stock, and the value of buildings.

An illustration is provided of the 210 acre [85 ha] farm taken up by
Emerson Dalley in 1892 under ORP [Occupation with Right to Purchase]
conditions (Figure 7.1). The land had a capital value of £325 and annual
rent of £17/1/13.[27] The farm was inspected by the ranger in 1894 at which
time it was still 80 percent forest covered, although 42 acres [17 ha] had
been felled and planted in grass and a temporary dwelling erected. By 1899
when the ranger returned, the forest had been reduced to 64 percent of the

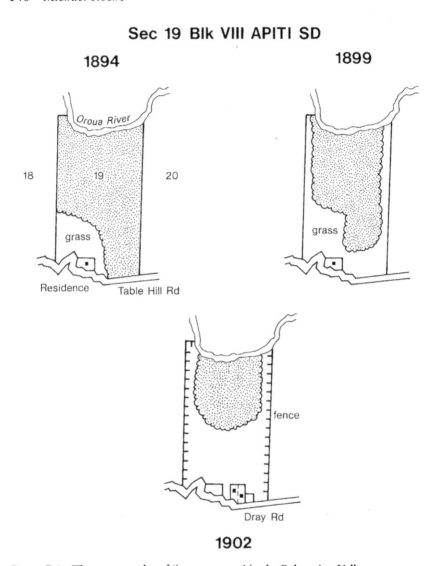

Figure 7.1   The cartography of 'improvement' in the Pohangina Valley.

Source: Author's rendering of original located in Archives New Zealand, Wellington, LS-W 9/5 ORP 401–498.

farm area, an average rate of clearance of just under 5 acres [2 ha] per year with the side boundaries cleared of trees. On the ranger's last inspection in 1902, the forest had further been reduced to 36 percent of the property and had been cleared at a faster average rate of 16 acres [6 ha] per annum with most of the remaining 124 acres [55 ha] in grass. Importantly in terms of meeting the requirements of the legislation, by 1902 130 chains [2.6km] of boundary fences had been erected along with a modest farmhouse valued at £20 and a £12 shed separated from the rest of the farm by internal fences in addition to a well and orchard/garden.[28] Dalley transferred the property to another settler, H.W. Hayward, in 1911.[29]

Removal of forest cover counted as an improvement, a perspective that gained pragmatic sanction because remnant areas of forest tended to easily degrade and retreat under the impact of cattle grazing and opening to wind. For some, this phenomenon was explained in Darwinian terms of the displacement of species, whereby a stronger invading flora was supplanting a weaker indigenous one, although local botanists disputed this idea from the 1900s. A minority of officials pressed for change. Phillips Turner, the inspector of scenic reserves, in 1901, for instance, urged that the Land Act be amended "so that every future selector of second and third class rural holdings be compelled to leave in forest 10 percent of the holding 'securely fenced without being charged any rent for this but being able to source firewood and some building timber from it."[30]

By chance one of the Pohangina Valley settlers, Charles Wildbore was an accomplished amateur photographer, and he reproduced many facets of day-to-day life at this latter bush frontier in New Zealand, and these greatly complement the cartographic and statistical framing of land settlement in the valley. One of his most evocative images was that of a bush burn in the valley in 1908 (Figure 7.2). Various official statistical series enable the appearance of pioneer settlement in the Pohangina Valley to be captured from 1895 onward (Table 7.1). The statistics are not without limitations, for instance, as part of a government economy no new agricultural census data was collected from 1909 to 1914, and the 1908 data was merely repeated (see sown grass, grain, and plantation data). The column "Sown grasses not previously ploughed" serves as a proxy for the course of deforestation, reflecting a 51 percent decline in forest area from 1895 to 1908. Sheep numbers and to a lesser extent grain crop areas provide other indicators of the steady expansion of settlement in the valley, with the former nearly tripling in number over 20 years and amounting to an impressive 80 head per person by 1914. There is unfortunately no dairy equivalent to the sheep returns as this was also an important land use in the valley in 1906. The data on plantations, although a very minor land use, does point to one of the paradoxes of farming under the Crown's 'improvement' conditions: Obliged to fell all the indigenous forest on the farms, some owners responded by quickly planting small areas of exotic plantations as shelter belts and windbreaks.

The Pohangina Valley is not presented as a statistically representative case study of closer land settlement, though it possibly does fulfill some of these criteria. Rather it is used as a means of illustrating some of the ideas of improvement that powered much land settlement in New Zealand in the nineteenth century and into the twentieth. This scale of analysis also reveals some tendencies and connections that, as Gordon Winder has shown, can be lost in dealing only with national aggregates.[31]

Figure 7.2   The bush burn—Pohangina Valley, 1908.

Source: Palmerston North Public Library 2008_Bf2_1408.

Table 7.1 Pohangina County: Settlement indicators 1895 to 1914.

Year	Sown grasses not previously ploughed (total acres)	Sheep (no.)	Oats and wheat for grain (acres)	Plantation trees (total acres)	Population (census years)
1895	48577	64276	4	-	
1896	53251	72994	6	3	1351
1897	58681	80545	61	15	
1898	65894	102693	18	3	
1899	69802	101998	4	3	
1900	75828	115847	7	3	
1901	79688	120171	26	3	1536
1902	83826	128940	34	2	
1903	87445	104574	11	8	
1904	87279	98165	3	8	
1905	91956	116675	7	25	
1906	92750	121941	41	7	1797
1907	92319	140873	32	20	
1908	95539	144965	31	9	
1909	95539	151931	31	9	
1910	94329	149075	118	63	
1911	94329	156810	118	63	1797
1912	94329	151960	118	63	
1913	94329	167835	118	63	
1914	94329	171742	118	63	2079

Sources: Statistics of New Zealand Production, Sheep Returns H23 *AJHR*
NB: The population figure for 1914 is an estimate.

TRADING ENVIRONMENTS AND RESISTANCE TO TRANSFORMATION VIA NATIONAL PARKS AND SCENIC RESERVES

> *The axe bites deep. The rushing fires streams bright;*
> *Swift beautiful and fierce it speeds for Man,*
> *Nature's rough-handed foeman, keen to smite*
> *And mar the loveliness of ages. Scan*
> *The blackened forest ruined in a night,*
> *The sylvan Parthenon that God will plan*
> *But builds not twice. Ah bitter price to pay*
> *For Man's dominion—beauty swept away!*[32]

Although one of New Zealand's early forestry officials ruefully summed up the dominant settler view in the 1920s as a desire to fell two trees to plant one blade of grass, there were some challenges to the hegemony of productive agricultural and pastoral land use. At a utilitarian level, on Crown Land these had dated back to the 1870s with the gazetting of hill country forests as 'Climatic Reserves,' and other areas for the Growth and Preservation of Timber, the latter for future use by saw millers and thereafter being turned over to land settlement, but land settlement where the land could support it was accorded priority over other uses.

Only from the late 1880s were some mountainous areas set aside under the Domains Act later to become the basis of national parks. And since many of the scenic areas were in remote areas of limited value for land settlement, there is a prima facie case for invoking Alfred Runte's 'worthless lands hypothesis' in New Zealand. A national park, along the US Yellowstone model, was created in New Zealand in 1887, but herein there were significant departures from Runte's hypothesis. The Maori owners of the sacred volcanoes were seeking to meet their own ends by gifting Mt. Tongariro to the state as the country's first national park in order to prevent it from ever falling into private settler ownership. At a more mundane level, the Land Act, 1892 included a provision for the creation of scenery reserves so that small, largely forested areas would be preserved as surrounding Crown Lands were opened for settlement. The Scenery Preservation Act, 1903 continued these efforts in a more concerted way with powers to repurchase freehold land and purchase Maori land for scenic reserves. Overtime this became the mainstream state vehicle for protecting scenic areas, which numbered 713 at 366,483 acres [148,307 ha] by 1922.[33]

The motives for preservation included an amalgam of scientific advocacy to protect representative areas of a largely endemic vegetation, proto eco-nationalist sentiments for projecting settler 'New Zealandness' through the use of symbols such as ferns and kauri trees (and native birds) as a way of differentiating themselves from Britain, and finally to protect the scenery that was admired for its picturesque qualities. The last of these motivations also splits into two not entirely compatible strands. On the one hand, there was a desire to retain areas as scenic reserves to beautify the colonial environment and to provide sites for passive recreation such a picnicking for locals, while on the other the more spectacular scenic areas were already part of an incipient revenue-generating overseas tourist circuit, in which the state was an early participant through a Tourist and Health Resorts Department established in 1901, which owned hotels at some of the key sites.

Government officials were only too well aware that they faced pressure from saw millers to protect forest land from settlement for felling in the future, from settlers to release it for burning and clearance for farm land, as well as having responsibility for retaining areas of Crown Land in perpetuity to protect scenic features for locals and for tourism. The general principles that emerged for scenery preservation by 1907 were first, to protect the scenery on main travel routes and second, as Crown Lands were opened up for closer land settlement, to preserve scenic areas unsuited for farming as reserves. Third, as far as peri-urban forest reserves were concerned, the department expected some local contribution to the purchase price of what were typically remnants on previously freeholded lands. Where areas had both settlement and scenic potential, the situation was straightforward:

> it must clearly be understood that it has never been the practice of the Department to unduly withhold from settlement areas of rich soils and well adapted for pastoral or agricultural pursuits merely because they are also suited for scenic purposes.[34]

Lands Department officials discussed the value of scenic reserves as commodity in two ways in recognizing that future generations would appreciate their foresight in preserving scenic areas as well as highlighting the wider role that scenic reserves in forested country played in soil conservation and flood protection.[35] Using the forest near Taihape as an example, the Under-Secretary of Lands observed that,

> two or three hundred acres [81 to 121ha] of bush, so long as it is kept intact, may be valued at £100,000: but should it be destroyed and the land denuded of forest covering, the damage done to streams and the surrounding country would be very large indeed.[36]

No attempts were, however, made to estimate the value of scenic reserves to tourism, particularly of the 'ribbon reserves' beside the North Island Main Trunk Railway line, flanking the Whanganui River, and along other major route ways and around lakes, though these were regarded as essential attractions by the Tourist and Health Resorts Department. This may well have been beyond the conception of officials at the time, and in any case, there was a paucity of data. The Tourist and Health Resorts Department introduced a third way in which scenery was a commodity—for consumption by an international tourist industry. Of interest here is the degree to which the colonial state moved to take control of the tourist infrastructure rather than leaving this completely to the private sector.[37]

It is possible to compare the prices that the Crown under the Land for Settlements Act paid to purchase or compulsorily acquire land for subdivision and release to closer land settlement with those paid for freehold land for scenic reserves. Taking 1910 as an example (Table 7.2), in that year, the Crown purchased 48,287 acres [19,540 ha] for £260,793 or an average of £5/5/- per acre. These ranged from £3 per acre for the poorest grazing country to £20 for dairying and over £40 for the best agricultural land.

Table 7.3 assembles land purchase data from 1905 to 1907 and serves to make the point that, in terms of average land values, the Crown paid comparatively low prices for scenic reserves compared to expenditure on settlement land of even the most limited potential; less than £1 compared to £3 to £4 per acre for the poorest grazing land. The point should also be made that area of scenic reserves was miniscule compared to Crown repurchases of farmland and the expenditure similarly small. A complicating factor is

Table 7.2 Land purchased under Land for Settlements Act in year ended March 31, 1910.

Land District	Acres	£/- per acre	Total price (£)	Land Quality
Hawkes Bay	8433	5/14	48433	grazing
	9734	4/10	43803	grazing
	10693	7/5	77466	grazing
	120	9	1078	pastoral
Canterbury	1585	5	7925	agricultural & pastoral
	271	41	11262	agricultural
	70	43	3023	agricultural
	3050	11	52412	agricultural & pastoral
	2402	4/5		agricultural & pastoral
	2526	3		agricultural & pastoral
	574	25		dairying
	409	20		dairying
	4424	9		agricultural & pastoral
	75		51	agricultural
Otago	1177	4	3531	agricultural & pastoral
	2744	4/5	11647	agricultural & pastoral
Total	48287		260793	

Source: AJHR C5 1910.

Table 7.3 Land purchases under the Scenery Preservation Act.

Land District	Name	Area (acres)	Purchase price (£)	Price /acre (£/-)
Hawkes Bay	Lindsay Settlement	22	310	14/-
Taranaki	Tututuramokai Pa	14	385	25/2
Wellington	Paraparaumu Bush	185	300	1/12
Canterbury	Raincliff Bush	62	497	8/-
Otago	Baileys Flagstaff	24	208	8/14
Southland	Edendale Settlement	205	1335	6/10

Year	Area (acres)	Number	Purchase price (£)	Price shillings/acre (£/-)
1904–05	914	6	216	4/6
1905–06	13640	55	3336	5/-
1906–07	11233	27	7855	14/-

Source: AJHR C6, 1906, 1907.

that the published reports do not systematically link the prices paid with individual blocks of land, and the process of formally gazetting reserves was typically not completed until several years after the sale so that it is difficult to connect these back to the actual purchases. Table 7.3 also includes some available purchase price data for 1906, which reinforces the point that, similar to the lands for closer settlement acquisitions, there was a range of purchase prices and that in a few instances considerable sums were expended for 'valuable' scenic areas, for instance, pa sites (fortified Maori earthworks), but overall, price-wise, scenery was valued at less than land for settlement.

Hall in reviewing national park establishment suggested that Runte's 'worthless land hypothesis,' that US parks were established as much because of what they lacked in terms of resources than for powerful aesthetic or ecological arguments, could be applied effectively in Australia.[38] To some extent, it also applies to New Zealand and operates as a palliative to the more nationalistic accounts of park creation.[39] But can scenic reserves in New Zealand be treated simply as small-scale 'national parks' to which a 'worthless lands' hypothesis can in turn be applied? The Crown through the Lands Department, while proactively reserving small areas as scenery reserves from the early 1890s, gave preference to releasing lands that had settlement potential, even if they had scenic qualities. The government's Tourist and Health Resorts Department, from its inception in 1901, also pushed for the preservation of forest along major scenic rail and road route ways in order to maintain the scenic attractiveness of the country, even if this only amounted to screening off the 'bush burn' landscape from the view of railway bound visitors. The Lands Department, which administered the forested scenic reserves, also recognized that the reserves had a value over and above their 'scenery,' which resided in their capacity to prevent floods and considerable costly damage to downstream farmlands.

Did scenery preservation represent a good investment on the part of the state? This is difficult to answer, bedeviled as it is by issues of intrinsic value versus other sorts of valuation data and of a paucity of economic information. Overseas visitor numbers were put at over 5,233 in 1903 increasing to 8,982 within only six years (Table 7.4). Scenic areas of New Zealand had a value as a commodity to be consumed by the early tourists. This involved not only the state-run geothermal resorts such as Rotorua and the alpine national parks such as Mt. Cook and the volcanoes of Tongariro National Park but also took in many of those scenic reserves that were protected in ribbons along the main truck railway line and along some of the major highways.[40] Using an estimate of £50 expenditure per overseas visitor, officials placed the tourist revenue at £449,000 for 1909, a still considerable sum even alongside meat exports of £3.6 million, butter of £1.5 million, and £1 million of cheese.[41] The direct revenue to the Tourist and Health Resorts Department at around 5 percent of the overseas visitor expenditure or £23,787 in 1909 was considerably in excess of the amounts spent on purchase of land for scenic reserves. Scenery equated with revenue generating potential and thus became a commodity. Over half of the overseas visitors

Table 7.4 Overseas visitors to New Zealand and expenditure on scenic reserve purchase.

Year	Overseas visitors	Estimated £ spent	Direct income to Tourist and Health Resorts Department	£ spent on land purchase for scenic reserves
1903–4	5233	261500	15344	—
1904–05	5992	299000	16018	216
1905–06	7142	357000	15820	3336
1906–07	9604	484000	18203	7856
1907–08	8602	430000	20487	4286
1908–09	8982	449000	23787	3813

Source: AHJR H2 and C6.

were from Australia with a sizable proportion of the remainder from the United Kingdom, although there were small numbers from the United States and Canada and Europe. That said, the majority of the scenic reserves were however created for local nonmonetary benefit.

The reevaluation of ideas around land development manifest in creation of scenic reserves in particular and their place in a revenue-generating tourist circuit occurred comparatively early in a New World settlement context but also represented an important challenge to the primacy of land settlement. The recognition of the protection offered by the forestry element of scenic reserves and the importance of scenery to tourism transcends the comparatively small areas set aside and in conceptual terms makes this the most interesting of the three trading environment case studies elaborated on in this chapter, because it challenged the hegemonic land development ethos.

TRADING ENVIRONMENTS AS ENTERPRISE: TEMPORARY 'VICTORY OVER ENVIRONMENT'—WEST TAUPO AND WHANGANUI HILL COUNTRY

> *indeed, the only limit to the extent of the country the farmer could stock is the limit of his purse.*[42]

The difficulties facing pioneer farmers in the counties to the west of Lake Taupo in the central North Island constitutes the third case study. Here the focus is on land deterioration, a situation where 'victory over environment' proved to be very short lived, but it is also linked to events beyond New Zealand, particularly the 'slump' of 1921–1922 when the end of the commandeer produced a short, sharp depression as New Zealand primary produce returns fell sharply. A second round of 'victories' were gained here and in other areas after 1945 through the widespread use of aerial topdressing techniques.[43] It ought to be acknowledged that the hill country was not to be the last frontier; the 'bush sick' lands of the Volcanic plateau of the central North Island represented another, later frontier of settlement expansion, which was delayed until the trace element deficiency of cobalt was discovered in the 1930s.

The 'bush burn' techniques employed in New Zealand since the 1860s on the lowland forests served well enough to clear the forests of the hill country and, as before, the sudden release of pot ash from the bush burn provided good conditions for pasture growth in the first couple of seasons. The general wetness of the land, however, made it difficult to get the cut vegetation dried out sufficiently by the end of summer to achieve the 'hot burn' necessary to kill the seed bank in the soil so that newly sown pastures soon became over run with invading bracken and scrub. Environmental learning was slow. Cumberland in *Landmarks* attributed much of the problem to settler ignorance of how to farm in a deforested hill country environment and did so by concentrating on the plight of the discharged soldier settler farms, part of a scheme set up to reward and rehabilitate returned soldiers after WWI.[44] Indeed, he inadvertently ended up conveying the impression that all soldier settlement was situated at the frontier of settlement, when this was not the case.[45]

By 1925, the government had passed the Deteriorated Lands Act and established a Committee of Inquiry to investigate and report on the problem with particular reference to Whangamomona, Ohura, Waitomo, Otorohanga, Kawhia, Raglan, Kaitieke, and Waitotara counties, all located in North Island 'hill country' areas. Four types of land deterioration were recognized by the Department of Agriculture at this time ranging from replacement of valuable stock vegetation by less valuable species, through replacement of superior vegetation for stock feed by species of no use (for instance bracken fern) and grassland depletion where species were reduced in number to the point of bare ground showing through to, finally, accelerated soil erosion involving the removal of the soil.[46] The Committee of Inquiry published a report in 1925 based on inspection and interviews and offered a diagnosis of the problem and some, by its own admission, incomplete but still indicative, statistics.[47] The districts under review amounted to 874,700 acres [353,971 ha] taking in 1990 farms, largely on leasehold tenures on Crown Land. Abandoned farms numbered 75 (3.8 percent of farms) and 42,905 acres [17,362 ha] (4.9 percent by area). Detailed information was available only from the 310 circulars returned by settlers seeking easement of their rents and payments. This amounted to 15.5 percent of the total land holdings in question. They were believed by officials to be a 'fair estimate' of the wider situation in the counties under review. The area of reverted land was estimated at 232,500 acres [94087 ha] or 27 percent of the total.

The Committee of Inquiry considered that deteriorated land had multiple intersecting causes. They listed as the 12 'most potent' factors:

1. Wet climatic conditions preventing hot burns and favoring regrowth of fern and scrub
2. Inefficient fencing that prevented controlled stocking of country

3. Injudicious stocking
4. Sowing of grasses and clover not adapted to the country
5. Depletion of fertility
6. Boom and slump periods
7. High maintenance costs
8. Lack of knowledge of local conditions
9. Difficulties in providing winter feed
10. Aspect and steepness of the land
11. Lack of road access
12. Lack of capital

The first two of these were interrelated in that the inability after the burn off to manage concentrated grazing with spelling by cattle gave the fern and scrub the opportunity to become established. The rule of thumb for successful grazing of regrowth by cattle was that paddocks needed to be no more than 10 percent of the total size of the property. This situation was exacerbated by poor choice of 'first class English grasses' when other varieties were better suited to the hill country and excessive grazing by sheep, which gave better short-run economic returns. But sheep did not graze evenly thus enabling secondary growth to gain a further foothold.[48] Considerable importance was attributed to the fact that the environmental knowledge built up over a generation of bush burn farming on the lowland forests was not applicable to breaking in the hill country. Grass seed varieties, research, and the environmental history of pastoralism in New Zealand more generally has been the subject of Brooking and Pawson's *Seeds of Empire*, which is particularly strong on the conversion of the tussock grasslands in the South Island, but more perhaps awaits to be said about the grassland environments of the North Island hill country.[49] The economic context was not, however, completely overlooked by the Committee which recognized that land deterioration had been accentuated pre-WWI by many leases being transferred for excessive amounts, which in the immediate postwar land boom and slump left many farmers highly indebted and unable to farm effectively.

The Committee's remedy was predicated on the axiom that since large amounts of capital had already been spent on breaking in the country "caution should be used before abandoning any of this class of country."[50] To abandon land was to fly in the face of the settler ethos of improvement and development extending back to the mid-nineteenth century. Instead the Committee recommended some other, rather unpalatable, solutions, which included a revaluation of the land, the postponement of and remission of rents. These were options that the Land Department already had recourse to under the Land Act, but which tended to be used on a case-by-case basis and not on such a large scale. A downward revaluation of the value of the land had the effect of reducing the rentals, and if backdated, would also reduce the arrears of rent. Postponements of rents and writing off of amounts owing also gave the occupiers an opportunity to farm themselves out of difficulties, as did other associated measures, such as reducing mortgages and interest rates. Accepting a reduced valuation did, however, reduce the value of the lease and the 'goodwill' that might be secured in the future in transferring it to another would-be farmer. Official estimates put indebtedness on land at £1/7/6 per acre to the state and £1/6/10 to private and institutional lenders. For land on which forest had been recently felled, these figures were somewhat higher at £2/-/5d and £1/19/9d per acre respectively. Loans for stock were also considerable at 1/1d to the state and 8/2d to private firms respectively giving a total indebtedness per acre of £7/14. For the counties under review, this was extrapolated to sums of £1.2 million owed to the state and £1.17 million to private sources along with £0.49 million of stock mortgages.[51]

The full extent of what this meant at the farm level is somewhat disguised in the aggregate data. To bring this into clearer relief, the case of a 1,003 acre [406 ha] leasehold property applied for in 1920 in partnership by ex-soldiers William Russell and William Gray under the Discharged Soldiers Settlement Act in the Retaruke Survey District, adjacent to the infamous Mangapurua block, a site of a failed soldier settlement, is instructive.[52] The initial rent of this Crown leasehold property was set at £73/7/- p.a. Both men had previous farming experience and their efforts at felling the heavy bush and establishing pasture then stocking with sheep were commended by officials. Between 1920 and 1923, Russell and Gray borrowed to the maximum allowable limit of £2500 under the conditions of the Discharged Soldiers Settlement Act (Table 7.5). The land that had originally been completely in forest had been quickly cleared and carried 400 breeding ewes, 598 lambs, 40 hoggets, 20 wethers, and 8 rams, along with 20 heifers and 4 horses. In 1924, their 'improvements' meant that the capital value of the farm was £1630, though the total debt owing to the state was now £4042. Concerned by this, Russell and Gray sought a revaluation of the property from the Dominion Revaluation Board, established in 1923 to review soldier settler farms. The Board found 97 acres [39 ha] of bush had been felled, another 440 acres [178 ha] felled and burnt, and 4 1/2 acres [1.8 ha] stumped along with 440 acres [178 ha] sown in grass. Some 30 acres [12 ha] of pasture it assessed as 'worn out' probably a sign of overstocking. The total value of improvements as freehold they put at £3230. The board reduced the original capital value of £1630 by £530 to £1100 and postponed current account interest repayments for five years. Set against the Committee's 1925 report, Russell and Gray had too few cattle to keep back regrowth and insufficient fencing for managed grazing. In 1924, they dissolved the partnership, and Gray took over the entire farm. Russell took £600 for his share of which £400 was paid in cash. In 1927, Gray applied for relief under the Deteriorated Lands Act and this further reassessment reduced the capital value by another £730 to £370. This had a sizable impact on the half yearly rents, reducing them from £24 to £8. Tellingly, the appraisal noted that the farm had 500 acres [202 ha] of bush 'not worth felling,' that is unsuited for conversion to pasture, 500 acres [202ha] felled and grassed but that this was 'worn out pasture,' in other words 'depleted' pasture, and that the land was suitable only for sheep grazing. Gray's debts, although somewhat reduced, were still considerable, and in 1928, he forfeited the property by which time it was valued at £767. The Lands Department promptly offered the farm for selection, the official description providing subtle clues as to its deteriorated state. It was described as poorer 'light quality land' and a hilly section with 'high broken ridges' of which 500 acres [202 ha] were in bush, 300 acres [121 ha] had reverted to scrub, and 203 acres [82 ha] were in grass (LS 1 26/13032 Sec 2 Blk XIV Retaruke S.D.).[53] Bearing in mind that the farm had been cleared of forest in 1924, the extent and speed of regrowth was impressive. The halving of the capital value of a farm affected by the regrowth of fern and scrub in the space of four years and the owner's forfeiture of the property are more poignant measures of the human and environmental costs of land deterioration than the aggregate figures provided by the Deteriorated Land Committee.

Table 7.5 Loans, improvements, and forest clearance on Russell and Gray's farm 1920 to 1923.

Date	Soldier settlement loan £	Total loan £	Bush felling £	Grass seed £	Stock £	Improvements £	Bush felled (acres)
24/1/20	145	145	85	60			42.5
18/3/20	75	220		75 for 1190lb			
17/1/21	330	550	330				144
25/2/21	270	820		270 to sow 144 acres			
20/7/21	40	860		20 to sow 43 acres		20	
2 /9/21	340	1200	140		200 for 500 lambs		100
8/12/21	300	1500	300				200
20/1/22	100	1600	100				63
21/3/22	460	2060		460			263
19/8/22	60	2120			60 for 85 Romney ewes		
29/11/22	300	2420		110	270		97.5
5/12/23	80	2500		80 for 100 acres			100

Source: Compiled from loan application forms LS 1 26/13032 Section 2 Blk XIV Retaruke SD.
NB: The total area of estimated bush felled actually slightly exceeds the farm size by 6.5 acres.

The further scientific inquiry that the Deteriorated Land Committee of Inquiry recommended bore fruit in the form of geologist Norman Taylor's influential 1938 paper "Land Deterioration in the Higher Rainfall Districts of New Zealand," which affirmed many of its original interpretations, although with rather greater emphasis on the classification of soil erosion types and discussion of rates of erosion.[54] This flowed on to a further official Committee of Inquiry on *Maintenance of Vegetative Cover in New Zealand with Special Reference to Land Erosion* published in 1939 and, in turn, a comprehensive Soil Conservation and Rivers Control Act, 1941.[55] Taylor's perceptive observation that hill country land deterioration would never be controlled while "farmers are forced to 'mine' their land in order to pay their debts" was only partly addressed by the 1941 legislation.[56]

CONCLUSION

Massive and rapid environmental change accompanied the European colonization of New Zealand, whereby a forested land was transformed into grassland. Refrigeration technology cemented New Zealand's place as a pasture-based, food and fiber producer for Britain and, if anything, heightened earlier settler mentalities about progress and improvement.

Brooking and Pawson in *Seeds of Empire* convincingly make the point that the attention given to the loss of the forests has diverted detailed attention away from the complexities of creating the grassland economy that replaced it, especially moving into the twentieth century.[57] Elsewhere, Winder has highlighted the importance of looking behind the national aggregate measures.[58] The Pohangina case study builds on both these sets of concerns and is emblematic of the pioneer farming experience in the North Island hill country, which tends to be overshadowed by the more expansive South Island High country historiography. With qualifications, I would agree with the view, though not of the celebratory tone, of Prof. George Jobberns, also a South Islander, who observed that the,

> making over of the accessible parts of the North Island inland forest was the outstanding achievement of our people in the making of the present grassland landscape . . . The achievements of all these ordinary struggling people make the really significant history of the North Island.[59]

The Crown Lands Rangers charted this making over in dispassionate form using simple sketch maps showing the progress of farm improvements.

The dominant narratives of land settlement, improvement and development, did not, however, as the second case study on scenic reserves makes clear, exist unopposed. By the 1890s, coincident with the Liberal government's closer land settlement policies, active though limited official moves were made to protect selected areas of the country as national parks and scenic reserves where these lands were deemed unsuitable for settlement.

Scenic reserves were an important element as landscapes of consumption for the early tourist industry and the financial contribution of tourists to the economy was considerable even when compared to the sums contributed by meat and dairy exports. The value of a scenic remnant to future generations as well as their contribution to soil conservation and flood protection was also recognized, even if this value could not be precisely calculated. In a small way, this also signals that New Zealand was not completely configured as an overseas farm for British consumers: There was still scope for local eco-nationalist projects.

Deteriorated land, explored in the third case study, represented a loss of value in terms of absolute and capital value and as such was an anathema to the discourse of improvement. Various revaluation and debt restructuring options were employed by the state to enable occupiers to eventually farm themselves out of debt or at least to save the farms if not the actual farmers. But in some ways, larger social and economic concerns were not addressed and instead the state tended to place emphasis on science and later on legislation in order to put in place nationwide soil conservation and rivers control legislation in 1941. These later developments were influenced by some large-scale dramatic events, particularly the Esk Valley floods of 1938, which coincided with new political interest in these matters that together made land deterioration in the West Taupo hill country seem slow moving.[60] The connection between local land deterioration, land degradation, and erosion problems in New Zealand on the one hand and the demands of British consumers linked by commodity chains on the other was not well apprehended by officials and scientists. Instead, the problem of environmental learning was constructed more narrowly in terms of 'nature's revenge' with applied science leading the fight back to pacify the environment and securing further victories for a generation after 1945 via aerial topdressing.

It was not, however, simply a case of global commodity chains, especially those for meat, dairy, and wool, being buyer led and driving land deterioration of various kinds in New Zealand from half a world away. In any case, the Ottawa Agreement of 1932 instituted quotas on New Zealand primary exports to the United Kingdom and thus ended the era of unrestricted access to an apparently bottomless market. But many if not most local producers and officials were both complicit in wanting to continue to sell in the United Kingdom and oblivious to local environmental consequences. Neither was it simply a consequence of the power of buyer-led, agri-commodity chains, for there were continuous efforts at the New Zealand end to find new markets for its limited range of agrifood exports. But in endeavoring to build commodity chains into new markets, some local farmers continued to deplete environments as a consequence of structural relationships and in other instances by again seeking to expand the margins of the settlement frontier. Price fluctuations in UK markets were particularly damaging, not only in terms of reduced financial returns but because they could lead to overstocking and repeat cropping of land, which in turn can accelerate land degradation.

The dominant settler ideas around progress and improvement combined with the development of a grassland economy whereby New Zealand functioned as one of Britain's overseas farms, though there were at least three sorts of 'trading environments' in action during the course of the nineteenth century. This however ought not to obscure the point that there were some reactions, in the form of the creation of scenic reserves, against the dominance of entirely productionist views. This was achieved to some extent despite the assumptions behind 'translation' and 'transformation,' including the unforeseen consequences of various mistranslations (for example, necessitating pest destruction efforts) notwithstanding the consequences of transformation. Cumberland appreciated these issues in the South Island high country and North Island hill country where they accelerated erosion and triggered land degradation. Trading environments as 'enterprise' could persist but, especially from the 1920s when export prices fell and local production was increased to maintain revenues, this was achieved only at the expense of land deterioration especially at the settlement frontier.[61]

NOTES

1 Alfred W. Crosby, *Ecological Imperialism, the Biological Expansion of Europe 900–1900* (Cambridge: Cambridge University Press, 1986).
2 Peter Holland, *Home in the 'Howling Wilderness': Settlers and Environment in Southern New Zealand* (Auckland: Auckland University Press, 2013).
3 Kenneth Cumberland, "A century's change: Natural to cultural vegetation in New Zealand," *Geographical Review* 31 (1941): 554.
4 Eric Pawson, "Creating public spaces for geography in New Zealand: Towards an assessment of the contributions of Kenneth Cumberland," *New Zealand Geographer* 67 (2011): 102–115.
5 See for example Judith A. Johnston, "The New Zealand bush: Early assessments of vegetation" *New Zealand Geographer* 37(1981): 19–24.
6 James Beattie, "Environmental anxiety in New Zealand 1840–1941: Climate change, soil erosion, sand drift, flooding, and forest conservation," *Environment and History* 9 (2003): 379–392.
7 Holland, *Home in the 'Howling Wilderness'*, and Eric Pawson and Tom Brooking (eds.), *Making a New Country* (Dunedin: Otago University Press, 2013).
8 Eric Pawson, "Plants, mobilities and landscapes: Environmental histories of botanical exchange," *Geography Compass* 2 (2008): 1464–1477.
9 Robert Peden, "'The exceeding joy of burning': Pastoralists and the Lucifer match: Burning the rangelands of the South Island of New Zealand in the nineteenth century, 1850 to 1890," *Agricultural History* 80 (2006): 17–34 and Robert Peden, *Making Sheep Country: Mt Peel Station and the Transformation of the Tussock Lands* (Auckland: Auckland University Press, 2011).
10 Eric Pawson and Tom Brooking (eds.), *Making a New Country* (Dunedin: Otago University Press, 2013).
11 Tom Brooking, *Lands for the People? The Highland clearances and the colonization of New Zealand, a biography of John McKenzie* (Dunedin: Otago University Press, 1996), 75.

12 Tom Brooking, "Busting up the greatest estate of all: Liberal Maori land pol-
    icy, 1891–1911," *New Zealand Journal of History* 26 (1992): 78–98 and Tom
    Brooking, "Use it or Lose it. Unravelling the land debate in late 19th century
    New Zealand," *New Zealand Journal of History* 30 (1996): 141–162.
13 Russell Stone, *Makers of Fortune: A Colonial Business Community and Its
    Fall* (Auckland: Auckland University Press, 1974) and Duncan Waterson,
    "The Matamata Estate, 1904–1959: Land transfers and subdivision in the
    Waikato," *New Zealand Journal of History*, 3 (1969): 32–51.
14 For example Anne Brower, 2008, *Who Owns the High Country? The Contro-
    versial Story of Tenure Review in New Zealand* (Nelson: Craig Potton Publish-
    ing, 2008); Michelle Dominy, *Calling the Station Home: Place and Identity in
    New Zealand's High Country* (Lanham, MD: Rowman and Littlefield, 2001);
    Roberta McIntyre, *Whose High Country? A History of the South Island High
    Country of New Zealand* (North Shore: Penguin, 2008); Peden, *Making Sheep
    Country*, Stone, *Makers of Fortune* and Waterson, "The Matamata Estate,
    1904–1959."
15 Richard Le Heron, "A political economy perspective on the expansion of New
    Zealand livestock farming, 1960–1984 — Part I. Agricultural policy," *Journal
    of Rural Studies* 5 (1989): 17–32 and Richard Le Heron "A political eco-
    nomy perspective on the expansion of New Zealand livestock farming, Part II.
    Aggregate farmer responses—Evidence and policy implications 1960–1984,"
    Journal of Rural Studies 5 (1989): 33–43.
16 Michael Roche, "Internationalisation as company and industry colonialisa-
    tion: The frozen meat industry in New Zealand in the 1900s," *New Zealand
    Geographer* 49 (1993): 2–7.
17 Cumberland, "A century's change."
18 John C. Weaver, *The Great Land Rush and the Making of the Modern World
    1650–1900* (Montreal McGill-Queens University Press, 2003), 81.
19 Les Heathcote, *Back of Bourke: A Study of Land Appraisal and Settlement in
    Semi-Arid Australia* (Melbourne: Melbourne University Press, 1965).
20 *Appendicies to the Journals of the House of Representatives* (hereafter *AJHR*)
    B17B (1915), ix.
21 Weaver, *The Great Land Rush and the Making of the Modern World
    1650–1900*, 87.
22 Thomas Kelly. "Taranaki forest and forest farming," *New Zealand Country
    Journal* 1(1877): 244.
23 Land Act, 1892, section 125 (Wellington: Government Printer Wellington,
    1892).
24 Land Act, 1892, section 2.
25 Land Act, 1892, section 2.
26 Norman Thrower, *Original Survey and Land Subdivision* (Chicago: Mono-
    graph Series of the Association of American Geographers, 1966) and Hilde-
    gard B Johnson, *Order Upon the Land: the US Rectangular Land Survey and
    the Upper Mississippi Country* (New York: Oxford University Press, 1976).
27 Rangers' note books—Apiti, Umutoi, Pohangina, Mangahoa, 1901–1915
    LS-W 29 48/50 Archives New Zealand, Wellington.
28 LS-W 9/5 ORP 401–498 Tenure Files, Archives New Zealand, Wellington.
29 Pohangina County, *Feilding Star*, 13 March 1911.
30 *AJHR* C6 (1910): 7.
31 Gordon Winder. "Grassland revolutions: Disaggregating a national story,"
    New Zealand Geographer 65 (2009): 187–200.
32 William Pember Reeves, "The passing of the forest," in William F. Alexan-
    der and A.E. Currie (eds.), *A Treasury of New Zealand Verse* (Auckland:

Whitcomb and Tombs, 1926), 58. [The poem was originally published in 1898].

33 *AJHR* C6 (1922): 2.
34 *AJHR* C6 (1907): 2.
35 *AJHR* C6 (1913): 2.
36 *AJHR* C6 (1913): 2.
37 Margaret McClure, *The Wonder Country, Making New Zealand Tourism* (Auckland: Auckland University Press, 2004).
38 C. Michael Hall, "The 'Worthless lands hypothesis' and Australia's national parks and reserves," in *Proceedings of the First National Conference on Australian Forest History* (Canberra: Department of Geography and Oceanography, Australian Defence Force Academy, 1988), 441–458.
39 David Thom, *Heritage, Parks for the People*, (Auckland: Lansdowne Press, 1987).
40 *AJHR* C6 (1907).
41 *New Zealand Official Year Book* (Wellington: Government Printer, 1910).
42 W. Downie Stewart, "Land tenure and land monopoly in New Zealand," *Journal of Political Economy* 17 (1909): 82–91.
43 Michael Roche, *Land and Water: Water and Soil Conservation and Central Government in New Zealand, 1941–1988* (Wellington: Historical Branch, Dept. of Internal Affairs, 1994).
44 Kenneth Cumberland, *Landmarks* (Surry Hills NSW: Readers Digest, 1981).
45 Michael Roche, "Failure deconstructed: Histories and geographies of soldier settlement in New Zealand circa 1917–39," *New Zealand Geographer* 64 (2008): 46–56.
46 J. Connell, "Land deterioration is a grave phase of our national economy," *New Zealand Journal of Agriculture* 59 (1939): 4–12.
47 Committee of Inquiry, "Deterioration of Crown Lands," *AJHR* C15 (1925).
48 Committee of Inquiry, *AJHR* C15, 4.
49 Tom Brooking and Eric Pawson (eds.), *Seeds of Empire, the Environmental Transformation of New Zealand*. (London: IB Tauris, 2010).
50 Committee of Inquiry, *AJHR* C15 (1925): 7.
51 Committee of Inquiry, *AJHR* C15 (1925): x.
52 LS 1 26/13032 Sec 2 Blk XIV Retaruke Survey District, Archives New Zealand, Wellington.
53 LS 1 26/13032.
54 Norman Taylor, "Land deterioration in the heavier rainfall districts of New Zealand," *New Zealand Journal of Science and Technology* 11 (1938): 657–681.
55 *Committee of Inquiry on Maintenance of Vegetative Cover in New Zealand with Special Reference to Land Erosion* (Government Printer, 1939) and Roche, *Land and Water*.
56 Taylor, "Land deterioration in the heavier rainfall districts of New Zealand": 657.
57 Brooking and Pawson, *Seeds of Empire*.
58 Winder, "Grassland revolutions."
59 George Jobberns, "Life and landscape in New Zealand: Fifty years in retrospect," in Michael Roche (ed.), *A Geographer by Declaration, Selected Writings by George Jobberns* (Christchurch: Canterbury University Press, 2010), 75.
60 Roche, *Land and Water*.
61 For a contrary view for the South Island High country see Peden, *Making Sheep Country*.

8 Reimagining the Tropical Beef Frontier and the Nation in Early Twentieth-Century Colombia

Shawn Van Ausdal

On the eve of World War I, the future of global beef supplies appeared uncertain. The world's largest exporter at the beginning of the century, the United States, had become a net importer. While Argentina's success at replacing the United States in international markets was remarkable, people with an eye on the beef trade feared that the expansion of domestic consumption and agriculture on the Pampas would curtail further growth of exports.[1] With North Atlantic demand continuing to rise, especially after the onset of war, there was an urgent need to develop new sources of supply. In this context, the possibilities of tropical ranching began to generate much interest.[2] In 1914, noted author and editor of the *Boston Evening Transcript*, Joseph Edgar Chamberlin, reported on the bright prospects for raising cattle in Colombia. With "more cheap and unused grazing land than any other country in the world," he noted, "Colombia alone could feed us [the multiplying millions of the United States] with beef for many years."[3]

Chamberlin was not alone in his prognostication that Colombia could become a major exporter. Numerous people with an interest in the beef trade, such as British expatriate E. Lloyd Owen, claimed that the Caribbean lowlands of Colombia "must be the great meat producing district of the future."[4] Intrigued, the British Board of Trade sent Robert Cunninghame Graham, the Scottish author and adventurer with extensive experience on the grasslands of Argentina and Venezuela, on a secret reconnaissance mission. His reports were highly favorable: the grass grew exuberantly, the cattle were well shaped, pests and diseases were limited, and recently introduced British beef breeds appeared to be doing well. "In my opinion," asserted Cunninghame Graham, "the future of Colombia lies in cattle-raising."[5] All that was needed to develop Colombia into a commercial and globally integrated ranching frontier was a modern slaughterhouse. By then, meatpacking interests from Europe and the United States had begun exploring the possibility of establishing operations there. In 1918, the Colombian Products Company (CPC), a joint venture between Colombian ranchers and the International Products Company, won the concession to build and operate the country's first 'packing house,' as it was called locally. The optimism that Colombia could follow Argentina on the path to beef-led prosperity was palpable. The Minister of Agriculture and Commerce, Luis Montoya, predicted that, "with the establishment of the meat exporting business, the development of wealth in Colombia will be fabulous . . ."[6]

Despite the bright prospects, integrating Colombia into North Atlantic beef markets was not self-evident. Because wiry, tropical cattle were considered inappropriate for northern palates, most internationally traded beef came from British breeds raised in temperate regions. Colombian cattle might have been favorably esteemed in Havana, but it was not clear how their meat would be received in London's Smithfield market. Nor was the possibility of upgrading native herds by crossing them with British beef breeds a straightforward proposition given the difficulties of acclimatization. And while the exuberant growth of tropical grasses may have seemed fantastic, by the early twentieth century, doubt about the productive potential of the tropics was starting to spread. As early as 1908, Francisco de Villa complained that Colombia's grasses were "rachitic and parched" and that much of its territory was "infertile."[7] By the early 1920s, Lucien Febvre, cofounder of the Annales School, denounced the "illusionary riches" of the tropics more generally.[8]

In the end, the naysayers prevailed. The packing plant, which took three times longer than anticipated to build, never initiated operations. Unable to establish a profitable market for Colombian beef, the CPC decided to shutter the plant rather than export at a loss. Instead of turning Colombia into a second Argentina, the packing plant became a symbol of national failure, prompting reevaluations about the country's tropical environment and the best method to develop its ranching potential and the nation as a whole.

This tale of hype and failure raises the issue of how resource frontiers in the tropics are imagined and constructed. A useful place to start is David Arnold's notion of 'Tropicality.'[9] This concept highlights the long-standing way that Europeans depicted the tropics as either a terrestrial paradise or living hell. Both sides of this Janus-faced discursive formation had the effect of highlighting the essential difference and deviance of such regions from a temperate norm, thereby justifying outside intervention. Various studies have shown how such ideas were central to Europe's incorporation of distant lands.[10] Not only did they color the perspectives of travelers, artists, scientists, and colonial officials, who in turn reshaped and reinforced them, but investors also fell under their influence. The concept of Tropicality, then, can also be of service in tracing the development of commercial knowledge and business ventures. Although doubts existed about the potential of the Colombian tropics to become an important beef exporter, in the context of impending scarcity and the fears of missing out on a valuable opportunity, the deep-rooted belief in tropical fecundity could be recycled into a narrative of commercial potential.

Nonetheless, while the concept of Tropicality originated as an effort to emphasize landscapes rather than just peoples or cultures in Europe's ordering of the nontemperate world, the particularities of tropical environments tend to be subsumed within the larger discursive formation. Discourses shape actions and have real implications, but it is equally important to avoid losing sight of the material and ecological underpinnings of history. In this case, I suggest that the failure of Colombia's first packinghouse was rooted in the tangible challenges of ranching in the tropics rather than simply the false expectations generated by a faith in tropical exuberance. The slow growth of native cattle, which made Colombian beef relatively expensive and of poor quality, along with the difficulty of introducing European breeds, undermined the country's competiveness.

The failure of the packinghouse had the effect of inverting perceptions about Colombia's tropical environment and its potential to be a global beef producer. From faith in their natural fecundity, the tropics came to be seen as debilitating and unproductive. While this radical shift was consistent with Tropicality's dualistic vision, the actors who reimagined the Colombian tropics were primarily local. This case thus highlights the need to understand how the discourse operated domestically rather than simply framed European or American perceptions and domination. On the one hand, by defining the tropics as deviant from temperate standards, government officials and ranching modernizers highlighted their 'essential' difference. But similar to the way that Latin American elites understood racial qualities to be mutable rather than intrinsic, they also insisted that the tropics could be tempered. Backed by the authoritative power of modern science, officials and modernizers thus justified state interventions in an effort to transform the environment, ranching, and the nation. There was also a 'subversive' tinge to this discourse, since their portrayal of ranchers as backward and inefficient fanned critiques of the *latifundio* and encouraged Colombia's initial attempt at land reform in the 1930s. On the other hand, the reevaluation of the tropics generated a curious trans-species politics of race. Given the concern of many Colombian elites about the physical and moral inadequacy of the masses, they embarked on a concerted effort of racial revitalization. One strategy to reinvigorate the population was to raise domestic beef consumption. This required that ranchers produce more and cheaper beef, which, in turn, depended on their ability to domesticate the tropics and import European breeds. 'Whitening' Colombia's cattle, therefore, was a means to 'whiten' the nation. Ranchers, however, were more interested in crossing their animals with zebu, which symbolized, for modernizing boosters, acquiescence to Colombia's tropical environment and the maintenance of outdated ranching practices. The product of a region even more diseased and debilitating than Colombia's, zebu not only threatened the country's cattle herd but the nation itself and needed to be banned. Although the prohibition lasted less than a decade, from 1931 to 1939, it demonstrates the commingling of Tropicality, eugenics, and veterinary science.

THE 'PACKING HOUSE' AT COVEÑAS

Plans to build a meat packing plant in Colombia grew out of a conflu-
ence of global and local interests. Officials from North Atlantic economies
worried about rising pressure on internationally traded cattle stocks. As
beef consumption in Europe rose, and the United States entered global markets as a competing importer, the ability of Argentina or Australia to significantly increase their exports seemed doubtful.[11] Furthermore, because
of wartime demand and destruction, Lord Harcourt, president of Britain's
Board of Trade, predicted that "After the war there will be a general scarcity of meat—almost a war famine."[12] Britain was particularly vulnerable
since 40 percent of its consumption consisted of imports. To secure a steady
stream of beef, Harcourt looked for new sources of supply, dispatching
Cunninghame Graham to Colombia. By then, numerous meatpacking interests were also examining Colombia's potential.[13]

In Colombia, the prospect of future scarcity was embraced with alacrity.
"For many years so favorable an opportunity will not present itself again,"
wrote Luis Montoya.[14] Yet the idea of establishing a beef export industry
also promised to resolve a number of pressing domestic problems. From
the mid-nineteenth century, Colombian economic growth was punctuated
by a series of tropical commodity booms and busts. The latest was coffee,
whose long-term prospects at the beginning of the twentieth century were
still far from certain. There was an urgency to find a stable export commodity and, to many, cattle seemed to be the most promising. Since beef
was an 'indispensable' food, reasoned a congressional commission, its consumption would only increase over time, "something that does not happen
with coffee."[15] A meatpacking plant also promised to resolve a looming
crisis in the country's most important cattle-raising district, the plains of
the Caribbean coast. Manuel Dávila Flórez, senator from the Caribbean
department of Bolívar, argued that despite the export of about half a million animals to Cuba between 1898 and 1906 (to help restock the island
following the Spanish American War), local herds rebounded quickly on
the region's extremely fertile soil and abundant grasses, causing prices to
fall and the industry to stagnate.[16] Furthermore, most everyone agreed that
Colombia had large extensions of undeveloped land that was good for raising cattle and that was within easy reach of Caribbean ports. If only an
export outlet could be found, the cattle population of the Caribbean plains
could easily increase from one to five or even ten million head, and Colombia could duplicate Argentina's beef-led prosperity.[17] Yet given the restrictions on exporting live animals to the United States and Europe, the only
way to access those markets was by shipping frozen or chilled carcasses.

The Colombian government, therefore, passed a series of laws designed
to attract the capital and expertise required to build a meatpacking plant.
The final version offered a subsidy of £10,000 per year for ten years to the

first company that constructed a plant on the Caribbean coast within two years of winning the concession. The plant had to be modern and capable of processing 50,000 cattle per year and converting the waste to commercial products like fertilizer. Additionally, the meat it produced could only be exported, and the company was required to provide £150,000 worth of long-term, low-interest loans (for five years at 9 percent annually) to ranchers in the region. It promulgated the offer around the United States and Europe and three groups submitted bids by the 1918 deadline: one led by English Liberal politician, Sir Robert Perks, who served as the front man for Poels and Brewster, beef importers at Smithfield market; the Compañía Agraria del Caribe, composed of prominent estate and cattle owners from the Colombian interior; and the Colombian Products Company, a joint venture between four ranching operations from the Caribbean coast and the US-based International Products Company, with large-scale cattle and forest interests in Paraguay.[18]

Despite the lingering anti-Americanism over the loss of Panama, the CPC won the concession. Backed by foreign capital already in the meatpacking business and by prominent ranchers from the Caribbean coast, the government thought that the CPC had more organizational capacity than the Colombian-owned Compañía Agraria del Caribe.[19] The CPC also promised to complete construction within two years, a time line that Perks was unwilling to commit to, given the wartime restrictions on the export of capital from the United Kingdom. Additionally, the CPC offered to build a plant with twice the required capacity and volunteered to match any offers to accept fewer subsidies, which the Perks group had reduced from a total of £100,000 to £30,000. The company declared that it would build its plant at Coveñas, on the southern edge of the Gulf of Morrosquilla and about 110 kilometers southwest of Cartagena.

Construction problems plagued the CPC from the start. Although it intended to begin construction one month after signing a contract with the Colombian government, wartime constraints on the export of capital and materials from the United States prevented the CPC from breaking ground for over a year. The company then ran into shipping delays because of labor struggles in the United States and had trouble recruiting workers in Colombia. The delays forced the CPC to request extensions from the Colombian government.[20] There was pressure within Colombia to declare the contract void, but other than the forfeiture of a bond equivalent to about US$5,000, the government had not made provisions for noncompliance. Because it could not retroactively collect customs duties on imported construction materials and machinery, and it would lose the power to oblige the CPC to export all of its product and to make long-term, low-interest loans to local ranchers, the government felt compelled to grant the extensions.[21] It was not until December 1923 that the company's American engineers and some seven hundred workers finally finished building a modern meatpacking facility with the capacity to slaughter 9,000 cattle per month, cold storage for 6,000 carcasses, and a 1,900-foot wharf complete with railway line.[22]

Despite completing the plant, the CPC did not begin operations in 1924. A year later, 'reliable sources' told Lester Schnare, the US consul in Cartagena, that the company would start producing frozen carcasses in July.[23] The following year, Schnare's 'best available sources' indicated a probable start date in September 1926.[24] September came and went, and the slaughterhouse remained silent. The plant's archival trail then peters out, presumably as its supporters admitted that it was a lost cause. By 1938, at the end of its 20-year contract, the CPC was finally dissolved.[25] For some years, the company had shipped live cattle to Mexico and Peru, but it never exported beef carcasses.

Various theories circulated to explain the failure. The CPC initially blamed the construction delays. Others also noted the closure of the US market by protectionist tariffs in 1922. Some Colombians even suggested that it was a conniving plan by the International Products Company to prevent Colombian cattle from competing against their Paraguayan operation.[26] The immediate cause, however, was the global market situation: beef prices collapsed because of the postwar depression (1920–1921) and the projected supply shortfalls never materialized, partly because Argentine beef exports, by far the world's largest, kept growing.[27] But the fundamental problem was that Colombian cattle were not competitive on the international market. When the plant was ready to operate, the CPC sent samples to buyers around Europe. English importers graded them poorly, the equivalent to second-class frozen carcasses from Australia; neither they nor the Germans expressed much interest. The Italians, who could not afford to be so discerning, offered to buy five hundred tons monthly. But the price they offered, the equivalent of about $32 pesos per steer, would have caused the CPC to lose money.[28] Meanwhile, Fernando Vélez, the company's president, noted that the CPC could sell live animals in Mexico and Peru for $40 pesos per head.[29] And ranchers who fattened cattle in Bolívar were getting up to $46 pesos for their cattle in the Medellín (Antioquia) market. So long as 'second-class' cattle sold for 8¢ per kilogram in Colombia, compared to 6.8¢ per kilogram for the best Creole-European crosses in Argentina and Uruguay, Vélez said, "it is obvious that the packing-house cannot start operating yet."[30]

Two interrelated problems undermined the competitiveness of Colombian beef: breed and age. Colombian cattle were descendants of the original stock brought to the country by the Spanish at the beginning of the colonial period. Cunninghame Graham remarked that, for range cattle, they fattened relatively well and yielded a good proportion of meat. For these reasons, Cuban buyers at the turn of the century paid a small premium for Colombian cattle over Mexican and Central American animals. But they were still Creole range cattle, with lean, stringy meat and heavy on the less valuable cuts from the forequarters. That their meat was inferior in both quality and yield to the European breeds or even the Creole-European crosses raised in Argentina was primarily due to genetics. English breeders had created animals that produced tender meat interlaced with fat deposits and had proportionally larger hindquarters, where the most valuable cuts are located. They also dramatically lowered the time it took these breeds to reach maturity, both increasing the productivity of meat production and creating more tender and more valuable beef. In 1924, Lester Schnare noted that in Argentina, with their English breeds and alfalfa pastures, "a grower can produce in the same length of time thrice the quantity of beef, sell it at a lower price per pound, and realize more than double the amount of money, as compared to a grower in this district."[31] Although he expected European markets to improve in the future,

> it does not appear possible that the cattle rearing industry can be of constant and permanent value to Colombia or become a competitor in the world's markets for packed meats and live cattle until radical changes shall have been made in the care and treatment of cattle and the herds shall have been greatly improved by large importations of blooded cattle and careful breeding.[32]

The radical transformation that Schnare envisioned never came, although a very different one, based on the diffusion of zebu blood, had already begun. In fact, instead of becoming a prominent beef exporter just the opposite occurred. By 1926, rising domestic demand turned Colombia into an importer of thin cattle from the *llanos* or plains of Venezuela. The CPC foundered on misplaced expectations common to the development of resource frontiers: that local demand was negligible and that global scarcity alone would ensure their success.

IMAGES AND REALITIES OF TROPICAL RANCHING

Given the spectacular failure of the CPC, as well as Colombian ranchers to satisfy even domestic demand by the mid-1920s, what accounts for the prior optimism? Why did so many people believe that Colombia could duplicate Argentina's success as the world's largest beef exporter? The answer, I suggest, lies in the way inherited ideas of tropical fecundity fused with a speculative urgency.

From Europeans' early encounters, the trope of earthly paradise has shaped their image and understanding of the region that they later defined as the tropics. Bathed by the sun and perpetual warmth, blessed with exuberant and varied vegetation, these were lovely and sweet-smelling lands, similar, no doubt, to the Garden of Eden. Nature was benevolent there: crops grew effortlessly, fruit ripened year round, and one's few wants were easily satisfied. By the eighteenth century, " 'a full-fledged myth of tropical exuberance' had become established in Europe."[33] A key figure in the construction and propagation of this image, especially for Latin America, was Alexander von Humboldt.[34] His assessment of the natural abundance and surprisingly fertile soils of the tropics indicated their potential value. The wave of British investment in Latin America following the Wars of Independence was predicated on the belief that, by removing the shackles of Spanish colonialism, the natural riches of the region could be turned into a source of tremendous wealth. The economic boom never came, leaving much of the continent mired in debt, but the expectations did not die down. The fervor of mid-century liberalism was driven by similar ideas, only now couched more in the language of comparative advantage. They also became integrated into foundational myths, promulgating a streak of optimism about latent national destiny.[35]

In Colombia, the postcolonial economy finally started to revive in the late-1840s as the country found North Atlantic markets for a series of (quasi) tropical commodities. These export booms, however brief, served to reorient the interest of many Colombian elites from staid professional activities in the old colonial centers to the potential riches that were possible by exporting tropical commodities. Given that many of these elites had to leave the comforts of the capital and brave the primitive conditions and adversities of the lowlands, they stressed their own heroic efforts to make a tropical wasteland productive.[36] Such views parallel long-standing European perceptions of the tropics as inhospitable and disease-ridden. As David Arnold notes, "Whether naturalists found the forests of Amazonia grand or gloomy, they understood them to be an obstacle to progress and the advance of civilization."[37] To unlock their riches, both Europeans and Colombian elites emphasized the need to domesticate the environment, deploy the emerging field of tropical medicine to render it safe, and maintain their own moral fiber in face of the threat of degeneration. These challenges, however, did not undermine the persistent belief in the country's unrivaled fertility.

This inherited faith in the natural exuberance of the tropics generated much of the optimism that Colombia could become a prominent beef exporter. Discussions about the packinghouse project repeatedly refer to the fertility of the country's soils and its rich forage base. Cunninghame Graham described the vegetation of the coastal plains as 'very luxuriant' with guinea and pará grasses quickly growing over two and four feet respectively.[38] "This is quite one of the finest cattle countries in the world," he wrote, "and it would be a sin to lose such an opportunity."[39] Utah rancher Lester Magnum was convinced that the extensive property he managed south of Mompós could be made into the most productive cattle operation in the world.[40] Lloyd Owen suggested that the millions of acres of 'splendidly watered' savannahs gently rising to the foothills of the Andes were just waiting for an export outlet to fill with cattle.[41] Dávila Flórez claimed that the 'very fertile' soils, on which new pastures of 'superior quality grasses' could easily be established, would allow the regional herd to grow five-fold without exhausting the productive base.[42] Luis Montoya extolled "that nature herself has indicated the cattle industry, for the quality of the land, the abundance of water, the environmental conditions, to be at the center of our economic upsurge."[43] M. T. Dawe, British agricultural advisor to the Colombian government, concurred: "If half of what I've been told regarding the resources and facilities to raise cattle on the Coast is true, Colombia is destined to be a second Argentina."[44]

This optimism was also generated by investor anticipation and anxiety, both typical of the speculative mentality associated with the development of resource frontiers.[45] The reports highlighting Colombia's cheap rangeland, prolific grasses, and promising environment were remarkably vague and anecdotal given the substantial sums to be invested. While they constructed the image of valuable resources waiting to be tapped, it was also the expectation of future scarcity and knowledge of prior beef fortunes that made for a compelling story. The wealth generated running cattle on the free grass of the Western United States following the Civil War, the economic might of Chicago's Big Four, and the sensational rise of Argentina's beef exports intensified the sense of urgency: get in before prices rose and the best lands were taken. Doubts about whether the cattle population of the Caribbean region was large enough to support the packing plant were easily dismissed. And Cunninghame Graham's comment that Colombian beef was "good and juicy" seemed to satisfy the concern of the Perks group about its quality and eventual market price.[46]

Contrary to the frequent emphasis on northern perceptions of the tropics, much of the optimism about Colombia's ranching potential was generated locally. There has been some effort to correct this Eurocentric bias within the notion of Tropicality by incorporating subaltern voices, although the shift sometimes just casts local actors in supporting roles, missing both the way such discourses circulate within tropical regions and how people from the tropics helped shape northern impressions.[47] European views, particularly those advanced by Humboldt, encouraged Colombians to imagine the unlocked potential of their tropical environment. But later, as Europeans and Americans began investigating the possibilities of raising cattle for export in Colombia, local perceptions and faith in tropical fecundity influenced their assessments. Although Cunninghame Graham spent a couple of months in Colombia, he gleaned much of what he reported by talking to local ranchers. While he could speak directly to the quality of Colombian beef or the calm disposition of the cattle, he could judge the prospects and challenges of cattle raising primarily from the information that ranchers provided him. M. T. Dawe was even more explicit when he qualified his prediction that Colombia could become a second Argentina on the veracity of what he had been *told*. In turn, however, the statements of foreign experts served to reconfirm local views and hopes. At times this circuit of recycled images appears to have been consciously manipulated. For example, it is likely that newspaper editor Joseph E. Chamberlin received information about the favorable outlook for raising cattle in Colombia from the Colombian Information Bureau, a New York office set up by the Colombian government to promote commercial ties. The Bureau then quoted Chamberlin in an article that it published to generate foreign interest and investment in Colombian ranching.[48]

Whatever its origin, supporter's faith in the productive potential of Colombia's coastal plains ran headlong into the challenging realities of tropical ranching. While Colombia's Caribbean coast has decent alluvial soils, contra Lloyd Owen and Dawe, there were not millions of acres of prime savanna land just waiting to be grazed. Most of the unused land was covered by forest, which first had to be cleared and planted in pasture. While undeveloped land could be acquired relatively cheaply, it cost a good deal to make it productive. And although the grasses did grow quickly in the tropical conditions, this was a problem as much as a blessing. Their prolific growth helped ranchers conquer the forest, but it also caused their protein content to decline quickly. This was exacerbated by the predominance of large, continuously grazed pastures and a mistaken belief that favored forage quantity over quality. Thus, while some of the difficulties of ranching in the tropics were self-imposed, tropical grasses tend to be less nutritious than their temperate counterparts.[49]

Furthermore, the limits to Colombia's competiveness had more to do with its cattle than its forage base. The European breeds on which the Argentine industry was based fared poorly in the tropical conditions of the Colombian lowlands. Disease, pests, and parasites represented an important obstacle. Range management did not help matters either. But a primary obstacle was simply the heat of Colombia's coastal plains where daytime temperatures average about 32 degrees Celsius year round and do not drop significantly at night. Such heat levels are a problem for most European breeds, which have a solid layer of subcutaneous fat that helps keep them warm through cold winters but causes them to overheat in the tropics. By contrast, this layer of fat is discontinuous in Creole cattle, facilitating the escape of body heat; and zebu lay on fat between their muscles rather than under the skin. Improved European breeds were also bred to digest forage efficiently. In the tropics, however, their high metabolism rate is a disadvantage since it increases their internal body temperature, especially given the coarse quality of tropical grasses. To compensate, they not only seek shade and reduce their movements but also eat less. As a result, European cattle in the tropics tend to grow more slowly and breed less frequently than in temperate regions. Heat-suppressed appetites lower their resistance to disease and parasites, which is further exacerbated by their comparatively thin hides. And they tend to acquire larger heads, thicker necks, and stunted loins and rumps after several generations. In other words, in the hot tropics, European breeds lose many of the qualities for which they were originally bred and introduced. Colombians were not the only ones who experienced such problems: North American and European ranchers did no better in Colombia or elsewhere in the tropics. "That many types of livestock originating in the Northern Hemisphere do not thrive in tropical and subtropical environments can no longer be denied," concluded South African cattle expert Jan Bonsma in 1955.[50]

Colombian ranchers did introduce some European cattle, but the scale of such imports paled in comparison to those of Argentina. By 1895, close to one third of the cattle on its Pampas region were European breeds or crosses, and in the early 1920s, Argentine ranchers imported up to 150,000 pure-breds from the United States and Europe annually.[51] By contrast, Colombian ranchers imported less than one hundred purebred cattle per year during the 1920s, and over half of these were dairy breeds destined for the highlands.[52] As a result, they had to rely on autochthonous breeds that, though well adapted to the rigors of the tropics, grew and multiplied slowly. Reaching maturity at four to five years, their meat was already too tough for better European markets. And the slow turnover of capital—in both animal and grass—raised production costs despite the seemingly cheap land. While it took Colombian ranchers about five years to produce a steer that yielded 250 kilograms of meat, their Argentine counterparts could raise a steer in two-and-a-half years that yielded 340 kilograms of better quality beef.[53] The CPC was thus squeezed between the relatively high cost of Colombian cattle and the relatively low quality of its beef.[54]

REIMAGINING TROPICAL RANCHING

In the wake of the packing plant fiasco, disillusionment with the country's tropical environment set in. The rich forage base that boosters once empha-sized withered into nutritionally deficient grasses. "[O]ne of the obstacles to the improvement of ranching in these [tropical lowlands] is the poor and unvaried food," remarked the head of the National Livestock Depart-ment in 1930.[55] Similarly, the natural fertility of the soil became eclipsed by its mineral deficiencies. Instead of the 'unimprovable quality' of native breeds, as noted by a congressional commission in 1915, officials com-plained about their 'inferior characteristics,' "the outcome of the feed and environmental conditions."[56] Manuel Gómez Rueda, head of the National Livestock Department, warned that "the heat, humidity, lack of seasons . . . and other tropical characteristics make our environment very favorable for the development of a great variety of parasitisms . . . which [if they] don't always immediately kill the organism [cattle] . . . they do annihilate its development."[57] Whereas many people believed that livestock diseases were of minor importance through the early-1920s, by the following decade they threatened to "ruin the livestock industry."[58] Rather than a source of comparative advantage, government officials had to admit that "ranching in tropical regions is difficult due to the inherent environmental conditions."[59]

Government officials and industry boosters, however, believed that it was possible to transform the environment by adopting modern man-agement practices. Although little was known about tropical ranching at the time, they scoured foreign livestock journals and initiated research on local conditions as the basis of their recommendations. To counteract the soil deficiencies, they promoted the use of mineralized salts. To improve diets, they encouraged ranchers to grow a variety of grasses and to propagate, rather than remove, the spontaneously growing legumes in their pastures. To combat pests and disease, the government began subsidizing the construction of tick-dipping tanks and requiring that cattle be vaccinated against a number of diseases. Officials extolled the virtues of "technical and scientific care and management" through government publications, radio shows, and state veterinarians.[60] While such practices promised to raise productivity levels, they were also said to minimize the environmental hurdles to importing European breeds, which the government had begun to subsidize. Only by upgrading the cattle population, officials argued, could Colombia become a prominent beef exporter. But even just attending to the rapidly growing home market required domesticating the tropics through the application of the latest scientific principles.

By promoting scientific authority at the cost of traditional knowledge and local autonomy, these recommendations form part of a much broader tendency in the history of efforts to develop the tropics. In this case, however, modernizers directed their contempt at one of the country's most powerful groups. "The transformation of the environment," complained Washington Bernal, "depends on the preparation of the human element, and among us this makes it very difficult, especially in the lowlands."[61] Annoyed at the slow pace of progress, government officials blamed ranchers for failing to adopt their suggestions: most cattle estates still lacked orderly management plans, the pastures remained impoverished, and cattle fended for themselves. Ranchers were also said to ignore the "laws of diet, inheritance, zootechny and the environment," and only halfheartedly participated in the government's pest and disease eradication campaigns.[62] Not only do we have to deal with "the prejudices of the masses," complained Guillermo Londoño, Minister of Agriculture and Commerce, but we also have to struggle "against the inexplicable resistance of landowners of the most elevated social position, [yet] no less reticent to scientific initiatives."[63] Instead of improving, the cattle industry remained mired in "backwardness and routine."[64]

In their frustration, officials began to associate ranching with nature and extraction more than with labor and production. They described ranchers as 'empirical' rather than scientific or progressive, and derided them for relying on nature's bounty rather than attempting to transform their tropical environment. "Ranchers simply use cattle to take advantage of natural grasslands," despaired Manuel Gómez Rueda. "The bull works alone and then the ranchers round up the offspring, count, brand, and capitalize the result."[65] They likened ranchers to nature-based rentiers in a world where the new mantra had become "produce more cheaply."[66] For this reason, Raúl Varela, director of the Division of Rural Economy in the Ministry of Agriculture, lamented the lack of "real ranchers or real ranching."[67] While critiques of ranching were not entirely new, they gathered force in the wake of the packing plant fiasco.

The image of retrograde ranchers also fed into the growing critique of the *latifundio* in Colombia. This also has old roots that gathered momentum in the 1920s and '30s. By then, the conflicts over the settlement of the agrarian frontier had intensified. Many municipalities reported that cattle ranchers often occupied all or most of their public lands. And laws designed to protect peasant settlers, such as granting them squatting rights and excluding their holdings from subsequent adjudications, were often flaunted in practice. To make matters worse, the requirement that frontier lands be made productive in order to establish property rights, generally by converting forest to pasture, was only marginally successful, as many large cattle estates remained only partially developed. As peasants clamored for access to land, as the state lost control of its agrarian frontier, and as rising domestic demand forced up food prices, the problem of the *latifundio* acquired greater significance.[68] Social critic, Alejandro López, identified ranching as the source of many of the country's problems. Raising cattle, he argued, was socially unproductive: low labor demands failed to generate employment and stymied regional development, which depended on a denser population and a more equitable land tenure structure.[69] Critiques of this sort spurred the Minister of Industries to defend ranching from this 'national hyperesthesia.' While cattle ranches monopolized large parts of the countryside, he wrote, "it is an absolute error to believe, as some have been preaching, that ranching, instead of a source of wealth, is a cause of impoverishment."[70] But in the early 1930s, momentum was temporarily against ranchers and other landed elites as President López Pumarejo, however timidly, pushed through the country's first attempt at land reform.

RACE AND NATION

The reevaluation of the tropics and Colombia's ranching potential also intersected with concern for the future of the nation. Like their counterparts throughout Latin America, Colombian elites worried about the country's racial makeup. They imagined that the predominantly indigenous, black, and racially mixed roots of the masses that formed the bulk of the population were decidedly inferior. What's more, many also believed, like psychologist Miguel Jiménez López, that "all the races that comprise our current population were once superior to what they are today."[71] Signs of this racial degeneration included small stature, cranial deformations, physical weakness, reproductive abnormalities, sickness, imbecility, and childish temperaments.[72] How could they hope to build a strong, modern nation state with such a weak and ignorant population? "With racial mediocrity," and "biological forces barely sufficient to vegetate," lamented Laurentino Muñoz in *The Biological Tragedy of the Colombian People*, "we will never achieve prosperity or civilization."[73]

Yet Colombian elites tended to reject the scientific discourses emanating from the United States and Europe that essentialized racial characteristics and defined a country's potential in terms of the genetic composition of its people or, for that matter, its environmental conditions.[74] Abiding by such theories meant that the path to progress was effectively closed, because local populations were not up to the task. Unable to face such dismal prospects, and steeped in the Lamarkian tradition, Colombian elites held out for the possibility of racial transformation.

There were three main avenues through which elites hoped to improve the racial character of the masses and set the nation on the path toward modernity.[75] The first was by crossbreeding. "The radical cure for our decadence," wrote Jímenez López, is "a good and large [wave of] immigration."[76] By good he meant white, preferably from Northern Europe. Not only would they bring skills and strong work habits but, contrary to European fears that racial mixing necessarily led to degeneration, many Colombian elites believed that white blood was inherently dominant and that miscegenation would lead to a 'whitening' of the citizenry. The second strategy was to cleanse the environment of degenerating and debilitating influences. Acclimatization debates demonstrated that Europeans and Americans could not flourish in the tropics: They too suffered from the heat, parasites, diseases, and low morality.[77] Therefore, environmental rather than just racial characteristics were part of the problem. One solution to the poor health, vitality, and behavior of the Colombian people was to promote hygienic conditions and practices. "To govern is to sanitize," affirmed future president, Mariano Ospina Pérez.[78] The third path was dietary improvement.[79] The "deficient diet of our working class," wrote Pablo García, "should lead us to reflect on the dire consequences that this has not only on the individual and collective health but on the future of the race."[80] Protein intake appeared particularly deficient, so increasing it was a direct way to invigorate the masses. While Mexican elites encouraged the masses to consume wheat rather than corn because they assumed it contained more protein, in Colombia experts promoted the consumption of meat, especially beef.[81] For instance, Carlos Michelsen, author of the first Colombian text on nutrition, claimed that "the size, power, strength, and morality of well-managed nations develop in direct proportion to the consumption of beef."[82] Within Colombia, García compared the "weak, anemic, and lazy" highlanders, who ate little meat, to the virility of the *llaneros* or inhabitants of the Eastern plains, who consumed lots of beef.[83]

The Beef Question was therefore not just about establishing an export industry; it also addressed the issue of insufficient domestic consumption. The problem was that much of the population could afford to eat meat only occasionally. To encourage beef consumption, the government tried to increase cattle stocks by periodically banning the slaughter of reproductive-age cows. More important were its efforts to improve the productivity of ranching. Ranchers, it argued, needed to produce more and cheaper beef, and the most promising strategy was to 'sanitize' the tropical environment, making it safe for the introduction of fast-maturing European breeds. In other words, the future of the nation depended, to a significant degree, on the 'racial' composition of its cattle.

The problem was that most ranchers were more interested in crossing their animals with zebu rather than European breeds. Over the years, a number of ranchers attempted to upgrade their herds with European animals, but, outside of the highlands, the results were generally disheartening: They required an inordinate amount of care, performed poorly or died, and did little for the long-term improvement of Colombian cattle. By contrast, ranchers were enthusiastic about the results of crossbreeding with zebu. Given its origins on the Indian subcontinent, the zebu is well adapted to tropical environments and poor forage. A wide range of physiological adaptations—from lower basal temperatures and metabolic rates to various properties of it skin and cells—help it avoid overheating under the tropical sun. A thick hide, which it can shake vigorously, helps it resist pests and the transmission of insect-borne diseases.[84] Furthermore, because the zebu (*Bos indicus*) is a different species from Colombia's 'native' cattle (*Bos taurus*), crossing the two took advantage of heterostasis, or hybrid vigor, in which the offspring tend to grow faster and larger than their parents.

Colombian ranchers were fairly quick to recognize the advantage of upgrading their herds with zebu. The Eder family imported the first zebu bull in 1901 for its Cauca Valley sugar plantation. In line with the initial global diffusion of zebu to Jamaican or South African sugar plantations and Brazilian coffee estates, their main interest was producing strong draft animals. It was only in 1914, however, that a second zebu bull was imported with an eye to improving Colombia's beef cattle. The previous efforts of Adolfo Held, the German merchant-turned-rancher, to improve his cattle by introducing European beef breeds had failed. So he asked the Hamburg commercial house of Carl Hagenbeck, the dealer in exotic animals to Europe's zoos and circuses, for advice. Hagenbeck recommended the zebu, which had worked well for the French in Algeria.[85] The results proved promising and Held later imported more zebu bulls, and a few cows, from Texas, Brazil, and even India. Other ranchers, following the success of Held and colonial breeding programs in the Caribbean, also began to import zebu from Jamaica and Trinidad. But despite these connections between Colombia and European or colonial circuits of knowledge production and animal distribution, it was in fact Brazil that quickly became the most important zebu breeder and booster outside of Asia. Between 1890 and 1921, Brazilian ranchers imported over five thousand zebu cattle; and by the late 1930s, there are estimates that half the national herd, some 22 million head, was composed of zebu crosses.[86] Colombian imports of zebu cattle were on a much smaller scale, but the popularity of their offspring nonetheless spread rapidly among lowland ranchers. By 1938, veterinarian Carlos Alberto Rojas noted that "All the ranchers of the hot and temperate lands [below

2000 meters] show themselves to be partisan to the zebu breed, and have dedicated themselves to breeding and rebreeding it, obtaining a mixture that almost never goes above ½ zebu blood."[87]

The diffusion of zebu was anathema to ranching modernizers. Some of their concerns were practical. Following European and American critics, they warned that zebu meat was tough and insipid.[88] If Colombian ranchers retained any hope of breaking into European markets, then they needed to avoid the zebu at all costs. In addition to being difficult to handle and poorly shaped, the zebu was said to grow slowly, a poor choice for a nation looking to lower the cost of beef production. Zebu cows also produced little milk, which discouraged people who had begun to envision the dairy industry as a cheap, alternative source of protein. Furthermore, officials feared that zebu would prove a vector for the introduction of cattle diseases. Precedents elsewhere had them on alert: In 1906, zebu imported from India to the United States were found to have surra; and in 1921, Brazil banned further imports of zebu (until 1930) following the introduction of rinderpest.[89] Given the weakness of the Colombian state, and "the still deficient livestock sanitary stations," explained Fidel Ochoa, head of the National Livestock Department, "what hope do we have left" other than outright prohibition?[90] Following an outbreak of trypanosomiasis in 1931, which was traced back to the importation of cattle, including a number of zebu, from Venezuela, the government banned further imports of zebu into Colombia.[91]

But much of the concern about the zebu appears to have been more ideological than practical. For instance, it was not clear whether it was zebu or *criollo* cattle that arrived infected from Venezuela. By contrast, the introduction of brucellosis along with European dairy cows did not generate campaigns to ban the importation of European breeds. While the admirable qualities of a Hereford or Angus represented a shining beacon of modernity and human prowess, critics thought that the zebu was shaped by nature rather than by people. Antonio Zapata called it a "wild animal," emphasizing its otherness with respect to domesticated cattle.[92] Its Indian origin—even more tropical than Colombia—elicited fears of dangerous, exotic diseases and degenerating influences. As with human immigrants, there was concern about the wrong kind of miscegenation.[93] Because zebu attributes were thought to dominate, crossbreeding threatened to eliminate any admirable traits that native breeds might possess. European blood could improve Colombian cattle, but the zebu's would cause them to degenerate.

Furthermore, the relatively rapid diffusion of the zebu was symptomatic of the backwardness of Colombian ranching. To veterinarians and government officials, ranchers preferred zebu because changing the animal to fit the environment was easier than transforming the environment or their own ranching practices. While modernizing boosters were well aware that European breeds needed more care, that was partly the point. Successfully introducing specialized beef breeds required ranchers to combat ticks and pests through chemical dipping and pasture rotation, to drain swampy land

and provide access to clean water, to improve their forage base, rationalize pasture management, use supplemental feed, and provide more attentive care. In other words, they needed to make the environment hospitable to these more demanding breeds of cattle. Thus the modernization of ranching and the domestication of the tropics went hand in hand. By contrast, the diffusion of zebu represented the renunciation of both such efforts. "It is an error to believe," Zapata complained,

> that ranching on the [Caribbean] coast can be improved by developing it extensively and carelessly. In this, many ranchers from Bolívar are mistaken, and for this reason they are inclined to mix their herds with zebu, in order to make their cattle more resistant and to care for them as little as possible.[94]

Thus while there were some legitimate concerns about the introduction of zebu into Colombia, issues such as disease and meat quality were invariably seen through the prism of such larger debates about race and progress.[95]

Although ranching modernizers hoped that, with the zebu ban in place, they could promote the Europeanization of Colombia's cattle population, by the late-1930s they had to concede defeat. As ranchers previously recognized, most acclimatization efforts ended badly and upgrading the national herd in this manner was unrealistic. Industry modernizers regrouped, but they did not rehabilitate the zebu. Instead, perhaps paralleling the rise of *mestizo* nationalism, they began to reevaluate the qualities and potential of Colombia's native cattle. One veterinarian suggested that, "If we give our creole breeds the kind of feed and care they need to survive in our environment, many of their physical deficiencies will largely disappear, and this new breed (now sick, degenerated, and malnourished) will move into the high ranks of those exported."[96] As part of this shift, the government opened various breeding farms around the country to begin the work of improving Colombian cattle through selection rather than crossbreeding. They still urged ranchers to provide better care, but because local breeds were hardy, the chances of success seemed greater.

This shift in emphasis did not diminish the frustration of many ranchers and even some officials who increasingly pressured the government to lift the ban on zebu imports. By the late 1930s, a couple of factors were in their favor. First, zebu had gained greater acceptance internationally. Veterinary experts from the United States and Europe, in addition to Brazil, increasingly supported the use of zebu to improve (sub)tropical cattle operations. Consumers also demonstrated that they were willing to buy zebu beef, giving its proponents in Colombia more credibility. Additionally, the concerted effort of ranchers and livestock scientists to improve zebu breeds and crosses made it harder to argue that they were simply the product of nature. Second, the earlier fears of degeneration had to contend with the actual results that ranchers obtained by using zebu to upgrade their herds. Early data from Colombia is hard to find, but a study carried out by a Brazilian experimental station allowed one booster to argue that because zebu-creole crosses resisted tropical parasites better than creole steer, by 24 months the former were 170 percent larger. With such impressive, zebu-based productivity gains, he projected that "we could start to export this article."[97] As a result of such evidence, growing pressure, and the de facto diffusion of zebu blood through Colombia, in 1939 the government rescinded the prohibition on importing zebu.

By the early 1950s, most cattle in the lowlands were zebu-creole crosses.[98] The Zebu Question did not disappear, however. Instead it metamorphosed into a debate about the most appropriate way to utilize the animal. Underlying the dispute was the persistent effort to improve the productivity of Colombian ranching and lower the cost of beef for a rapidly growing population.[99] (Dreams of becoming a prominent beef exporter were put on hold following the introduction of foot-and-mouth disease in 1950.) Some veterinarians maintained that the best results were obtained by crossing zebu with native breeds in order to take advantage of hybrid vigor. But this strategy required ranchers to maintain two separate 'lines' of cattle, something that most were reluctant to do. Instead, they chose to improve their herds by adding progressively greater amounts of zebu blood. Behind this 'zebuization' drive was a new image of what was considered progressive and modern—the large zebu bull—fostered by breeders and the growing influence of livestock shows. As Colombian ranchers neglected the country's native breeds, government livestock stations, originally designed only to improve them through selective breeding, soon became one of the few remaining repositories of an increasingly endangered genetic stock. By 1976, 95 percent of Colombia's beef herd was predominately zebu, and less than a quarter century later, only 1,522 *Costeño con cuernos*, the native breed of Colombia's Caribbean lowlands, remained.[100] The genetic transformation of the Colombian cattle herd was essentially complete.

CONCLUSIONS

How does the failure of the meatpacking plant at Coveñas and debates about the genetic transformation of Colombia's cattle herd help us think about the broad issue of trade and the environment? One aspect highlights the relationship between environmental knowledge and commercial success. The development of resource frontiers requires more than just paying attention to market demand or production techniques; it also necessitates understanding local ecologies. In this case, however, investors were willing to risk significant capital on a project about which they had only superficial information. Merchants and capitalists commoditize and transform nature as they draw resources into global circuits of trade, but their investment decisions can be influenced by preconceptions about the environment, the material properties of commodities, methods of production and extraction, and so on. Recycled notions about the productive potential of the tropics substituted for meager market research. Blinkered by the allure of fertile soils, luxuriant grasses, and cheap, undeveloped land, the packinghouse at Coveñas fell prey to the long-standing myth of El Dorado or the hope of finding hidden treasures in a lush landscape.

In addition, the context of impending scarcity generated an equally crucial speculative urgency. The outlook for global demand of beef appeared solid and meatpacking, in the early-twentieth century, was a leading industrial sector where vast fortunes had been made. There was also an interest, especially by the British, who were being displaced from control of the Argentine trade by American meatpackers, in developing commercial ties that would ensure a steady flow of carcasses to domestic butchers. The nature of many frontier resources, including beef—their finite supply, uneven quality, limited accessibility—meant that the window of opportunity could shut quickly: the best lands could be taken, the cost of raw materials might rise, competitors could be faster to grab market share. As a result, limited information had to suffice, and doubts about the size of Colombia's cattle herd, the quality of its rangelands, or the productive potential of the tropics more generally fell by the wayside.

The failure of the packinghouse encouraged a radical shift in perceptions about the Colombian tropics and the potential of its cattle industry. In some ways, however, this move from buoyancy to gloom was restrained. On the one hand, the negative characterizations of the tropics and the proposed methods of overcoming their challenges were also based on limited information and excessive optimism. On the other, the seemingly opposed views about the prospects for tropical ranching fit neatly within the Janus-faced pattern by which Europeans described the tropics either as a garden of earthly delights or as putrid, pestilential, and unruly. Such contradictory portraits, according to Arnold, "were a potent form of othering"; they marked off the tropics as fundamentally distinct from "the perceived normality of the northern temperate zone."[101] Such projected differences lay at the heart of how Europe, or America, understood the tropics and justified their colonial and commercial interventions. While much of the scholarship on Tropicality has focused on the production of images and knowledge about the tropics by travel writers, artists, scientists, and colonial officials, the concept also serves to explore the attitudes and actions of northern investors looking to develop new resource frontiers.

At the same time, the Coveñas packinghouse fiasco and its repercussions highlight some of the limits to Tropicality's Eurocentric origins. While there have been calls to pay "greater attention to the ways in which European conceptions of the tropics may have been shaped by interactions with indigenous peoples and places," the results are still limited and tend to privilege northern agency.[102] In this case, European and American assessments of the potential of Colombian ranching relied on the experience and perceptions of local ranchers and officials. Ultimately, though, the traffic in ideas was circular: The perceptions that Colombians had of their tropical environment drew on, and were reinforced by, the European impressions that they had helped shape.

More significantly, the circulation of ideas about the tropics did not just move between Colombia and temperate latitudes; much of it occurred within the country. In this sense, the discourse of Tropicality was more than a way for the North to frame, incorporate, and perhaps dominate the South; it also responded to hopes, concerns, and debates within the tropics themselves. Faith in the bright prospects of Colombian ranching generated considerable investment by locals, not just foreigners, forcing cattle prices up significantly and leading to a wave of bankruptcies when they later collapsed. Government officials took advantage of the negative perception of the tropics, and the solutions offered by modern science, to promote the role and authority of a weak but growing state. Such modernization efforts could threaten the power of landed elites, a twist that focusing on European images of the tropics might miss. This also holds for the way that local understandings of the tropics intersected with eugenics and veterinary science in a project of national regeneration. Fundamental to this project was a belief in the possibility of transformation: the faith that the tropics could be domesticated and the racial makeup of its population could be improved. At the same time, the emphasis on national projects hid the way that images of the tropics were internally differentiated in Colombia—what Michael Taussig calls the 'moral topography' of the nation—with the 'temperate' highlands, where wealth and power were concentrated, counterposed to the dangers and disorder of the 'tropical' lowlands.[103] In turn, such geographic differentiation facilitated the intertropical prejudices that surfaced with the perceived threat of 'racial' degeneration of the country's cattle herd by Indian zebu.

The issues of agency and scale also surface with respect to trade. While the wheels of commerce transform landscapes by drawing new regions into their sphere of orbit, this case helps qualify the tendency to emphasize North Atlantic capital, markets, science, and boosters as the driving forces behind such metamorphoses. The effort to extend the North Atlantic beef frontier to Colombia was not just the result of foreign capital searching for new resources; local elites also pushed hard to develop such linkages. Although colonial veterinary science helped promote zebu in Colombia, firsthand experimentation by local ranchers played a leading role. In the end, it was the domestic market, not international trade, that generated much of the debate about the tropics as well as their actual transformation. The failure of the meatpacking plant at Coveñas did not eliminate cattle from the Caribbean lowlands from wider circuits of trade. Some were exported to neighboring countries, where the lack of cold chains helped to maintain the regional segmentation of global markets, but most made their way to the main population centers in the interior of the country. It was this domestic trade that kept prices high, diverting potential surpluses from foreign markets, that encouraged ranchers to clear pastures out of the tropical forests and that stimulated the genetic transformation of the country's cattle.

Lastly, while recycled notions about the productive potential of Colombia's Caribbean coast, as well as the power of modern science, fostered a false sense of optimism, ultimately it was the intractability of the tropics themselves that doomed the projects. Nature is not necessarily the ultimate arbiter. By planting African grasses, introducing new breeds, constructing tick-dipping tanks, and the like, Colombian ranchers managed to increase the productivity of the cattle industry.[104] Nonetheless, the failure of the meatpacking plant was rooted more in natural than social factors. Given the cost of clearing the forest and planting grass, the only way that Colombian ranchers could have competed against Argentina or Australia was by introducing rapidly maturing European cattle breeds. Colombia's tropical environment, however, precluded this possibility. Such 'natural limits' have social roots—such as the belated efforts to improve native breeds, the paucity of research on tropical ranching, a poor state with inadequate veterinary and extension services—and can disappear over time. But during the time period I explore in this chapter, there was no way that ranchers could have radically altered their productive base. The tropics matter as an idea as well as a material reality.

NOTES

1   George K. Holmes, *Meat Situation in the United States. Part I. Statistics of Live Stock, Meat Production and Consumption, Prices, and International Trade for Many Countries* (Washington, DC: United States Department of Agriculture, 1916), 169–170.
2   Holmes, *Meat Situation*, 173–187; Albert W. Pearse, *The World's Meat Future* (New York: E.P. Dutton, 1920); Gary S. Dunbar, "African Ranches Ltd., 1914–1931: An ill-fated stock raising enterprise in northern Nigeria," *Annals of the Association of American Geographers* 60(1970): 102–123; I.R. Phimister, "Meat and monopolies: Beef cattle in southern Rhodesia, 1890–1938," *The Journal of African History* 19(1978): 391–414.
3   Quoted in Colombia Information Bureau, "The cattle industry in Colombia and its possibilities," *Bulletin of the Pan American Union* 40(1915): 198.
4   E. Lloyd-Owen, "Memorandum: RE: Cattle Business in the Republic of Colombia," Meat supplies: Cattle Resources of Colombia Report, 1917, 13/81, Records of the Board of Trade and successor and related bodies (BT), Public Records Office (PRO), The National Archives of the UK (London).
5   Robert Cunninghame Graham, "Meat Report, CG: A Short Report upon the Meat Resources of Colombia. Confidential," Nov. 1916, 13/81, BT, PRO.
6   Ministerio de Agricultura y Comercio, *Memoria del Ministro de Agricultura y Comercio al Congreso de 1917* (Bogotá: Imprenta Nacional, 1917), LXVIII.
7   Cited in Stefania Gallini, "El Atila del Ganges en la ganadería colombiana," *Nómadas* 22(2005): 189.
8   Cited in David Arnold, "'Illusory riches': Representations of the tropical world, 1840–1950, *Singapore Journal of Tropical Geography* 21(2000): 16.
9   David Arnold, *The Problem of Nature: Environment, Culture, and European Expansion* (Oxford: Blackwell, 1996), 141–168.

10 Felix Driver and Brenda Yeoh, "Constructing the tropics: Introduction," *Singapore Journal of Tropical Geography* 21(2000) 1–5; Felix Driver and Luciana Martins, *Tropical Visions in an Age of Empire* (Chicago: University of Chicago Press, 2005); Greg Bankoff, "First impressions: Diarists, scientists, imperialists and the management of the environment in the American Pacific, 1899–1902," *The Journal of Pacific History* 44(2009), 261–280; Gavin Bowd and Daniel Clayton, "Tropicality, Orientalism, and French colonialism in Indochina: The work of Pierre Gourou, 1927–1982," *French Historical Studies* 28(2005): 297–327; James Duncan, *In the Shadows of the Tropics: Climate, Race and Biopower in Nineteenth Century Ceylon* (Burlington, VT: Ashgate, 2007); Stephen Frenkel, "Jungle stories: North American representations of tropical Panama," *Geographical Review* 86(1996), 317–333; Nancy Leys Stepan, *Picturing Tropical Nature* (Ithaca, NY: Cornell University Press, 2001); Susie Protschky, *Images of the Tropics: Environment and Visual Culture in Colonial Indonesia* (Leiden: KITLV Press, 2011).
11 Holmes, *Meat Situation*, 170, 173.
12 Cited in Pearse, *The World's Meat*, 1.
13 These included the British and Argentine Meat Company, Smithfield and Argentine Meat Company, the Vesteys, International Cold Storage and Ice Company, Schwarzschild & Sulzberger, Swift, and Svenska Aktiebolaget. Swiss capital, which US officials feared was a cover for German interests, offered to back a group of Colombian investors. See Belden to SecState (Confidential), Dec 27, 1918, v. 215, 1918, Colombia, General Correspondence, Consular Records, Record Group (RG) 84, National Archive and Record Administration (NARA, College Park, MD).
14 Ministerio de Agricultura y Comercio, *Memoria 1917*, LXVII.
15 "Proyecto de ley por la cual se adiciona la número 21 sobre packing-houses [Ley 60]," f. 230, vol. V, Leyes Sancionadas, Senado, 1917, Archivo del Congreso (AC), Archivo General de la Nación (AGN, Bogotá).
16 "Ley 82 de 1915 por la cual se fomenta el establicimiento de carnicerías y refrigeradoras (Packing Houses) para la exportación de carnes," f. 355, vol. VI, Leyes Autografas, 1915, AC.
17 "Ley 82 de 1915," f. 355, AC; Ministerio de Agricultura y Comercio, *Memoria 1917*, LXIX.
18 Ministerio de Agricultura y Comercio, *Memoria del Ministro de Agricultura y Comercio al Congreso de 1918* (Bogotá: Imprenta Nacional, 1918), 173. For information on the Perks group, see "The meat trade: A new competitor enters the lists," *Manawatu Standard*, January 25, 1910, 2. For more information on the Compañía Agraria del Caribe, see "Colombia Packing Concessions", Sept 3, 1918, 1918/368/1894/151134, Foreign Office (FO), PRO. A large part of the International Products Company was owned by the American International Corporation and G.F. Sulzberger, Percival Farquhar, and Minor C. Keith served as vice-presidents. Its Colombian partner was Ganadería Colombiana, which was composed of Velez Danies & Co. and Diego Martínez & Co., each with a 40 percent share, and Julián Patrón and Caledonio Piñeres, each with ten percent. For more information on the International Products Company, see Belden to SecState, June 30, 1918, v. 215, 1918, Colombia, General Correspondence, Consular Records, RG 84, NARA.
19 Ministerio de Agricultura y Comercio, *Memoria 1918*, 173–177; "Colombia Packing Concessions," PRO.
20 "Packing House at Coveñas," Aug. 25, 1920, Box 133, Colombia, Narrative Reports 1904–1939, Foreign Agricultural Service (FAS), RG 166, NARA; "Nota del Ministerio de Comercio y Agricultura . . . relacionado con el establicimiento del packing-house en la Costa Atlántica," f. 85, vol. IX, Memoriales y Telegramas, Senado, 1920, AC.

21 "Informe de la comisón que visitó el Packing House de Coveñas," ff. 568–592, vol. IV, Asuntos Varios, Cámara de Representantes, 1922, AC.

22 Ministerio de Industrias, *Memoria del Ministerio de Industrias al Congreso en las sesiones ordinarias de 1924, Anexos* (Bogotá: Imprenta Nacional, 1924), 23; S.J. Fletcher, "Re: Establishment of a Packing House in the Dept. of Bolivar (Confidential)," Box 133, Colombia, Narrative Reports 1904–39, FAS, RG166, NARA. See also Gabriel Moré, *Rancho Grande. La Historia de Coveñas* (unpublished), http://covenas-sucre.gov.co/apc-aa-files/6465373634646336303462653566396 4/historiacovenas.pdf; Adalberto Machado, "La exportación de carne y el Packing House de Coveñas, 1918–1938" (BA thesis, La Corporación Tecnológica de Bolívar, 1989).

23 Lester Schnare, "Voluntary Report: Operation of Meat Packing Establishment at Covenas: Prospects of," March 6, 1925, Box 133, Colombia, Narrative Reports 1904–39, FAS, RG 166, NARA.

24 Lester Schnare, "Operation of Packing House at Coveñas, Colombia," Feb. 12, 1926, Box 133, Colombia, Narrative Reports 1904–39, FAS, RG 166, NARA.

25 Moré, *Rancho Grande*, 85.

26 Carlos Escobar to Carlos E. Restrepo, March 13, 1923, ff. 286–288, Document 13, Box 57–2, Correspondencia Recibida, Archive of Carlos E. Restrepo (Universidad de Antioquia, Medellín).

27 Lynn R. Edminster, *The Cattle Industry and the Tariff* (New York: Macmillan, 1926), 74–75, 150.

28 Lester Schnare, "Monthly Report," (Cartagena consular district), Dec. 18, 1923, Box 133, Colombia, Narrative Reports 1904–39, FAS, RG 166, NARA; Lester Schnare, "Cattle Raising in the Cartagena Consular District," Dec. 19, 1924, Box 133, Colombia, Narrative Reports 1904–39, FAS, RG 166, NARA; W. Boaz, "Cattle Industry in Colombia," Dec. 18, 1925, Box 133, Colombia, Narrative Reports 1904–39, FAS, RG 166, NARA; Rodolfo Freyre, "La industria del ganado vacuno en Colombia," *Revista Nacional de Agricultura* 267–268(1926): 29–31; Eduardo Posada-Carbó, *El caribe colombiano. Una historia regional, 1870–1950* (Bogotá: Banco de la República, Ancora Editores, 1998), 190.

29 Ministerio de Industrias, *Memoria del Ministerio de Industrias al Congreso en las sesiones ordinarias de 1924* (Bogotá: Imprenta Nacional 1924), 40; Schnare, "Cattle Raising," NARA; Boaz, "Cattle Industry," NARA; Lester Schnare, "For Fourth Quarter, 1925," Jan. 14, 1926, Box 133, Colombia, Narrative Reports 1904–39, FAS, RG 166, NARA.

30 Quoted in Ministerio de Industrias, *Memoria 1924*, 39–40. See also Schnare, "Cattle Raising," NARA.

31 Schnare "Cattle Raising," NARA. See also Ministerio de Industrias, *Memoria 1924*, 37–40.

32 Schnare "Cattle Raising," NARA.

33 Arnold, "Illusory riches," 7, citing Philip Curtin.

34 Mary Louise Pratt, *Imperial Eyes: Travel Writing and Transmigration* (London: Routledge, 1992), 109–140; Stepan, *Tropical Nature*.

35 Jerry Hoeg, "Andrés Bello's 'ode to tropical agriculture': The Landscape of independence," in Beatriz Rivera-Barnes and Jerry Hoeg, *Reading and Writing the Latin American Landscape* (New York: Palgrave Macmillan, 2009), 53–66.

36 See Medardo Rivas, *Los trabajadores de tierra caliente* (Bogotá: Banco Popular, 1972).

37 Arnold, "Illusory riches," 10.

38 Robert Cunninghame Graham, "Report for Garnham Roper: On the Cattle Resources of the Republic of Colombia," March 1, 1917, 11/10, BT, PRO.

39 Robert Cunninghame Graham to Macrosty, March 31, 1917, 13/81. BT, PRO.
40 Lester Magnum to Jennie Magnum, May 12, 1925, Folder 1, Box 46, Ramona Wilcox Cannon Archive (The University of Utah, Salt Lake City).
41 Lloyd Owen, "Memorandum Cattle Trade," PRO.
42 "Ley 82 de 1915," f. 355, AC.
43 Ministerio de Agricultura y Comercio, *Memoria 1917*, LXVII-LXVIII.
44 M.T. Dawe, "Relación de un viaje por el río Magdalena, por el Departamento del Magdalena y por la peninsula de la Goajira (Colombia)," in Ministerio de Agricultura y Comercio, *Memoria 1917*, 116.
45 Anna L. Tsing, *Friction: An Ethnography of Global Connection* (Princeton, NJ: Princeton University Press, 2011).
46 Cunninghame Graham, "Report for Garnham Roper."
47 Felix Driver, "Imagining the tropics: Views and visions of the tropical world." *Singapore Journal of Tropical Geography* 25(2004): 1–17; Driver and Yeoh, "Constructing the tropics"; Gavin Bowd and Daniel Clayton, "Fieldwork and tropicality in French Indochina: Reflections on Pierre Gourou's Les Paysans du Delta Tonkinois, 1936," *Singapore Journal of Tropical Geography* 24(2003), 147–168; John Kleinen, "Tropicality and topicality: Pierre Gourou and the genealogy of French colonial scholarship on rural Vietnam," *Singapore Journal of Tropical Geography* 26(2005): 339–358. See also Victor R. Savage, "Tropicality imagined and experienced," *Singapore Journal of Tropical Geography* 25(2004): 26–31; Stepan, *Tropical Nature*; Pratt, *Imperial Eyes*.
48 Colombia Information Bureau, "Cattle Industry."
49 Shawn Van Ausdal, "Pasture, power, and profit: An environmental history of cattle ranching in Colombia, 1850–1950," *Geoforum* 40(2009): 707–719. See also T.H. Stobbs and P.A.C. Thompson, "Milk production from tropical pastures," in *Ruminant Nutrition: Selected articles from the World Animal Review* (Rome: FAO, 1978). Accessed February 3, 2015, http://www.fao.org/docrep/004/X6512E/X6512E04.htm.
50 Jan C. Bonsma, "Degeneration of the British beef breeds in the tropics and subtropics," in A.O. Rhoad (ed.), *Breeding Beef Cattle for Unfavorable Environments* (Austin: University of Texas Press, 1955), 17. See also William J.A. Payne, *An Introduction to Animal Husbandry in the Tropics* (Essex: Longman Scientific & Technical, 1990), 11–24; Shawn Van Ausdal, "Productivity gains and the limits of tropical ranching in Colombia, 1850–1950," *Agricultural History* 86(2012): 1–32.
51 Osvaldo Barsky and Julio Djenderedjian, *Historia del capitalismo agrario pampeano. Tomo I: La expansión ganadera hasta 1895* (Buenos Aires: Siglo XXI, Universidad de Belgrano, 2003), 429; R.H. Whitbeck, *Economic Geography of South America* (New York: McGraw-Hill, 1926), 230.
52 Ministerio de Industrias, *Memoria 1924*, 86–93; Ministerio de Industrias, *Memoria del Ministerio de Industrias al Congreso en las sesiones ordinarias de 1925* (Bogotá: Imprenta Nacional, 1925), 127–139; Ministerio de Industrias, *Memoria del Ministerio de Industrias al Congreso en las sesiones ordinarias de 1927* (Bogotá: Imprenta Nacional, 1927), 99–101; Ministerio de Industrias, *Memoria del Ministerio de Industrias al Congreso en las sesiones ordinarias de 1930* (Bogotá: Imprenta Nacional, 1930), 293–294; Rafael Flórez, *Fases de Colombia* (Bogotá: Editorial Minerva, 1926), 51.
53 Ministerio de Industrias, *Memoria 1924*, 37–40; NARA, RG 166, FAS, Narrative Reports 1904–1939, Colombia, Box 133, "Cattle Raising in the Cartagena Consular District," Dec. 19, 1924, L. Schnare; Freyre, "Industria del ganado."
54 In the mid-1920s, the high cost of Colombian cattle was also function of rapidly rising demand that stemmed from a revival of the coffee economy and an inflationary period of foreign lending and infrastructure development known as the "Dance of the Millions."

55   Ministerio de Industrias, *Memoria 1930*, 290.

56   "Ley 82 de 1915," f. 345, AC; Ministerio de Industrias, *Memoria 1930*, 10.

57   Manuel Gómez Rueda, "Informe del Departamento Nacional de Ganadería al Señor Ministro de la Economía Nacional," *Boletín de Ganadería* 1(1939), 13.

58   Ministerio de Agricultura y Comercio, *Memoria del Ministro de Agricultura y Comercio al Congreso de 1935* (Bogotá: Imprenta Nacional, 1935), 58–59.

59   Ministerio de Economía Nacional, *Informe del Ministro de la Economía Nacional presentado al Congreso de 1944* (Bogotá: Editorial Minerva, 1944), 78.

60   Luis Marulanda "Intereses ganaderos," *El Agricultor Caucano* 3(1935), 674–675.

61   Washington Bernal, "La granja de selección de ganado criollo en Montería y su orientación," *Boletín de Ganadería* 1(1939), 25.

62   Manuel Gómez Rueda, "Producción pecuaria de Colombia," *Revista Agropecuaria: Órgano Oficial de Divulgación Agrícola del Departamento de Santander* 9(1938), 35.

63   Ministerio de Agricultura y Comercio, *Memoria 1935*, 58–59.

64   Gómez Rueda, "Producción pecuaria," 35.

65   Gómez Rueda, "Producción pecuaria," 37.

66   Salvador Franco, "Plan de organización agrícola en Colombia," in Ministerio de Industrias (ed.), *Agricultura y ganadería. Plan de organización agrícola en Colombia y la industria del ganado vacuno en Colombia* (Bogotá: Imprenta Nacional, 1926), 14.

67   Raúl Varela, "Memorándum sobre el Departamento del Atlántico," *Boletín de Agricultura* 3(1930), 630.

68   Catherine LeGrand, *Frontier Expansion and Peasant Protest in Colombia, 1850–1936* (Albuquerque: University of New Mexico Press, 1986).

69   Alejandro López, *Problemas colombianos* (París: Editorial París-América, 1927), 53–54.

70   Ministero de Industrias, *Memoria 1930*, XLI.

71   Manuel Jiménez López, "Algunos signos de degeneración colectiva en Colombia y en los países similares," in Luis López de Mesa (ed.), *Los problemas de la raza en Colombia* (Bogotá: El Espectador, 1920), 24.

72   Manuel Jiménez López, "Algunos signos."

73   Laurentino Muñoz, *La tragedia biológica del pueblo colombiano. Estudio de observación y de vulgarización.* (Editorial América: Cali, 1935), 14.

74   Nancy Leys Stepan, *"The Hour of Eugenics:" Race, Gender, and Nation in Latin America, 1890–1916,* (Ithaca, NY: Cornell University Press, 1991).

75   Catalina Muñoz, "Más allá del problema racial: el determinismo geográfico y las 'dolencias sociales'," in Catalina Muñoz (ed.), *Los problemas de la raza en Colombia* (Bogotá: Editorial Universidad del Rosaio, 2011), 11–58; Claudia Leal, "Usos del concepto raza en Colombia," in Claudia Mosquera, Agustín Laó-Montes and César Rodríguez (eds.), *Debates sobre ciudadanía y políticas raciales en las Américas negras* (Bogotá: Universidad Nacional, Universidad del Valle, 2010), 389–438; Alvaro Villegas, "Nación, intelectuales de elite y representaciones de degeneración y regeneración, Colombia 1909–1937" *Iberoamericana* 7(2007): 7–24.

76   Manuel Jiménez López, "Algunos signos," 36.

77   Warwick Anderson, "Climates of opinion: Acclimatization in nineteenth-century France and England," *Victorian Studies* 35(1992): 135–57; David Livingstone, "Tropical climate and moral hygiene: The anatomy of a Victorian debate," *British Journal for the History of Science* 32(1999): 93–110.

78   Mariano Ospina Pérez, " 'El problema sanitario de Colombia es el primero dice el Dr. Mariano Ospina Pérez' (Bogota 23 ago 1934)," in Muñoz, *Tragedia*

Biológica. See also Sandra Pedraza, *En cuerpo y alma. Visiones del progreso y la felicidad* (Bogotá: Ediciones Uniandes, 1999).

79 Stefan Pohl-Valero, " 'La raza entra por la boca': Energy, diet, and eugenics in Colombia, 1890–1940," *Hispanic American Historical Review* 94(2014): 455–486.

80 Cited in Pohl-Valero, "La raza entra," 459.

81 Jeffrey Pilcher, *Que Vivan los Tamales!: Food and the Making of Mexican Identity* (Albuquerque: University of New Mexico Press, 1998), 77–97.

82 Cited in Pohl-Valero, "La raza entra," 460. Also see Anonymous, "La carne y el trabajo intelectual," *Ganadería de Bolívar* 43–44(1937): 1269.

83 Cited in Pohl-Valero, "La raza entra," 460.

84 P.J. Hansen, "Physiological and cellular adaptations of Zebu cattle to thermal stress," *Animal Reproduction Science* 82–83(2004): 349–360.

85 Aug. Tietjen, "El ganado zebú en Colombia," *Revista Nacional de Agricultura* 33(1939): 336–337.

86 James O. Sanders, "History and development of Zebu cattle in the United States," *Journal of Animal Science* 50(1980): 1193; Olimpio Arenas, "El zebú y sus ventajas en el trópico," *Revista Nacional de Agricultura* 33(1939): 322; Robert Wilcox, "Zebu's elbows: Cattle breeding and the environment in central Brazil, 1890–1960," in Christian Brannstrom (ed.), *Territories, Commodities and Knowledges: Latin American Environmental Histories in the Nineteenth and Twentieth Centuries* (London: Institute for the Study of the Americas, 2004), 218–46.

87 Carlos Alberto Rojas, "Estado actual de la ganadería de Santander y sus perspectivas," B.S. thesis, Universidad Nacional de Colombia (1938), 16.

88 Antonio Zapata, "El ganado de raza cebú," *Boletín de Agricultura* 4(1931): 125–128.

89 Fidel Ochoa, "Porqué se prohibió la importación de ganado cebú," *Boletín de Agricultura* 4(1931): 535–540; Sanders, "History of Zebu," 1193, 1195.

90 Ochoa, "Porqué se prohibió," 537.

91 Ochoa, "Porqué se prohibió."

92 Zapata, "Ganado de raza cebú," 125.

93 I have not found explicit references to the racial inferiority of the zebu in the Colombian sources. By contrast, geographer R.H. Whitbeck wrote: "This black-skinned animal is, like the negro, an adaptation to a tropical climate" in "The agricultural geography of Jamaica," *Annals of the Association of American Geographers* 22(1932): 25. Australian ranchers in the 1930s were also more unequivocal in their fears of "mongrelization." See Beverly Angus, "The history of the cattle tick *Boophilus microplus* in Australia and achievements in its control," *International Journal for Parasitology* 26(1996): 1348.

94 Zapata, "Ganado de raza cebú," 126.

95 See also Greg Bankoff, "A question of breeding: Zootechny and colonial attitudes toward the tropical environment in the late nineteenth-century Philippines," *The Journal of Asian Studies* 60(2001): 413–37.

96 Eugelio Velasco, "Desconcierto ganadero," *Revista Agrícola y Ganadera* 3(1939): 14–17.

97 Jaime Villegas, cited in Virgilio Echeverri, "El problema ganadero del Valle," *Revista Nacional de Agricultura* 33(1939): 241.

98 Cortes G. Randall, *La industria ganadera en Colombia* (Washington, DC, 1953).

99 See Lovell S. Jarvis, *Livestock Development in Latin America* (Washington, DC: World Bank, 1987).

100 Stefania Gallini, "El Atila del Ganges en la ganadería colombiana," *Nómadas* 22 (2005), 187; R.A. Martínez et al., "Genetic variability in Colombian Creole cattle populations estimated by pedigree information," *Journal of Animal Science* 86(2007): 545.

101   Cited in Bowd and Clayton, "Tropicality, Orientalism," 297–98.
102   Driver and Yoeh, "Constructing the Tropics," 3.
103   Michael Taussig, *Shamanism, Colonialism, and the Wild Man: A Study in Terror and Healing*, (Chicago: University of Chicago Press, 1987), 287.
104   Van Ausdal, "Productivity gains."

Part IV

Competing Modernist Logics

9 Industrializing Forests and Naturalizing Industrialization

Forests, Pulp Wood, and Environmental Transformations, 1860–1930

Mathias Mutz

Paper is made out of water and wood, and the pulp and paper industry, therefore, is an ideal example to illustrate the interconnectedness of industry and environment. Paper production has long been notorious for its intensive resource usage, high energy consumption, and dismal pollution record.[1] While water consumption has significant local effects on the natural water balance and water quality, the industry's demand for wood resulted in a transnational trade system with far-reaching ecological effects. Today it is mainly the global impact of pulpwood production that is targeted by environmental activists. For example, German environmental organizations regularly publish an *Alternativer Waldschadensbericht* (Alternative Forest Damage Report) arguing that growth and recovery of forests in Germany are only possible at the expense of forests in other parts of the world.[2]

Looking at the statistical data, wood from German forests is not crucial for the national paper production and consumption anymore. In recent decades, used paper has become the industry's main resource with a share of 74 percent in 2013. But it is technically unavoidable to add fresh fibers, which—in the German case—come mostly from abroad, that means from boreal coniferous forests or tropical regions. While the German paper industry could satisfy the demand of the home market on its own, two-thirds of Germany's demand in wood cellulose is covered by imports.[3] Apart from that, German pulp mills also import large amounts of unprocessed wood. During the last decades, an accelerating shift toward cellulose production in plantations, consisting of eucalyptus trees, became apparent. Today this accounts for over a third of the total global cellulose output. Eucalyptus is fast growing and well suited for paper production. On the down side, these plantations have a severe impact on biodiversity, soil quality, and water balance.[4]

In many ways, today's international system of paper, pulp, and pulpwood trade is a continuation of strategies and structures developed in the nineteenth and early twentieth centuries. This makes a long-term perspective indispensable to understand (and probably improve) modern patterns of natural resource consumption. In this case, history might not only raise awareness for the path dependencies that remain formative until today, but a closer look at the industry's environmental relations in the period of high industrialization could also help to reconsider "the business-environment connection" as an integral part of our economy.[5] Since business practices and environmental issues evolved in tandem, theoretical approaches should not consider ecology and economy as separated spheres. It is unsatisfying to see nature merely as a victim of industry or an obstacle that needs to be overcome. At least in the case of the pulp and paper industry, environmental issues were at the core of the production process: nature was not only exploited or consumed, it also became the source of commercial knowledge and origin of economic learning processes. This chapter encourages new approaches to nature's place in the process of industrialization.

The following discussion of this environmental frontier of business history concentrates on four tasks that the German pulp and paper industry had to deal with while establishing a completely new resource regime at the end of the nineteenth century—switching from rags to wood as new raw material. Within a few decades, there was not only a rapid increase of production following mechanization but also a far-reaching reset of the industry's 'learning base.'[6] First of all, paper manufacturers had to reconsider their location choices with regard to new raw material sources, while, second, also adapting their technology to the processing of wood. Third, enterprises had to establish trade connections between forests and factories and fourth, they also had to come up with innovative ways to customize wood production to their special needs. In short, they had to open up space, incorporate materiality, manage resources, and industrialize nature.

These four challenges, in the end, add up to a fifth task—this time for environmental and economic historians: the need to naturalize industrialization. The case of the paper industry is especially illustrative, since the expanding use of resources in the industrial age coincided with the emergence of wood as a new raw material for paper production. Wood did not become significant before the 1860s, since paper was mostly made out of rags at that time. The following 'wooden revolution' and its effects on the paper industry's organization are decisive starting points, when examining the entanglement of environment and business in the industrialization process. Overcoming the bottleneck of traditional paper manufacturing, the new source for fibers opened up new frontiers for production and consumption.

Once a luxury good, paper eventually became a product for mass consumption during the nineteenth century. In 1800, per capita demand in Germany was half a kilo. This figure rose to 24 kilos in 1913 and 48 kilos in 1938. Production figures increased simultaneously from 15,000 to over two million tonnes in the interwar period.[7] This change was not only a matter of quantity but also a result of a qualitative change in consumption, since new fields of application for paper, such as packaging or sanitary products, created new markets. To supply and promote those new demands, radical technical changes were necessary, which were connected to new machinery as well as new raw materials. Traditionally, rags were processed in paper mills using hand-operated vats. But after the invention of the papermaking machine in 1799, the production of 'endless paper'—that is, paper rolls—became commonplace in Europe until the mid-nineteenth century. The limited supply of rags posed a major threat to the industry's further development. An important first step to enlarge the resource base was the introduction of chlorine bleaching around 1800. Later, Friedrich G. Keller from Saxony invented the ground-wood process, which enabled the industry to produce, for the first time, low-grade paper from wood in 1843. This turn to wood later gained momentum through new chemical methods to extract cellulose. In Germany, Alexander Mitscherlich's sulfite process (patented in 1874) became the nucleus of a completely new industry. By the end of the century, wood had replaced rags as the industry's main raw material. According to estimates for northern and western European countries, the share of wood in paper production rose from 10 percent in 1880 to 38 percent in 1900 and to 60 percent in 1913.[8]

As a result, the period before the First World War not only saw the paper industry emerge as big business, as was the case in other sectors, its enterprises also faced extraordinary technological challenges. The new material basis increased the usual tasks connected with industrial mass production and resource extraction, but at the same time it created new opportunities. Due to its abundance of wood, the paper industry experienced a boom in the Kingdom of Saxony. The region became the largest cluster of German pulp and paper mills and accounted for approximately one quarter of the total national production throughout the German Kaiserreich. By 1910, almost 60 percent of all newsprint (mainly made out of ground-wood) came from there.[9] The dynamic development is most evident in the number of new enterprises founded at that time. In the 1860s, 81 new production facilities were set up, in the 1870s and '80s, the figures rose to 150 and 232 respectively.[10] In the 1890s, another 187 factories were newly created. Then after a final wave of new establishments at the beginning of the twentieth century, the Saxon paper industry entered a period of stagnation, although it maintained its extraordinary position within Germany. For a limited time, especially between 1860 and 1880, natural location factors had opened a window of opportunity for the local paper industry, and this could be transferred into lasting success. In this constellation, Saxony is an ideal research area, especially because it provides several well-documented case studies.[11]

OPENING UP SPACE

Saxony was at the core of Germany's new paper economy. It had always been a papermaking region, but in the course of the nineteenth century its contribution to national production doubled. Back in the seventeenth century, Saxony already had a remarkably high density of mills. However, the total number of production facilities stagnated thereafter, since available water power could not support an unlimited number of mills. After 1830, Saxony was able to reclaim its leading role in paper production, because now the papermaking tradition coincided with early industrial impulses. Apart from Württemberg, most early German papermaking machines were situated there. After the transition to wood as a raw material, some three hundred wood-milling operations and nine pulp factories were established. The new factories in the valleys of the Erzgebirge made it clear to any observer that "ground-wood production follows the forest."[12] Moving closer to the mountain range helped to avoid otherwise long and costly transport. Paper factories often followed suit, as ground-wood produced there, with 60 percent water content, was also difficult to handle. Initially there were no dehydrating facilities, and once they were available later on, they would have raised the overall production costs—especially since dried ground-wood had to be redissolved at the factory. These technical dependencies, which also applied to chemical pulp, ideally resulted in a tight interweaving between the various branches of paper production.[13]

Together with the continuous growth of domestic production, the transition to wooden paper led to an enormous rise in resource use. In the late 1880s, after only a few decades, estimates for Germany assumed an annual consumption of 1.5 million solid cubic meters. Later on, in the years before the First World War, German pulp and paper mills consumed 5 to 6 million, in the interwar years between 4 and 10 million solid cubic meters of pulpwood. For Saxony, the numbers are even more impressive. Its paper industry consumed 450,000 solid cubic meters in the 1880s, which is equivalent to the production of 125,000 hectares of forests operated in a sustainable manner or—purely arithmetical—one fourth of Saxony's forest area. Half a century later, consumption had tripled, making self-sufficient supply illusionary—theoretically, that is, by disregarding other usages, Saxon forests could provide for only a third of the local demand.[14] Interestingly enough, Alexander Mitscherlich, the German holder of the patent for sulfite pulp, had already anticipated the problem of resource scarcity in the early 1870s. According to his licensing requirements, no other pulp mills were allowed within a "rayon" of 50 kilometers of an existing sulfite factory so as to secure the raw material supply of the license holders. As Saxony was densely populated with paper mills, this hindered a faster diffusion of the new technology, although this had no long-term effect because patent protection ended in 1884.[15]

Spatial expansion and trade became the alternative solutions. More efficient production procedures led to such an increase in the demand for raw materials that individual factories could no longer purchase wood (or ground-wood) at the local level alone. At the advent of the First World War, individual enterprises like *Kübler & Niethammer*, Saxony's largest producer of newsprint, consumed more than 100,000 solid cubic meters annually.[16] Initially, the result was a split system in pulpwood supply. Wood-grinding enterprises, with their limited capacity, primarily relied on the regional market. Most of the wood from the Erzgebirge went to small ground-wood mills situated directly in the narrow valleys of the mountain range. Large factories, on the contrary, began to obtain their wood from abroad. They were especially making use of inexpensive waterways from Russia and Scandinavia. Apart from that, Saxon mills were also using the railroads coming from neighboring Bohemia.[17] Between 1908 and 1910, the *Leonhardt Söhne Zellstoffabrik* in Crossen, for instance, received on average 5,500 solid cubic meters per month. The largest share came from Russia (35.6 percent), followed by Bohemia (26.0 percent), Bavaria (21.4 percent), and Austria (15.8 percent). On average, only 26 solid cubic meters came from Saxony and nearby Thuringia.[18] As this trend of internationalization continued, it put additional pressure on the production sites in the Saxon low mountain ranges. Wood exporting countries in Northern and Eastern Europe used their natural advantages and built up their own capacities in pulp and paper production.[19]

Wood availability continued to be a decisive criterion for location, since "approximately half the production costs for both the ground-wood pulp and chemical pulp industries" were tied to the acquisition of wood.[20] But the direction in which wood functioned as a location factor changed. In order to maintain high-speed production, enterprises had to expand their supply chains, which created the demand for a highly developed transportation system. New location considerations began to take center stage. In the late nineteenth century, direct railway connections and nearby waterways became critical factors in determining the location of pulp and paper factories. There is hardly any paper mill established after the 1870s that did not consider transportation questions from the beginning. Older factories that were far from existing railway lines either tried to initiate state or private construction projects, or they established connecting lines on their own. This created costs of approximately 30,000 Mark per kilometer.[21] The large pulp mills in Pirna and Heidenau, founded around 1900, were directly situated at the riverside of the Elbe, and they had their own unloading devices for wood and coal. Obviously, as the owner of the mill in Crossen put it in 1933,

> the question of a paper mill's economic profitability has become merely a question of location. In Germany, a paper mill can be profitable only where there is a cheap supply of raw materials (especially coal) and cost-effective means of transport (such as navigable rivers).[22]

As a result, no large-capacity mill was built in Saxony after the First World War. New factories were concentrated at sites along the Rhine or near the Baltic Coast.

Within a short period of time, the Saxon paper industry had turned its head start into a threat to further growth. The strategy of spatial expansion could help to overcome these shortages, but this did not mean that the Saxon paper industry became independent of natural factors. One major aspect was the fact that infrastructure systems and trade were dependent on nature as well. For example, factory location in the mountain range complicated railway engineering. Weather and transport conditions made year-round logging impossible. Additionally, water transport was periodically interrupted by spring floods or summer droughts, and during the winter, the Elbe was usually closed to ships for several months due to drifting ice.[23] The resulting supply variations necessitated extensive wood storage, with stockpiles often exceeding a factory's annual production capacity.[24] The complex issue of storage, which was closely linked to specific characteristics of forest products, proved to be one to which a firm's standard managerial practices and accumulated expertise could not be applied directly.

INCORPORATING MATERIALITY

By the start of the First World War, industrial mass production of paper was well established and had initiated a tremendous change in the utilization of natural resources. The crucial point, however, is that the successful innovation of wooden paper was not inevitable or automatic. Wood-based paper was merely the market opportunity to which the industry had to adapt. Despite the affordability of pulpwood and the invention of wood pulp in the 1840s, the new production method did not become commonplace until the end of the 1860s. Mill owners needed time to retool their facilities, and most of the potential customers were skeptical about the new product. As the industry's first trade journal observed in 1866, it was a common belief that "solid wood could never be made into a fiber flexible enough to be formed into sheets."[25] Manufactures had to further improve their products and convince paper converters. Specific technical, operational, and entrepreneurial knowledge had to be acquired, and new managerial capabilities had to be built. This new learning base altered the technical processes of production and simultaneously influenced the industry's organizational structures.

Wood was a challenging raw material. Looking back from 1922, Carl Gustav Schwalbe, a leading expert in wood and paper chemistry, exemplified the exercise:

> The chemical and physical characteristics of these fibers [. . .] differed substantially from the ones processed before. They also showed extraordinary differences among themselves. The sulfate cellulose, which resembled cotton, and Mitscherlich's sulfite cellulose, which resembled linen [. . .], required a different treatment compared to well-known linen, hemp, or cotton rags in traditional paper-making.[26]

Apart from basic differences, the material characteristics of individual tree species played a decisive role. The percentage of cellulose, the length of the fibers, and the resin content determined which species could be used for paper production and what type of production facility needed to be built. While wood had to be fresh for mechanical pulping, aged wood was preferable for chemical pulp (as storing helped to reduce resin content). In the beginning, spruce was the only species suitable for grinding and producing sulfite cellulose. Thus Saxony, where spruce covered the Erzgebirge, had secondary advantages to become a center of paper production. Later on, new production methods such as sulfate cellulose broadened the resource base, as sulfate was most suitable for pine. Changes in the industry's location preferences now reflected a diversifying raw material basis. At the same time, natural characteristics and the chosen methods dictated possible uses of the end product, as they defined its quality characteristics.[27]

These fields of work forced the owners of paper mills to acquire new knowledge closely related to wood as a natural resource. Environmental learning, in this case, the creative use of natural resources, became a crucial basis of innovation, while technology management asked for new organizational solutions. Gottfried Keller had initiated wood processing as an outsider to papermaking. In the initial phase, further contributions to the industrial use of wood often came through the work of individual entrepreneurs applying the trial-and-error method. But in the long run, the materiality of the raw material contributed to a more systematic and professional approach to environment-related knowledge. Chemical research began to play an important role in the industry's development. Or as Heino Castorf, director of the paper mill in Penig, put it in 1897: "Like a torch chemistry illuminated the deep darkness of inherited papermaking empiricism."[28] Alexander Mitscherlich, a professor of chemistry at the Prussian Forestry Academy in Münden, combined expertise in chemistry and forestry and so was perfectly equipped to discover the sulfite process. Thereafter, it became common practice to employ chemists and for paper mills to establish their own quality control and research laboratories.[29]

Within individual enterprises, the growing importance of knowledge management contributed to corporate growth, vertical integration, and departmental specialization, but the professionalization of the pulp and paper industry was also promoted by trade associations and public institutions that functioned as hubs of knowledge transfer. In Saxony, the *Höhere Technische Bildungsanstalt* in Chemnitz offered the first university-level courses in paper technology in 1893.[30] Organizations like the *Verein Deutscher Papierfabrikanten* (Association of German Paper Manufacturers, founded in 1872) or the *Verein Deutscher Zellstoffabrikanten* (Association of German Pulp Manufacturers, founded in 1880) established special working groups on subjects such as tariff policy, wood chemistry, or transportation matters, thus highlighting the significance of environment-related expertise.[31]

In the interwar years, this development culminated in the establishment of new research institutes and industrial research investments. Enterprises such as *Kübler & Niethammer* or the *Vereinigte Papierfabriken* (United Paper Mills) in Bautzen enlarged their research departments and developed new research agendas for alternative raw materials and production methods.[32] The Saxon paper industry as a whole subsidized the *Technische Hochschule* (Institute of Technology) in Dresden, which in 1926 established a new professorship for fiber and paper technology. It also helped to finance the venerable *Forstakademie* (Forest Academy) in nearby Tharandt. Professor Hans Wislicenus had made wood chemistry a major research topic there. It appealed to the pulp and paper industry that he redefined forestry as "large-scale forest-plant production and plant utilization."[33] He was rewarded for his efforts in 1928, when the mill owners of Saxony offered to establish a Society for Wood Research, which they would endow with an annual grant of 100,000 Mark. The research program of the society deeply reflected the interests of the paper industry, declaring four aims of research:

> First, to identify foreign alternatives to the domestic spruce [. . .]; second, to calculate the transportation costs of shipping wood from abroad to German harbors; third, to accelerate wood production in German forests through increased planting and intensified soil fertilization; and fourth, to breed a plant with fibers similar to spruce, such as an annual grass, which could be cultivated on wasteland and used as a surrogate or additive."[34]

This agenda was never realized because of the Great Depression. Nonetheless, it symbolizes a new level of scientific penetration of the pulp and paper industry at that time.

The limits of a scientific approach, however, are not only visible in the fact that spruce remains an essential raw material for paper today. It is important to acknowledge that successful manufacturing processes were always the "result of *long-lasting*, *tedious* and *dearly bought* endeavors."[35] For one, digesting wood in pulp mills depended on the right combination of temperature, pressure, boiling time, and the composition of the chemicals used. Entrepreneurs had their own empirical values and did not trust in standard recommendations. Scientific knowledge remained limited. In 1925, the *Verein der Zellstoff- und Papierchemiker* emphasized that there are "still many dark spots, especially regarding wood as a raw material and cellulose."[36] This is more than an academic attempt to aggrandize the importance of future research. In the end, wood remained a natural resource in its truest sense. Its quality depended on local factors such as climate, soil conditions, and the forest technology applied. The inconsistency of the raw material demanded flexible approaches. For example, it was important to remove the bark properly and drill out knotholes, as all impurities could damage the digesting process. Developing mechanical solutions for this task turned out to be rather difficult. Other problems were connected with storage and the danger of wood pests.[37] Dealing with the materiality of wood became everyday business to most paper manufacturers. Nonetheless, it required human and financial resources, as well as elaborated strategies. Connecting business in material terms to its resource base remained an enduring process of adaptation and learning.

MANAGING RESOURCES

Learning to work with wood was not the only new frontier to paper production. The managerial capabilities to handle the natural aspects of pulpwood were not limited to producing knowledge or finding technological fixes. Professional trade—that is, the spatial extension of supply and organizational integration into the enterprise—were part of the same story. Along with scientific and operational challenges, pulp producers needed to become familiar with contemporary methods of forest management and timber trading. Since the eighteenth century, the market for forest products had become more and more sophisticated. This was especially true in Saxony, where scientific forestry was established very early (dating back to Carlowitz' *Sylvicultura oeconomica*, which first mentions the concept of sustainability in 1713). Since the Middle Ages, mining and woodworking created an ongoing demand for wood and timber, which was further increased in the industrial age.[38] At the same time, 48 percent of the forests of Saxony were state owned, and in the Erzgebirge, the percentage was even higher. This made public authorities the leading supplier for new pulp-producing facilities. They sold their felling on public sales or by secret bid. Later, so called 'free-hand sales' were an exception designed to support local customers.[39]

In this trading environment, paper manufactures had to learn how to bargain with timber traders and how to find the size or category of wood best suited to their purposes. Customs and usances for pulpwood trade had to be negotiated. Delivery conditions and fitting differed regionally and internationally. There was no exact definition of pulpwood at all, since pulping didn't require a standardized category of wood. It was not until the early twentieth century that some German authorities began to designate particular types as 'pulpwood' or 'fiber wood,' but the Prussian *Holzmarktordnung* (Timber Market Regulations) of 1911 rather inexactly ruled "round timber of species suitable for wood pulp and cellulose in lengths of one to four meters; at both ends cut with a saw, sound, few knotholes; put in stacked cubic meter."[40] Many participants complained about this imprecision, but there was no accurate solution to the problem. It only reflected the fact that the usage of pulpwood was not alone defined by natural characteristics but also by prices and alternative offers. The logs and branches used in pulp mills could also be sold as firewood or timber. In Saxony, despite the importance of its pulp and paper industry, there was no standardization at all. Mill owners had to compete for the best types available. Of course, this does not mean that—as some observers put it—Saxon authorities "did not take business needs into account."[41] More likely, buyers and sellers accepted the limited sense of standardizing nature.

During the 1860s and 1870s, wood trade became everyday business for all the small ground-wood mills in the Erzgebirge. With only a few local suppliers, however, it could still be managed rather easily. As soon as this local pulpwood economy reached its limits, regional, national, and international trading became indispensable for medium-sized businesses. At this point, intermediary traders entered the stage. They selected the desired categories and negotiated with individual suppliers or local wood merchants. Some of them specialized in pulpwood and developed long-standing relationships with pulp and paper mills. When the *Verband Deutscher Papierholzhändler* (Association of German Pulpwood Traders) was founded in 1918, the number of specialized pulpwood traders in Germany was estimated at 180. Although purchasing wood from these traders became routine for paper manufacturers, it remained a distinctively bureaucratic process that required considerable management resources. Deliveries usually came in small batches, each of which had to be recorded, inventoried, and paid for.[42]

Larger, well-capitalized firms established their own purchasing or even shipping departments or set up subsidiary companies to handle these operations. While this approach carried additional financial risks, it enabled firms to minimize pulpwood costs and to streamline their supply systems. For many companies it seemed "inevitable to free pulpwood supply from the contingencies of the market."[43] The pulp and paper mills in Crossen proudly declared in 1936:

> The company of Leonhardt Söhne, from the beginning, established its own wood purchasing organization for its factories that now exist for over 45 years; it was upgraded according to special service requirements as well as experience we gained, and, therefore, we could always rely on it with success, especially when buying foreign wood.[44]

Going even further, some companies used foreign direct investments to secure their raw material supply, buying forest areas abroad and establishing subsidiary factories there. For example, the *Zellstoffabrik Waldhof* founded a subsidiary in Pernau (Estonian: Pärnu) in 1898 and began to buy up large forests in Russia.[45] The *Aschaffenburger Zellstoffwerke* relied on a "generous purchasing and storage policy, but also the acquisition and management of forests, especially in Russia with a special office in St. Petersburg."[46] The strategy of completely integrating the supply chain was much more difficult to apply in Germany itself, where forests were usually closed to industrial ownership by traditional property and management structures. Here foreign investments were also a loophole to escape from the strict application of sustainable forest management in German forests.

Local supply, intermediary traders, purchasing departments, and direct investments in forests often occurred as a chronological succession, but this was not always so. For instance, the *Feldmühle AG*, then Germany's third largest producer of cellulose, did rely on intermediary traders until the 1930s.[47] None of the larger Saxon pulp mills (*Hoesch & Co.* in Pirna and Heidenau, *Leonhardt Söhne* in Crossen, and *Kübler & Niethammer* in Gröditz) got involved with foreign direct investments. They were all family enterprises lacking the financial resources to do so. Nonetheless, they tried to secure their pulpwood supply by long-term contracts with Russian authorities in the years before 1914.[48] In the end, while approaches differed from firm to firm, they all agreed on the strategic importance of pulpwood supply and invested in organizational solutions.

The paper industry's special interest in a spatial expansion of their supply chain became visible once more, when, during the First World War, the German military government was asked to provide additional pulpwood from occupied areas in Eastern Europe. Despite extensive planning, detailed negotiations, and considerable investments by individual firms, this undertaking achieved only limited results before the German defeat in 1918.[49] What became apparent in the discussions among German paper industrialists, however, was the role of expert knowledge and local embeddedness in trade negotiations. It is reported that "especially the larger pulp mills were unwilling to share the operating experience which they had acquired over the years without further ado."[50] For them, it was important to keep their strategic advantages and be able to react in a flexible manner. As soon as the war ended, the German pulp and paper industry began to reestablish its international purchasing networks. By the early 1920s, pulpwood supply had normalized, although the political changes in Eastern Europe and the newly established Soviet Union altered the conditions of trade and made Finland, Poland, and Czechoslovakia Germany's most important suppliers.[51] The established system proved capable of adjusting to the vulnerability of commercial networks. Nevertheless, the experience of war spurred the German pulp and paper industry to reevaluate the possibilities of domestic supply, as already indicated by the Society for Wood Research plan.

INDUSTRIALIZING NATURE

By no means did the German pulp and paper industry ignore the forests in its own backyard, but in general, the existing institutional setting hindered the pulp and paper industry from taking over control of its resource base directly. The industry's way into the forest was to some extent closed by traditional forest policies, but pulp wood trade had noticeable impacts on scientific forestry and the cultivation of forests. Despite their sometimes anti-capitalist attitude, at least some foresters were responsive to industrial interests. In the long run, the new demand for fast growing, small-dimensioned wood, especially spruce, altered the utilization strategies of state and private forest administrations. Looking at Saxony, where we find both the heart of the German paper industry and the forerunner of modern forestry, these changes can be described as an 'industrialization' of forests insofar as structure and utilization of forests were adapted to the needs of the emerging industrial society. Erhard Schuster, one of the first historians of forestry who analyzed (in the words of a Marxist scientist) the "impact of the economic development of emerging capitalism on timber use and choice of tree species in forest management," did consciously select Saxony as his research area.[52] Already in 1961, he identified the three trends of industrialized forests he defines—a shift from firewood to timber, a new emphasis on small-dimensioned wood categories and a growing share of spruce monocultures—so all of these became visible early on.

Additionally, detailed figures can be provided for the Saxon case. Private demand for firewood decreased from 0.5 to 0.08 square cubic meters per capita between 1820 and 1900. While timber made up for 17 percent of public wood harvesting in the years 1817–1826, this share rose to 64 percent in 1864–1873 and 80 percent in the interwar period. Besides, the last third of the century saw a significant rise of sales in small-dimensioned timber. In the 1880s, wood with diameters below 15 centimeters comprised 23.8 percent of softwood sold, and in the first decade of the twentieth century, it made up 36.3 percent.[53] And while the trend toward extensive spruce monocultures can be traced back to medieval Saxon forestry, the degree of so-called *Verfichtung* ('sprucification') reached new levels in the nineteenth century. With a total share of 53 percent in 1883 and 64 percent in 1937 respectively, Saxony had the highest proportion of spruce among all German states.[54]

As a matter of fact, all of these changes had positive effects for paper manufacturing. Modern forestry practices, in essence, fitted the needs of the new industry. It is more difficult to judge whether industrial demand directly drove environmental transformation. For a long time, forest planning had mainly ignored changing consumer needs, still concentrating on producing high-grade timber. At least there is some evidence that local foresters were aware of the significance of the emerging pulpwood supply regime. At times forest authorities made concessions to the needs of ground-wood mills, which asked for freshly cut wood and commanded additional felling.[55] Moreover, in several scientific articles published in the 1870s and 1880s, the Saxon forester Zschimmer described the new market opportunity to his colleagues, stating that pulp and paper mills were "an industry that deserves the attention of foresters and their sympathy to a great extent, [. . .] an industry whose blooming and flourishing is closely connected to the blooming and flourishing of our forests."[56] Obviously, Zschimmer hoped to commercialize environmental expertise and transfer ecologic into economic capital.

Despite its self-portrayal, scientific forestry knew its business. The fact that forest officials continually tried to restrict pulpwood imports by asking for prohibitive tariffs is a strong indicator of how important pulpwood revenues were to German forestry.[57] Especially the sales crisis of the inter-war period reminded foresters of the pulp and paper industry as a potential customer. To increase economic efficiency, experts proposed "cultivating fast-growing species especially suited for pulpwood production."[58] Before that, the paper industry had triggered the industrialization of Germany's forests in a more indirect manner. The development was based on a coincidence of interests rather than direct interference. The paper industry stimulated ambitions of rationalizing and intensifying timber production that were intrinsic to the forest reform policies of the early nineteenth century.

This can be exemplified by discussing how spruce became the main resource of the German forest economy. In the beginning of modern forestry, it was chosen for reforestation measures because of its fast growth and modest requirements. Planting spruce monocultures was seen "clearly as a temporary interim solution," while rising demand and consumer preferences made it a steady development.[59] If you asked paper manufactures what they needed, their answers were predictable: "only spruce or exclusively spruce, preferring spruce, spruce most valued, reluctantly fir, pine not at all, or pine is unusable."[60]

At the same time, pulpwood helped to make the practice of thinning cost-efficient. In order to increase total forest growth, small and feeble trees were routinely cut and sold to pulp mills, which became major buyers of this type of wood. Thinning was recommended by the classical authors of the early nineteenth century, but it was hard to establish. During the 1850s, most of Saxony's local forest authorities did not apply any measures at all, and the central forest administration had to threaten foresters that "those noticeably lacking behind with this kind of economic operation might easily face inconveniences."[61] The main argument against thinning was its lack of profitability, and this only changed with the emergence of pulpwood demand. Now the percentage of state forests in which thinning was applied grew from 0.44 percent annually in 1850–1854 to 2.9 percent in 1889. Instead of 7.5 solid cubic meters per hectare, 20 solid cubic meters were extracted.[62] At the time, about a quarter of the forest administration's revenues came from so called "intermediate usage," and thinning had been "intensified so much that it needed to be mitigated."[63] In 1932, once more, the *Forstwirtschaftliches Centralblatt* appreciated the distinct connection between forestry and the paper industry:

> The possibility to use small-dimensioned spruce as pulpwood gave forest owners the possibility of a better thinning record and, therefore, a more intensive forest maintenance. [. . .] Selling pulpwood is the precondition to establish first-class forest stands.[64]

It is clear enough that forestry did not oppose industrialization in principle; there is rather a coevolution of forestry and industry. For Germany, however, it is appropriate to speak of a limited industrialization of forests, because

industrial interests did not reach the forests unfiltered. While spruce plantations and thinning corresponded to the intrinsic logic of modern forestry,
German foresters did not turn forests into cellulose plantations. As long
as forest authorities had alternative sales opportunities for high-grade timber, they could afford to deliberately refuse price competition with foreign
pulpwood producers. Additionally, their commitment to the principles of
sustainability arguably limited short-term productivity.[65] Pulpwood imports
softened industrial pressure and allowed German forestry to block a higher
degree of forest conversion. Here the environmental impact of trade became
multidirectional. It did not only exploit the resources of ever more regions,
which were integrated into the supply chain, it also allowed for alternative supply strategies and helped—in comparison, at least—to conserve
resources.

That forest authorities called for protective tariffs indicates that this
conserving effect of trade exceeded the interest of forestry. To sell pulpwood or not to sell it was rather a question of price than of principle. After
all, diverging interests did not hinder a growing symbiosis of forestry and
paper industry in general. As shown earlier, they were not only tied together
by overlapping needs in various fields but also by shared research interests and facilities. Here many different agents—entrepreneurs, researchers,
forest administrators—worked independently and collaboratively to manage resources more efficiently. Obviously, scientific research and trade were
appealing strategies to further advance large-scale production as the core of
industrialization. Wood as a raw material had the backing of scientific forestry, thus giving the paper industry a partner with outstanding human and
financial resources.[66] At the same time, the growing mutual dependence laid
the groundwork for future approaches to environmental issues. Focusing
on technical issues of pulpwood processing limited the scope of alternatives
discussed, and, at least to some extent, professional resource management
excluded other stakeholders. This became especially visible when paper sur-
rogates turned into a main focus of forestry research in the interwar period,
and forest scientists began to experiment with alternatives to spruce, such
as bamboo, eucalyptus, and poplar.[67] In the long run, this reaffirmed wood
as the central element of the paper industry's learning base.

NATURALIZING INDUSTRIALIZATION

The story of the Saxon pulp and paper industry can hardly be told without
its environmental implications. Here the task of integrating the environment, with its manifold physical aspects, into the production process is central to modern industrial practice. The way Saxon pulp and paper industry
incorporated wood as a new raw material exemplifies various dimensions of
this interconnectedness. Wood did not only affect the spatial structure of the
pulp and paper industry; with regard to the efforts to secure wood supply,

it also influenced the strategic and organizational development of industrial enterprises. This became visible in ecological restrictions, technological innovation, environmental learning, and management capabilities. Pulp and paper mills did not only adjust their location, they also tried to improve nature by establishing infrastructure and trade networks. They set up a new learning base to produce environment-related knowledge. Even more important, the industry transferred this asset into commercial knowledge in order to organize trade and fit itself into existing institutional arrangements.

The pulp and paper industry aimed at vertically integrating raw material production or at least making the process more suitable for mass production. This objective might have been overly ambitious; but environmental issues became a decisive driving force for corporate change and economic development. At the core of this process were two interrelated aims: on the one hand, the need to learn and create new commercial knowledge, on the other hand, the desire to improve nature and adjust it to economic workflows. Both aims envisioned a rationalization of business-environment relations, but each approached the problem from a different viewpoint, respectively adapting or reengineering. While both elements can be found in different fields of business activities, it seems as if the pulp and paper industry became more and more self-assured after the new resource regime was established at the end of the nineteenth century. Following successful adaptation, the logical next step was to bring commercial and environmental practices to perfection. New patterns of resource and knowledge management emerged that were stabilized by economic success and long-lasting institutional settings. The resulting incorporation of environmental issues into the business sphere, nevertheless, was neither trouble-free nor permanent.

The exceptional case of an industry that made the transition from one basic raw material to another within a few decades highlights the amount of knowledge and skill that was necessary to make economical use of nature. In other industries, the use of natural resources might not have had similar effects; however, business history should not turn a blind eye to the impact of environmental issues there as well.[68] In the paper industry, natural resources required new organizational capabilities not only because of input quantity but also because of management tasks specifically related to ecological issues. Obviously, purchasing and manufacturing wood differed from purchasing and manufacturing rags. The strategies applied here—professional expertise, vertical integration, or scientific research—were not limited to environmental issues or a specific type of business activity, but they needed to be carefully adapted. In the end, the various tasks connected with wood as raw material made growth and vertical integration successful strategies for pulp and paper mills, but they also highlight the importance of organizational adaptation. The resulting regime of pulpwood supply clearly indicates that natural preconditions never stood for themselves. The close and multilayered dependency between industrial enterprises and environmental change was embedded into organizational structures and managed by social actors.

Exactly the large variety of environmental relations and their openness to historical change ask for a more ecological interpretation of industrialization. It is not only a technological revolution or the unleashing of market powers but also a new mode of using the environment. In retrospect, the paper industry became an important driving force of so called rational forestry and modern forest management. Forests were rebuilt following the modernist logics of standardization and profitability in the paper industry. As different as they may seem, the challenges of opening up space, incorporating materiality, managing resources, and industrializing nature all produced new connections between forests and factories. In the long run, this led to more intensive, accelerated and efficient paths of using and consuming resources. The business strategies applied followed the modernist mindset of growth and high-speed throughput. Industrialization, however, is not about eliminating nature or bringing it into line: ecology is part of a coevolutionary development. New possibilities and objectives of resource use increased the complexity of human-environment relations and called for an active involvement with environmental issues. Economic, technological, and institutional change owed many impulses to environmental challenges and interactions.

Focusing on the adoption of industrial enterprises to the natural environment, this chapter calls for a broader understanding of industrialization. The impact of wood on the pulp and paper industry highlights the role of nature as a precondition and object of industrialization. The paper industry reshaped nature and depended on natural premises at the same time. The economy of the nineteenth century could not detach itself from ecological questions (even if it tried to do so, as in the cases of energy usage and pollution). Often enough it had to adapt itself to its ecological surrounding. In this line, Sara B. Pritchard and Thomas Zeller recently requested historians to give the environment a more active role in the industrialization process:

> Naturalizing industrialization [. . .] highlights the ways in which industrial processes were embedded within, and thus ultimately dependent upon, natural resources, environmental processes, and ecosystems. [. . .] Naturalizing industrialization also stresses the way in which industrialization involved not only significant social, economic, and technological change but also fundamental shifts in how people in industrializing societies perceived and interacted with nonhuman nature.[69]

Of course, 'naturalizing industrialization' does not mean that nature alone determined the course of economic developments. Nor should it be confused with a 'greening' of industrialization. The idea is not to make pollution and exploitation look harmless, but to stress the reciprocity as well as the historicity of human-environment relations. Or with other words: Paper is not nature's product just because it is made of water and wood; the way we produce and use paper is man-made and subject to historical change.

In the age of industrialization, resource usage was far from an idealized detachment of nature. At least, we need to realize that—historically—industrializing nature has been a tedious and complex process. It is clear that organizational and technical adaptation did not always succeed. On the one hand, environmental challenges themselves were dynamic and could not be managed with static solutions. Arguably, the dynamics of both economic and ecological change simply do not allow for an 'end of history.' Neither scientific research nor management facilities could completely control the materiality of wood or the vulnerability of trade networks. On the other hand, institution building often entailed the risk to produce lock-in situations, as might be argued in the case of pulp and wood research. For the pulp and paper industry, incorporating nature remained a moving target, and environmental issues were relevant in more ways than we usually think of.

From a business perspective, nature became a frontier line of activities that created risks and opportunities and asked for long-term commitment. This insight of mutual dependency, of course, does not offer any direct answers for contemporary problems. In today's economy, business and environmental interests collide often enough. Nonetheless, the history of industrialization—not only of papermaking—exemplifies how the way we look for solutions is specified by the past. In the case of wood as a raw material, not only the problems but also the solutions of today's paper industry clearly remind us of the ones chosen earlier. The strategies and structures developed in the nineteenth century turned into path dependencies and patterns of thought that remained influential until today. Reevaluating the interdependence of economy and ecology and redrafting our explanatory models might help us to look for alternatives.

NOTES

1 The industry's ecological record has been a major focus of contemporary environmental policy since the 1970s. See Council on Economic Priorities (ed.), *Paper Profits: Pollution in the Pulp and Paper Industry* (Cambridge, MA: MIT Press, 1972); OECD (ed.), *Pollution by the Pulp and Paper Industry: Present Situation and Future Trends* (Paris: OECD, 1973).

2 Cf. urgewald e.V. (ed.), *Update zum Alternativen Waldschadensbericht 2010* (Sassenberg: urgewald e.V., 2012). Download at https://urgewald.org/sites/default/files/update_wsb_2010.pdf (15.12.2014).

3 In 2013, German demand for paper and cardboard amounted to 19.9 million tonnes (or 247 kilos per capita), while German paper mills produced 22.4 million tonnes. German pulp mills produced 1.6 million tonnes of cellulose, while 3.5 million tonnes were imported. Cf. Verein Deutscher Papierfabriken (ed.), *Papier-Kompass 2014* (Bonn: VDP, 2014). Download at http://www.vdp-online.de/de/publikationen/angebot.html (15.12.2014).

4 Cf. Ricardo Carrere and Lawrence Lohmann, *Pulping the South: Industrial Tree Plantations and the World Paper Economy* (London: Zed Books, 1996); Marcel Rejmánek and David M. Richardson, "Eucalypts," in Daniel

Simberloff and Marcel Rejmánek (eds.), *Encyclopedia of Biological Invasions* (Berkeley: University of California Press, 2011), 203–209.

5 So Cristine Meisner Rosen, "The business-environment connection," *Environmental History* 10(2005): 77–79.

6 For this concept, cf. Alfred D. Chandler Jr., *Inventing the Electronic Century: The Epic Story of the Consumer Electronics and Computer Industries* (New York: The Free Press, 2001), 4–6.

7 For basic information on the following, see Günter Bayerl and Karl Pichol, *Papier: Produkt aus Lumpen, Holz und Wasser* (Reinbek: Rowohlt, 1986), 99–176; Peter. F. Tschudin, *Grundzüge der Papiergeschichte*, 2nd edition (Stuttgart: Hiersemann, 2007), 166–195. On paper production in general, Dard Hunter, *Papermaking: The History and Technique of an Ancient Craft* (New York: Dover, 1978); and Juha-Antti Lamberg, Jari Ojala and Mirva Peltoniemi (ed.), *The Evolution of Global Paper Industry 1800–2050: A Comparative Analysis* (Dordrecht: Springer, 2012).

8 Data taken from Wilhelm von Nöllenburg, *Das Papier auf dem Weltmarkt: Statistische Zusammenstellung und geoökonomische Untersuchungen* (Leipzig: Neue Deutsche Papier-Zeitung, 1926), 193.

9 See Julius Schultze, *Die Papierfabrikation im Königreich Sachsen unter besonderer Berücksichtigung ihrer Beziehungen zu den Holzschleifereien* (Tübingen: Kloere, 1912), 97. In regard to population, Saxony's share was about 7 percent in the German Kaiserreich and 9 percent in the Weimar Republic.

10 Cf. Jürgen Blechschmidt and Alf-Mathias Strunz, "Papierindustrie in Sachsen," in Bildungswerk der Sächsischen Wirtschaft (ed.), *Wirtschaft—Innovation—Bildung: Beiträge zur Darstellung von 100 Jahren Industrie- und Wirtschaftsentwicklung in Sachsen* (Chemnitz: Bildungswerk der Sächsischen Wirtschaft, 2000), 156–163.

11 Cf. Mathias Mutz, "Managing resources. Water and wood in the German pulp and paper industry (1870s–1930s)," *Jahrbuch für Wirtschaftsgeschichte* 50(2) (2009): 45–68; Mathias Mutz, "Nature's product? An environmental history of the German pulp and paper industry," in Bernd Herrmann and Christine Dahlke (eds.), *Elements—Continents: Approaches to Determinants of Environmental History and their Reifications* (Halle/Saale: Deutsche Akademie der Naturforscher Leopoldina, 2009), 259–264.

12 Richard Staudt, Die Standortwahl der deutschen Papierindustrie in theoretischer und historischer Untersuchung" (PhD diss., Köln, 1930), 29. The industry virtually "invaded" areas such as the upper valley of the Zwickauer Mulde River and its confluents. In 1860, there had been just six paper-producing facilities; by 1880, there were 43, and by 1900 there were 70. Cf. Mathias Mutz, "Naturale Infrastrukturen im Unternehmen. Die Papierfabrik Kübler & Niethammer zwischen Umweltabhängigkeit und Umweltgestaltung," *Saeculum. Jahrbuch für Universalgeschichte* 58(2007): 59–87.

13 Cf. Mutz, "Managing resources," 49–53.

14 For data sources, see Zschimmer, "Holzstoff- und Holzcellulosefabrikation in Beziehung auf Ausnutzung und Verwerthung der Hölzer," *Tharandter Forstliches Jahrbuch* 40 (1890): 239–259; Gerhard Diamant, *Deutschlands Papierholzeinfuhr im Rahmen seiner Papierholzbeschaffung* (Leipzig: Moltzen, 1936), 20; Nöllenburg, *Papier*, 86. For technical details, see Bayerl and Pichol, *Papier*, 121–132, 137–141; and Jürgen Blechschmidt and Alf-Mathias Strunz, "Der Beginn eines neuen Zeitalters der Papierfaserstoff-Erzeugung: Die Erfindung des Holzschliff-Verfahrens durch Friedrich Gottlob Keller," in Frieder Schmidt (ed.), *Papiergeschichte(n): Papierhistorische Beiträge Wolfgang Schlieder zum 70. Geburtstag* (Wiesbaden: Harrassowitz, 1996), 139–150.

15 Cf. Frieder Schmidt, "Tilghman, Mitscherlich und der Fall des Reichspatents 4179," *IPH Congress Book* 9(1992): 26–32.

16 Cf. Sächsisches Wirtschaftsarchiv (Saxon Business Archives, SWA), dept. U 47, no. 900, Statistik über Holz, Holzmasse, Zellulose, 1911–1915.

17 Cf. Gerhard Reinhold, *Die Papierholzversorgung* (Berlin: Carl Hofmann, 1927), 143. For German pulpwood supply, see also Martin Reinhold, "Forstwirtschaft und Papierindustrie," *Forstwissenschaftliches Zentralblatt* 54(1932): 113–131 and Kurt Mantel, *Holzmarktlehre: Ein Lehr- und Handbuch der Holzmarktökonomie und Holzwirtschaftspolitik* (Melsungen: Neumann-Neudamm, 1973), 153–157, 242–254.

18 Cf. Staatsarchiv Chemnitz (State Archives Chemnitz, StAC), dept. 33063, no. 1370, Holzverbrauch, 1908–1910.

19 Cf. Bruno Birkhahn, "Die Standortverschiebungen in der papiererzeugenden Industrie Europas" (PhD diss., Kiel, 1935).

20 Birkhahn, *Standortverschiebungen*, 21.

21 Cf. Schultze, *Papierfabrikation*, 247.

22 StAC, dept. 33063, no. 616, Note Carl Friedrich Leonhardt, January 17, 1933.

23 Cf. Max Thielemann, *Die Eisverhältnisse der Elbe und ihrer Nebenflüsse* (Halle/Saale: C.A. Kaemmerer & Co., 1907).

24 Cf. StAC, dept. 33063, no. 1369, Note Leonhardt Söhne: Unterhaltung eines Papierholz-Werklagers zwingendes Erfordernis, 1936.

25 Carl Adolf Alwin Rudel, "Zur Disputation über die Surrogate in der Papierfabrikation," *Central-Blatt für die deutsche Papier-Fabrikation* 17(1866): 89–91, 97–99, here 91.

26 Carl Gustav Schwalbe, "Die chemischen Arbeiten der Papierfabrikation während der letzten 50 Jahre," in Verein deutscher Papierfabrikanten (ed.), *Festschrift zum 50jährigen Jubiläum des Vereines: Der Verein deutscher Papierfabrikanten* (Berlin: Eigenverlag, 1922), 211–216, here 211.

27 Cf. Horst Niethammer, "Papier: Rohstoffe und Arten einst und jetzt," *Abhandlungen und Berichte des Deutschen Museums* 22(1954): 45–54.

28 Heino Castorf, *Die Patentpapierfabrik zu Penig. Ein Beitrag zur Geschichte des Papieres* (Magdeburg: Penig Eigenverlag, 1897), 95.

29 Justus von Liebig, the pioneer of agro-chemistry, foretold this trend when he advised his editor, Friedrich Vieweg, in 1855 to employ a chemist and not a papermaker as managing director of the publishing house's paper mill. See letter Liebig to Vieweg, Munich, March 28, 1855, in Margarete Schneider and Wolfgang Schneider (eds.), *Justus von Liebig: Briefe an Vieweg* (Braunschweig, Friedrich Vieweg & Sohn, 1986), 288–289.

30 Some German technical academies founded institutes for paper chemistry or technology, starting with Darmstadt in 1905. A more practical training was available at several technical schools for papermakers. While none of these schools was situated in Saxony, two of them—in nearby Altenburg and Köthen (both founded in 1905)—had close connections with the Saxon paper industry.

31 On the importance of business associations, see Christian Kurtz, *Verbände der deutschen papiererzeugenden Industrie 1870–1933* (Berlin: Duncker & Humblot, 1966).

32 Cf. Kübler & Niethammer (ed.), *Papier aus Kriebstein* (Darmstadt, Heppenstedts Wirtschafts-Archiv, 1956), 57, 60; Gustav Wilhelm Stegemann, *Die Papierherstellung der Vereinigten Bautzener Papierfabriken, Bautzen* (Leipzig: Übersee-Post, 1934), 45–48.

33 Universitätsarchiv Dresden (University Archives Dresden), dept. Forstliche Hochschule Tharandt, no. B 715, Letter Prof. Wislicenus to Councillor of the Forest Academy, November 16, 1927.

34 Ibd., Letter Dr. Friedrich Zacharias to Prof. Wislicenus, February 9, 1928.
35 C.M. Rosenhain, *Holz-Cellulose in ihrer geschichtlichen Entwicklung: Fabrikation und bisherigen Verwendung* (Berlin: Polytechnische Buchhandlung, 1878), 9. Cf. Franz Schaefer, *Die wirtschaftliche Bedeutung der technischen Entwicklung in der Papierfabrikation* (Leipzig: Klinkhardt, 1909), 117–151.
36 "Hauptversammlung des Vereins der Zellstoff- und Papierchemiker und-Ingenieure, Berlin, 4.–6. Dezember 1930," *Zeitschrift für angewandte Chemie* 44(1931): 86.
37 Cf. StAC, dept. 33063, no. 1369, Note Leonhardt Söhne: Unterhaltung eines Papierholz-Werklagers zwingendes Erfordernis, 1936.
38 In Saxony, a high degree of market integration is indicated by a high level of prices and a strong correlation with cyclical business fluctuations. Cf. Mantel, *Holzmarktlehre*, 495.
39 Mutz, "Managing resources," 51–53.
40 Leopold Hufnagel, *Handbuch der Kaufmännischen Holzverwertung und des Holzhandels*, 10th ed. (Berlin, Ulan Press, 1929), 35–36; also Leopold Hufnagel, *Handbuch der Kaufmännischen Holzverwertung und des Holzhandels* (Berlin: Ulan Press, 1905), 31–32.
41 Paul Heuel, "Die Papierholzversorgung Deutschlands" (PhD diss., Freiburg, 1921), 12.
42 See Reinhold, *Papierholzversorgung*, 82–87. As a matter of fact, only very few records on purchasing wood can be found in business archives, but what has been passed on fills folders.
43 Bayerisches Wirtschaftsarchiv (Bavarian Business Archives, BWA), dept. F 66, box 6, Die Entwicklung der Aschaffenburger Zellstoffwerke AG bis zum Zusammenschluss mit der Zellstofffabrik Waldhof zu den Papierwerken Waldhof-Aschaffenburg. Manuscript, 1972, 12.
44 StAC, dept. 33063, no. 1369, Stellungnahme der Firma Leonhardt Söhne, Crossen, January 7, 1936.
45 In 1914, the corporation owned more than 40,000 hectares of forest there. See Karl Eisemann, "Grundlagen, Aufbau und Organisation der deutschen Zellstoffindustrie" (PhD diss., Heidelberg, 1930), 49.
46 BWA, dept. F 66, box 6, Entwicklung der Aschaffenburger Zellstoffwerke AG, 12. In 1907, for the first time, the firm bought 19,000 hectares in Russia.
47 For the organizational development of the German pulp industry, cf. Eisemann, "Grundlagen," 38–57.
48 Cf. SWA, dept. U 47, no. 614, Contract Kübler & Niethammer and Hoesch & Co., Kriebstein/Pirna, January 2 and 3, 1914.
49 It was the task of the "Papierholzbeschaffungsstelle GmbH" (founded in 1916) to organize these deliveries. See Bundesarchiv Berlin (Federal Archives Berlin, BArch), dept. R 8756, Papierholzbeschaffungsstelle, 1916–1920.
50 BArch, dept. R 8756, no. 2, Besprechungen mit Abteilung VII B Oberost über Erwerbung von Waldobjekten im besetzten Gebiet, January 31, 1918.
51 For a statistical analysis of international pulpwood trade in the interwar period, see Reinhold, *Papierholzversorgung*, 87–96.
52 Cf. Erhard Schuster, "Der Einfluß der wirtschaftlichen Entwicklung des aufstrebenden Kapitalismus auf Holznutzung und Baumartenwahl in der Forstwirtschaft, dargestellt vor allem am Beispiel Sachsens," *Archiv für Forstwesen* 10(1961): 1208–1227.
53 Deicke, "Die Preisbewegung beim Stamm- und Klotzholz in den Königl. Sächs. Staatsforsten von 1880 bis 1912 und die Beziehungen zwischen beiden Sortimenten," *Tharandter Forstliches Jahrbuch* 64(1911): 256–288.
54 Alfred Wobst, *Forstgeschichte Sachsens 1919–1945* (Hannover: Schaper, 1967), 10; Klaus Dittrich, "Der sächsische Wald: Sachsens Wald zwischen Tradition und Gegenwart," *Der Wald* 42(1992): 221–223, 416–419.

55 So Bernhard Dropisch, *Holzstoff und Holzcellulose. Ihre Herstellung und Verarbeitung für die Zwecke der Papierfabrikation* (Weimar: Voigt, 1879), 14.
56 Zschimmer, "Holzstofffabrikation," 251. Also Zschimmer, "Eine neue Holzverwendung," *Tharander Forstliches Jahrbuch* 25(1875): 25–28; Zschimmer, "Mittheilungen über die Fabrikation von Cellulose," *Tharander Forstliches Jahrbuch* 31(1881): 104–107.
57 In 1892, the German government abolished import tariffs on pulpwood (established in 1879). Pulpwood up to 1 meter in length and 20 centimeters in diameter was made tariff-free. Although this exemption was highly disputed and opposed by the forest authorities, it remained intact and was even widened. Cf. Reinhold, *Papierholzversorgung*, 99–104.
58 Rubner, "Steigerung der Papierholzproduktion Deutschlands durch waldbauliche Maßnahmen," *Wochenblatt für Papierfabrikation* 69(42) (1931): 1–10, here 3.
59 Dittrich, "Der sächsische Wald," 223.
60 Zschimmer, "Holzstofffabrikation," 252.
61 StAC, dept. 30301, no. 143, Oberforstmeisterei Schwarzenberg to Oberförster des Forstbezirks, May 23, 1857.
62 So Zschimmer, "Holzstofffabrikation," 250.
63 Wobst, *Forstgeschichte*, 59.
64 Reinhold, "Forstwirtschaft," 131.
65 For a general interpretation of German forest history see Karl Hasel and Ekkehard Schwartz, *Forstgeschichte: Ein Grundriss für Studium und Praxis*, 2nd ed. (Remagen: Kessel, 2002), 264–289.
66 Cf. Rubner, Steigerung der Papierholzproduktion."
67 For example, this was a research topic at the newly established "Institut für Ausländische und Koloniale Forstwirtschaft" (Institute for Foreign and Colonial Forestry) in Tharandt. Cf. Franz Heske, "Forstwirtschaftliche und ingenieurtechnische Voraussetzungen zur modernen Erschließung des Kolonialwaldes," in *Wochenblatt für Papierfabrikation* 75(4) (1941): 47–48.
68 Cf. Christine Meisner Rosen and Christopher C. Sellers, "Business and the environment," in Regina Lee Blaszczyk and Philip B. Scranton (eds.), *Major Problems in American Business History: Documents and Essays* (Boston and New York: Houghton Mifflin, 2006), 28–35; Hartmut Berghoff and Mathias Mutz, "Missing links. Business history and environmental change," in *Jahrbuch für Wirtschaftsgeschichte* 50(2) (2009): 9–21.
69 Sara P. Pritchard and Thomas Zeller, "The nature of industrialization," in Martin Reuss and Steven H. Cutcliffe (eds.) *The Illusory Boundary: Environment and Technology in History* (Charlottesville, VA: University of Virginia Press, 2010), 69–100, here 70.

10 Trading Degradation for Conservation

Revaluing Rural Landscapes in the American South

Craig E. Colten

One ambitious New Deal project sought to wrest rural families from impoverished situations and resituate them to better circumstances. The object was to move them off forlorn farms and relief rolls and then to restore the vacated properties to more productive uses. While national in scope, the Resettlement Administration oversaw this effort and gave considerable attention in the American South. The first step in this process was to create a new geography of the land that had locked farm families into poverty or to revalue the rural landscape by reclassifying lands where farming was viable as "submarginal."[1] Declaring a landscape worthless was the easy step.

Once redefined, the Resettlement Administration could proceed with rehabilitating both places and people. But to begin that process, it had to make a case that there were better uses than small-scale farming or timber removal and that the submarginal locations would benefit from a massive makeover. Pressing a clear conservation agenda, federal authorities proclaimed that much of the exhausted land would be more productive as wildlife conservation tracts, federally managed forests or pasture, or recreation areas—the latter for the restoration and conservation of the spirit of the area's inhabitants. Thus as quickly as the land received a 'submarginal' classification, managers had to restore its value and this time as worthy and productive through wise use. This double revaluation was quite a feat, but not out of keeping with the grand plans of the New Deal and its enthusiastic leaders who sought to trade the degradation produced by private property owners for the benefits of federally managed conservation.

This chapter draws on the planning documents of the Resettlement Administration and considers how they imposed a federal classification on rural property: first to justify federal acquisition and second to convert it to other uses. Although similar efforts took place nationwide, the programs of the South are especially poignant, because the relabeling of the landscape provided a sharp critique of social practices frowned upon by the New Dealers and reinforced the view that the South writ large was a sprawling 'problem area.' This effort represented a renewed criticism of small farmers with antebellum precedents and one embraced by local elites who ultimately joined in the chorus initiated by federal planners. While there are important economic

implications wrapped up in this process, this is an examination of the historical process that revalued the landscape, a process that eventually produced
a patchwork of parks and other federal properties dedicated to conservation
principles and that reflected a powerful national agenda in terms of land-use
planning and recreational spaces across the American South.

CREATING PLACES AND LANDSCAPES

Geographer Yi-Fu Tuan discusses how affixing names to an undifferentiated
landscape imbues places with meaning and value.[2] Tuan's approach suits the
Resettlement Administration's use of language to degrade and then rehabilitate rural lands. Beyond attaching meaning to places, the intentional designation of family farms as 'submarginal' exhibits the power of a central authority
to impose its own order on the landscape. This has the impact of 'norming'
the landscape, unifying it under a nationalist agenda. Renaming places and
landscape features typically accompanies colonization, military conquest,
or political regime change. Those who attach new names may impose their
exotic language, remind the conquered who is in power, or promote their
own ideological and political objectives as they mangle words taken from
native languages.[3] Even the National Park Service, through its shifting interpretive and management emphasis, has reordered the landscape.[4] With submarginal lands, it was essential for New Dealers to redefine the landscape
as worthless first, and then restore its value as part of a national rehabilitation program through a combination of text and actions on the land. These
efforts contributed to one of the most ambitious landscape transformations
by the US government since the creation of the land alienation system.[5] And
although the impact of the Resettlement Administration was a modest part of
the overall New Deal agenda, it had a huge impact on certain locales.

Federal officials used a narrative that was sharply critical, not just of the
eroded slopes, incinerated cutover lands, and the dilapidated housing found
on submarginal lands, but it directly attacked the social conditions that contributed to them. There was an undercurrent in their critique that the poor
quality lands were a major factor in the degraded quality of life found there. At
the critique's core was the notion that these submarginal lands could only support poverty and that they needed to be taken out of private ownership. This
was a familiar account with roots in antebellum reform efforts, but one that
also rearticulated the federal economic recovery and conservation mission.
Steven Stoll makes the case that antebellum agricultural 'improvers' saw government management as a path toward more orderly development and that
these efforts laid the foundation for later conservation.[6] Nineteenth century
agricultural reformer Edmund Ruffin scolded small farmers for abusing their
land while he advocated state activism to guide improvements.[7] While Ruffin
and reformers of his era were unable to achieve the reforms they desired, they
saw a relationship between poor farmers and degraded landscapes.

Depression-era federal administrators saw a similar pattern of poor farmers and degraded land, and in the early years of the New Deal, the liberal reformers assailed the former plantation economy that bound sharecroppers and tenants into an untenable existence.[8] Beyond that, Rex Tugwell, an early administrator of the Resettlement Program, and others went so far as to criticize the nation's broader 'laissez-faire' economic system.[9] While the Resettlement Administration's initial liberal economic agenda encountered strong political resistance that forced its leaders to pull back on cooperative farms and resettlement projects in particular, the conservation impulse in land-use change remained a fundamental element of the program.[10] Many of the early New Deal agricultural programs benefited larger farmers more than their impoverished neighbors. Nonetheless, at its outset, the Resettlement Administration made the case for its programs by casting both the poor land quality and an oppressive economic framework as responsible for the blighted landscape. Salvation for these lands required the 'retirement' of abusive practices—namely those carried out in the name of laissez-faire economics—and restoration of the lands and people through new centrally planned and publicly beneficial practices. The rehabilitation of the South would blend conservation goals with economic development, and federal administrators sold it to local elites using carefully crafted metaphors and wording intended to gain their acceptance.

One practice that promised renewal was recreational land use. The rich planning documents allow us to retrace the textual demolition and restoration of selected landscapes. Through a literal reading, they reveal an explicit disdain for the traditional Southern economic hierarchy that was not always in alignment with the program's outcomes, all the while holding out promise for conservation-oriented reforms that were not always ecologically sound. In this way, the Resettlement Administration sought to trade destructive land uses for productive ones, and in doing so, nurture practices that would produce sustainable yields of forest, pasture, and recreation. The ambition of the New Deal reformers, like previous reformers, exceeded their ability to rework the physical terrain and economic system as extensively as they reshaped it with their words. Yet with the investment of over $43 million in land purchases, they prompted local leaders to adopt their language and embrace some of their objectives. This success enlarged federal holdings in the South by over 2 million acres (809,000 hectares), enabled states to create park systems and expanded conservation programs across the countryside, and boosted forest product and recreational economic activities at the local level for decades to come.[11]

DEFINITION AND SCOPE OF SUBMARGINAL LANDS PROGRAM

Franklin D. Roosevelt's administration placed tremendous emphasis on federal planning to chart the country's long-term economic recovery, and planning entailed imposing a classification system on the landscape that would guide federal programs. As part of this effort, the National Land Use Planning Committee's (NLUPC) 1933 report defined submarginal lands as "those areas that are not clearly adapted to use for farming."[12] Among the traits that characterized submarginal, or problem, lands were decayed farming systems that had deteriorated due to drought, erosion, pest infestation, depleted soil fertility, or cutover forests. The NLUPC recognized that the social and economic milieu contributed to those conditions and pointed out that land tenure systems in the South, along with repressive tax policies and credit systems, impacted the stewardship of rural lands.[13] In its 1936 annual report, L. C. Gray wrote that the Resettlement Administration was

> the first comprehensive program aimed primarily at acquiring land not for a special purpose but at correcting the pathological conditions of land use which have developed through the years as a result of a laissez-faire policy of land use and settlement.[14]

He also hit hard at one of the sacred principles of American land policy—the homestead acts.

> For a long time there was a tacit assumption underlying our land policy that if we would make it easy to acquire land either from the Federal Government or by purchase from private owners, farm families could be trusted to find suitable locations and to utilize the land to best advantage not only to themselves but also to the general welfare. The Nation has now learned from sad experience [the dust bowl on the Great Plains and soil erosion in the South] that this assumption is largely fallacious.[15]

Not only had farmers been poor judges of the quality of land and its ability to support their families, but scattered settlement had imposed costs on government in the form of inefficient roads, schools, and other public services. Prudent centralized planning, however, could reverse these economic 'maladjustments.' Such assertions did not sit well with farmers or politicians, but they reflect the position of the bureaucrats seeking to redefine the rural landscape who considered small farmers as poor land stewards. As Cole Harris has argued for resettlement of indigenous peoples in colonial Canada, the overlay of a new cadastral geography reordered space. In this case, poor farming families in the South were the impacted group and many were African American. Although promoted as democratic, the Resettlement Administration's revaluing of the landscape worked primarily to the advantage of the region's elite and not for the dispossessed.[16]

The NLUPC called for appropriate adjustments that centered on public acquisition of submarginal lands and their removal from private agricultural or forest uses. Promoters of this policy argued that it was essential to create a new public domain and that private adjustments could never produce the necessary large-scale transformation. Only when reassembled in federal hands could these lands be rehabilitated and put to more productive uses. As described in internal documents, the effort was

> a program of land conservation and utilization, including the retirement of lands which are unsuited for cultivation, in order to correct maladjustments in land use, and to assist in controlling soil erosion, protecting watersheds of navigable streams, and protecting the public lands, health, safety and welfare.[17]

It was also "directed primarily toward changing, by means of public purchase, existing patterns of land use which cause, or are likely to cause, rural poverty, waste of public funds, unduly expensive or inefficient local government, or waste or misuse of land resources."[18] Public management, the program presumed, would provide superior oversight to private stewardship.

President Roosevelt authorized $25 million in 1934 to begin acquiring submarginal lands and to commence their conversion from worthless to productive and thereby reverse the value of the rural landscape.[19] Early resettlement projects encountered political opposition and forced a shift toward conservation-oriented projects—national forests and recreational uses. Nonetheless, by April 1937, there were 206 land acquisition projects, encompassing over 9 million acres (3.6 million hectares), pressing the agenda forward nationwide. This group included 46 recreational areas containing over 400,000 acres (161,874 hectares).[20] Within the total number, 99 resettlement projects remained (involving both land acquisition and relocation of residents), and 61 of those were in the South.[21] By the end of 1937, this number stood at 122 active resettlement projects.[22] Most of the better-known resettlement projects sought to consolidate rural families in urban settings or attempted to reassemble farmers into rural cooperatives.[23] In addition to those, there were many small multipurpose rural land utilization projects that uprooted somewhere in the neighborhood of 100–500 families per project area and aided their relocation to better farmland nearby.[24] In addition to the resettlement recreation projects, there were recreational demonstration projects carried out by CCC crews and the massive multipurpose TVA project.[25] Overall, the South was a major target for and beneficiary of aid for recreational projects—a reflection of the intent to bring the region into social and economic alignment with national goals. While the Resettlement Administration programs had less overall economic impact than hoped for, and indeed met political and popular resistance after 1936, the process of relabeling the landscape was effective.[26]

What was obvious from the outset was that denuded forests and gullied farms were not ideal recreational properties—hardly sublime settings (Figure 10.1). As historian Phoebe Culter put it, New Deal programs "transformed unlikely and downright inhospitable settings across the land into vignettes evocative of the Eastern woodland resort."[27] While it might be

Figure 10.1 Eroded Mississippi landscape typical of the property classified as 'sub-marginal' across the South.

Source: Farm Security Administration, LC-USF342-T01–003046-A. Courtesy Library of Congress.

a stretch to compare some of the Southern rural recreation areas to the grand resorts of the Adirondacks or Blue Ridge Mountains, transformation was considerable for certain locales. The NLUPC recognized a hierarchy in recreational lands and acknowledged that national parks had "scenery of supreme and distinct quality" and that state parks had scenic characteristics that were "better than average."[28] It was the CCC-recreation demonstration projects that frequently became key components in state park systems. Beyond the locations with dramatic scenery, there were areas within the submarginal lands with value for active recreation "but lacking in qualities of scenic, prehistoric, historic, or scientific interest" that deserved a lesser title such as recreation grounds.[29] Reporting on one such project, the proposed Natchez Trace, a Resettlement Administration official noted that "It is impossible to call the area beautiful for the land is poor, the hills eroded, the building too delapidated [sic], and the inhabitants too poverty stricken." Nonetheless, he recommended rehabilitation for recreation. An unidentified local official wrote about a proposed Louisiana site, "The project would be very fine as [a] desirable location to demonstrate recreation use for practically worthless agricultural land."[30] Through public acquisition, prudent planning, and conservation-minded management, transformation was possible. In the South, with fishing and hunting two prime recreational activities, reforestation and wildlife propagation were tantamount to a recreational paradise—regardless of the scenery.

DEVALUING THE AGRICULTURAL LANDSCAPE

To create a submarginal lands project, regional Land Utilization Division (LUD) officials first had to identify and describe potential sites. This involved multiple stages of investigation and proposals to document the degraded condition of the property. Instructions for selecting likely sites provided language cues to devalue land by labeling it as submarginal. In a 1936 discussion of its procedures, the LUD pointed their teams toward several sections of the South:

> The most striking land use problems have arisen in the cut over regions bordering on the Great Lakes, *the Gulf of Mexico* [emphasis added], and the northern part of the Pacific coast; the eastern highlands region resulting principally from attempts to farm rough land; *the southeastern hilly cotton and tobacco regions resulting from a one crop system of farming which has depleted the soil to such a state that profitable agricultural production is in many sections impossible under normal conditions* [emphasis added].[31]

Maladjustments produced soil erosion, denuded forests, and depleted mines. These conditions all contributed to land abandonment and tax delinquency that produced local financial distress.[32] Proposals detailed the qualities of a particular location that could make profitable farming impossible, and they highlighted two main problems: poor natural conditions or human-induced degradation. Numerous reports suggested both conditions conspired to create submarginal conditions.

Poor soil fertility and drainage factored into the natural conditions that made an area agriculturally unviable. In coastal Georgia, a plan noted that soils and drainage inhibited farming. A combination of depressions in a relatively flat landscape, underlain by sterile sands with a clay hardpan a foot beneath the surface trapped water during wet seasons but became excessively parched during dry weather.[33] The report argued that such conditions, while not suited to agriculture, could support forests, which the authors presented as a superior land use. The Sandhills project in North Carolina encompassed similar areas with readily drained sandy soils, which the authors claimed were better suited to pine trees than annual row crops.[34] In a Piedmont location in Alabama, the plan reported, "By and large the soil types [with some exceptions] are not capable of maintaining families living on them under the present system of farm organization."[35] Low fertility was the prime concern in this location, as it was in Claiborne Parish in North

Louisiana. The preliminary documents indicated, "the soil in the acreage is of the poorest type. The surface is covered with deep sand. . . . The entire area reflects depleted soil conditions."[36]

In Arkansas, rugged topography impeded cultivation. The Magazine Mountain tract, which became a state park, consisted of "ridges and mountains having very little land suitable for farming." Consequently, "drainage in the area is excessive, and damage from drought occurs almost every year."[37] The Northwest Louisiana project had steep slopes that contributed to rapid drainage and flood risks in the small valleys along its watercourses. Eroded soils filled wetland basins that contributed to the set of local problems.[38] Bottomland flooding presented a key criterium for the submarginal declaration in Mississippi:

> These bottoms are generally comparatively narrow and almost level. Thus when water from the hills comes into the valleys, these streams cannot take care of the rush of water. This makes the bottoms, although comparatively fertile, impractical for farming.[39]

In Northeast Georgia, regular inundations also provided planners with a justification for submarginal designation.[40]

Authors of reports saw pestilence lurking in the environment and thought it contributed to submarginal conditions. Environmental maladies were nothing new to accounts of the rural South, but they provided Resettlement Administration officials with another argument. In coastal Georgia, officials found "The majority of the people have malaria, and hookworm and pellagra [a dietary deficiency] are frequent occurrence, especially among the negro population."[41] At the Tuskegee, Alabama, site, investigators found that in addition to dietary deficiencies, "communicable diseases like malaria, typhoid, social diseases diphtheria are intensified by the open wells, unsanitary toilets, lack of knowledge about simple care of the sick and manure pits which breed millions of flies."[42]

As soil conservation advocate Hugh Hammond Bennet trumpeted the need to arrest soil erosion at the national level; the regional officers of the Resettlement Administration frequently found eroded land a primary problem across the South.[43] The proposal for a multipurpose tract in Northwest Louisiana described the land as "steeply eroded to hilly over the major portion of the area. The upland has been severely eroded and is now or is rapidly approaching submarginal condition."[44] The land acquisition plan pointed out the acreage represented "misspent human effort and funds as conditions [grew] worse year by year from the effects of erosion and lack of fertility to produce farm crops sufficient to finance operations."[45] Likewise about the Tuskegee, Alabama, project,

> Soil erosion is a pertinent factor in hastening the submarginality of the purchase area. The slope of the land, together with the poor methods of the land management, have intensified erosion.[46]

In an effort to establish a recreation area for African Americans in central Arkansas, a proposal noted:

> that the fertility of the soil has been almost entirely exhausted—it is now incapable of producing sufficient [income] to provide proper living standards. The character of the soil makes it susceptible to severe sheet erosion. Many portions of it are now badly washed and gullied. (Figure 10.1)[47]

In North Louisiana, planners assailed past practices: "The problem area consists of lands which for approximately eight decades have been in cultivation under one crop type system, and which consequently are depleted of practically all of the fertility that they may have originally possessed."[48] The document critiqued farming practices: "many farmers have attempted to cultivate such lands, resulting in extreme sheet and gully erosion and finally abandoning same. This practice has continued for many years resulting in a large per cent [sic] of wooded land cleared for cultivation, causing the area to be depleted of its natural fertility and resources, and becoming an unfit area to depend on for an income."[49] In Western Alabama, "serious economic and social maladjustments" existed prior to the depression, "because of the unsuitability of the land for agriculture" and the persistence of cotton farming on small worn-out farms.[50] Observers reported traditional Southern field rotation practices in a negative light. "When crop land can no longer produce, it is a general practice to clear another location."[51] While criticizing current practices, the proposal noted that forest and game management would be more appropriate land uses.[52] The phrasing both declared the land useless for agriculture and pointed toward better ultimate uses—thus beginning the verbal rehabilitation.

Fire, in the eyes of federal planners, presented another human abuse of the rural landscape that produced submarginal conditions. In West Alabama, "Some of the wooded hills are badly eroded due to annual burning which prevents reforestation and destroys vegetation and humas [sic]."[53] Fires in cutover land also inhibited the economic well-being in coastal Georgia.[54] In Northeast Georgia, despite "the absolute lack of forest ground cover the constant occurrence of these fires[,] the lands are more susceptible to erosion, the natural accumulation of soil fertility is retarded, and in a great many instances the young timber is wholly destroyed."[55] Lacking an appreciation for the ecological importance of fire to sustain Southern forests, New Deal reformers castigated the Southern customs of 'burning the woods' and used this practice as another device to condemn the landscape.

Deforestation constituted another abusive practice according to the federal officials. In Eastern Alabama, a proposal declared "The forest resources have been woefully abused." It continued, "the forests have been raped, and the land and natural resources have been brutally exploited."[56] In the proposed Georgia coastal flatwoods area, authors of the proposal stated:

"as the timber was gradually cut out and as the fertility of the cleared land declined, the economic and social problems increased." It noted further that "large tracts of land are being completely denuded of timber by mill operators, followed by fire; such practices will tend to reduce rather than increase employment."[57]

Small farms, or inefficient operations, also were an element of existing land use that the program sought to rectify. Planners in Arkansas argued that: "a large part of the land which is clearly submarginal under the present system of farming might furnish a fair income under a more extensive system."[58] With average farm sizes of only 29 acres, the plan recommended that in order to earn a fair income, each farmer should receive 67 acres of cropland along with 13 acres of woodland pasture, while cattlemen should receive 370 acres (149 hectares) for pasture plus 50 acres (20 hectares) for hay and another 400 acres (161 hectares) for reforestation. Rugged topography in the area, along with the small farm size had contributed to excessive farm abandonment (109 of 629 farms in the area).[59] Abandonment reflected not just physical conditions, but a failed settlement system.

Frequently, the tenant-sharecropper farming system of the Cotton Belt received blame for land degradation.[60] After the arrival of the boll weevil disrupted cotton production in Alabama's "Black Belt in the early twentieth century," sandy soils near Tuskegee had responded to fertilizers and encouraged some farmers to begin tilling these hilly forested lands. But this shift in cultivation merely brought in absentee landlords and tenant operators to the proposed land utilization area. "Following a farm management system of laissez faire, the hills, which a generation ago responded to 'quick acting commercial fertilizers,' are now for the most part dormant." The report chastised the "crop-lien" system as a major factor in soil erosion and land degradation. "Under this system the tenants have been so busy trying to meet their current obligations they have not had time nor inclination to think seriously of soil erosion, and the conservation of the resources in their midst."[61]

In Northeast Georgia, traditional farming practices also became the object of the verbal assault. "The mode of living and methods of farming used by these people are practically the same as they were 50 years ago."[62] According to the plan, these antiquated practices contributed to erosion, soil exhaustion, and field abandonment—all of which led to impoverished conditions and a degraded landscape. The plan also noted illiteracy and criminal behavior, which inflated social costs.[63] In many locations, the reports argued mismanagement was a principal contributor to untenable landscapes.

Within the smaller space of the individual homestead, plans also critiqued sanitary conditions and housing. For the West Alabama project, the report indicated that "less than one percent of the homes on the acreage to be purchased have sanitary conveniences"—or toilets. It also observed most water came from shallow wells or springs and in some cases it arrived at the house after flowing through "troughs made of hollowed out logs. Neither the wells nor the springs are protected from contamination."[64]

Houses too became the object of derision. In West Alabama, where 80 percent of residents reportedly had inadequate housing, "Most houses are seriously in need of repair. Many of them are so badly dilapidated that they hardly provide protection from the elements."[65] In coastal Georgia, housing stock received similar treatment:

> houses are small, flimsy and inadequately screened. During parts of the year many mosquitoes and flies are found in the area, but few houses are screened to keep them out. Not more than 2 per cent of the houses are painted; many have leaky roofs.

The same report went on to claim, "Houses are single floored, with no heating, cooking or lighting arrangements other than fireplaces. Buildings are in a bad state of repair, with sagging corners, poor roofing, and crumbling foundations."[66] Planners saw little hope for reusing old farm structures in the new recreational areas. The budgets for the two North Louisiana projects, included as a basic cost the 'obliteration' of preexisting farmsteads.[67]

CONSERVATION AND A REVALUED LANDSCAPE

Each submarginal lands plan included statements about future uses, and these served as the core texts for declaring the potential for revaluing the landscape. In a proposal for a particularly ambitious parish-wide project in the rolling hills of North Louisiana, the planners argued that a resettlement project would "serve as a demonstration of how millions of acres of worn-out discarded land in the 'Deep South' can be brought back to productive uses."[68] In Northern Mississippi, similar sentiments appeared. "While the area is certainly submarginal for farming now and for the immediate future conditions can be foreseen, it is extremely well suited for the production of pine timber."[69]

Rehabilitation in words, as with the critiques, focused on several key elements, including restoring the land by controlling erosion and establishing forests or pasture, eradicating forest fires and abusive timber extraction, consolidating land and people into larger communities, and providing recreation as a means to uplift the population (Figure 10.2). L. C. Gray noted the conservation-minded objectives in the Resettlement Administration's 1936 annual report but also pointed out how the submarginal lands program would accelerate the benefits.

> Conservation, however, looks largely to the future. It became gradually apparent that in addition to conserving resources for the future through avoidance of unnecessary waste, it is also important to achieve a more

Figure 10.2 Corney Lake in North Louisiana was created after farmers were relocated from submarginal lands. The property includes a national forest managed under conservation principles and a lake used for fishing.

Source: courtesy Claiborne Public Library.

adequate utilization in the present. In fact, inadequate or improper use of our lands is essentially wasteful, and adequate use for the present in large measure is not incompatible with conservation for the future.[70]

His statement revealed an impatience with a slowly unfolding conservation program and a desire to implement more immediate changes.[71]

Comments on the specifics of rehabilitation generally began with reforestation and its associated conservation-oriented benefits.[72] The expansive Bienville Parish, Louisiana, project plan stated that three of its purposes were "to reclaim land damaged by soil erosion and gullies by placing them in permanent forests and pastures," "to retire from cultivation such tracts of land which are submarginal for private ownership, and which are necessary to make the best use of land in the project area," and to "prevent continued burning of forest lands."[73] Effusive commentary about restorative benefits appeared in the coastal Georgia plan. "The area is particularly adapted for propagation and conservation of wild life, particularly deer, wild turkeys and quail. Considerable swamp acreage is included in the proposed area, which furnishes ideal cover for these species. The area also furnishes an ideal environment for fur-bearing animals." A secondary site within the proposed area "affords the opportunity for developing one of the best inland lake wild life refuges in the South." The century-old, human-made lake covered about 11,000 acres (4,451 hectares). But it "was drained several years ago for the misguided purpose of obtaining a large revenue from the sale of the numerous fish, chiefly bass, which the lake contained." Planners observed that "very little labor and materials will be necessary to restore the dam to it former condition" and thereby restoring a valuable fish and waterfowl habitat.[74]

In addition to habitat restoration, "the Purchase Area is in a region considered by foremost authorities as being the best timber-producing region in the South, especially for slash pine and long leaf pine." According to the plan, this area was seriously degraded due to poor fire protection, open range grazing, and poor extractive practices; and it argued that with improved management, the area would reach its full potential. Reflecting the ill-informed obsession with eradicating forest fires and open grazing, the plan called for the establishment of a fire protection system that would halt the "prevalence of uncontrolled burning, resulting chiefly from practices of the grazing interests in annually burning over the woods for pasture." Additional efforts would include culling diseased, dead, or deformed trees, thinning overly dense stands, and planting favored species.[75] Through such transformative efforts, the land utilization program would enable the landscape to flourish—at least for commercial forestry.

Likewise, near Tuskegee, Alabama, planners foresaw forest rehabilitation functioning to reduce erosion but also to provide local revenue from recreational hunting and fishing that would follow improved game management. The plan explicitly proclaimed that the land will be devoted to: "Forestry, including erosion control necessary for reforestation and for maintenance and restoration of the land." It also forecast economic benefits: "a managed forestry program will serve as a definite income base for the project." Both pine pulp and turpentine, along with recreational revenue, pointed toward renewed prosperity.[76]

Along with restoration of the physical landscape, New Deal planners claimed the submarginal lands program would serve as a tool for rehabilitating populations on the land. In one of the earliest statements, the National Land-Use Planning Committee declared:

> As a long run program the acquisition or retention of submarginal farms may be advantageous where such acquisition results in the regrouping of population that will make possible economies in local government, while promoting more favorable relationship between supply and demand of farm products, removing the opportunity for exploitative resale of such farms to misguided purchasers, and retarding the development of continuance of "slum" conditions in these areas.[77]

Through the "elimination and prevention of sparse and scattering occupancy" or eliminating low rural population density, the program would reduce local government costs for small schools, dispersed roads, and other services, but it would provide residents with greater educational opportunities and reduce social isolation.[78]

In the plan for the Northwest Louisiana project, the authors proclaimed that the

> actual purpose of the Submarginal Land Project is to relieve distressed and suffering humanity by lifting them from a hopeless condition on poor eroded soil. This improved situation will bring about a reduction of families on relief, increase family production and income.[79]

Likewise in Mississippi, the plan projected that by removing families from submarginal lands "we may be able to take numbers off the relief rolls and generally aid the communities affected."[80] For the Tuskegee, Alabama, project, planners commented that: "The influence of education and American progress is not commonly a part of their standard of living. Here is a large opportunity to rehabilitate many needy persons in our general plan of development."[81] Although these programs never lifted many families from poverty, the planning documents reveal the early enthusiasm of the New Deal liberals.[82]

Recreation prominently figured into social restoration. In 1938, the Resettlement Administration boasted that the "development of recreation areas in connection with land-use projects has made play areas available to local populations badly in need of such facilities."[83] These facilities would offer experiences previously unavailable to an impoverished rural population. In Alabama, planners lamented that residents had access only to church gatherings and hunting and fishing as recreational outlets. It projected that "our proposed development plans recreation facilities [that] will be provided to care for a much neglected phase of their activities."[84] Several planned campsites and picnic grounds would provide a means to raise the residents' standards and provide "adequate living and better citizenship."[85] In coastal Georgia, before the submarginal program began

> No organized recreational facilities [were] available and only the crudest types of recreation [were] indulged in, and this only by a small percentage of the population. Hunting and fishing [were] the chief recreation for the male members of the families, and [was] carried out without regard for conservation laws and regulations.[86]

Among the African Americans, the plans reported, "secret lodges" provided "obsessive" recreational interest. Proposed facilities for the Georgia site included a recreation center, picnic shelters, a boat dock, and wayside parks along highways. Hunting and fishing would take place within a conservation framework and outdoor activity would rejuvenate the area's residents.[87] The Northwest Louisiana plan authors also noted that "the only recreational advantages offered these people are occasional visits to a nearby town on Saturday or visiting with each other on Sunday or perhaps going to some rural church once a month."[88] To remedy this deprived condition, the final plan called for a lake with a public campground. Another common feature was land dedicated to scouting or 4-H organizations that strove to instill secular, national values in their young members. The Caney Lake project in Webster Parish, Louisiana, for example, included land dedicated for a Boy Scout camp. The Claiborne Parish, Louisiana, project converted cutover forests and abandoned farms with eroded fields into a human-made lake to provide "excellent boating, bathing, and fishing, and a protection harbor for wild fowl."[89] With an emphasis on outdoor recreation, the submarginal lands would enable socially impoverished farm families to escape the drudgery of their lives and find enjoyment and rejuvenation in nature.

The Northwest Arkansas tract provided perhaps the most scenic territory, and planners emphasized its recreational potential and how public facilities would improve access to recreation. It declared,

> A recreational project should attempt to provide for the various interests of a great many people; some people from the standpoint of recreation want to play in the ordinary way; some want to rest; some want to hunt; others to fish, hike, ride, go boating and swimming. The Ozark Region provides opportunity for the satisfaction of these interests under private ownership for a limited number. It is necessary, however, to have publicly owned enterprises of these kinds if the population in this part of America is to be provided with recreation facilities.[90]

Intended to serve local residents, the project reflected the desire to uplift rural residents through outdoor activities.

The Resettlement Administration plans called for expressions of support and cooperation from locals—both leaders and the citizens likely impacted by relocation. Not surprisingly, written testimony came from government officials, educators, and business leaders. The planning documents commonly reported local citizens facing resettlement welcomed federal intervention, but they contained no letters from relocated farm families. Endorsements for the Claiborne Parish project came from the superintendent of schools, the county agricultural agent, a district judge, the police jury, the mayor, the clerk of court, the sheriff and several businessmen and attorneys.[91] This limited cross section was typical of the community members who provided letters of support and reflects the process of dispossession by accumulation by the elite. Gilbert Fite reports that opposition by uprooted farm families was common, however, if ineffective.[92]

In the collection of supporting letters for each site, correspondence from local elites contained remarkably similar language to that used by the Resettlement Administration. A banker in Northwest Louisiana, noted that the submarginal lands program would "remove from the relief rolls families that are unable to sustain themselves on worn out lands," while helping them escape from under oppressive mortgages. He added, "I believe it will be of great benefit to relocate them on lands that are much more productive than the lands in this submarginal area." He also commented on business opportunities that relocation would create for his bank—namely, new homes and new levels of productivity that would enable families to pay off mortgages. He closed by observing that the reforestation of and game management on submarginal lands would "contribute to the welfare of the community."[93] A local educator wrote:

> The progress of our community depends on agriculture and the proper use of our lands. I am familiar with the lands covered by the rehabilitation area and know them to be unsuited to their present use [agriculture]. The condition of the people and their homes in this area clearly demonstrates the need for a more proper land use.[94]

Letters from the town mayor and police jury president expressed similar sentiment. Such support underscored the immediate recognition that this program, while touted as a means to address poverty, would benefit those with greater financial resources as well. And it would benefit the government by reducing the number on relief roles.

A group of businessmen endorsed the project near Paris in Northern Arkansas. They claimed to speak on behalf of the families to be resettled:

> We are of the opinion there are 250 families living in and around Magazine Mountain who can not [sic] make a comfortable living on their farms; that they cannot move to more profitable farming communities; that the majority are on the 'Relief' now and will continue to be so situated; that they would be glad to move to better communities.[95]

These businessmen obviously wanted to convert the residents to be more robust consumers in the local economy. Leaders of the business community of nearby Yell County proclaimed:

> we endorse the move as one with far-reaching and valuable features, especially for the farmers of the area. This land is worn out, and will no longer make crops worthwhile. It seems ideally fitted for the purpose for which it is intended as a land utilization project.[96]

The county agent noted that serious erosion had rendered the land incapable of supporting agriculture.[97] The state secretary of the game and fish commission chose to emphasize the recreational and conservation potential of the project: "All of these streams furnish suitable places for the construction of dams and the impounding of waters that will be extremely valuable for recreational purposes and that will materially increase the supply of fish in that locality."[98] In sum, local endorsements emphasized the worn-out quality of

land and its inability to support the farmers. They voiced few critical comments about the inhabitants themselves but condemned the landscape and
touted the projected rehabilitation through conservation-oriented practices.
All the while, they recognized that recreational revenue would flow to local
businesses and business owners.

While the plans for Southern projects contained no letters from the
potentially displaced, local leaders sometimes claimed to speak on their
behalf. The Tuskegee, Alabama, plan reported that "perhaps no group of
people are more loyal to the purpose and objective of the project than those
in the neighborhoods adjacent to it."[99] Yet, even in this case, the support
seems to come from the leaders at Tuskegee Institute and "leading farmers"
who were willing to sell portions of their property to the federal government. More commonly, the plans included brief statements about the preferences of the residents to be displaced. Among six items in a list of local
endorsements, the coastal Georgia plan noted "Residents of the Purchase
Area favor the project." Among the other supporters were state and local
officials, agricultural specialists, relief agency personnel, and school officials.[100] One Louisiana project ground to a halt due to the reluctance of
residents to sell their land at the government price. They sought not just
compensation for the land, but for the mineral rights in an area where rich
oil deposits had been discovered.[101] Another muted expression of opposition
appeared many years after the completion of a small resettlement project in
North Louisiana. As part of a campaign to secure federal funds to maintain
Corney Lake in the 1970s (Figure 10.2), a constituent wrote to Senator J.
Bennett Johnston to remind him that some landowners were reluctant to
sell their lands as part of the resettlement project in the 1930s and did so
only with the promise of a recreational lake.[102] The writer encouraged the
senator to honor the long-forgotten federal commitment. This letter suggests that opposition was more widespread than is obvious in the historical
record. Not all affected by resettlement embraced the redefinition of the
landscape.

CONCLUSIONS

In many respects, the revaluaton of the Southern rural landscape was
another step toward subjugation of a 'problem area' and followed a long
tradition of criticizing the poor stewardship of small farmers while calling for government intervention. Plans declared traditional agricultural
practices abusive and the resulting condition of the landscape a reflection
of failed economic activities. Degraded soils resulted from inept farming
on lands ill suited to cultivation. Denuded forests were the consequence of
rapacious timber harvests with no conservation efforts. Burning the woods,
according to prevailing conservation thinking, aggravated the consequence
of forest removal and inhibited restoration. And of course, by wasting the

countryside, Southern farm families found themselves mired in poverty and on relief. Through their isolation, they lacked adequate education and found recreation in uncontrolled hunting and fishing, fundamental religion, or secret lodges. The debasement of the landscape and its inhabitants was thorough and effective.

By converting the landscape to more productive uses, New Deal program managers, as previous reformers, sought to impose a new authority over portions of the South, to overcome the failures of free-market capitalism, and substitute centralized planning. Erosion control, reforestation, and game management would introduce conservation principles to the South. Converting land to the purposes it was best suited to, given prevailing concepts of ecology, would increase incomes and the region's overall productivity. The submarginal lands program would impose a new growth regime on the landscape. Just as the elite and scientific community sought to improve the landscape through drainage in Scandinavia (see chapter by Ruuskanen in this volume), conservation-oriented management would bring renewed vitality to the rural South. The resettlement program and its revaluation of the countryside would in effect force rural Southerners to abandon their social isolation and climb into the national economy in a productive way.

Recreation was a big part of this grand plan. Recreation areas created through this program would help restore the worn-out spirit of farm families. Paralleling the 'worthless lands' thesis, submarginal lands would provide a new use as recreational spaces and would function as valuable commodities that served a nationalist agenda after their recalibration—much as the scenery reserves in New Zealand (see chapter by Roche in this volume). They would offer secular diversions from emotional religion and secretive social societies and enable residents an opportunity to appreciate nature. Establishing youth camps would facilitate the introduction of a national culture to rural youth. And although the plans assailed traditional hunting and fishing, Southern males would be allowed to continue their traditional pursuits on federally owned and managed areas but within a conservation framework. Federal guidance toward establishing a new social order permeated the recreation plans.

Those who have studied the impacts of the New Deal in the South argue that it had limited economic impacts, particularly for the rural poor.[103] Program support eventually benefited the Southern elite more than the disenfranchised poor. And certainly, the relatively small number of Southerners affected by submarginal lands programs and the limited social changes they produced supports this argument. Nonetheless, the two-stage revaluation of rural landscape as submarginal and then productive was remarkably effective. Equally as important, the national and state forests continue to support local timber products economies, and state parks established during the program became much more important in local economies in the years after World War II. The dispossessed families may not have been uplifted but local economies did see benefits in the long term.

NOTES

1 Conceived of by the National Land-Use Planning Committee in 1933, the submarginal lands project, or land utilization program, fell under the Resettlement Administration between 1935 and 1937. Ultimately, before being phased out, it found its home in the Soil Conservation Service.
2 Yi-Fu Tuan, "Language and the making of place: A narrative-descriptive approach," *Annals of the Association of American Geographers* 81(4) (1991): 684–696. See also, Jeffrey Davis, "Representing place: 'Deserted Isles' and the reproduction of Bikini Atoll," *Annals of the Association of American Geographers* 95(3) (2005): 607–625; Christian Brannstrom and Matthew Neuman, "Inventing the 'Magic Valley' of South Texas, 1905–1941," *Geographical Review* 99(2) (2009): 123–145; and Steven Hoelscher, "Making place, making race: Performances of Whiteness in the Jim Crow South," *Annals of the Association of American Geographers* 93(3) (2003): 657–686.
3 Stuart Horsman, "The politics of toponyms in the Pamir Mountains," *Area* 38(3) (2006): 279–91; R.D.K. Herman, "The Aloha State: Place names and the anti-conquest of Hawai'i," *Annals of the Association of American Geographers* 89(1) (1999): 76–102; and Saul B. Cohen and Nurit Kliot, "Place names in Israel's ideological struggle over administered territories," *Annals of the Association of American Geographers* 82(4) (1992): 653–680. See also Lawrence D. Berg and Robin A. Kearns, "Naming as norming: 'Race,' gender, and the identity politics of naming places in Aotearoa/New Zealand," *Environment and Planning D: Society and Space* 14(1996): 99–122. For a critical review of place name literature see Ruben Rose-Redwood, Derek Alderman, and Maoz Azaryahu, "Geographies of toponymic inscription: New directions in critical place-name studies," *Progress in Human Geography* 34(4) (2010): 453–70.
4 Justin Reich, "Re-creating wilderness: Shaping narratives and landscapes in Shenandoah National Park," *Environmental History* 6(1) (2001): 95–117; and Terence Young, "False, cheap and degraded: When history, economy, and environment collided at Cades Cove, Great Smoky Mountains National Park," *Journal of Historical Geography* 32(1) (2006): 169–189.
5 Wilbur Zelinsky, "The imprint of central authority," in *The Making of the American Landscape*, ed. Michael P. Conzen (Boston: Unwin Hyman, 1990), 311–334.
6 Steven Stoll, *Larding the Earth: Soil and Society in Nineteenth Century America* (New York: Hill and Wang, 2002), 178–183.
7 Jack Temple Kirby, *Poquosin* (Chapel Hill, NC: University of North Carolina Press, 1995), 147 and John Majewski, *Modernizing a Slave Economy: The Economic Vision of the Confederate Nation* (Chapel Hill, NC: University of North Carolina Press, 2009), 54–59.
8 See, William C. Holley, Ellen Winston and T. J. Woofter Jr., *The Plantation South, 1934–1937*, Works Projects Administration Research Monograph 22 (Washington: Government Printing Office, 1940) and Charles S. Aiken, *The Cotton Plantation South Since the Civil War* (Baltimore: Johns Hopkins University Press, 1998).
9 Rexford G. Tugwell, "The resettlement idea," *Agricultural History* 33(4) (1959): 159–164. The Resettlement Administration looked abroad for precedent. See Erich Kraemer, *Land Settlement Techniques Abroad* (Washington, DC: Resettlement Administration, 1936). An earlier experiment in resettlement sought to reform peasant agriculture in Russia. See Peter Holquist, " 'In accord with the state interests and the people's wishes': The technocratic ideology of Imperial Russia's Resettlement Administration," *Slavic Review* 69(1) (2010):

151–79. Also, for a discussion of Germany's postwar resettlement effort see D. J. Alexander, "Some features of West German policy for improving the agriculture structure," *Journal of Farm Economics* 46(4) (1964): 791–804.

10 Sarah T. Phillips, *This Land, This Nation: Conservation, Rural America and the New Deal* (New York: Cambridge University Press, 2007), 81–82; Sara M. Gregg, *Managing the Mountains: Land Use Planning, the New Deal, and the Creation of a Federal Landscape* (New Haven, CT: Yale University Press, 2010), 175–212; and Roger Biles, *The South and the New Deal* (Lexington: University of Kentucky Press, 1994), 48–49.

11 See, Phillips, *This Land, This Nation*; Gregg, *Managing the Mountains;* and a thorough analysis of the historical roots of New Deal conservation appears in Neil M. Maher, *Nature's New Deal: The CCC and the Roots of the American Environmental Movement* (New York: Oxford University Press, 2008), especially chapters 1 and 2; and, Resettlement Administration, Letter from the Administrator, Senate Document 213, 74th Cong., 2nd sess., 12 May 1936, 25–31. Table 1a lists acreage and projected expenditures.

12 National Land-Use Planning Committee, *The Problems of "Submarginal" Areas, and Desirable Adjustments with Particular Reference to Public Acquisition of Land*, Publication 6 (Washington, DC: Government Printing Office, 1933), 1.

13 National Land-Use Planning Committee, *Problems of "Submarginal" Areas*, 2.

14 Gray, "The Program of Land Use Adjustment and Conservation," 3.

15 Ibid.

16 Farmers on the Great Plains rejected the criticism that they had caused farm failures and instead blamed it on the drought. See Phillips, *This Land, This Nation*, 128. Opposition by Southern congressmen prompted the Resettlement Administration to reorient its efforts to preserving, rather than dismantling, the family farm, Roger Biles, *The South and the New Deal* (Lexington: University of Kentucky Press, 1994), 48–49. And, Cole Harris, "How did colonialism dispossess? Comments from an edge of empire," *Annals of the Association of American Geographers* 94(1) (2004): 165–82.

17 Resolution, 13 January 1934, 1, Soil Conservation Service, Land Utilization Records, Record Group 114, Box 4, History Files, NARA-DC.

18 Ibid.

19 Ibid.

20 U.S. Department of Agriculture (hereafter USDA), Resettlement Administration, *Report of the Administrator of the Resettlement Administration, 1937* (Washington: U.S. Department of Agriculture, 1937), 9–10.

21 Roger Biles, *The South and the New Deal* (Lexington: University of Kentucky Press, 1994), 48.

22 USDA, Resettlement Administration, *Report of the Administrator of the Resettlement Administration*, 14.

23 Robert D. Leighninger, Jr., *Long-Range Public Investment: The Forgotten Legacy of the New Deal* (Columbia: University of South Carolina Press, 2007); Greta de Jong, *A Different Day: African American Struggles for Justice in Rural Louisiana, 1900–1970* (Chapel Hill, NC: University of North Carolina Press, 2002); and Donald Holley, "Old and New Worlds in the New Deal Resettlement Program: Two Louisiana projects," *Louisiana History* 11(2) (1970): 137–165.

24 USDA, Soil Conservation Service, Register of Land Utilization Projects, 1939, Soil Conservation Service, Land Utilization Records, National Archives, Record Group 114, Box 6, History Files, Washington, DC.

25 Clayton, "Program of the Federal Government," 60. For an extensive discussion of the CCC, see Maher, *Nature's New Deal*. Phoebe Cutler, *The Public Landscape of the New Deal* (New Haven, CT: Yale University Press, 1985), 157.

On the TVA see, Michael J. McDonald and John Muldowny, *TVA and the Dispossessed* (Knoxville: University of Tennessee Press, 1982). See also Donald Holley, "The Negro in the New Deal Resettlement Program," *Agricultural History* 45(3) (1971): 179–193 and *Uncle Sam's Farmers: The New Deal Communities in the Lower Mississippi Valley* (Urbana: University of Illinois Press, 1975).

26 Phillips, *This Land, This Nation*, 119. See also Sara M. Gregg, "Uncovering the subsistence economy of the twentieth century South," *Agriculture History* 78(4) (2004): 417–437 and Marion Clawson, "Resettlement experience on nine Resettlement projects," *Agricultural History* 52(1) (1978): 1–92. See also, Gilbert C. Fite, *Cotton Fields No More: Southern Agriculture, 1865–1980* (Lexington: University of Kentucky Press, 1984), 143–148.

27 Cutler, *Public Landscape*, 66.

28 National Land-Use Planning Committee, "Problems of 'Submarginal' Areas," 8. A discussion of the typical inheritance of abused land by state parks appears in Geoffrey L. Buckley, "The environmental transformation of an Appalachian Valley, 1850–1906, *Geographical Review* 88(2) (1998): 175–198.

29 National Land-Use Planning Committee, "Problems of 'Submarginal' Areas," 9.

30 Handwritten note, ca. 1935, Soil Conservation Service (hereafter SCS), Land Utilization Files, RG 114, Box 211, Natchitoches file, National Archives, Fort Worth, Tex. (Hereafter NARA-FW).

31 Resettlement Administration, Methods and Basis for Establishing Land Use Projects, January 1936, p. 1, SCS, Historical Files 1933–40, RG 114, Box 4, NARA-DC.

32 L.G. Gray, The Program of Land Use Adjustment and Conservation, Draft Annual Report for Resettlement Administration, June 1936, 4–5, SCS, Historical Files 1933–40, RG 114, Box 4, NARA-DC.

33 Resettlement Administration, The Final Plan for Georgia Coastal Flatwoods Upland Game Project for Planned Land Use, 1935, 3–4 and 13, SCS, Land Utilization Project Files (Hereafter LU Files), Box 103, GA-3 folder, RG 114, Box, NARA-DC.

34 Resettlement Administration, Submarginal Land Program, Agricultural Demonstration Project: Sand Hills Submarginal Lands Project, 1935, p. 2, SCS, LU Files, Box 303, NC A-1 file, NARA-DC.

35 Resettlement Administration, Final Plan for Tuskegee Planned Land Use Demonstration, 1935, p. 8, SCS, LU Files, RG 114 Box 3, AL-8 file, NARA-DC. See also, Sarah Warren and Robert Zabawa, "The origins of the Tuskegee National Forest," *Agricultural History* 72(2) (1998): 478–508.

36 Resettlement Administration, Development Plan: Claiborne Parish, Louisiana, Land Use and Population Adjustment, 1938, p. 1, SCS, Submarginal Lands Files, RG 114, WG8(h) file, NARA-FW.

37 Agricultural Adjustment Administration, Tentative Plan in Memorandum of Proposed Project: Magazine Mountain Forestry, Grazing, Game, and Recreation Project, Arkansas A-1, 1935, p. 5, SCS, RG 114, LU Files, Box 17, Ak-1 file, NARA-DC.

38 Agricultural Adjustment Administration, Memorandum of Proposed Project, Louisiana A-1, 1936, p. 4, SCS, RG 114, LU Files, Box 155, La-1 file, NARA-DC.

39 Resettlement Administration, Summary Report on Project Plan and Application: Mississippi A-1, 1935, p. 2, SCS, RG 114, LU Files, Files, Box 209, Ms–9 file, NARA-DC.

40 Agricultural Adjustment Administration, Summary of Information: Northeast Georgia Upland Game Conservation Project, 1935, p. 2, SCS, RG 114, LU Files, Box 99, Georgia A-1 file, NARA-DC.

41 Resettlement Administration, The Final Plan for Georgia Coastal Flatwoods, 19.
42 Resettlement Administration, Final Plan for Tuskegee Planned Land Use, 20.
43 Hugh Hammond Bennett, *Soil Conservation* (New York: McGraw Hill, 1939), and Hugh Hammond Bennett, *Soils and Agriculture of the Southern States* (New York: Macmillan, 1921).
44 Agricultural Adjustment Administration, Louisiana Proposal No. A-1, Northwest Louisiana Forestry and Pasture Making Project, 1934, 5, SCS, RG 114, Submarginal Lands Files, Box 281, LA-1 file, NARA-FW.
45 U.S. Department of Agriculture, Land Acquisition Plan: Northwest Louisiana Forestry and Pasture Making Project, 1938, 6, SCS, RG 114, LU Files, Box 155, LA-1 file, NARA-DC.
46 Resettlement Administration, Final Plan for Tuskegee Planned Land Use, 8.
47 National Park Service, Land Program Division, Pine Bluff Regional Negro Park: Proposed Submarginal Land Purchase, Jefferson County, Arkansas, 1936, 2–3, SCS, RG 114, Box 210, Proposed Negro Park folder, NARA-FW. There was often public resistance to parks proposed for African Americans. See William O'Brien, "Jim Crow NIMBYs: White resistance to proposed sites for state parks for African Americans," paper presented to the annual meeting of the American Society for Environmental History, 26 Feb 2009, Tallahassee, Fla.
48 U.S. Department of Agriculture, Land Acquisition Plan: Northwest Louisiana Forestry and Pasture Making Project, 1938, 3.
49 Ibid., 4.
50 Resettlement Administration, Preliminary Plan for Land Acquisition: West Alabama Planned Land Use Demonstration Project, 1936, 5, SCS, RG 114, LU Files, Box 7, Alabama 9 file, NARA-DC.
51 Resettlement Administration, Preliminary Plan for Land Acquisition: West Alabama Planned Land Use Demonstration Project, 7.
52 Resettlement Administration, Preliminary Plan for Land Acquisition: West Alabama Planned Land Use Demonstration Project, 2. It is precisely these arguments that echo antebellum critiques of small farmers. See Kirby, *Poquosin*, and Majewski, *Modernizing a Slave Economy*.
53 Resettlement Administration, Preliminary Plan for Land Acquisition: West Alabama Planned Land Use Demonstration Project, 7.
54 Resettlement Administration, The Final Plan for Georgia Coastal Flatwoods Upland Game Project for Planned Land Use, 7.
55 Resettlement Administration, Summary of Information: Northeast Georgia Upland Game Conservation Project, 6.
56 Quotes from Resettlement Administration, Final Plan for Tuskegee Planned Land Use, 2 and 4.
57 Quotes from Resettlement Administration, The Final Plan for Georgia Coastal Flatwoods Upland Game Project for Planned Land Use, 3 and 7.
58 Agricultural Adjustment Administration, Tentative Plan in Memorandum of Proposed Project: Magazine Mountain Forestry, Grazing, Game, and Recreation Project, quote from 1, 1–2 and 5–6.
59 Agricultural Adjustment Administration, Tentative Plan in Memorandum of Proposed Project: Magazine Mountain Forestry, Grazing, Game, and Recreation Project, quote from 1, 1–2 and 5–6.
60 For a discussion of critique of tenancy in the South, see Paul E. Mertz, *New Deal Policy and Southern Rural Policy* (Baton Rouge: Louisiana State University Press, 1978).
61 Resettlement Administration, Final Plan for Tuskegee Planned Land Use, 4 and 9.
62 Resettlement Administration, Summary of Information: Northeast Georgia Upland Game Conservation Project, 1935, 6, SCS, RG 114, LU Files, Box 99, Georgia A-2 file, NARA-DC.

63 Resettlement Administration, Summary of Information: Northeast Georgia Upland Game Conservation Project, 7.

64 Quotes from Resettlement Administration, Preliminary Plan for Land Acquisition: West Alabama Planned Land Use Demonstration Project, 10.

65 Resettlement Administration, Preliminary Plan for Land Acquisition: West Alabama Planned Land Use Demonstration Project, 10.

66 Quotes from Resettlement Administration, The Final Plan for Georgia Coastal Flatwoods Upland Game Project for Planned Land Use, 7–8 and 18.

67 Budget of 1938 attached to Agricultural Adjustment Administration, Louisiana Proposal No. A-1, Northwest Louisiana Forestry and Pasture Making Project.

68 Resettlement Administration, Project Proposal for Bienville Parish Project, 1938, 3, SCS, RG 114, Submarginal Lands files, Box 211, Bienville Parish folder, NARA-FW.

69 Lewis Long (Regional Administrator, Agricultural Adjustment Administration) to C.F. Clayton (AAA, Washington), Memo regarding "Alcorn-Prentiss Forestry, Game, and Recreation Project (Mississippi), 18 May 1935, 2, SCS, RG 114, General Records, Box 213, Proposed Mississippi Project file, NARA-FW.

70 L.G. Gray, The Program of Land Use Adjustment and Conservation, Draft Annual Report for Resettlement Administration, June 1936, 2, SCS, Historical Files 1933–40, RG 114, Box 4, NARA-DC.

71 Maher argues that New Deal conservation could trace its roots to Progressive Era conservation ideas. See Maher, *Nature's New Deal*, 43–77. Also, Samuel Hays, *Conservation and the Gospel of Efficiency: The Progressive Conservation Movement, 1890–1920* (Cambridge, MA: Harvard University Press, 1959).

72 Maher notes that the CCC began its program with an emphasis on reforestation too. Maher, *Nature's New Deal*, 54–55.

73 Resettlement Administration, Project Proposal for Bienville Parish Project, 1938, 3–4, SCS, RG 114, Submarginal Lands files, Box 211, Bienville Parish folder, NARA-FW.

74 Quotes from Resettlement Administration, The Final Plan for Georgia Coastal Flatwoods Upland Game Project for Planned Land Use, 34–35.

75 Quotes from Resettlement Administration, The Final Plan for Georgia Coastal Flatwoods Upland Game Project for Planned Land Use, 36–39.

76 Resettlement Administration, Final Plan for Tuskegee Planned Land Use, 29, 37, and 40.

77 National Land-Use Planning Committee, *Problems of "Submarginal" Areas*, 7.

78 Resettlement Administration, Methods and Basis for Establishing Land Use Projects, January 1936, 2 and Gray, The Program of Land Use Adjustment and Conservation, Draft Annual Report for Resettlement Administration, 9.

79 Agricultural Adjustment Administration, Memorandum of Proposed Project, Louisiana A-1, 10.

80 Resettlement Administration, Summary Report on Project Plan and Application: Natchez Trace Forestry, Pasture, Game, and Recreational Project, 1935, 12, SCS, RG 114, LU Files, Box 209, MS-9 file, NARA-DC.

81 Resettlement Administration, Final Plan for Tuskegee Planned Land Use, 11.

82 Phillips, *This Land, This Nation*, 80–81, makes the case that the TVA never benefitted the poorest farmers and Fite, *Cotton Fields No More*, 153, argues that few small farmers gained from the Resettlement Administration programs.

83 Resettlement Administration, Report of the Administrator, 10.

84 Resettlement Administration, Final Plan for Tuskegee Planned Land Use, 20.

85 Ibid., 20 and 29.

86 Resettlement Administration, The Final Plan for Georgia Coastal Flatwoods Upland Game Project for Planned Land Use, 8.
87 Ibid., 19 and 39. Where parks were opened Blacks seldom had equal access. See O'Brien, "Jim Crow NIMBYs."
88 USDA, Land Acquisition Plan LA-1, 7.
89 Resettlement Administration, Claiborne Parish Land Use and Population Adjustment Project, LA-2, n.d., 1; SCS, RG 114, Submarginal Lands Records, Box WG8(H), LD-LA- file, NARA-FW.
90 Resettlement Administration, Northwest Arkansas Forestry, Grazing, and Recreational Project: Report LD AK 2, 1937, 1–2; SCS, RG 114, Submarginal Lands Records, Box 238, WPA Report file, NARA-FW.
91 Resettlement Administration, Claiborne Parish Land Use and Population Adjustment: Final Plan, Schedules I and II, 1935, 10, SCS, GR 114, Land Utilization Project Records, LA-2 file, NARA-DC.
92 Fite, *Cotton Fields No More*, 146.
93 C.O. Holland (President Peoples Bank and Trust, Minden, Louisiana) to W.W. Porter, correspondence, 20 February 1935, included in Resettlement Administration, Preliminary Plan: Louisiana A-1, SCS, RG 114, Land Use Project Files, Box 155, LA-1 file, NARA-DC.
94 E.S. Richardson (Superintendent Webster Parish Schools) to Dan Gray (USDA), correspondence, 10 November 1934, included in Resettlement Administration, Preliminary Plan: Louisiana A-1, SCS, RG 114, Land Use Project Files, Box 155, LA-1 file, NARA-DC.
95 Paris Business and Professional Men's Club to Dan Gray (University of Arkansas), correspondence, no date (circa 1934), in Agricultural Adjustment Administration, Memorandum of Proposed Project: Magazine Mountain Forestry, Grazing, Game and Recreation Project, Arkansas A-1, SCS, RG 114, Land Use Project Files, Box 17, Ak-1 file, NARA-DC.
96 J.B. Mitchell and others to Agricultural Adjustment Administration, endorsement letter, 19 September 1934, in Agricultural Adjustment Administration, Memorandum of Proposed Project: Magazine Mountain Forestry, Grazing, Game and Recreation Project, Arkansas A-1, SCS, RG 114, Land Use Project Files, Box 17, Ak-1 file, NARA-DC.
97 G.S. Boggan to B. M Gile (University of Arkansas), endorsement letter, 19 September 1934, in Agricultural Adjustment Administration, Memorandum of Proposed Project: Magazine Mountain Forestry, Grazing, Game and Recreation Project, Arkansas A-1, SCS, RG 114, Land Use Project Files, Box 17, Ak-1 file, NARA-DC.
98 Guy Amsler (Arkansas Secretary of Game and Fish Commission) to Dan Gray (University of Arkansas), correspondence, 25 September 1935, in Agricultural Adjustment Administration, Memorandum of Proposed Project: Magazine Mountain Forestry, Grazing, Game and Recreation Project, Arkansas A-1, SCS, RG 114, Land Use Project Files, Box 17, Ak-1 file, NARA-DC.
99 Resettlement Administration, Final Plan for Tuskegee Planned Land Use, 33.
100 Resettlement Administration, The Final Plan for Georgia Coastal Flatwoods Upland Game Project for Planned Land Use, 31.
101 T. Roy Reid (Regional Director, Farm Security Administration) to Will Alexander (Administrator, Farm Security Administration, D.C.), correspondence, 4 October 1937, SCE, RG 114, Box WG-(h), file LD-LA1, NARA-FW.
102 F.C. Haley correspondence to Senator J. Bennett Johnston, 1 February 1973. In Russell Long Papers, Collection 3700, Box 314, folder 10, Hill Memorial Library, Louisiana State University, Baton Rouge, Louisiana.
103 Biles, *The South and the New Deal* and Phillips, *This Land, This Nation*.

11 Destruction of the American Fishing Industry

Carmel Finley

The island nations of Japan and Iceland are among the world's most accomplished fishing nations. Both countries have a long and deep history of involvement in the sea. Their fishermen are celebrated for their contributions to the nations' unique cultures, and both countries also owe part of their postwar fishing success to the United States and its foreign policy objective of defeating the expansion of Communism. For both Japan and Iceland, fish was the vehicle to tilt from Asian and European influence toward the United States during the Cold War.[1] Fishing has always been about much more than just catching fish.

One of the foundational pillars of American postwar policy was that Japan join the West to stand against the Soviet Union and Communist China. With the start of the Korean War in 1949, American spending rapidly transformed Japan's economy. One of the few early Japanese exports to the United States was canned, and then frozen, tuna. As exports accelerated during the 1950s and American tuna fishermen and processing plants were put out of business, the industry sought relief from tariffs. But the government was committed to open markets and both the Departments of State and Defense objected to tariffs on trade with allies.

Fish also played an important role in a second major foreign policy objective, bringing crucial European allies deeper into the Western sphere. The most critical ally was Iceland, where the Americans had built a strategically important air base. In signing a 1943 defense agreement with Iceland, the Americans committed themselves to helping the Icelandic economy. As imports from Iceland joined those of Canada after 1945, the fishing industry in New England, already suffering from depleted waters near home, could not compete and sought government assistance.

These two US foreign policy objectives involved Japanese tuna and Icelandic cod. The fish were a means to an end, used to achieve political and economic objectives. They could be traded to achieve other priorities. Developing fisheries was a way to modernize and industrialize. While there is language about 'conservation' in many of the postwar fisheries and whaling treaties, it is conservation as it was understood in the Progressive Era, with its emphasis on the rational exploitation of resources.[2] Fish were a resource that only had value if they could be harvested. Fishing expanded under the assumption that uncaught fish simply died and that it was immoral to waste them when they could contribute to easing hunger problems in a war-torn world.[3]

Fishing is an inherently volatile industry, responding to sharp changes in the availability of fish, resulting in price rises and crashes. As small buyers went out of business, fishing was increasingly dominated by large-scale industrial companies. The development of marine refrigeration in the 1930s greatly expanded the ability of fishermen to fish farther from home and stay longer at sea. American tuna boats were increasingly fishing for bait off Mexico, Peru, Chile, and Ecuador. The Japanese expanded fishing through the Pacific during the 1930s, into Alaskan waters in the north, and into Australian waters in the south. The expanded fishing created political tensions that thrust fishing issues, most inconveniently, into foreign policy. One result was an escalation in the ways that governments found to subsidize fishery's expansion.

With the end of World War II, many of the technologies developed during the war were transferred to the civilian sector. Shipyards transitioned from building military vessels to building fishing boats and merchant marine vessels. Floating motherships had been used for decades to process fish, especially in Japan. Now these vessels industrialized, with the launch of the first factory processor ship, the *Fairtry*, in 1954. Colonial empires dwindled on land, but they were recreated at sea, as nations sought to expand fisheries, both in local waters and, for Japan, in distant waters as well.

This dramatic expansion took place at a time when little was known about stocks of fish in the ocean. Scientists attempted to estimate how many fish could safely be harvested. They assumed that when harvests declined, boats would stop fishing, because it was no longer economic. But with the expansion of subsidies to build boats, the correlation between expenses and profits was eroded, allowing boats to continue to fish even if it was not economic. Thus government intervention at the policy level added additional complexity to the fisheries, by lessening the incentive of fishermen to leave the industry. The industry was overcapitalized, and as fishing capacity increased, there were few places in the oceans where fishermen and their increasingly sophisticated technology could not follow.

Alfred E. Eckes, a former chairman of the US International Trade Commission during 1981 to 1990, wrote that during the Cold War, the US traded export opportunities to achieve foreign policy objectives. He suggests the government sacrificed thousands of domestic jobs to create employment elsewhere in the noncommunist world.[4] These postwar diplomatic alliances greatly shaped the emergence of the modern fishing industry. Government involvement was critical during this postwar time, as the industry transitioned from salted and dried fish to frozen fish, causing a shift in the traditional markets. Postwar trade agreements stimulated increased imports into the US government, which were increasingly invested in the expansion of fishing, especially in Japan and Iceland, where fishing played an unusually large role in the domestic economy. The 1943 trade agreement between Iceland and the United State created a loophole that the Japanese were able to use after 1948 to accelerate their tuna exports to the United States. The American fishing industry appealed to Congress for tariff relief but was unable to muster the votes. This paper examines how Cold War politics link Japan and Iceland, tuna and cod in the globalization of the world fisheries.

THE ICELANDIC FISHERIES

Fish have always been at the heart of Iceland's relationships with the world. For centuries, it was the main export and the most important source of foreign funds. Like Japan, Iceland was blessed with the oceanographic conditions that produced abundant fish populations, but, unlike Japan, the government did not have the resources to systematically develop the fishing industry until the 1940s. Following independence from Denmark in 1918, Iceland remained one of the poorest countries in Europe, with a near feudal economy, struggling to sell salted and dried fish in Southern Europe. World War II not only transformed Iceland's global status, but its society, politics, and economics. It became a strategically important nation in the midst of unprecedented prosperity, with new demands for its fish and its labor.

Iceland had a long tradition of neutrality and tried to avoid involvement in World War II, a stance that was challenged, first by the invasion of British troops in 1939, then by the arrival of Americans in 1941. Iceland's negotiations over the Keflavik air base in 1946, participation in the Marshall Plan between 1948 and 1953, and the entry into NATO were all grounded in its desire to protect its fish populations from other nations and to expand markets for its fish supplies.[5] While the development of fish and fish processing ultimately brought postwar prosperity, fish remained a fluctuating resource, a difficulty for a government counting on export sales.

The continental shelf around Iceland is wide, extending over 150 kilometers in some areas. In other areas, the shelf is cut by many subsea canyons. Beyond the shelf, the sea floor falls away from 200 to 400 meters on the shelf to a depth of more than 1000 meters. Three major current systems influence fish production off Iceland: the warm and saline Irminger Current, an offshoot of the Gulf Stream flowing from the south, the very cold and less saline East Greenland Current from the northwest, and the intermediate East Icelandic Current from the northeast. The East Greenland Current flows directly from the Arctic, but the East Icelandic Current is made up from the merging of cold Arctic waters and the warmer Atlantic waters. The Irminger Current flows around the western, northwestern, and northern parts of Iceland, but along the way mixes with the colder currents.[6] The currents make for a productive system for fisheries. Iceland's waters are home to some three hundred species of fish, but the most important have traditionally been cod and herring.[7] While the waters off Iceland are enormously productive, the country still produces only about 2 percent of world fish production and about 12 percent of all West European and Scandinavian fish exports.[8]

With the development of steam engines into fishing boats in the 1880s, more Europeans boats began to fish in Icelandic waters. Steam engines allowed fishermen to use larger nets and to fish in deeper water farther from home. Concern over the widespread decline in stocks in the North Sea and North Atlantic led to the creation of the first organization devoted to fishery science, the International Council for the Exploration of the Seas (ICES), based in Copenhagen, in 1902. As fish stocks declined in the North Sea, British boats began traveling to Iceland in 1891.[9] This was the extreme range of steam trawlers, and the crews crammed coal into every nook for the outward journey. Until larger vessels were built, Iceland was a summer fishery, as the winter fogs made the voyage too hazardous.[10] By the turn of the century, French, German, English, and Norwegian ships were all fishing in Icelandic waters.[11]

With a population of just 80,000 and with scant capital to build larger boats or fish processing facilities, Iceland could do little to police fishing in its waters[12] Icelandic historian Jon Th Thor placed the expansion of fishing within the context of British imperialism:

> The trawlerman sailed hither equipped with the most modern fishing gear known at that time and were backed by the most powerful naval force in the world. On the coast of Iceland they met people who for all practical purposes were in great contrast to themselves, people who hardly kept alive under the most primitive conditions, many surviving near starvation-limits and still remaining at stage of industry befitting the Middle Ages. Off their coast these people possessed some of the world's richest fishing grounds, but they had neither the funds nor the equipment to utilize them.[13]

Nevertheless, the Althing, Iceland's parliament, was aggressive in trying to defend its fish stocks. An 1889 act forbade trawling within near shore waters, but it could not be enforced. A stronger act was passed in 1894, banning vessels with trawls from entering local waters or putting in at Icelandic ports, except in emergencies. Despite British trawlers arguing that this was contrary to international law, a string of British crews were arrested, fined, and had their gear confiscated for illegally fishing off Iceland and the Faeroes.[14]

Iceland was not the only nation to chaff at foreign boats fishing off its coast. Fish belonged to whoever caught them, a loose arrangement that sprang from the three-mile limit—the distance a cannon ball could fly. Beyond three miles were the high seas, with freedom to navigate—and to fish. But the three-mile limit had never been formally codified, and it was clearly inadequate in the face of increased fishing pressure. The League of Nations held a conference in 1930 to see if there was any consensus on how the growing number of fishery disputes could be handled. While nations such as Iceland urged restrictions, the United States, Britain, and Japan were opposed to any regulation. There was no agreement, and boats from a dozen nations continued to fish in Icelandic waters, producing an estimated 17 to 21 percent of total European fish production.[15]

The Icelandic government pushed ahead with efforts to develop its own industry. During the 1920s and 1930s, much of the catch was cod caught by fishermen in rowboats. The fish was salted and dried for sale in Portugal, Italy, Spain, Brazil, and Cuba, although some salted fish also went to Britain, France, and Argentina. Most of the herring catch was cured for sale to Sweden, and only small amounts of fish were frozen. With the outbreak of the Great Depression, markets in Southern Europe deteriorated. The Spanish Civil War disrupted imported fish from Iceland. Britain and Germany imposed quotas on fish imports. As demand fell, so did fish prices.[16] The result was widespread unemployment in Iceland, a factor in the rise of the Icelandic Communist party, which controlled 10 of the 52 seats in Parliament in 1942, the peak of its political power.[17]

The government made another attempt to deal with overfishing in 1937, this time trying to use science as a way to conserve stocks. It persuaded scientists at the International Council for the Investigation of the Seas (ICES) that Faxa Bay, an important nursery area on the western coast, was being hit hard by foreign trawling. ICES suggested an experiment: a ten-year moratorium on fishing. The proposal included having an international conference, which was never held. Britain declined to participate.[18]

Since the majority of Icelandic fishermen were poor, with small boats, the government moved to support the industry with an experimental frozen fish plant in 1929. Between 1935 and 1939, 19 quick-freeze plants were put into operation. By 1944, Iceland had 62 freezing plants.[19] The government also created a community around the herring processing plant at Skagastrond, on the north coast.[20] But the herring fishery, which had been so profitable during the war and played such a pivotal role in providing profits, almost failed in 1945, and catches would be poor in the three subsequent years, developments that would cause severe financial and political problems for the government.[21]

It is difficult to overstate the importance of fishing to the Icelandic economy during the 1940s. With the outbreak of war, Iceland's problems in marketing its fish disappeared. The German Navy began to blockade British ports, greatly curtailing fishing. Icelandic fishermen, willing to run to Britain to deliver, received premium prices for their catch. Through the war, the industry supplied 70 percent of the fish consumed in the United Kingdom. Fishermen caught a record 880 million pounds (399,161 tonnes) of fish in 1944, with 512 million pounds (105,233 tonnes or 26.4 percent) of it exported.[22]

The government passed Act No. 34, creating a Fisheries Fund in 1943, capitalized at 100 million Kroner. The fund was an independent institution under the supervision of the minister in charge of fisheries and managed by the Fisheries Bank of Iceland.[23] Iceland went on a boat-buying binge, ordering 45 new boats from Sweden, and a second order for another 50 boats was proposed for 1945.[24] Thirty new trawlers were built in Great Britain at a cost of $500,000 each and delivery began in 1947.[25] The boats were sold to fishermen at a preferential rate, which would plague the government throughout the next decade.[26] The Icelandic fleet totaled some 732 vessels by 1947.[27] And as a sign of things to come, one of the new trawlers broke the world record for catching fish, securing 380 tons (386 tonnes) in just seven days.[28]

Iceland's strategic importance grew throughout the 1930s. The German airline Lufthansa applied for transit rights during 1939, and the government sent a cruiser to visit Icelandic waters. The request was refused, but it was certainly noted in London and Washington, DC.[29] As tensions deepened with Germany, Iceland's strategic importance as the 'king pin of the Atlantic' increased. Its ports did not freeze in winter and it was on the great circle air routes from American and Canadian airfields to Britain and the Soviet Union. Both countries were determined to keep Iceland as part of their mutual defense system.[30] This determination deepened in April of 1940, when Hitler's armies invaded and occupied Denmark and Norway.[31] A few weeks later, British and Canadian troops invaded Iceland on May 10, 1940, taking control of Reykjavik and dropping leaflets that apologized for the 'disturbance' and noted the hope that it would not last long. The Icelandic government made a formal protest against the violation of its neutrality and independence. Then it urged its citizens to treat the invaders as guests, displaying the greatest courtesy.[32]

By the following June, the British had suffered a military defeat in Greece and its troops were bogged down in North Africa. The United States had not yet entered the war, but within a month, it concluded a defense agreement that provided a legal basis for protection of Iceland for the duration of the war. American troops finally arrived on July 7, 1941. The agreement contained eight clauses, the most important of which promised the withdrawal of American troops "immediately on the conclusion of the present war."[33]

The agreement promised that the United States would support Iceland in its claim of independence from Denmark, keep Iceland supplied with goods during the war, and make "favorable commercial and trade agreements with it."[34] Among those favorable agreements was a 1943 trade agreement that lowered tariffs on a number of items, including fish canned in anything except oil. The normal US tariff rate on fish canned in oil was 45 percent. The new trade agreement set a tariff of 12.5 percent on fish canned, for example, in water. It was a minor clause and it is doubtful if anybody paid much attention at the time.

The Americans built a major naval base at Hvalfjörður and the Keflavik airfield at Reykjavik became one of the largest wartime bases, crucially important for antisubmarine activities. The Iceland bases allowed the Allies to provide greater protection of allied conveys to Britain. "Winning the battle of the Atlantic, to a large extent fought from Iceland, prevented the fall of Britain and made it possible to ship the desperately needed manpower and supplies from the United States to England for the invasion of France," according to Icelandic diplomat Einar Benediktsson.[35] In Iceland, the US base was a source of political tension:

> It supplied hard currency to the Iceland economy, but it also increased inflation. It provided good-paying jobs, but it also contributed to the depopulation of the hinterlands and concentration of persons near Reykjavik. The base was favored by those who supplied it and worked for it . . . It was bitterly opposed by many.[36]

With the end of the war, Iceland wanted the American occupation to end. They had spent centuries freeing themselves from Danish control and did not want to become an American colony.

The end of the war brought its own set of tensions. The 1941 defense agreement had specified "that we would depart, bag and baggage, upon the cessation of the emergency."[37] Nothing had been said about continued rights during peacetime. Iceland saw the war as being over. The Americans saw their troops stationed in Germany and Italy and that the Iceland airbases were still central to 'American defense' as new Cold War priorities and realities emerged.[38] Without Iceland, the North Atlantic air route was unreliable and unsafe. The capacity for military air transport would be reduced by 20 percent on eastbound routes and 60 percent on westbound ones. Flights by single-engine aircraft would be suspended. The United States was maintaining troops in Britain, France, and Africa. Withdrawing from Iceland would set an undesirable precedent. It was also unacceptable that the airfields might fall under the control of the Soviets.[39] The Americans suggested a 99-year lease.

The presence of the Americans at Keflavik, so close to Reykjavik, was a major irritation to some Icelanders, especially the Communist members of Parliament. The Icelandic Communist Party was relatively strong during the 1930s, with members railing that Iceland had been victimized by British capitalists.[40] Two of the six cabinet posts were held by Communists. As negotiations around the airbase dragged on, the Soviet Union announced it would buy Iceland's entire 1947 fish exports, setting off a torrent of telegrams between the American embassy and Washington. Could the Americans at least buy some of the fish for the US zone in Germany?[41] But the German fishing industry was also recovering from the war and increasingly able to supply its own markets, and the US military did not have funds to buy fish from Iceland.

The two countries signed an agreement that the bulk of the American troops would leave by June 15, 1946, and that a new agreement would be drawn up to allow the airbase to continue operations, paid for by the Americans. The new agreement was signed on Oct. 7, 1946, granting the Americans military air transit rights for six and a half years. In Iceland, however, the agreement was still controversial. After the Althing approved it, the Communist members of the parliament withdrew their support from the government, forcing Prime Minister Olafur Thors to submit his resignation. It took until February of 1947 for there to be enough compromise for a three-party coalition to form a new government.[42]

The Icelandic government did want preferential status for exports to the United States, a status that went against the whole thrust of the new American enthusiasm for free trade.[43] It might be legal for the United States to buy Icelandic fish and resell it in the United States but that was inconsistent with government procurement policies and would pit the government against private fishing company. An American study showed it cost Iceland 15.3 cents to produce frozen fillets, while American fillets cost 24 cents to produce. Fish from Iceland entered the United States with a 2.5-cent tariff per pound for the first 15 million pounds; then the tariff was reduced to 1.78 cents a pound. The Americans suggested it would be best for Iceland to market its own fish in the Unites States.[44] Iceland wanted a bilateral government agreement.[45]

Iceland's fishermen were still making money. The British fishing industry was in disarray, and Icelandic fish continued to be welcome in British ports. Starting in 1946, the Soviet Union, Czechoslovakia, and Poland began to buy fish from Iceland. A third of Iceland exports in 1946 went to Britain, but the Soviets took 20 percent of the catch, while the United States, Sweden, and Denmark took 14 percent each.[46] The British were rebuilding their own fishing fleets and anxious to supply their own markets. Iceland had suffered inflation during the war and now the Kroner was overvalued compared to the economies in its traditional markets. The balance of trade worsened, and there was no market for Iceland's main export. The government didn't want to devalue the Kroner, so it implemented a series of guaranteed minimum prices for various goods, including fish. If the fish sold on the world market for less than the guaranteed price, the government would make up the difference.[47]

In these circumstances, an offer from the Soviets to buy most of the 1947 catch was welcomed by the government in Reykjavik, but the Soviets backed out of their offer to buy the 1947 production. The US embassy had seen the offer as politically motivated. But if there was no country to buy Iceland's fish, the government could fall, opening the door to a new government with two cabinet posts held by the Communists—possibly even the aviation ministry. The embassy thought the Russians were stalling over the negotiations, counting on the deteriorating economic situation to bring down the government. In a secret telegram, it urged the State Department to find a market for the fish.[48]

"It can be assumed that a principal aim of Communist cabinet ministers would be to do everything in their power to embarrass the United States and to nullify the special rights we have under the Airport Agreement," wrote Hugh S. Cumming Jr., chief of the State Department's Division of Northern European Affairs.[49] He also urged the British to do what they could to buy more Icelandic fish. The US War Department came up with $1 million to buy Icelandic fish for the relief program in the Mediterranean countries.[50] It offered to buy between 15,000 and 20,000 tons of wet salted fish, but would only pay 13.5 cents a pound. The Icelandic government had guaranteed its producers a price of 17 cents a pound, creating a gap of $3.5 million.[51] Despite heavy lobbying from the embassy about the political importance of the deal to Iceland, it fell through.

To the Americans, the failure to sell Iceland's 1947 fish catch had the potential to bring down the Icelandic government, offering an opportunity for the Communists to reenter the cabinet and jeopardize Iceland's relationship with the United States by opening the door to change the Keflavik agreement. The embassy pressed the State Department to sell the fish in Germany.[52] With nobody willing to buy the fish (and pay the 17 cents a pound), the government was vulnerable to charges that it had failed to sell the fish. The embassy pushed again in a May 2, 1947 telegram, saying it was in the American interest to assist the Icelandic government in disposing of the fish—and not selling fish to the Soviets.[53] Compounding the problem was steep inflation in Iceland, at least partly because of American military spending during the war.[54] To make matters worse, the all-important late herring season got off to an unexpectedly slow start. The Iceland government borrowed £1.5 million sterling it intended to repay by exporting herring oil and now owed £65,000 to British firms.[55] Meanwhile, the Icelandic Communists argued that the government could solve its problems by exporting fish to Eastern Europe.[56]

The Americans worried about a Communist coup d'état and queried the Icelandic government about countermeasures it had prepared to prevent the Communists from taking over. Many in Iceland thought they would be better off without the airport, which made them a potential target of attack. The airport agreement did not cover its use as a future military base, and the government refused to discuss amending the agreement.[57] The Americans pushed the Icelandic government to make definite plans to combat a Communist coup d'état.[58] The United States drew up a contingency plan to deploy American forces to Iceland "to support a democratic system of government against internal Communist subversion." The wording was later changed to "protect U.S. and North Atlantic security interests in Iceland in the event of an emergency."[59]

For the 1948 catch, the United States was instrumental in arranging an agreement with the British to buy 70 tons of fish for "Bizonia," as the merger between the US and British occupation zones in Germany was called, which was announced on May 29, 1947.[60] The British were reluctant and it took "insistent prodding" by the United States to get the fish agreement signed in London on December 13, 1947. Iceland hoped for a similar agreement for the 1949 catch. As Donald Nuechterlein later summarized:

> It would be in the interest of the United States Government to help Iceland dispose of her fish elsewhere than in the Union of Soviet Socialist Republics, in order to prevent the Soviet Union from gaining any influence in Iceland. The United States War Department has a vital interest in Icelandic air-rights, since Iceland is strategically located.[61]

Why was it so difficult for Iceland to sell its fish on the world market? With the resumption of fishing in Europe at the end of the war, world demand had declined, and Icelandic fish was generally priced above other fish, especially fish from Norway. Wages and the cost of living in Iceland had increased some 310 percent since 1939, pricing Icelandic fish out of the market. In order to keep production up, the government was forced to continue the "Guaranteed Minimum Price Law," which had been introduced as an emergency measure in 1946. It was incorporated into an economic bill passed in December of 1947, with the government guaranteeing to make up the difference if fish sold for less. The law cost the government $3.5 million in 1947. The price supports would continue to be a major problem for the government. Export subsidies grew from 30 million Kroner in 1951 to 118 million in 1955 and 247 million in 1956, a measure of the disparity between Iceland's costs and the export prices at which Iceland had to sell its fish and agricultural products to compete on the world market.[62]

Iceland needed outside help to keep its economy afloat. Assistance came in June of 1947. The Marshall Plan, named after American Secretary of State George Marshall, was directed not "against any country or doctrine but against hunger, poverty, despair and chaos."[63] Iceland signed the Marshall Plan on July 3, 1949. The United States had already given $600,000 in Marshall Plan aid during 1948, along with a $1.9 million loan. Other loans followed from US foreign aid agencies, the International Bank for Reconstruction and Development, and the European Payments Union. The United States lent Iceland nearly $20 million after 1948.

The government drew up a four-year plan to build herring liquefaction plants, a fertilizer plant, several fish meal factories, and several refrigeration plants. It pledged to expand its fishing fleet and increase fish production by 34 percent from 552,000 tonnes in 1947 to 738,000 tonnes by 1952. Iceland also used an ECA loan of $2.3 million to buy a fish processing factory ship, the *Haeringer*, which arrived in Reykjavik in October of 1948.[64]

The infusion of money did not solve either the problems with the fishery or those of the Icelandic economy. The government was forced to devalue the Kroner by 42.5 percent in March of 1950, hoping to make exported fish more competitive on the world market. The policy of guaranteeing minimum prices for fresh fish and subsidizing the export price of frozen fish was leading to turmoil in the fishing industry and had the potential to collapse the entire economy.[65] Making things more difficult were that herring catches on the north coast grounds were poor, when the government had counted on good catches as a much-needed source of revenue.[66]

The next quandary for Iceland was if it was going to join the proposed military alliance of Western nations, the North Atlantic Treaty Organization (NATO). The alliance had not yet formed, but the Icelandic Communists, as well as the National Preservation League, waged a vigorous opposition campaign, arguing NATO would force Iceland to participate in a military alliance that would involve accepting military bases and foreign troops. It was difficult for the government to refute the claims, because it did not know what the provisions of the NATO alliance would be. Others argued Iceland should return to its traditional neutrality.[67] The debate was bitter and divisive. Voting on the NATO provisions came on March 30, 1949, amid a Communist-led riot outside the Althing building. Despite the shower of rocks and stones thrown through the windows, the voting was decisive, 37 votes in favor of the government's resolution, and 13 against, with two abstentions.[68] With an agreement in place, the Americans spent $73 million at Keflavik air base to upgrade its facilities for use as a major air base by NATO.[69]

As British trawlers once again appeared in Icelandic waters, the old grievances were abraded. In 1951, Iceland closed Faxa Bay to all fishing by both Icelandic and British fishermen. Britain responded by banning Icelandic trawlers from making deliveries in British ports. Britain had been taking about a quarter of Iceland's fresh fish catch and finding a replacement market was a significant issue that affected the entire economy.

Sensing an opportunity, the Soviet Union offered Iceland a bilateral clearing agreement to buy large quantities of frozen fish and in return supply lumber and cement, which Iceland had been importing from Western nations. The terms of the trade were highly advantageous and by 1955, the Soviet Union would become the largest single importer of Icelandic fish and Iceland's second largest trading partner, after Britain.

The expanded trade stimulated the development of fish processing jobs in Iceland, increasing employment and increasing the value of fish products.[70] The deal increased Communist prestige and influence in Iceland, and as far as the Americans were concerned, it was motivated by the desire to separate Iceland from NATO and eliminate the air base.[71] One peculiar result of the situation was that Iceland, a member of NATO, in reacting to a trade boycott from another NATO country, developed strong trading ties with the Soviet bloc.[72]

Ultimately, the Icelandic government leveraged the air base at Keflavik for the chance to modernize and develop Iceland's fisheries, long imagined in Reykjavik as the nation's resource frontier opportunity. A combination of foreign loans and devaluation in the context of Cold War rivalries facilitated government-led industrialization of the fisheries. This took place with scant regard for stock assessments or for conservation, at least as far as the US State Department and embassy records are concerned. In turn, Iceland's fish were traded for economic goals and to secure national identity and sovereignty in the face of new perceived threats. As a dependent player, its fish were traded off in government offices in Washington, DC, Moscow, and London, as well as Reykjavik. And that had repercussions in Tokyo.

THE JAPANESE FISHERIES

Just as Iceland was the beneficiary of bountiful oceanographic conditions, so was Japan. A resource-poor island nation with little agricultural land, Japan had always been forced to rely on the sea. After American Admiral Perry sailed into Tokyo Bay in 1854, Japan had sought to modernize itself. The new Meiji government in the 1880s developed a series of subsidies to encourage the development of fisheries. The expansion into the high seas began in 1893, when Japan began hunting for North Pacific fur seals.[73] After defeating Russia in the 1905 war, Japan won substantial fishing concessions off Sakhalin Island and Kamchatka. Government resources poured into fisheries, funding the introduction of Western technology, including engines and fishing gear such as trawl nets. Other subsidies included bounties to build sea-going vessels, rebates on the salt excise duty, rebates on the import duty on oil for canned goods, the establishment of closed periods for fishing, and protective measures for fishermen, including a program of weather warnings.[74] Additional bills funded the construction and improvement of fishing ports, installation of refrigeration equipment, and increased exportation of marine products.[75] By the 1930s, Japan was the world's leading fishing country.

With the end of World War II, the Japanese fishing empire was systematically dismantled and Japanese boats confined to coastal waters. Historian Edwin O. Reischauer wrote:

> Once stretching a sixth of the way around the globe from northern Manchuria to the eastern extremities of the Marshalls, the Japanese Empire has been reduced to a thin sliver, scarcely one eighth of its former width and less than half its former length.[76]

Some of its most profitable fisheries were gone: the high-seas salmon fishing off Kamchatka, the bottomfish and king crab of Bristol Bay, herring and salmon off Sakhalin, tuna from the Marshall, Caroline, and Mariana Islands, and the catches off Korea and China that had provided so much of the daily food supply. For the Japanese fishing industry, the loss of the war looked like ruin indeed.

Yet the fleet was rebuilt with enormous speed. The Supreme Commander Allied Powers (SCAP), in charge of the American occupation, made rebuilding the fishing fleet one of its priorities. The Japanese people were starving, and there was a clear need to expand sources of protein. SCAP policies had made fuel and material available to the industry, which was rapidly rebuilt by early in 1947. Overlooked by SCAP was that the prewar fleet had been too big to operate only in Japanese waters. Many of the larger boats had been engaged in distant water fisheries, shipping fish back to Japan. Now all fishing was confined to a small zone around Japan and catches soon began to decline, especially in the East China Sea. SCAP began to push to expand the waters the Japanese could fish, despite objections from other nations, such as North Korea and the Soviet Union. In 1949, SCAP sent the Japanese longline fleet back to waters it had pioneered in the 1920s near the Marshall, Mariana, and Caroline Islands, now under the control of the United States.[77]

In December of 1947, SCAP opened a trade office in New York to make it easier to see Japanese commodities in the United States. One of the few Japanese products that Americans wanted was cheap canned tuna.[78] By the end of 1948, small amounts of Japanese canned albacore reached the New York market, drawing protests from the United States' West Coast tuna industry. Large tuna schools, observed the *Pan-American Fisherman*, "provide the Japanese with plenty of ammunition with which to gun down American prices."[79] The industry was opposed to free trade and the reduction of the current duty on tuna, then 22.5 percent, but its leaders knew it was only a matter of time before the Japanese would be dominating their market.[80]

By July of 1950, cans of Japanese tuna were entering the US market at $10.85 a case, compared to $13 for West Coast tuna. Japanese light meat tuna was selling in supermarkets for 29 cents a can, compared to American advertised brands selling for between 35 to 39 cents a can.[81] Even more ominous was the price of a new product, tuna packed in brine, which entered the United States at a 12.5 percent tariff, rather than the 22.5 percent for tuna packed in oil. Brined tuna fish sold for $8.60 a case.[82] It was an inferior product, since the fish often got hard in the can, but it was cheaper than anything the American industry could produce.[83] The displacement of American tuna from supermarket shelves had begun.

The Japanese exploited the Icelandic loophole, for fish canned in anything except oil, and sharply escalated exports of tuna canned in brine. They also increased exports of frozen and fresh tuna to the United States. There was no tariff governing these new products. Fresh tuna had not existed as a commodity when the previous tariff agreements were negotiated, and frozen tuna had made up a small part of the imports. By 1951, there were four different kinds of tuna products imported into the United States with three different tariff structures, and almost all of it was cheaper than tuna caught by American boats and canned at Southern California canneries. In San Diego and San Pedro, the canneries were idled, the workers unemployed, the boats tied to the dock.[84]

In September of 1951, the *Commercial Fisheries Review* reported that large Japanese fishing companies would only guarantee a minimum monthly wage of 5,000 to 6,000 yen, about $13.90 to $16.40 in American dollars. Fishermen averaged well over 10,000 yen ($27.78) per month in 1947, even though the company received 60 percent of the value of the catch and the fishermen 40 percent.[85] Cheap labor was a substantial advantage that American processing companies could not match.

American fishermen had been plagued for decades by imports from countries with cheaper labor. Japanese cod had hurt American markets on the West Coast in the 1920s. Cheap fish from Canada undercut prices for fishermen in New England. A major government study published in 1945 found that imported fish from countries with lower standards of living and subsidized boats had the capacity to "completely demoralize the North Atlantic fishing industry and drastically affect the fishing industry in other sections of the country."[86]

The fishing industry on both coasts appealed to the Tariff Commission for relief. The industry would have to establish that the domestic fishermen had been hurt before a tariff could be increased to provide relief. The American Tuna Association (ATA), based in San Diego, testified that Japanese imports threatened the very existence of the industry. There were some 200 bait boats that used hooks to catch tuna and another 100 purse seiners that fished with nets. As California sardine catches collapsed after the war, more purse seiners went fishing for tuna.[87]

The Commission held a series of hearings in early 1952. The State Department objected that a tariff, even of three cents, would seriously impair Japan's second most important export, and that it would be resented by the Latin Americans, who might retaliate against the America tuna fleet operating off Central America. The State Department reasoned that if it supported tariffs against allies, they could retaliate by placing restrictions on American boats, and a precedent on a fishing boat would be used as a further precedent for military vessels and submarines. The Japanese government announced that it would voluntarily place a quota on its tuna exports to the United States, effective on May 1, 1952. In return, the Ministry of Trade and Industry asked Congress not to vote on import duties.

Congress passed a bill to place an emergency three-cents-a-pound tariff on all imports of fresh and frozen tuna, a measure that would last for a year while the secretary of the interior and the US Tariff Commission investigated the situation, with a report due to Congress by January 1, 1953. But the bill stalled in the Senate for months, and then it was soundly defeated by a vote of 43–32. The foreign policy concern of the State Department trumped the domestic pressure from coastal lawmakers. The most the industry could get were orders to the US Tariff Commission and the Department of the Interior, to conduct investigations into the impact of tuna imports on the domestic industry.[88] In the meantime, Japanese tuna continued to pour onto the shelves of American grocery stores. Even if the tariff had passed, the industry recognized that three cents would not have made up for the substantial advantage of cheap Japanese labor on fishing boats.

The US Tariff Commission issued its report on March 23, 1953. It declined to issue recommendations, but it drew a number of conclusions. The Commission was not sympathetic. Many domestic industries had to adjust to imports from abroad. Sales of tuna were projected to continue to increase, and commercial tuna fishing was construed as an entrepreneurial activity that simply involved greater risk than most other domestic enterprises. One of the few Japanese commodities with a ready market in the US was tuna. The Commission decided that the imports had not caused serious injury to the industry. A dissenting statement came from the Commission's Chairman, Walter F. George of the Senate Committee on Finance, who said the report should have been delayed until a more thorough investigation could be made.[89] But that was all.

A further tariff commission decision came in June of 1953, involving East Coast cod and other groundfish. The New England fleet had also argued that imports threatened the complete destruction of their industry. The Commission recommended that the tariff on imported groundfish fillets be raised from 1 ⅞ cents a pound to 2 ½ cents.[90] There was a storm of protest. The Canadian government warned that increasing the tariff could have serious consequences, not only for trade, but for the overall relationship between the two countries.[91] The Foreign Operations Administration weighed in, warning that the operation of US bases in Iceland depended on the goodwill of the nearby fishing communities and reminding them that Iceland had recently signed a trade agreement with the Soviet Union. The State Department said there was no justification for a quota or a tariff. Either action would:

> conflict with our military security system to some extent in Norway, more in Canada, and worst of all in Iceland. As one Icelandic official has put it, in commenting on the Tariff Commission's proposal, 'Iceland cannot live on military agreements alone.'[92]

The ultimate decision was made by President Eisenhower, who declined to increase the tariff. While he recognized the pain within the industry, he saw expanding markets for fish products as the way to solve the industry's problems. Since the tariff commission had decided to study the issue, the demand for fish sticks had greatly increased, perhaps bringing about an increase in American per capita consumption of fish, a figure that had held between 10 and 12 pounds per person for almost 50 years. Increasing the tariff would reduce the supply of raw material for fish sticks, hampering the development of this promising new market. Expanding the market for fish sticks "appears to hold the best prospect for a vigorous, healthy domestic industry that also best serves our international relations."[93] At the same time, Eisenhower pledged additional assistance to the industry, with research in fishing technology, conservation, and marketing.

Fish sticks were indeed popular. Demand was so great during 1953 that producers were unable to keep up with orders, and a number of new companies started making the precooked, breaded food. During the first quarter of 1954, production rose to 9 million pounds (9,140 tonnes) of fish sticks and the US Fish and Wildlife Service estimated that output would exceed 40 million pounds (40,640 tonnes). "Consumer acceptance of fish sticks has been so widespread that some sources expect them to do for the fishing industry what fruit juice concentrates have done for the citrus fruit trade."[94] While new markets were good, New England groundfish catches were falling and boats had to travel farther to fill their nets, increasing their costs. Recent evidence suggests that New England catches peaked about 1860 and the general trend has been downward.[95] It was going to prove impossible for New England fishermen to grow their way out of their problems by catching more fish.

There was a further round of tariff hearings in 1956. The Commission recommended escape-clause relief for New England fishermen, but once again, the State Department refused to agree. Foreign policy considerations and a desire to encourage trade relations in Iceland, in hopes of steering it away from selling fish to the Soviet Union, were more important than domestic dislocations. According to the International Cooperation Administration, a 50 percent tariff on fish would "strengthen those elements in Iceland which wish to drive out U.S. NATO troops. As fish goes, so goes Iceland."[96]

New England fishermen were denied tariff relief, but Southern California tuna fishermen were luckier. The Commission recommended relief on tuna and President Eisenhower issued a proclamation doubling the duty on tuna canned in brine from 12.5 percent to 25 percent ad valorem, whenever imports exceeded 20 percent of the previous years' US pack of canned tuna of all varieties. The proclamation followed an agreement by Iceland to withdraw tuna canned in brine from the 1943 trade agreement and an invocation of the rights reserved by the United States in the GATT agreement. [97] But the tariff was too little, too late for the Southern California processing industry.

CONCLUSION

By June of 1956, the White House announced a package of measures designed to help the fishing industry. There was an administrative reorganization, and the US Bureau of Commercial Fisheries was created to take over the responsibilities of the US Fish and Wildlife Service. A broader research program was set up to investigate all phases of the industry and to develop new resources, improve the efficiency of fishing, and promote new fishery commodities. A $10 million loan fund was set up to make loans for maintenance, repairs, and equipment of boats at a 3 percent interest rate.[98]

A report to Eisenhower in January of 1957 said 88 applications had been made for loans, but the amounts only totaled $2.5 million.[99]

It was clear to American tuna fishermen that they were being sacrificed to create jobs for Japanese fishermen, but they were unable to do anything about it. As the decade wore on and the cannery jobs onshore dwindled, American tuna fishermen continued to chase tuna on the high seas. Between 1954 and 1960, Congress enacted a series of laws and directed agencies to create programs to address fishery's problems. Early laws provided funds for research, loans for vessel owners were adopted in 1956, and a program of vessel construction subsidies began in 1960. By the mid-1960s, there were programs on safety, training of fishermen, research and development, and loans and vessel construction subsidies. The glory days after World War II, when the American fishing industry believed that wages in other countries would increase to American levels and that free enterprise would triumph, were over. Americans began importing more and more fish from other countries.

The high seas were shrinking. It was not just expanded fishing throughout the oceans, but trade, economics, and politics that drew fishing and non-fishing countries together, however unwillingly. If the high seas had ever been a commons, it was rapidly disappearing because of the deliberate actions of nations, motivated by a range of issues. Postwar trade was structured by political alliances, binding countries and fisheries together, with impacts that could not be foreseen, especially for the world's fish stocks.

Historians are slowly uncovering the environmental effects of the postwar industrialization, the 'Great Acceleration' when countries sharply increased their extraction of resources from the natural world.[100] Heady with the scientific and technical knowledge developed during the war, nations dammed rivers, moved mountains, and tried to change ocean currents and alter weather patterns. All of these events created unprecedented changes in the natural environment, altering the biosphere itself. Human activity has changed the ocean, not only close to shore but, as historian Naomi Oreskes argues, "in its entirety."[101]

There has been very little study of the linkages between war and fishing. Historian Poul Holm argues that World War II had fundamental consequences for the European fishing industry in the North Atlantic.[102] Holm does not go far enough. The impacts of war in the North Atlantic rippled westward and southward from Britain to Iceland, Iceland to Japan, Japan to American Samoa, and back to the United States, directly setting the stage for the decline of the New England fisheries in general, and the destruction of the Southern California tuna processing industry.

The Cold War created an environment where trade policies were implemented with little thought that there might be negative environmental consequences. The targeted aid to both Iceland and Japan allowed the fishing industries in both nations to rapidly industrialize and modernize. Government money greatly facilitated the spread of technologies, including sonar, radar, bigger engines, and more efficient nets, increasing the ability of fishermen to find fish.

Government money expanded fisheries, creating employment in coastal areas and providing fish for export. Fishery scientists sought to make fishing gear more efficient, while food technologists perfected preservation techniques, and home economists showed consumers how to cook the fish. As historian Paul Josephson has argued, governments play important roles in shaping fisheries, "not only in setting the rules, but in development of new product forms, marketing campaigns, and school lunch programs, and funding researchers looking at how to perfect refrigeration, processing, shipping of products."[103] There was really only one component of this industrializing process that was much harder to figure out, and that was predicting how many fish could be caught.

NOTES

1 W.R. Mead, "Renaissance of Iceland," *Economic Geography* 21(2) (1945): 141.
2 Samuel P. Hays, *Conservation and the Gospel of Efficiency*, (Cambridge, MA: Harvard University Press, 1959), 3.
3 Wilbert M. Chapman, "Report on Activities with Respect to High Seas Fisheries, 1949," RG 59 811.245/1–950, Box 4425, NARA.
4 Alfred E. Eckes, "Trading American interests," *Foreign Affairs* 71(4) (1992): 135–154, 135.
5 Valur Ingimundarson, "Buttressing the West in the North: The Atlantic alliance, economic warfare, and the Soviet challenge in Iceland," *The International History Review* 21(1) (1956–1959): 82.
6 "Icelandic Fisheries—Oceanography," http://www.fisheries.is/ecosystem/oceanography/, downloaded Feb. 16, 2015.
7 "Icelandic Fisheries—Oceanography," http://www.fisheries.is/ecosystem/oceanography/, downloaded Feb. 16, 2015
8 Robert Loring Allen, "Public finance analysis," *New Series* (1958–59): 443.
9 Jon Thor, *British Trawlers in Icelandic Waters: History of British Steam Trawling off Iceland, 1889–1916.* (Reykjavik: Fjolvi Publishers, 1992), 15.
10 Robb Robinson, *Trawling: The Rise and Fall of the British Trawl Fishery* (Exeter: University of Exeter Press, 1996), 105.
11 Hannes Jonsson, *Friends in Conflict: The Anglo-Icelandic Cod Wars and the Law of the Sea*, (London: C. Hurst, 1982), 6.
12 Einar Benediktsson, "At Crossroads: Iceland's Defense and Security Relations, 1940–2011." Strategic Studies Institute, United States Army War College website, accessed February 16, 2015, http://www.strategicstudiesinstitute.army.mil/index.cfm/articles/Icelands-Defense-and-Security-Relations-1940–2011/2011/8/18
13 Thor, *British Trawlers in Icelandic Waters*, 15.
14 Robinson, *Trawling: The Rise and Fall of the British Trawl Fishery*, 108.
15 *Commercial Fisheries Review* 8(5) (1946): 44.
16 Olafur Björnsson, "Economic development in Iceland since World War II," *Weltwirtschaftliches Archiv* 98(1967): 221.
17 Donald E. Nuechterlein, *Iceland, Reluctant Ally* (Ithaca, NY: Cornell University Press, 1961), 4.

18 Jonssen, *Friends in Conflict*, 51.
19 *Commercial Fisheries Review*, 8(5), May (1946): 44.
20 *Commercial Fisheries Review*, December (1946): 48–49.
21 Bjornsson, 223.
22 *Fisheries Market News*, June (1945): 46–47.
23 "Fisheries Fund of Iceland," box 5114, April 14, 1954, RG59, NARA
24 *Fishery Market News*, June (1945): 46–47.
25 *Commercial Fisheries Review*, 10(7) (1948): 34.
26 Allen, "Public finance analysis," 444.
27 *Commercial Fisheries Review*, 10(7) (1948): 37.
28 *Commercial Fisheries Review*, December (1948): 33.
29 Nuechterlein, *Iceland*, 21.
30 Hans W. Weigert, "Iceland, Greenland, and the United States," *Foreign Affairs* 23(1) (1944): 113.
31 Nuechterlein, *Iceland*, 23.
32 Ibid., 24.
33 "U.S. military requirements in Iceland," box 4767, May 1, 1946, RG 59, NARA.
34 Nuechterlein, *Iceland*, 29.
35 Benediktsson, "At crossroads: Iceland's defense and security relations, 1940–2011," 18.
36 Morris Davis, *Iceland Extends Its Fisheries Limits: A Political Analysis* (Universitetsforlaget, 1963), 19.
37 "Iceland Bases," box 5114, Dec. 3, 1945, RG 59, NARA.
38 "U.S. Military Requirements in Iceland," box 4767, May 1, 1946, RG 59, NARA.
39 General Hilldring to Mr. Acheson, May 22, 1947, "OMGUS Purchase of Icelandic Fish," box 5114, RG 59, NARA.
40 Ragnheiður Kristjánsdóttir, "Communists and the national question in Scotland and Iceland, c. 1930 to c. 1940," *The Historical Journal* 45(3): 605.
41 Airgram, Box 5114, Nov. 4, 1946, RG 59, NARA.
42 Nuechterlein, *Iceland*, 71.
43 John H. Morgan to Mr. Hickerson, Dec. 3, 1945, box 5114, RG 59, NARA.
44 Outgoing telegram, Dec. 6, 1946, box 5114, RG 59, NARA.
45 Incoming telegram, Dec. 10, 1946, box 5114, RG 59, NARA.
46 *Commercial Fisheries Review* 10(2) (1948): 29.
47 Bjornsson, 223.
48 Reykjavik to Secretary of State, April 18, 1947, box 5114, RG 59, NARA.
49 Hugh S. Cumming Jr. to Mr. Hickerson, April 28, 1947, box 5114, RG 59, NARA.
50 "Developments on U.S. Purchase of Iceland Fish," June 12, 1947, box 5114, RG 59, NARA.
51 "OMGUS Purchase of Icelandic Fish," May 20, 1947, box 5114, RG 59, Iceland.
52 Incoming Telegram, April 18, 1947, box 5114, RG 59, NARA.
53 Outgoing Telegram, May 2, 1947, box 5114, RG 59, NARA.
54 Incoming Telegram, Aug. 8, 1947, box 5114, RG 59, NARA.
55 Reykjavik to Secretary of State, Aug. 8, 1947, box 5114, RG 59, NARA.
56 William C. Trimble to Secretary of State, Sept. 12, 1947, box 5114, RG 59, NARA.
57 Richard P. Butrick to John D. Hickerson, American Legation, Aug. 18, 1948, box 5114, RG 59, NARA.
58 Richard Butrick to John D. Hickerson, Aug. 18, 1948, box 5114, RG 59, NARA.
59 George H. Butler to Mr. McWilliams, June 15, 1949, box 5114, RG 59, NARA

60 "Report on Iceland," Papers of Wilbert M. Chapman, box 18, folder 10, University of Washington Special Collections.
61 Chapman papers, Report on Iceland.
62 Allen, "Public finance analysis," 446.
63 Adolf Augustus Berle Jr., "The Marshall Plan in the European struggle," *Social Research* 15(1) (1948): 3.
64 *Commercial Fisheries Review* January (1949): 33.
65 Reykjavik 178, May 16, 1950, Current Outlook of Iceland's Fishing Industry, NARA.
66 Reykjavik 564, June 27, 1951, Icelandic Summer Herring Fishery.
67 Nuechterlein, *Iceland*, 74.
68 Ibid., 87.
69 Allen, "Public finance analysis," 450.
70 Nuechterlein, *Iceland*, 147.
71 Allen, "Public finance analysis," 451.
72 Bruce Mitchell, "Politics, fish, and international resource management: The British-Icelandic Cod War," *The Geographical Review* 66(2) (1976): 127–138
73 Kurkpatrick Dorsey, *The Dawn of Conservation Diplomacy: U.S.-Canadian Wildlife Protection Treaties in the Progressive Era* (Seattle: University of Washington, 1998), 144.
74 F.A. Nicholson, *Note on Fisheries in Japan* (Madras: The Superintendent, Government Press, 1907), 40.
75 The Japan Times and Mail, *Japan's Fisheries Industry 1939* (1939), 21.
76 Edwin O. Reischauser, *The United States and Japan* (Cambridge, MA: Harvard University Press, 1950), 241.
77 Bell M. Shimada, "Japanese tuna-mothership operations in the Western Equatorial Pacific Ocean," *Commercial Fisheries Review* June (1951): 2.
78 *Commercial Fisheries Review*, December (1947).
79 *Pan-American Fisherman*, December (1948):11–12.
80 *Pacific Fisherman*, January (1949): 47.
81 *Pacific Fisherman*, July (1950): 40.
82 *Pacific Fisherman*, June (1950): 17.
83 U.S. Tariff Commission Testimony, June 26, 1952. Box 18, Folder "Committee on Reciprocity Information. Files of the American Tuna Association, Scripps Institution of Oceanography.
84 The ATA before the U.S. Tariff Commission, June 26, 1952. Box 18, Folder "U.S. Tariff Commission. American Tuna Association files, Scripps Institution of Oceanography.
85 *Commercial Fisheries Review*, September (1951): 29–30.
86 *Commercial Fisheries Review*, January (1945): 54.
87 Statement of Harold F. Cary, Committee on Reciprocity Information, December, 1954, Box 18, ATA Files, Scripps Institution of Oceanography.
88 *Pacific Fisherman*, August (1952): 87.
89 *Commercial Fisheries Review*, April (1953): 74–77. *Tuna Fish—Report on Investigation Conducted Pursuant to a Resolution by the Committee on Finance of the United States*, 74–77.
90 Margaret E. Dewar, *Industry in Trouble: The Federal Government and the New England Fisheries* (Philadelphia: Temple University Press, 1983), 48.
91 White House Central Files, Box 786, Folder 149-B-2 Fish (1).Eisenhower Library.
92 Subject Series, Box 94, Folder "Trade Agreements and Tariff Matters, Fish (1)," Subject Series, Eisenhower Presidential Library.
93 Eisenhower to Millikin and Reed, June 25, 1953, Box 786, Folder 149-B-2 Fish (1), White House Central Files, Eisenhower Presidential Library.
94 *Commercial Fisheries Review*, July (1954): 36.

95 James Acheson, "Coming up empty: Management failure of the New England groundfishery," *Mast* 10(1): 58.

96 Eckes, "Trading American Interests," 147.

97 Papers of Phillip Areeda, Box 9, folder "Tuna Fish (2)." White House press release, March 17, 1956, Eisenhower Presidential Library.

98 White House Press Release, June 4, 1956. OF 624 Folder 122-I (2), Eisenhower Presidential Library.

99 Memorandum, Jan. 4, 1957, Subject Series Box 12, Fish and Wildlife (Fisheries Loans (2)), Eisenhower Presidential Library.

100 D. Schimel, C. Redman, J. Dearing, L. Graumlich, R. Leemans, C. Crumley, K. Hibbard, W. Steffen and R. Costanza, "Evolution of the human-environment relationship," in *The Encyclopedia of Earth*, May 2 (2007).

101 Naomi Oreskes, "Scaling up our vision," *ISIS* 105 (2) (2014): 384.

102 Poul Holm, "World War II and the 'great acceleration' of North Atlantic fisheries," GE, 66–91.

103 Paul R. Josephson, "The ocean's hot dog: The development of the fish stick," *Technology and Culture* 49(1) (2008): 42.

Part V
Environmental Trading

12 Frontier Exchanges
Commercial Calculation and Environmental Transformation

Gordon M. Winder and Andreas Dix

Trading Environments' collective approach permits some summary and discussion of wide-ranging characteristics of environment and trade as distant environments were rapidly integrated into the circuits of emerging world markets. These we discuss here in terms of the work of valuing environments, discovering nature and natural limits in business, the power of calls for improved environments, and the surprising characteristics and work of trading environments, before addressing the contribution of the volume to further research in environmental history. However, since each chapter investigated a specific combination of commercial knowledge, environmental transformation, settlement and technical frontiers, associated with specific trading environments, and each contributed findings constrained by these contexts, it is useful to briefly summarize these separate findings in terms of the trading environments, frontiers and knowledges discussed.

TRADE, ENVIRONMENT, KNOWLEDGE, AND FRONTIER

From the start, *Trading Environments* ran the risk of forcing the term and metaphor to carry such a heavy weight of potential meanings that it would lose its analytical usefulness. The volume has indeed collected findings from researching such diverse experiences of historical trading environments as merchant adventuring in South America, the warehouses of nature model for European-style consumerism and landscape transformation, Europe's international forestry congresses, and enterprise management of manufacturing and selling paper, and even harvesting machines. The loosely organized and thinly stretched networks that met in these trading environments, the institutions supporting them and the environmental learning and consequences associated with them are consistent with the contested networks of the wheat exchange and the abstracting and regularizing work that they accomplished that the volume first used to illustrate what a trading environment could be. But the US State Department's Cold War archives reveal the strategic rooms and corridors where the work of trumping domestic fisheries' market protectionism and environmental concerns over fisheries with geopolitical interests in a way that stretches 'trading environment' well beyond this initial illustrative example. In addition, *Trading Environments* has investigated diverse frontiers, whether the organizing of Fennoscandia peatland frontiers, the assembling of projects to integrate Colombia into North Atlantic beef markets, the environmental learning of the New Zealand settler government as it framed 'improvement' in terms of natural, improved, and acquired land value, or the two-stage revaluation of lands and people carried out by the USA's New Deal Submarginal Lands Program. Thus the places of trade and the material and envisioned environments that were traded in these places were diverse.

Consumers were produced by the creation of new trading environments, such as the department stores, exhibitions, and other 'warehouses of nature.' In addition, as Andreas Dix showed, rural landscapes became reorganized into both consumption and specialized production landscapes as imports replaced some local production and elites revalued and reworked the European countryside. The new landscapes of consumption included resorts and spas, recreational landscapes, and new production and consumption landscapes, such as those for wine and beer. Long-distance trade and tourism drove the landscape transformation and thus the rebuilding of cities and the replanting of rural districts meant that European nature and environment were put to the service of generating market opportunities.

Ships, shore stations, and merchant warehouses constituted the mobile and networked trading environments of merchant adventurers. Thus networks and mobility are emphasized over markets and environments in Stephen Bell's exploration of merchant adventuring in South America. Each adventurer utilized varied trading environments, and it was the coordination of them using foreign capital that permitted the extraction of profits. Whether adventuring in the context of infrequent and slow communications made more tenuous by political instability or of regular telegraphic and steamer communication, merchants profited from exploiting information and capital asymmetries made possible by their communication and mobility advantages and through acquiring commercial privileges from local governments. Bell's third case study, the beef extract enterprise at Fray Bentos, shows an increased scale of investment and exploitation of a technological frontier through the joining of scientific and commercial networks. But in each of his case studies, environments played a fifth fiddle to network, capital, mobility, and political power.

The international congresses where European officials met to discuss forests, forest management, and the timber trade constituted one set of trading environments. The forestry experts who met there traded no timber, even though they had timber prices in mind. Instead they shared their estimates of forest harvests and debated the prospect of a future international timber famine. That debate highlighted the tension between forests carefully managed for local timber supply under sustainable forest management regimes and the plunder economy stripping bare forests on the timber frontier. As

Western and Central European industrialization drove the expansion of timber trading networks and regions became more entangled, the ecological aspects of the timber trade became increasingly visible to forestry experts but were largely ignored by companies and governments, which relied on ever larger supply regions to meet timber demand. In these trading environments, sustainability was rescaled, but the hard realities of resource plundering on the timber frontier continued unabated. Eventually the calculative practices of sustainable forest yields would be applied in the resource hinterlands, but in the meantime the market forces and prices drove an unequal exchange between industrializing cores and distant resource peripheries with scant regard for ecological effects despite the warnings of the experts meeting in the trading environments. Here we find environmental learning but with little effect: these trading environments were circumvented.

Some manufacturers worked hard to coordinate diverse trading environments. The McCormick enterprise's trading environments spanned from factory and labor hiring hall, through fairs, exhibitions, patent offices and patent courts, warehouses, agencies and branches, legal offices, stock exchanges and banks, company trade catalogues, and diverse farms located around the world but notably within the 'hennequin-wheat complex' of Mexico, the Philippines, and North America. In their advertising, the McCormicks trumpeted the agricultural abundance and the civilization and urbanization that their harvesting machines brought: their machines would civilize nature. In reality, their manufacturing and business interests remained heavily marked by the difficulties that they encountered when they set about articulating and transforming diverse natures. Both their Chicago factory and their extensive and costly distribution network ran to seasonal beats. The materiality of their horse-drawn machinery locked them into an exhausting competitive environment. The calculative practices of their propertied interests came to dominate the business so that the machine civilized the family and enterprise, while civilizing nature remained at best a work in progress.

Organizing a resource frontier requires not only a visioning of nature but also promotional activity in a wide range of trading environments, or 'arenas' as Esa Ruuskanen calls them. He traces the scientific revisioning of mires and peatlands as a natural resource using theories about local, human-induced climate change to promote 'frost-preventing drainages.' To make mires valuable, the scientists had to win over and work with landowners, administrators, and politicians, a process that gained momentum in the second half of the nineteenth century as drainage projects connected with the identification of peat as a fuel with a commodity frontier. Beginning in the 1920s in Sweden and peaking in Finland in the 1960s and 1970s, drainage for a forest commodity frontier became a force on the landscape. The environmental results were changed peatland ecologies, biodiversity loss, and habitat destruction. In this case, rather than careful commercial calculation or market forces, initially false assumptions, combined with optimism and determination, and then the emergence of new commodity frontiers drove large-scale environmental transformations. Social, political, and cultural institutions provided the key trading environments.

In his reexamination of the environmental transformations wrought by settler society in New Zealand, Michael Roche finds that, despite the eagerness to transform forest into pasture that stamped this enterprise, other ideas about land value emerged. Visions of an expected outcome—the mixed pastoral landscape of Britain's southern farm—framed the land market. But the settler government calculated 'land improvement' in terms of the differences between natural value, improved value, and acquired value. As its officers recorded the improvements made to properties in their cartography of land settlement, they began to revise their expectations that all of New Zealand could be transformed into this idealized landscape. They designated land for scenic reserves and established several classes of rural land for lease or sale depending upon quality. Thus the environmental transformation was accompanied by environmental learning: uneven, partial, error-laden, still based on false assumptions, but nonetheless related to both ways of approximating economic returns and to ways of knowing environmental outcomes. Michael Roche argues for processes of translation and enterprise that accompanied the transformation story more usually associated with the making of farm landscapes in this settler society.

Prominent individuals assembled to subsidize and promote projects to integrate Colombia into North Atlantic beef markets spurred on by ideas about tropical fertility, improvement, speculative urgency, and impending scarcity. Shawn Van Ausdal shows that their aspirations foundered on inadequate market research and on limited understanding of the productive potential of the tropics, and thus ran headlong into social and natural limits to environmental transformation. Their efforts triggered debates about the best prospects for improvement in the tropics, and wound up fueling critiques of *latifundio*, confirming a regional segmentation of global beef markets, and reorientating discourses about Tropicality within the country. Ultimately, turning Colombia into a second Argentina proved to be a misplaced expectation.

Mathias Mutz encourages business historians to naturalize industrialization and shows what this could mean in the example of the Saxon pulp and paper industry. As the industry switched from rags to wood as raw material, manufacturers reset their 'learning base,' reconsidered their location choices, adapted their technology to the new material, established trade connections between forests and factories, and customized wood production to their special needs. This entailed, among other things, relocation of the industry to the resource areas, an expanding international timber trade, the holding of enormous stockpiles of wood, and an industrialization of German timber supply areas in terms of a shift from firewood to timber and a growing emphasis on small-dimensioned wood and spruce monoculture. Through ecological restrictions, technological innovation, environmental learning, and enhanced management capabilities, pulp and paper mills also tried to 'improve' nature. Further, the industry established infrastructure and trade networks and generated environmental and commercial knowledge, which in turn influenced the strategic and organizational development of industrial enterprises. Thus he sees industrialization as a process combining new commercial and environmental knowledge and both technological and geographical frontiers.

Craig Colten reports the work of a trading environment comprising the planning apparatus of the federal state, and its associated experts, reports and politics, a complex that pushed through an ambitious, two-stage revaluation of lands and people executed under the New Deal by the Resettlement Administration through its Submarginal Lands Program. First its experts reclassified parts of the landscape as 'submarginal'; that is, exhausted, deforested, infertile, eroded, and degraded, and thus unsuited for agriculture, the results of a failed settlement system that produced too many small and uneconomic farm units and left many people in poverty and suffering from health and social problems. In this way, they named past failed economic practices and simultaneously legitimated federal acquisition, in the process writing a new normative landscape. In a second revaluation, experts resorted to claims regarding the superiority of recreation, forestry, and conservation uses for such lands and expressed hope for 'restoration' through conservation, improvement, and forest and game management. Erosion control, reforestation, and game management would restore degraded lands. Forests and recreational land use, based on the landscape ideal of the Eastern woodland resort were designated as superior land uses to small farming, and their proper planning and management would install a new growth regime. The poor were to be resettled off of these lands and removed from relief rolls. The improvement of the remaining population would be completed through recreation and social restoration. The superior effects of central planning based on a reform agenda were sounded. In these ambitious landscape transformations, the "degradation produced by private property owners" would be traded "for the benefits of federally managed conservation" (see Colten this volume). The mistakes produced by the old settlement frontier would be wiped away by the restorative effects of a new recreation and conservation frontier. Again, social, political, and cultural institutions provided the key trading environments.

During the Cold War, the US State Department was a powerful trading environment, but one that functioned in its own surprising ways. Ignoring market calculations and economists' advice, its officials reallocated access to the US domestic fish market and international fishing stocks to Icelandic and Japanese fishers so as to secure strategic resources—the Reykjavik air base and the Japanese economy—and with devastating results for US fishing interests. These trades took place with little attention to the environment, to fish stocks, or to markets. In this case, as Carmel Finley argues, geopolitical interests trumped both national market realities and environmental concerns. As it were, in the offices and corridors of the State Department, narratives of geostrategic environments and resources were wedded to imagined Cold War frontiers and the imagined abundance of cheap produce lining the shelves of US supermarkets, so as to swing President, Senate and Congress behind measures that would, ultimately, sacrifice US fishing industry interests to Japanese and Icelandic ones.

THE WORK OF VALUING AND ASSEMBLING ENVIRONMENTS

Our inquiries reveal the weak commercial knowledge and, in the trading of environments that we have examined, no important role for price, market, or even business management in the trading of environments. To some extent, this is a result of our choices of case studies, only three of which are focused on businesses. In the first of these cases, merchant adventurers profited by identifying new markets for objects and through processes of environmental learning and transformation as well as market making and technological change developed more regular and larger scale trading relations related to large-scale environmental transformations. In the second case, sales price and machinery market considerations were dominated by the disproportionate costs of distribution to production costs. The latter became more important as competition intensified, but for the first three decades of its production history, the McCormick enterprise secured high levels of profit from the sale of each machine. Nevertheless, the firm remained locked into natural conditions for its business and particularly the seasonality of rural harvest seasons. Central Europeans responded to timber market price signals by developing both a sustainable forest production system and an ever-expanding timber frontier that operated in a far from sustainable manner. In each case, prices proved to be weak influences on the trading of environments.

Governments were busy framing, evaluating, regulating, and adjusting markets, especially land markets. The most unlikely government trader of environments was the US State Department, which ignored market and environmental considerations as it reshaped fishing industry futures for Cold War geopolitical gains. Michael Roche demonstrates that values were assigned to land classes in New Zealand in order to frame land markets. Further, individual farm histories reveal varied results, as the failures of some large and small New Zealand land developments testify. Craig Colten shows a US government reframing a wide land market through expert assessment of the failures of earlier settlement schemes, the designation of 'submarginal' lands, and their revaluation as lands for recreation. In several of the case studies, the profitability of economic units or activities was assumed in advance rather than demonstrated. This was clearly so in the cases of Colombian beef and Fennoscandia peatlands. In such cases, the result was environmental and market learning due to false assumptions, as well as waste of capital and damage to environments. Ambitious and inappropriate environmental transformations were partly the result of shortcomings of government and commercial practice, which consistently featured a lack of attention to environment. Even when sophisticated calculations of environments were available, as for example in Central European forestry, they proved inadequate to the new commercial realities, in this case, the expanding timber frontier.

Our volume points to the power of calls for improved environments. Representations of environments as improvable and improved were used to legitimize exploitation and in ways that obscured the ecological and social damage done. Commercial exploitation was designed to produce new environments that would facilitate long-term extraction of resources and profits, whether the target environment comprised Saxon forests, Great Plains wheat farms, or Scandinavian peatlands. Thus the human alteration of environments, the generation of new cultural landscapes, and 'socionatures' were well under way over large areas of the globe throughout the period under study here. This constituted testimony for the power of humans over nature and for the improvability of nature, findings that in turn served to legitimize further, heroically scaled interventions.

However, organizing any resource frontier requires not only a visioning of nature but also promotional activity in a wide range of trading environments or 'arenas,' as Esa Ruuskanen calls them. In his discussion of the mobilizing of Swedish and Finnish peatlands into frontiers, social, political, and cultural institutions provided the key trading environments. While we identified and worked with a wide range of trading environments, in fact these were organized either by business or by government and scientists. In each case, frontiers were organized and legitimized by assembling experts in support of government sanctioned projects. The assembled experts often promised some weak form of 'sustainability': the transformative project would produce a long lasting, improved productive landscape. But these forms of 'sustainability' often relied on both poor or inadequate environmental knowledge and the harnessing of webs of investors and consumers distanced from the environmental transformations taking place. So the new improved environments generated by historical frontiers tended to lack assessments of environmental impact and of sustainability.

Instead, diverse environments and frontier projects were entangled with each other through processes of long-distance teleconnection. Thus Central European rural and urban landscapes (for example, wine landscapes) were bound to frontier energy projects (coal and timber). Similarly, a sustainable forest management system in Germany was possible only because of the expansion of a timber frontier throughout Northern and Eastern Europe. Thus the transformation of Europe into specialized tourism, consumption, and production landscapes was possible within the context of other projects conducted elsewhere.

Further, this teleconnectivity was orchestrated using not only sophisticated trading environments and environmental knowledge but also various forms of mystification and idealization that accompanied and legitimized this assembling work. Thus while European officials met to discuss forests, forest management, and the timber trade at international congresses, they were unable to communicate environmental problems to their governments in ways that would alter the exploitative practices of the timber frontier. Similarly, the McCormicks sold their machines to US farmers by advertising the ideals of improvement and abundance illustrated with images of farm mechanization in other, less advanced lands. Environmental learning did occur and sometimes government interventions—as we saw in the cases of revaluations of land and settlement processes in New Zealand and the US South—designed to revalue and recategorize land so as to align specific parcels to new projects and their related 'markets' accompanied it. But environmental learning tended to be cast as an unwanted constraint on the efficacy of 'improvement' and was thus devalued in the workings of trading environments.

Despite the growing organizational capacities of businesses, enterprises struggled to coordinate diverse trading environments. Thus the ships, shore stations, and merchant warehouses loosely assembled by merchant adventurers had the advantages of winning arbitrage by shifting capital, goods, and products among separate trading environments. Mobility and networking among environments comprised a chief advantage for such loosely organized enterprises. In contrast, the McCormicks asserted centralized ownership and control whenever possible, but they were hard pressed to coordinate the diverse trading environments of the far-flung business. The McCormick enterprise's trading environments spanned from factory and hiring hall, through fairs, exhibitions, patent offices and patent courts, warehouses, agencies and branches, legal offices, stock exchanges and banks, company trade catalogues, and diverse farms located around the world. Similarly, the regularizing of information and material flows that underpinned the successes of the meat works at Fray Bentos required not only standardized information and goods but also a diverse array of places for trade, plus hidden trades of environments and environmental effects. Saxon pulp and paper interests learned to organize webs of enterprises to supply their mills from wide areas of Eastern Europe. Thus our focus on trading environments reveals the need to add investigation of the networking among numerous and diverse trading environments to studies of regional environmental transformations and business history.

By investigating trading environments, this volume discovered natural limits in business. Despite claims by many contemporaries about the ability of 'civilization' to overcome the constraints of nature on urbanization, cultivation, and commerce, nature remained a problem for manufacturers, merchants, and producers. Saxon pulp and paper manufacturers learned to rely on spruce—spruce was desired, only spruce would do and no other timber was adequate—even though this locked them into a specific forest production schedule and reliance on a far-flung timber supply region. Not all land in New Zealand was suitable for pastoral farming. Colombian ranchers found that Hereford cattle were not easily adaptable to their tropical environments. McCormick's manufacturing success required a proliferation of horses on farms, fiber imports from Mexico and the Philippines, and a production schedule keyed to the wheat harvest season.

Thus environments were not interchangeable or perfectly improvable. Instead, geography mattered: not in the usual limited sense in which 'geography' is used in environmental history (to refer to distance) but in the sense used in the discipline of geography that 'geography' refers to spatial and environmental differentiation, not only in terms of physical and biological environmental differences but also in terms of built environments, infrastructure, social, economic, political, and landscape variation. Environmental history will identify more geographic constraints on the transformation of environments and should do so without falling back into environmental determinism.

Similarly, environments were not simply interchangeable for businesses. Transformed or damaged environments had implications for commercial activity and deserve further attention. What practices commonly emerged when businesses found that they had transformed environments beyond recognition? Businesses are able to move on through such practices as resource abandonment, writing off capital and investment, or investment in new technologies. But, as we have seen, businesses rely on governments to revalue environments. So in what circumstances have governments and/or businesses been effective in rehabilitating damaged environments?

We call for a more systematic engagement by environmental historians with the practices that bind commercial and environmental knowledge together. This call involves a need for investigation of the effects of new forms of networking, network knowledge, and communication, as well as the effects of economic practices such as financialization, the establishment of production routines, standardization, and so on, on environments. But in addition to network knowledge, environmental knowledge needs to be a focus of attention. The effects of environmental learning, not to mention forgetting, of the development of practices designed to cope with risk and vulnerability, and efforts to remediate environmental degradation are also needed. Recent pressure on corporations to introduce environmental learning—for example, in the forms of triple bottom line reporting, the assessment of ecosystem services, the collection and analysis of environmental mega data, or through corporate social responsibility including waste reduction projects—may be having positive effects, but such calculative practices threaten to place future environments only in the hands of experts and to exclude other agents from decisions about landscape, economy, and environment. There needs to be further research into the effects, both direct and indirect, of commercial calculative practices on environments.

We believe that 'trading environments through frontiers' offers a promising multifaceted lens through which environmental historians can learn about the interactions among environmental transformations, commercial and knowledge frontiers, and environmental learning. Such an approach should highlight the ways investors equipped with new forms of commercial exploitation, governments planning for commercial-imperial imperatives, and scientists working to improve limited environmental knowledge, encountered and revalued environments. Where long-term ecological research and human-ecology history offer the merits and claims of seemingly 'timeless' and 'global' perspectives buttressed by the unique encompassing claims of ecological systems theory, the 'trading environments' metaphor and lens focuses on the histories and geographies of environmental and commercial knowledge production and circulation. It requires political economy, political ecology, and cultural perspectives on human environment relations, and it requires a recombination of histories and geographies of region and landscape with geographies and histories of networks and webs of enterprises. It offers an approach that could reexamine the propaganda of particular interests, the actual contributions to society and environment that were made, and the specific ideas and methods of thinking on sustainability that children of the European project of Enlightenment used.

Contributors

Stephen Bell is Associate Professor of Geography and History in the Department of Geography, University of California, Los Angeles. Following completion of his PhD in geography at the University of Toronto, he published on the historical geography and environmental history of Latin America, especially Brazil. His first book, *Campanha Gaúcha: A Brazilian Ranching System, 1850–1920* (Stanford University Press, 1998), was awarded the Warren Dean Memorial Prize of the Conference on Latin American History in 1999. It was followed by *A Life in 5 Shadow: Aimé Bonpland in Southern South America, 1817–1858* (Stanford University Press, 2010), his study of Alexander von Humboldt's first major research collaborator. In 2011, Professor Bell took up a Fellowship in the Rachel Carson Center for Environment and Society at the LMU Munich, where he researched the postwar Brazilian fieldwork of the German geographer Leo Waibel. His current major project examines the historical geography of Brazil between 1850 and 1950.

Craig E. Colten is Carl O. Sauer Professor at the Department of Geography and Anthropology, Louisiana State University, USA. With a doctorate in geography from Syracuse University, Professor Colten has published on environmental historical geography, urban environments, Louisiana, and the US South. Until recently, Professor Colten served as editor of *Geographical Review* and on the editorial board of *Environmental History*. The Association of American Geographers awarded him their J. B. Jackson Prize in 2005 and their Media Achievement Award in 2006. His book, *An Unnatural Metropolis: Wresting New Orleans from Nature* (LSU Press, 2005) was followed by *Perilous Place and Powerful Storms: Hurricane Protection in Coastal Louisiana* (University Press of Mississippi, 2009). His research interests are in water resources in the US South and community and regional resilience.

Andreas Dix is Professor of Historical Geography at the Institute for Geography, Otto-Friedrich-University Bamberg, Germany. He completed his

PhD (1993) and Habilitation (2000) at the Friedrich-Wilhelm University Bonn, the latter published as *"Freies Land." Siedlungsplanung im ländlichen Raum der SBZ und frühen DDR 1945 bis 1955* (Köln, Weimar 2002). He is a member of the board of the Working Group for Historical Cultural Landscape Research in Middle Europe (ARKUM Bonn), and a member of the scientific committee for the *Yearbook for the History of Rural Space* (JGLR St. Pölten). He was a Guest Research Fellow at the Chair of Historical Geography, Kokugakuin-University, Tokyo, Japan. He recently completed the research project "Historical Comparative Regional Analysis of Frequency and Magnitude of Landslides," within the "Early Warning Systems in Earth Management" project of the BMBF/DFG-Program "Geo-technologies." Professor Dix's research interests span historical geography, environmental history, natural hazards, reconstruction of historical cultural landscapes, and settlement and planning history.

Carmel Finley is Instructor in the School of History, Oregon State University, USA. She is an historian of science and is interested in the intersection of science and policy, especially in the oceans and the interactions of fish, fishermen, scientists, and managers. Dr. Finley received her PhD from the University of California San Diego in 2007, and she published *All the Fish in the Sea: Maximum Sustained Yield and the Failure of Fisheries Management* (University of Chicago Press) in 2011. She was a Fellow at the Rachel Carson Center for Environment and Society at the LMU Munich, where she worked on her next book, *All the Boats on the Ocean: The Politics of Fishing Subsides, 1945–1985*. With her extensive publishing on US and Canadian forest and fisheries policies, and on the history of fishing in the USA's Pacific Northwest, Dr. Finley has research interests in political ecology, marine and fisheries policy, Pacific fisheries history, marine conservation, environmental and maritime history, and the history of science and technology, generally.

Dr. Christian Lotz is conducting postdoctoral studies in the Leibniz Graduate School, at the Herder Institute, Marburg, Germany. In 2007 he gained his doctorate from the Historical Institute, University of Stuttgart with his work *Die Deutung des Verlust. Erinnerungspolitische Kontroversen im geteilten Deutschland um Flucht, Vertreibung und die Ostgebiete 1948–1972* (Böhlau-Verlag 2007). Before moving to Marburg, Dr. Lotz held research positions at the Institute for European History in Mainz and the German Historical Institutes in Warsaw and London. With Martin Zückert and Ulrike Plath he is editing a collected work, *Knowledge About Resources: Challenges of the Exploration and Exploitation of Resources in East Central Europe in the 19th and 20th Centuries*. His research, focused on the last two centuries, includes interests in German political and cultural history, environmental history, and the history of cartography, science, and international congresses.

Since April 2012, **Dr. Mathias Mutz** works at the RWTH Aachen, Germany, in the university's Economic, Social and Technology History Institute. He gained his doctorate in 2010 from the Georg-August University Göttingen before moving to the Institute for Historical Sciences, Humboldt University Berlin. With Wiebke Bebermeier and Anna-Sarah Hennig he edited the volume *Vom Wasser. Umweltgeschichtliche Perspektiven auf Konflikte, Risiken und Nutzungsformen* (Siegburg 2008) and he recently published *Umwelt als Ressource. Die sächsische Papierindustrie, 1850–1930* (Göttingen 2013) which brought together his postdoctoral research on the paper industry in Saxony. His research interests are in the environmental and technical history of industrialization, business and innovation, energy and resource history, and the technical and social history of time.

Michael Roche is Professor at the School of People, Environment and Planning, Massey University, New Zealand. Professor Roche gained his doctorate at the University of Canterbury, New Zealand, and his research into the historical geography of New Zealand's forest industries was published as *History of New Zealand Forestry* (Wellington, 1990). At Massey University he has lead the research projects "Hybrid Nature in New Zealand Domains," and "Soldier Home and Farm Loans," and was a member of the recent project "Biological Economies" funded by the Royal Society of New Zealand's Marsden Fund. Among his more recent works, Professor Roche counts the edited collections *A Geographer by Declaration: Selected Writings by George Jobberns (*Canterbury University Press, 2010), with Lindsay Proudfoot; *(Dis)Placing Empire: Renegotiating British Colonial Geographies* (Ashgate Publishing 2005); and with Caroline Miller, *Past Matters: Heritage and Planning History—Case Studies from the Pacific Rim* (Cambridge Scholars Publishing, 2007). He has published extensively on New Zealand's forest, agricultural, environmental and planning history, soldier land settlement schemes, and historical geography.

Dr. Esa Ruuskanen is Academy Research Fellow in the Department of History, University of Oulu, Finland and the person responsible for the minor in the Environmental Humanities in the Faculty of Humanities. He has been a Leibniz Graduate Fellow at the Herder Institute, Marburg, Germany and a Visiting Scholar at the University of Birmingham, United Kingdom. Together with Professor Park Seung-Joon of Kwansei Gakuin University, Osaka, he was engaged in a major research project "Energy Supply and regulation: Post-war Japan and Finland in Comparison", the results of which were brought out in an anthology published by Routledge. His research interests span the history of the utilization and protection of wetlands in the Nordic countries, the British Isles, and the Netherlands, 1750–2010; changes in energy production and consumption in postwar Finland; and the philosophy and theory of environmental history.

Dr. Shawn Van Ausdal is Assistant Professor of History and Geography at the Universidad de los Andes, Bogota, Colombia. With a doctorate in geography from the University of California, Berkeley, he was a Fellow at the Rachel Carson Center for Society and the Environment at the LMU Munich, where he explored the material practices, economic rationale, and political conflicts behind the transformation of Colombian lowland forests into a landscape of grass in his project, "The Logic of Livestock: Ranching Landscapes in Northern Colombia, 1850–1972." His research lies at the intersection of environmental history, agrarian and food studies, and development geographies.

Gordon Winder is Professor of Economic Geography and Sustainability Research at the Ludwig-Maximilians-University Munich, Germany. He received his PhD from the University of Toronto, and was Senior Lecturer in Geography at the University of Auckland before moving to Munich in 2008. He serves on the advisory board of the doctoral program at the Rachel Carson Center, LMU Munich, is an Honorary Research Fellow at the School of Environment, the University of Auckland, and a member of the editorial board of the *Journal of Historical Geography*. Professor Winder's recent book, *The American Reaper: Harvesting Networks and Technology* (Ashgate Publishing, 2012), investigates the dynamics of manufacturing networks within an industry characterized by dispersed production locations, technical constraints on the scale of production, and the use of licensing, subcontracting, and strategic alliances before 1890. As an economic and historical geographer, his research is focused on manufacturing networks, resource-based economies, and sustainability.

Archives Consulted

Colombia

Universidad de Antioquia, Medellín.
Archivo del Congreso (AC), Bogotá.
Archivo General de la Nación (AGN), Bogotá.

Finland

Kansallisarkisto (The National Archives of Finland), Helsinki.

Germany

Bayerisches Wirtschaftsarchiv (Bavarian Business Archives, BWA), Munich.
Bundesarchiv (BArch) (Federal Archives), Berlin.
Sächsisches Wirtschaftsarchiv (SWA), (Saxon Business Archives), Leipzig.
Staatsarchiv Chemnitz (StAC), (State Archives Chemnitz), Chemnitz.
Universitätsarchiv Dresden (University Archives Dresden), Dresden.

New Zealand

Archives New Zealand, Wellington.

Norway

Riksarkiv, Oslo.

United Kingdom

Public Records Office (PRO), London.
The National Archives of the UK, London.

USA

Drake Memorial Library, SUNY Brockport, Brockport, New York.

Eisenhower Presidential Library, Abilene, Kansas.

McCormick Collection, State Historical Society of Wisconsin (SHS), Madison, Wisconsin.

National Archives and Records Administration, (NARA), Maryland.

National Archives and Records Administration, (NARA-FW), Fort Worth, Texas.

National Archives and Records Administration, (NARA-DC), Washington, DC.

National Portrait Gallery, Washington, DC.

The University of Utah, Salt Lake City, Utah.

Hill Memorial Library, Louisiana State University, Baton Rouge, Louisiana.

Scripps Institution of Oceanography, University of California San Diego, California.

University of Washington Library, Seattle, Washington.

References

Acheson, James, "Coming up empty: Management failure of the New England groundfishery," *Mast* 10, no. 1: 58.

Adas, Michael, *Dominance by Design: Technological Imperatives and America's Civilizing Mission* (Cambridge, MA: Harvard University Press, 2006).

Ahtiainen, Marketta and Huttunen, Pertti, "Long-term effects of forestry management on water quality and loading in brooks," *Boreal Environment Research* 4 (1999): 101–114.

Aiken, Charles S., *The Cotton Plantation South Since the Civil War* (Baltimore: Johns Hopkins University Press, 1998).

Alexander, D. J., "Some features of West German policy for improving the agriculture structure," *Journal of Farm Economics* 46, no. 4 (1964): 791–804.

Allen, Robert Loring, "The vulnerability of Iceland's economy," *Finanz-Archiv: Public Finance Analysis*, New Series 3 (1959): 441–452.

Anderson, Kay, "White natures: Sydney's Royal Agricultural Show in post-humanist perspective," *Transactions of the Institute of British Geographers* 28, no. 4 (2003): 423.

Anderson, Mark L., and Taylor, Charles J., *A History of Scottish Forestry*, vol. 2 (London, Edinburgh: Nelson, 1967).

Anderson, Warwick, "Climates of opinion: Acclimatization in nineteenth-century France and England," *Victorian Studies* 35 (1992): 135–157.

Angell-Petersen, Ingerid, "Conservation and management of mires in Norway," in Asbjørn Moen and Richard Binns (eds.), *Regional Variation and Conservation of Mire Ecosystems* (Trondheim: Universitetet i Trondheim and Vitenskaapsmuseet, 1994), 11.

Angus, Beverly, "The history of the cattle tick *Boophilus microplus* in Australia and achievements in its control," *International Journal for Parasitology* 26 (1996): 1348.

Anonymous, "Congrès international d'agriculture de Vienne," *Revue des eaux et forêts* 46 (1907): 343f.

Anonymous, "Der VIII. Internationale landwirtschaftliche Kongress in Wien vom 20. bis 25. Mai 1907," *Allgemeine Forst- und Jagdzeitung* 83 (1907): 435–437.

Anonymous, "Fra den internationale Forstkongres i Paris 1900," *Tidsskrift for Skovbrug* 9 (1901): 13–18. [in Danish]

Anonymous, "La carne y el trabajo intelectual," *Ganadería de Bolívar* 43–44 (1937): 1269.

Anttila, Veikko, *Järvenlaskuyhtiöt Suomessa: kansatieteellinen tutkimus* mit Deutsches Referat (Helsinki: Suomen Muinaismuistoyhdistys, 1967). [in Finnish]

Appadurai, Arjun (ed.), *The Social Life of Things: Commodities in Cultural Perspective* (Cambridge: Cambridge University Press, 1986).

Ardrey, R. L., *American Agricultural Implements* (Chicago: R. L. Ardrey, 1894, facsimile by University Microfilms, Ann Arbor, MI, 1968).

Arenas, Olimpio, "El zebú y sus ventajas en el trópico," *Revista Nacional de Agricultura* 33 (1939): 322.

Arnold, David, "'Illusory riches:' Representations of the Tropical World, 1840–1950," *Singapore Journal of Tropical Geography* 21 (2000): 16.

Arnold, David, *The Problem of Nature: Environment, Culture, and European Expansion* (Oxford: Blackwell, 1996), 141–168.

Aspers, Patrick, *How Are Markets Made?* (Cologne: Max Planck Institute for the Study of Societies, 2009).

Åström, Sven-Erik, "English timber imports from northern Europe in the eighteenth century," *The Scandinavian Economic History Review* 18 (1970): 12–32.

Åström, Sven-Erik, "Northeastern Europe's timber trade between the Napoleonic and Crimean Wars: A preliminary survey," *The Scandinavian Economic History Review* 35 (1987): 170–177.

Auty, Richard M., *Sustaining Development in Mineral Economies: The Resource Curse Thesis* (London: Routledge: 1993).

Babo, Lambert von, *Der Weinstock und seine Varietäten. Beschreibung und Synonymik der vorzüglichsten in Deutschland cultivirten Wein- und Tafeltrauben, mit Hinweisung auf die bekannteren Rebsorten anderer europäischer Weinländer* (Frankfurt am Main: Brönner 1844).

Baghdiantz McCabe, Ina, *A History of Global Consumption 1500–1800* (London, New York: Routledge, 2015).

Bankoff, Greg, "A question of breeding: Zootechny and colonial attitudes toward the tropical environment in the late nineteenth-century Philippines," *The Journal of Asian Studies* 60 (2001): 413–437.

Bankoff, Greg, "First impressions: Diarists, scientists, imperialists and the management of the environment in the American Pacific, 1899–1902," *The Journal of Pacific History* 44 (2009), 261–280.

Baratay, Eric and Hardouin-Fugier, Elisabeth, *ZOOS. Histoire des jardins zoologiques en Occident* (XVIe-XXe siècle) (Paris: Edition de la découverte, 1998).

Barbier, Edward B., *Scarcity and Frontiers: How Economies Have Developed Through Natural Resource Exploitation* (Cambridge: Cambridge University Press, 2011).

Barnes, Trevor, "External shocks: Regional implications of an open staple economy," in John Britton (ed.), *Canada and the Global Economy: The Geography of Structural and Technological Change* (Montreal and Kingston: McGill-Queen's University Press: 1996), 48–68.

Barrán, José Pedro and Nahum, Benjamín, *Historia rural del Uruguay moderno, 1851–1885*, vol. 1 (in 2 bks.) (Montevideo: Ediciones de la Banda Oriental, 1967).

Barsky, Osvaldo and Djenderedjian, Julio, *Historia del capitalismo agrario pampeano. Tomo I: La expansión ganadera hasta 1895* (Buenos Aires: Siglo XXI, Universidad de Belgrano, 2003), 429.

Bauman, A., *Om våra torvmarker och deras tillgodogörande för odlingsändamål* (Stockholm: Fritze, 1925) [in Swedish].

Bayerl, Günter, "Die Natur als Warenhaus. Der technisch-ökonomische Blick auf die Natur in der Frühen Neuzeit," in Sylvia Hahn and Reinhold Reith (eds.), *Umwelt-Geschichte. Arbeitsfelder, Forschungsansätze, Perspektiven* (Wien, München: Verlag für Geschichte und Politik, 2001), 33–52.

Bayerl, Günter, "Prolegomenon der 'Großen Industrie'. Der technisch-ökonomische Blick auf die Natur im 18. Jahrhundert," in Werner Abelshauser (ed.), *Umweltgeschichte. Umweltverträgliches Wirtschaften in historischer Perspektive* (Göttingen: Vandenhoeck & Ruprecht, 1994), 29–56.

Bayerl, Günter and Pichol, Karl, *Papier: Produkt aus Lumpen, Holz und Wasser* (Reinbek: Rowohlt, 1986), 99–176.

Beattie, James, "Environmental anxiety in New Zealand 1840–1941: Climate change, soil erosion, sand drift, flooding, and forest conservation," *Environment and History* 9 (2003): 379–392.

Bell, Stephen, *Campanha Gaúcha: A Brazilian Ranching System, 1850–1920* (Stanford, CA: Stanford University Press, 1998).

Bell, Stephen, "Early industrialization in the South Atlantic: Political influences on the *charqueadas* of Rio Grande do Sul before 1860," *Journal of Historical Geography* 19, no. 4 (1993): 399–411.

Bell, Stephen, *A Life in Shadow: Aimé Bonpland in Southern South America, 1817–1858* (Stanford, CA: Stanford University Press, 2010).

Bell, Stephen, "Social networks and innovation in the South American meat industry during the pre-refrigeration era: Southern Brazil and Uruguay in comparison," *Scripta Nova: Revista Electrónica de Geografía y Ciencias Sociales* (Universidad de Barcelona) 69, no. 84 (2000): 1–10.

Bender, Oliver, *Analyse der Kulturlandschaftsentwicklung der Nördlichen Frankenalb anhand eines katasterbasierten Geoinformationssystems* (Leipzig: Deutsche Akademie für Landeskunde, 2007).

Bennett, Hugh Hammond, *Soils and Agriculture of the Southern States* (New York: Macmillan, 1921).

Bennett, Hugh Hammond, *Soil Conservation* (New York: McGraw Hill, 1939).

Berch, Anders (præses) and Fjellström, Carl (respondent), *Tankar om upodlings möjlighet i Lappmarkerna* (Stockholm: Salvius, 1760) [in Swedish].

Berg, Lawrence D. and Kearns, Robin A., "Naming as norming: 'Race,' gender, and the identity politics of naming places in Aotearoa/New Zealand," *Environment and Planning D: Society and Space* 14 (1996): 99–122.

Berg, Maxine, *Luxury and Pleasure in Eighteenth-century Britain* (Oxford: Oxford University Press, 2005).

Berghoff, Hartmut and Mutz, Mathias, "Missing links. Business history and environmental change," *Jahrbuch für Wirtschaftsgeschichte* 50, no. 2 (2009): 9–21.

Berle, Jr., Adolf Augustus, "The Marshall Plan in the European struggle," *Social Research* 15, no. 1 (1948): 3.

Bernal, Washington, "La granja de selección de ganado criollo en Montería y su orientación," *Boletín de Ganadería* 1 (1939), 25.

Berndt, Christian and Boeckler, Marc, "Geographies of circulation and exchange: Constructions of markets," *Progress in Human Geography* 33, no. 4 (2009): 535–551.

Bernstein, William J., *A Splendid Exchange: How Trade Shaped the World* (New York: Grove Press, 2008).

Biles, Roger, *The South and the New Deal* (Lexington: University of Kentucky Press, 1994), 48–49.

Björklund, Jörgen, *Den nordeuropeiska timmergränsen i Sverige och Ryssland* (Umeå: Umeå Universitet, 1998).

Birkhahn, Bruno, "Die Standortverschiebungen in der papiererzeugenden Industrie Europas" (PhD diss., Kiel, 1935).

Björklund, Jörgen, "Exploiting the last phase of the North European timber frontier for the international market 1890–1914. An economic-historical approach," in: Mauro Agnoletti and Steven Anderson (eds.), *Forest History. International Studies on Socioeconomic and Forest Ecosystem Change* (Wallingford: CABI, 2000), 171–184.

Björklund, Jörgen, "From the Gulf of Bothnia to the White Sea: Swedish direct investments in the sawmill industry of Tsarist Russia," *Scandinavian Economic History Review* 32 (1984): 17–39.

Björn, Ismo, "Takeover. The environmental history of the coniferous forest," *Scandinavian Journal of History*, 25 (2000): 281–296.

Björnsson, Olafur, "Economic development in Iceland since World War II," *Weltwirtschaftliches Archiv* 98 (1967): 221.

Blain, Bodil Bjerkvik, *Melting Markets: The Rise and Decline of the Anglo-Norwegian Ice Trade 1850–1920* (London: London School of Economics, 2006).

Blechschmidt, Jürgen and Strunz, Alf-Mathias, "Der Beginn eines neuen Zeitalters der Papierfaserstoff-Erzeugung: Die Erfindung des Holzschliff-Verfahrens durch Friedrich Gottlob Keller," in Frieder Schmidt (ed.), *Papiergeschichte(n): Papierhistorische Beiträge Wolfgang Schlieder zum 70. Geburtstag* (Wiesbaden: Harrassowitz, 1996), 139–150.

Blechschmidt, Jürgen and Strunz, Alf-Mathias, "Papierindustrie in Sachsen," in Bildungswerk der Sächsischen Wirtschaft (ed.), *Wirtschaft—Innovation—Bildung: Beiträge zur Darstellung von 100 Jahren Industrie- und Wirtschaftsentwicklung in Sachsen*, (Chemnitz: Bildungswerk der Sächsischen Wirtschaft, 2000), 156–163.

Blomqvist, A.G., "Skoghushållningens nationalekonomi och synpunkter i forstpoliti" (Helsingfors: G.W. Edlunds Förlag, 1893) [in Swedish].

Bonsma, Jan C., "Degeneration of the British beef breeds in the Tropics and Subtropics," in A.O. Rhoad (ed.), *Breeding Beef Cattle for Unfavorable Environments* (Austin: University of Texas Press, 1955), 17.

Bowd, Gavin and Clayton, Daniel, "Fieldwork and tropicality in French Indochina: Reflections on Pierre Gourou's Les Paysans du Delta Tonkinois, 1936," *Singapore Journal of Tropical Geography* 24 (2003), 147–168.

Bowd, Gavin and Clayton, Daniel, "Tropicality, Orientalism, and French Colonialism in Indochina: The work of Pierre Gourou, 1927–1982," *French Historical Studies* 28 (2005): 297–327.

Brandesten, Olof, *Lantbrukarnas organisationer: Agrart och kooperativt 1830–1930*. Skogs- och lantbrukshistoriska meddelanden nr 35. Eskilstuna (2005). [in Swedish]

Brandis, Dietrich, "Forstliche Ausstellung in Edinburgh, Tell I," *Allgemeine Forst- und Jagdzeitung* (1885): 97–106; Teil II: 242–248.

Brannstrom, Christian and Neuman, Matthew, "Inventing the 'Magic Valley' of South Texas, 1905–1941," *Geographical Review* 99, no. 2 (2009): 123–145.

Brechin, Gray, *Imperial San Francisco: Urban Power, Earthly Ruin* (Berkeley, Los Angeles, London: University of California Press, 1999).

Breckman, Warren G., "Disciplining consumption: The debate about luxury in Wilhelmine Germany 1840–1914," *Journal of Social History* 24 (1991): 485–505.

Breen, Timothy Hall, "The meaning of things: Interpreting the Consumer Society in the eighteenth century," in John Brewer and Roy Porter (eds.), *Consumption and the world of goods* (London, New York: Routledge, 1993), 249–260.

Brock, William H., *Justus von Liebig: The Chemical Gatekeeper* (Cambridge: Cambridge University Press, 1997).

Broda, Józef, "Gospodarka leśna (od połowy XIX w. do I Wojny Światowej)," in: Stanisław Arnold (ed.), *Zarys historii gospodarstwa wiejskiego w Polsce*, Vol. 3, (Warszawa, 1970), 607–657. [in Polish]

Brooking, Tom, "Busting up the greatest estate of all: Liberal Maori land policy, 1891–1911," *New Zealand Journal of History* 26 (1992): 78–98.

Brooking, Tom, *Lands for the People? The Highland Clearances and the Colonization of New Zealand, a Biography of John McKenzie* (Dunedin: Otago University Press, 1996), 75.

Brooking, Tom, "Use it or lose it: Unravelling the land debate in late 19th century New Zealand," *New Zealand Journal of History* 30 (1996), 141–162.

Brooking, Tom and Pawson, Eric (eds.), *Seeds of Empire: The Environmental Transformation of New Zealand* (London: IB Tauris, 2010).

Brower, Anne, 2008, *Who Owns the High Country? The Controversial Story of Tenure Review in New Zealand* (Nelson: Craig Potton Publishing, 2008).

Buckley, Geoffrey L., "The environmental transformation of an Appalachian Valley, 1850–1906," *Geographical Review* 88, no. 2 (1998): 175–198.

Burt, Ronald S., *Structural Holes: The Social Structure of Competition* (Cambridge, MA: Harvard University Press, 1992).

Çalışkan, Koray and Callon, Michel, "Economization, part 2: A research programme for the study of markets," *Economy and Society* 39 (2010): 1–32.

Callon, Michel, Méadel, Cécile, Rabeharisoa, Vololona, "The economy of qualities," *Economy and Society*, 31 (2002): 194–217.

Campbell, Colin, "Understanding traditional and modern patterns of consumption in eighteenth-century England: A character-action approach," in John Brewer and Roy Porter (eds.), *Consumption and the world of goods* (London, New York: Routledge, 1993), 40–57.

Canel, Eduardo, *Barrio Democracy in Latin America: Participatory Decentralization and Community Activism in Montevideo* (University Park, PA: The Pennsylvania University Press, 2010).

Cannavò, Peter F., "American contradictions and pastoral visions: An appraisal of Leo Marx, *The Machine in the Garden*," *Organization and Environment* 14, no. 1 (2001): 74–92.

Careless, James S., *Frontier and Metropolis: Regions, Cities, and Identities in Canada before 1914* (Toronto: University of Toronto Press, 1987).

Careless, James S., "Metropolis and region: The interplay between city and region in Canadian history," *Urban History Review* 78, no. 3 (1979): 108–118.

Carrere, Ricardo and Lohmann, Lawrence, *Pulping the South: Industrial Tree Plantations and the World Paper Economy* (London: Zed Books, 1996).

Carstensen, Fred V., *American Enterprise in Foreign Markets: Studies of Singer and International Harvester in Imperial Russia* (Durham, NC: Duke University Press, 1984).

Castorf, Heino, *Die Patentpapierfabrik zu Penig. Ein Beitrag zur Geschichte des Papieres* (Magdeburg: Penig Eigenverlag, 1897), 95.

Castree, Noel and Braun, Bruce (eds.), *Social Nature: Theory Practice and Politics* (Malden, Massachusetts: Blackwell: 2001).

Chandler, Jr., Alfred D. *Inventing the Electronic Century: The Epic Story of the Consumer Electronics and Computer Industries* (New York: The Free Press, 2001), 4–6.

Chandler, Jr., Alfred D., *Strategy and Structure: Chapters in the History of Industrial Enterprise* (Cambridge, MA: MIT Press, 1962).

Clapp, Alex, "The resource cycle in forestry and fishing," *The Canadian Geographer/Le Geographe canadien* 42, no. 2 (1988): 129–144.

Clawson, Marion, "Resettlement experience on nine Resettlement projects," *Agricultural History* 52, no. 1 (1978): 1–92.

Clayton, C. F., "Program of the Federal Government for the purchase and use of submarginal land," *Journal of Farm Economics* 17, no. 1 (1935): 55–63.

Cohen, Benjamin R., "Escaping the false binary of nature and culture through connection: Richard White's *The Organic Machine: The Remaking of the Columbia River*," *Organization and Environment* 18, no. 4 (2005): 445–457.

Cohen, Saul B. and Kliot, Nurit, "Place names in Israel's ideological struggle over administered territories," *Annals of the Association of American Geographers* 82, no. 4 (1992): 653–680.

Colombia Information Bureau, "The cattle industry in Colombia and its possibilities," *Bulletin of the Pan American Union* 40 (1915): 198.

Connell, J., "Land deterioration is a grave phase of our national economy," *New Zealand Journal of Agriculture* 59 (1939): 4–12.

Cook, Ian, "Geographies of food: Mixing," *Progress in Human Geography* 32 (2008): 821–833.

Cook, Ian and Crang, Philip, "The world on a plate. Culinary culture, displacement and geographical knowledges," *Journal of Material Culture* 1 (1996): 131–153.

Corden, W. Max, Neary, J. Peter, "Booming sector and deindustrialization in a small open economy," *The Economic Journal* 92(December 1982): 825–848.

Cotta, Heinrich, *Systematische Anleitung zur Taxation der Waldungen* (Berlin, 1804).

Council on Economic Priorities (ed.), *Paper Profits: Pollution in the Pulp and Paper Industry* (Cambridge, MA: MIT Press, 1972).

Cronon, William, *Nature's Metropolis: Chicago and the Great West* (New York and London: W.W. Norton, 1991).

Cronon, William, "The trouble with wilderness or getting back to the wrong nature," *Environmental History Review* 1, no. 1 (1996): 7–28.

Crosby, Alfred W., *The Columbian Exchange: Biological and Cultural Consequences of 1492* (Westport, CT: Greenwood Press, 1972).

Crosby, Alfred W., *Ecological Imperialism, the Biological Expansion of Europe 900–1900* (Cambridge: Cambridge University Press, 1986).

Crossley, J. Colin and Greenhill, Robert, "The River Plate beef trade," in D.C.M. Platt (ed.), *Business Imperialism, 1840–1930: An Inquiry Based on British Experience in Latin America* (Oxford: Clarendon Press, 1977), 284–334.

Cumberland, Kenneth, "A century's change: Natural to cultural vegetation in New Zealand," *Geographical Review* 31 (1941): 554.

Cumberland, Kenneth, *Landmarks* (Surry Hills NSW: Readers Digest, 1981).

Cutler, Phoebe, *The Public Landscape of the New Deal* (New Haven, CT: Yale University Press, 1985), 157.

Dahll, Marcus Bing, "Fra den internationale Forstkongres i Paris 1900," *Tidsskrift for Skovbrug* 9 (1901): 13–18. [in Danish]

Danby, Susan and Marx, Leo (eds.), *The Railroad in American Art: Representations of Technological Change* (Cambridge, MA: MIT Press, 1988).

Danckelmann, Bernhard, "Forstkongreß auf der Weltausstellung des Jahres 1900 in Paris," *Zeitschrift für Forst- und Jagdwesen* (1900): 104–16 and 605–15.

Daniels, Stephen and Cosgrove, Denis, "Iconography and landscape," in Denis Cosgrove and Stephen Daniels (eds.), *The Iconography of Landscape: Essays on the Symbolic Representation, Design and Use of Past Environments* (Cambridge, New York and Melbourne: Cambridge University Press, 1988), 1–10.

Daubrée M., (ed.), *Congrès international de sylviculture, tenu à Paris du 4 au 7 juin 1900* (Paris, 1900).

Davis, Jeffrey, "Representing place: 'Deserted Isles' and the reproduction of Bikini Atoll," *Annals of the Association of American Geographers* 95, no. 3 (2005): 607–625.

Davis, Morris, *Iceland Extends Its Fisheries Limits: A Political Analysis* (Universitetsforlaget, 1963), 19.

Dawe, M.T., "Relación de un viaje por el río Magdalena, por el Departamento del Magdalena y por la peninsula de la Goajira (Colombia)," in Ministerio de Agricultura y Comercio, *Memoria 1917*, 116.

Deicke, "Die Preisbewegung beim Stamm- und Klotzholz in den Königl. Sächs. Staatsforsten von 1880 bis 1912 und die Beziehungen zwischen beiden Sortimenten," *Tharandter Forstliches Jahrbuch* 64 (1911): 256–288.

Dewar, Margaret E., *Industry in Trouble: The Federal Government and the New England Fisheries* (Philadelphia: Temple University Press, 1983), 48.

Diamant, Gerhard, *Deutschlands Papierholzeinfuhr im Rahmen seiner Papierholzbeschaffung* (Leipzig: Moltzen, 1936), 20.

Dicken, Peter, "Geographers and 'globalisation:' (Yet) another missed boat?" *Transactions of the Institute of British Geographers* (NS) 29 (2004): 5–26.

Dicken, Peter, *Global Shift: Transforming the World Economy*, 3rd edition (New York: The Guildford Press, 1998).

Dicken, Peter, Kelly, Philip F., Yeung, Henry Wai-Chung, "Chains and networks, territories and scales," *Global Networks* 1 (2010): 89–112.

Dittrich, Klaus,"Der sächsische Wald: Sachsens Wald zwischen Tradition und Gegenwart," *Der Wald* 42 (1992): 221–223, 416–419.

Dix, Andreas and Schenk, W. (eds.), *Konsum und Kulturlandschaft.* (Bonn: Siedlungsforschung. Archäologie—Geschichte—Geographie, 2010).

Dix, Andreas, "Das Mittelrheintal. Wahrnehmung und Veränderung einer symbolischen Landschaft des 19. Jahrhunderts," *Petermanns Geographische Mitteilungen* 146 (2002): 44–53.

Dix, Andreas, "Die ökologischen Folgen der modernen Weltwirtschaft des 19. Jahrhunderts in Deutschland," *Archiv für Sozialgeschichte* 43 (2003): 81–99.

Dominy, Michelle, *Calling the Station Home: Place and Identity in New Zealand's High Country* (Lanham, MD: Rowman and Littlefield, 2001).

Domosh, Mona, "A 'civilized' commerce: Gender, 'race', and empire at the 1893 Chicago Exposition," *Cultural Geographies* 9 (2002): 181–201.

Domosh, Mona, *American Commodities in an Age of Empire* (New York and London: Routledge, 2006).

Domosh, Mona, "Uncovering the friction of globalization: American commercial embeddedness and landscape in Revolutionary-era Russia," *Annals of the Association of American Geographers* 100, no. 2 (2010): 427–443.

Dorsey, Kurkpatrick, *The Dawn of Conservation Diplomacy: U.S.-Canadian Wildlife Protection Treaties in the Progressive Era* (Seattle: University of Washington, 1998), 144.

Drache, Daniel (ed.), *Staples, Markets, and Cultural Change: Selected Essays Harold Innis* (Montreal and Kingston: McGill-Queen's Universisity Press, 1995).

Driver, Felix, "Imagining the Tropics: Views and visions of the Tropical world." *Singapore Journal of Tropical Geography* 25 (2004): 1–17.

Driver, Felix and Martins, Luciana, *Tropical Visions in an Age of Empire* (Chicago: University of Chicago Press, 2005).

Driver, Felix and Yeoh, Brenda, "Constructing the Tropics: Introduction," *Singapore Journal of Tropical Geography* 21 (2000): 1–5.

Dropisch, Bernhard, *Holzstoff und Holzcellulose. Ihre Herstellung und Verarbeitung für die Zwecke der Papierfabrikation* (Weimar: Voigt, 1879), 14.

Dumett, Raymond E. (ed.), *Mining Tycoons in the Age of Empire, 1870–1945: Entrepreneurship, High Finance, Politics and Territorial Expansion* (Farnham: Ashgate Publishing, 2009).

Dunbar, Gary S., "African Ranches Ltd., 1914–1931: An ill-fated stockraising enterprise in northern Nigeria," *Annals of the Association of American Geographers* 60 (1970): 102–123.

Duncan, James, *In the Shadows of the Tropics: Climate, Race and Biopower in Nineteenth Century Ceylon* (Burlington, VT: Ashgate, 2007).

Duncan, James and Duncan, Nancy, "(Re)reading the landscape," *Environment and Planning D: Society and Space* 6 (1988): 117–126.

Earle, Carville, "The last great chance for an American working class: Spatial lessons of the General Strike and the Haymarket riot of early May 1886," in C. Earle, *Geographical Inquiry and American Historical Problems* (Stanford, CA: Stanford University Press, 1992), 378–399.

Ebeling, Dietrich, *Der Holländerholzhandel in den Rheinlanden. Zu den Handelsbeziehungen zwischen den Niederlanden und dem westlichen Deutschland im 17. und 18. Jahrhundert* (Stuttgart: Steiner, 1992).

Echeverri, Virgilio, "El problema ganadero del Valle," *Revista Nacional de Agricultura* 33 (1939): 241.

Eckes, Alfred E., "Trading American interests," *Foreign Affairs*, 71, no. 4 (1992): 135–154.

Edminster, Lynn R., *The Cattle Industry and the Tariff* (New York: Macmillan, 1926), 74–75, 150.

Egerton, Frank, *Roots of Ecology: Antiquity to Haeckel* (Berkeley: University of California Press, 2012).

Eidloth, Volkmar, "Europäische Kur- und Badestädte des 19. Jahrhunderts. Ein konsumorientierter Stadttyp," *Siedlungsforschung. Archäologie—Geschichte—Geographie* 28 (2010): 15.

Eisemann, Karl, "Grundlagen, Aufbau und Organisation der deutschen Zellstoffindustrie" (PhD diss., Heidelberg, 1930), 49.

Eisenbach, Ulrich, *Wirtschafts- und Sozialgeschichte des Niederselterser Brunnenbetriebes bis zum Ende des Herzogtums Nassau* (Wiesbaden: Historische Kommission für Nassau, 1982).

Eliasson, Per, "Skogsdikning och skogsväxt under 1900-talet," in Leif Runefelt (ed.), *Svensk mosskultur: odling, torvanvändning och landskapets förändring 1750–2000* (Stockholm: Kungliga Skogs- och lantbruksakademien, 2008), 181–194. [in Swedish]

Endres, Max, "Über die Unzulänglichkeit der Nutzholzerzeugung auf der Erde. Bemerkungen zu dem Vortrage des Forstinspektors Mélard-Paris," *Forstwissenschaftliches Centralblatt* 22 (1900): 611–623.

Endres, Max, "Über die Unzulänglichkeit der Nutzholzerzeugung der Erde. Erwiderung [auf den Artikel von William Schlich, C.L.] von Universitätsprofessor Dr. Endres," *Forstwissenschaftliches Centralblatt* 23 (1901): 621f.

Ennals, Peter, *Opening a Window to the West: The Foreign Concession at Kōbe, Japan, 1868–1889* (Toronto, Buffalo, London: University of Toronto Press, 2014).

Evans, David, *A History of Nature Conservation in Britain*, 2nd edition (London, New York: Routledge, 1997).

Evans, Sterling, *Bound in Twine: The History and Ecology of the Henequen-Wheat Complex for Mexico and the American and Canadian Plains, 1880–1950* (College Station, TX: Texas A. and M. University Press, 2007).

Ewen, Stuart, *Captains of Consciousness: Advertising and the Social Roots of the Consumer Culture* (New York: McGraw-Hill, 1976).

Faggot, Jacob, "Afhandling om svedjande samt utväg til Hushållning med Skogar," *Kungliga Svenska Vetenskapsakademiens Handlingar* (1750): 138–150. [in Swedish]

Faggot, Jacob, "Beskrifning öfver Pernå Socken i Nyland," *Kungliga Svenska Vetenskapsakademiens Handlingar* (1754): 182–188. [in Swedish]

Faggot, Jacob, "Tankar om Fäderneslandets Känning oh Beskrifwande," *Kungliga Svenska Vetenskapsakademiens Handlingar* (1741): 6–29. [in Swedish]

Fellman, Susanna, "Growth and investment: Finnish capitalism, 1850s–2005," in Susanna Fellman, Martin Jes Iversen, Hans Sjögren and Lars Thue (eds.), *Creating Nordic Capitalism: The Business History of a Competitive Periphery* (Basingstoke: Palgrave Macmillan, 2008), 139–217.

Fite, Gilbert C., *Cotton Fields No More: Southern Agriculture, 1865–1980* (Lexington: University of Kentucky Press, 1984), 143–148.

Flórez, Rafael, *Fases de Colombia* (Bogotá: Editorial Minerva, 1926), 51.

Fourie, Johan and Uys, Jolandi, "Luxury product consumption in eighteenth-century cape colony households," *Tijdschrift voor Sociale en Economische Geschiedenis* 9 (2012): 29–60.

Fox, Richard Wightman and Lears, T. J. Jackson (eds.), *The Culture of Consumption: Critical Essays in American History, 1880–1980* (New York: Pantheon, 1983).

Fox, Robert and Turner, Anthony (eds.), *Luxury Trades and Consumerism in Ancien Régime Paris: Studies in the History of the Skilled Workforce* (Aldershot i.a.: Ashgate, 1998).

Franco, Salvador, "Plan de organización agrícola en Colombia," in Ministerio de Industrias (ed.), *Agricultura y ganadería. Plan de organización agrícola en Colombia y la industria del ganado vacuno en Colombia* (Bogotá: Imprenta Nacional, 1926), 14.

Frenkel, Stephen, "Jungle stories: North American representations of Tropical Panama," *Geographical Review* 86 (1996), 317–33.

Freyre, Rodolfo, "La industria del ganado vacuno en Colombia," *Revista Nacional de Agricultura* 267–268 (1926): 29–31.

Friedrich, Ernst, "Wesen und geographische Verbreitung der 'Raubwirtschaft'," *Petermanns Geographische Mitteilungen* 50 (1904): 68–79 and 92–95.

Friedrich, Josef, "Der VIII. internationale landwirtschaftliche Kongreß in Wien 1907," *Centralblatt für das gesamte Forstwesen* 33 (1907): 378–389, 434–440 and 475–484.

Fryjordet, Torgeir, *Skogadministrasjonen i Norge gjennom tidene*, vol. 2 (Oslo, 1962). [in Norwegian]

Gadd, Pehr Adrian, "Om ursprunget, beskaffenheten och nyttan af kärr, mossar och moras i Sverige," *Kungliga Svenska Vetenskapsakademiens Handlingar* (1776): 97–115. [in Swedish]

Gadd, Pehr Adrian (præses) and Agricola, Anders (respondent), *Oväldige Tankar om Jordens Svedande och Kyttande i Finland* (Åbo: Jacob Merckell, 1753). [in Swedish]

Gadd, Pehr Adrian (præses) and Hallenberg, Johan Heinrich (respondent), *Finska Ängsskötselens Hinder och Hjelp* (Åbo: Jacob Merckell, 1757). [in Swedish]

Gadd, Pehr Adrian (præses) and Foenander, Jacob (respondent), *Chemisk och Oeconomisk Uthandling om Bränne-Torf* (Åbo: Frenckell, 1759). [in Swedish]

Gadd, Pehr Adrian (præses) and Sjöstedt, Fredrik (respondent), *Academisk Afhandling om Medel at Underhålla och öka Skogväxten i Finland* (Åbo: Frenckellska Boktryckeriet, 1792). [in Swedish]

Gallini, Stefania, "El Atila del Ganges en la ganadería colombiana," *Nómadas* 22 (2005): 189.

Gamble, J. S., "The International Congress of Sylviculture," *Transactions of the Royal Scottish Arboricultural Society* Vol. XVI (1901): 262–274.

Gassan, Richard H., "The first American tourist guidebooks: authorship and the print culture of the 1820s," *Book History* 8 (2005): 51–74.

Gassan, Richard H., *The Birth of American Tourism. New York, the Hudson Valley and American Culture, 1790–1935* (Amherst: University of Massachusetts Press, 2008).

Gerding, M.A.W., *Vier eeuwen turfwinning: De verveningen in Groningen, Friesland, Drenthe en Overijssel tussen 1550 en 1950* (Wageningen: Landbouwuniversiteit Wageningen, 1995). [in Dutch]

Gereffi, Gary, Humphrey, John and Sturgeon, Timothy, "The governance of global value chains," *Review of International Political Economy* 12 (2005): 78–104.

Gereffi, Gary, and Korzeniewicz, Miguel (eds.), *Commodity Chains and Global Capitalism* (Westport, CT: Greenwood Press, 1994).

Gertler, Meric, "Harold Innis and the new industrial geography," *The Canadian Geographer/Le Géographe canadien* 37 (1993): 360–364.

Gibbon, Peter, Bair, Jennifer and Ponte, Stefano, "Governing global value chains: An introduction," *Economy and Society* 37, no. 3 (2008): 315–338.

Gibbon, Peter and Ponte, Stefano, "Global value chains: From governance to governmentality," *Economy and Society* 38, no. 3 (2008): 385–392.

Gibbs, David, "Prospects for an environmental economic geography: Linking modernization and regulationist approaches," *Economic Geography* 82 (2006): 193–215.

Giedion, Siegfried, *Mechanization Takes Command: A Contribution to Anonymous History* (New York and London: W.W. Norton and Company, 1969) (first published 1948): 130–168.

Glacken, Clarence J., *Traces on the Rhodian Shore: Nature and Culture in Western Thought from Ancient Times to the End of the Eighteenth Century* (Berkeley: University of California Press, 1967).

Gómez Rueda, Manuel, "Producción pecuaria de Colombia," *Revista Agropecuaria: Órgano Oficial de Divulgación Agrícola del Departamento de Santander* 9 (1938), 35.

Gómez Rueda, Manuel, "Informe del Departamento Nacional de Ganadería al Señor Ministro de la Economía Nacional," *Boletín de Ganadería* 1 (1939), 13.

González de Molina Navarro, Manuel and Toledo, Víctor Manuel, *The Social Metabolism. A Socio-Ecological Theory of Historical Change* (Cham: Springer, 2014).

Goss, Jon, "Geography of consumption I," *Progress in Human Geography* 28 (2004): 369–380.

Goss, Jon, "Geographies of consumption: The work of consumption," *Progress in Human Geography* 30 (2006): 237–249.

Göttlich, K-H., Richard, K.H., Kuntze, H., Eggelsmann, R., Günther, J., Eichelsdörfer, D. and Briemle, G., "Mire Utilisation," in A.L. Heathwaite and K.H. Göttlich (eds.), *Mires: Process, Exploitation and Conservation* (Chichester: Wiley, 1993), 325–415.

Gregg, Sara M., "Uncovering the subsistence economy of the twentieth century South," *Agriculture History* 78, no. 4 (2004): 417–437.

Gregg, Sara M., *Managing the Mountains: Land Use Planning, the New Deal, and the Creation of a Federal Landscape* (New Haven, CT: Yale University Press, 2010), 175–212.

Grewe, Bernd-Stefan, "Shortage of wood? Towards a new approach in forest history. The Palatinate in the 19th century," in Mauro Agnoletti and Steven Anderson (ed.), *Forest History. International Studies on Socioeconomic and Forest Ecosystem Change* (Wallingford: CABI, 2000), 143–152.

Grewe, Bernd-Stefan, "Das Ende der Nachhaltigkeit? Wald und Industrialisierung im 19. Jahrhundert," *Archiv für Sozialgeschichte* 43 (2003): 61–79.

Grierson, Cecilia, *Colonia de Monte Grande, Provincia de Buenos Aires: Primera y única colonia formada por escoceses en la Argentina* (Buenos Aires: Jacobo Peuser, 1925).

Grove, Richard H., *Ecology, Climate and Empire: Colonialism and Global Environmental History, 1400–1940* (Cambridge: White Horse Press, 1997).

Grove, Richard H., *Green Imperialism: Colonial Expansion, Tropical Island Edens and the Origins of Environmentalism 1600–1860* (Cambridge: Cambridge University Press, 1995).

Grove, Richard H., "The origins of environmentalism," *Nature* 345 (3 May, 1990): 11–14.

Grunsven, Leo. van, "Global commodity chains," in R. Kitchin and N. Thrift (eds.), *International Encyclopaedia of Human Geography* (Amsterdam: Elsevier, 2009): 539–547.

Guinnane, Timothy, Lamoreaux, Naomi R., Rosenthal, Jean-Laurent, "Putting the corporation in its place," *Enterprise and Society* 8, no. 3 (2007): 687–729.

Gunnarsson, Emelie, *Diken i skogsmark. Bedömning av produktionsnyttan i ett avrinningsområde i Västergötland* (Världsnaturfonden WWF, 2009). [in Swedish]

Gunzelmann, Thomas, "Bierlandschaft Bayern: Keller als historische Orte des Konsums," *Siedlungsforschung. Archäologie—Geschichte—Geographie* 28 (2010): 7–53.

Guttenberg, Adolf von, "Inwieweit ist bei dem heutigen Stande der Wirthschaft und der durch dieselbe bestimmten Forsteinrichtungs-Praxis die Forderung strengster Nachhaltigkeit der Nutzungen überhaupt noch aufrecht zu erhalten?" *Centralblatt für das gesammte Forstwesen* (1890): 364–372.

Haartman Johan, (præses) and Florin Johan Christian, (respondent), *Om Skärgårds Febren Omkring Åbo* (Åbo: Frenckell, 1781). [in Swedish]

Hall, C. Michael, "The 'worthless lands hypothesis' and Australia's national parks and reserves," in *Proceedings of the First National Conference on Australian Forest History* (Canberra: Department of Geography and Oceanography, Australian Defence Force Academy, 1988), 441–458.

Hånell, Björn, "Effektiv skogsskötsel på torvmarker," in M. Strömgren (ed.), *Växthuseffekt och skogsproduktion: hur ska vi hantera våra dikade skogsmarker* (SLU, Rapporter i skogsekologi och skoglig marklära 90, 2006). [in Swedish]

Hannikainen, P.W., *Wähäsen Metsistä* (Helsinki: Kansanvalistuseura, 1888). [in Finnish]

Hansen, P.J., "Physiological and cellular adaptations of Zebu cattle to thermal stress," *Animal Reproduction Science* 82–83 (2004): 349–360.

Harley, J. Brian, "Reading the maps of the Columbian encounter," *Annals of the Association of American Geographers* 82, no. 3 (1992): 522–542.

Harris, Cole, "How did colonialism dispossess: Comments from an edge of empire," *Annals of the Association of American Geographers* 94 (2004): 105–182.

Hartig, Georg Ludwig, *Anweisung zur Taxation und Beschreibung der Forste, 2., ganz umgearbeitete und stark vermehrte Auflage* (Gießen/Darmstadt, 1804).

Harvey, David, *The 'New' Imperialism: Accumulation by Dispossession* (Oxford: Oxford University Press, 2003).

Hasel, Karl and Schwartz, Ekkehard, *Forstgeschichte: Ein Grundriss für Studium und Praxis*, 2nd edition (Remagen: Kessel, 2002), 264–289.

Hassel, Henrik (præses) and Welin, Johan (respondent), *Velmente Tankar om landthushållningens Förbättrande i Finland* (Åbo: Frenckell, 1751). [in Swedish]

Hassler, M., "Commodity chains," in R. Kitchin and N. Thrift (eds.), *International Encyclopaedia of Human Geography* (Amsterdam: Elsevier, 2009), 202–208.

Hays, Samuel, *Conservation and the Gospel of Efficiency: The Progressive Conservation Movement, 1890–1920* (Cambridge, MA: Harvard University Press, 1959).

Hayter, Roger, "Environmental economic geography," *Geography Compass* 2–3 (2008): 831–850.

Hayter, Roger, Barnes, Trevor J. and Bradshaw, Michael J., "Relocating resource peripheries to the core of economic geography's theorizing: Rationale and agenda," *Area* 35, no. 1 (2003): 15–23.

Heathcote, Les, *Back of Bourke: A Study of Land Appraisal and Settlement in Semi-Arid Australia.* (Melbourne: Melbourne University Press, 1965).

Heaton, Herbert, "A merchant adventurer in Brazil, 1808–18," *Journal of Economic History* 6 (1946): 1–23.

Helphand, Kenneth I., "Learning from linksland," *Landscape Journal* 14 (1995): 74–86.

Herman, R.D.K., "The Aloha State: Place names and the anti-conquest of Hawai'i," *Annals of the Association of American Geographers* 89, no. 1 (1999): 76–102.

Heske, Franz, "Forstwirtschaftliche und ingenieurtechnische Voraussetzungen zur modernen Erschließung des Kolonialwaldes," in *Wochenblatt für Papierfabrikation* 75, no. 4 (1941): 47–48.

Heuel, Paul, "Die Papierholzversorgung Deutschlands" (PhD diss., Freiburg, 1921), 12.

Hoeg, Jerry, "Andrés Bello's 'Ode to Tropical Agriculture:' The landscape of independence," in Beatriz Rivera-Barnes and Jerry Hoeg (eds.), *Reading and Writing the Latin American Landscape* (New York: Palgrave Macmillan, 2009), 53–66.

Hoelscher, Steven, "Making place, making race: Performances of Whiteness in the Jim Crow South," *Annals of the Association of American Geographers* 93, no. 3 (2003): 657–686.

Hogarson, Kristin, "Cosmopolitan domesticity: Importing the American dream, 1865–1921," *American Historical Review* 107 (2002): 55–83.

Holden, J., Chapman, P.J. and Lapadz, J.C., "Artificial drainage of peatlands: Hydrological and hydrochemical process and wetland restoration," *Progress in Physical Geography* 28, no. 1 (2004): 95–123.

Holdsworth, D. and Tritch Roman, G., "From the pit to the globe: The reach of commodity exchanges," paper presented at the special session "The Urban Economy: Networks, Flows and Place," 12th International Conference on Urban History, Lisbon, Portugal, September 3–6, 2014.

Holland, Charles, *Noticias de Buenos Aires, el Paraguay, Chile y el Peru: cartas del ciudadano inglés Charles Holland, 1820–1826,* presentation and introduction by Leon Tenenbaum; trans. Mabel Susana Godfrid de Tenenbaum and Leon Tenenbaum (Buenos Aires: Fundación Banco de Boston, 1990).

Holland, Edgar Swinton, *A History of the Family of Holland of Mobberley and Knutsford in the County of Cheshire* (Edinburgh: Privately printed at the Ballantyne Press, 1902).

Holland, Peter, *Home in the 'Howling Wilderness': Settlers and Environment in Southern New Zealand* (Auckland: Auckland University Press, 2013).

Hollander, Gail M., *Raising Cane in the Glades: The Global Sugar Trade and the Transformation of Florida* (Chicago and London: The University of Chicago Press, 2008).

Holley, Donald, "The Negro in the New Deal Resettlement Program," *Agricultural History* 45, no. 3 (1971): 179–193.

Holley, Donald, "Old and New Worlds in the New Deal Resettlement Program: Two Louisiana projects," *Louisiana History* 11, no. 2 (1970): 137–165.

Holley, Donald, *Uncle Sam's Farmers: The New Deal Communities in the Lower Mississippi Valley* (Urbana: University of Illinois Press, 1975).

Holley, William C., Ellen Winston and T.J. Woofter, Jr., *The Plantation South, 1934–1937,* Works Projects Administration Research Monograph 22 (Washington, DC: Government Printing Office, 1940).

Holm, Poul, "World War II and the 'great acceleration' of North Atlantic fisheries," *Global Environment* 10 (2012): 66–91.

Holmes, George K., *Meat Situation in the United States. Part I. Statistics of Live Stock, Meat Production and Consumption, Prices, and International Trade for Many Countries* (Washington, DC: United States Department of Agriculture, 1916), 169–170.

Holquist, Peter, "'In accord with the state interests and the people's wishes': The technocratic ideology of Imperial Russia's Resettlement Administration," *Slavic Review* 69, no. 1 (2010): 151–179.

Hölzl, Richard, "Historicizing sustainability: German scientific forestry in the eighteenth and nineteenth centuries," *Science as Culture* 24 (2010): 431–460.

Hölzl, Richard, *Umkämpfte Wälder. Die Geschichte einer ökologischen Reform in Deutschland 1760–1860* (Frankfurt am Main/New York: Campus-Verl., 2010), 105–166.

Horsman, Stuart, "The politics of toponyms in the Pamir Mountains," *Area* 38, no. 3 (2006): 279–291.

Hounshell, David, *From the American System to Mass Production: The Development of Manufacturing Technology in the United States, 1850–1920* (Baltimore: Johns Hopkins University Press, 1984), 159.

Hufnagel, Leopold, *Handbuch der Kaufmännischen Holzverwertung und des Holzhandels* (Berlin: Ulan Press, 1905 and 1929), 31–32.

Humphreys, Robert A., *Tradition and Revolt in Latin America and Other Essays* (New York: Columbia University Press, 1969).

Hunter, Dard, *Papermaking: The History and Technique of an Ancient Craft* (New York: Dover, 1978).

Hutchinson, William E., *Cyrus Hall McCormick*, 2 vols. (New York and London: The Century Company, 1930 and 1935).

Ilvessalo, Lauri, "Ehdotus Suomen metsätieteellisen tutkimustoiminnan kehittämiseksi" with English summary, *Silva Fennica* 7 (1927): 1–18. [in Finnish]

Ingimundarson, Valur, "Buttressing the West in the North: The Atlantic Alliance, economic warfare, and the Soviet challenge in Iceland," *The International History Review* 21, no. 1 (1956–1959): 82.

Inglis Henry David, (pseudonym: Derwent Conway), *A Personal Narrative of a Journey Through Norway, Part of Sweden, and the Islands and States of Denmark* (Edinburgh, 1829), 127 and 158.

Innis, Harold A., *The Cod Fisheries: The History of an International Economy*, Revised edition (Toronto: University of Toronto Press, 1954, First edition 1940).

Innis, Harold A., *Essays in Canadian Economic History* (Toronto: University of Toronto Press, 1956).

Innis, Harold A., *The Fur Trade in Canada: An Introduction to Canadian Economic History* (Revised edition Toronto: University of Toronto Press, 1956, First edition 1930).

Jackson, Peter, "Commercial cultures: Transcending the cultural and the economic," *Progress in Human Geography* 26 (2002): 3–18.

Jacobs, Michael, *The Good and Simple Life: Artist's Colonies in Europe and America* (Oxford: Phaidon, 1985).

Jarvis, Lovell S., *Livestock Development in Latin America* (Washington, DC: World Bank, 1987).

Jayne, Mark, "Cultural geography, consumption and the city," *Geography* 91 (2006): 34–42.

Jentsch, Fritz, "Der VIII. internationale landwirtschaftliche Kongreß in Wien, 21. bis 25. Mai 1907," *Zeitschrift für Forst- und Jagdwesen* 39 (1907): 603–617, 680–690 and 745–755.

Jentsch, Fritz, "Holzproduktion und Holzhandel im Lichte der Pariser Weltausstellung von 1900," *Mündener forstliche Hefte* 10 (1901): 13–27.

Jobberns, George, "Life and landscape in New Zealand: Fifty years in retrospect," in Michael Roche (ed.), *A Geographer by Declaration, Selected Writings by George Jobberns* (Christchurch: Canterbury University Press, 2010), 75.

Johnson, Hildegard B., *Order Upon the Land: The US Rectangular Land Survey and the Upper Mississippi Country* (New York: Oxford University Press, 1976).

Johnston, Catherine, "Beyond the clearing: Towards a dwelt animal geography," *Progress in Human Geography* 32, no. 5 (2008): 633–649.

Johnston, Judith A., "The New Zealand bush: Early assessments of vegetation," *New Zealand Geographer* 37 (1981): 19–24.

Jong, Greta de, *A Different Day: African American Struggles for Justice in Rural Louisiana, 1900–1970* (Chapel Hill, NC: University of North Carolina Press, 2002).

Jonssen, Hannes, *Friends in Conflict: The Anglo-Icelandic Cod Wars and the Law of the Sea* (London: C. Hurst & Company, 1982), 6.

Josefsson, Torbjörn, Gunnarson, Björn, Liedgren, Lars, Bergman, Ingela and Östlund, Lars, "Historical human influence on forest composition and structure in boreal Fennoscandia," *Canadian Journal of Forest Research* 40 (2010): 872–884.

Josefsson, Torbjörn and Östlund, Lars, "Increased production and depletion. The impact of forestry on northern Sweden's forest landscape," in H. Antonsson and U. Jansson (eds.), *Agriculture and Forestry in Sweden since 1900: Geographical and Historical Studies* (Stockholm: Agriculture and forestry in Sweden since 1900, 2011), 338–353.

Josephson, Paul R., "The ocean's hot dog: The development of the fish stick," *Technology and Culture* 49, no. 1 (2008): 42.

Kalm, Pehr (præses) and Backman, Adolph (respondent), *Huru sådana kjärr kunna gjöras nyttiga, hvarifrån vatnet ej kan ledas med diken* (Åbo: Frenckell, 1757). [in Swedish]

Kalm, Pehr (præses) and Foeder, Adolph Magnus (respondent), *Tanckar om den Wärkan Som Et Lands Upodling har på des Climat* (Åbo: Frenckell, 1778). [in Swedish]

Kalm, Pehr (præses) and Kreander, Salomon (respondent), *Om Möjeligheten, Sättet och Nyttan at Utan Ängar Sköta Landbruket* (Åbo: Frenckell, 1775). [in Swedish]

Kalm, Pehr (præses) and Wegelius, Esaias (respondent), *Tankar om Nödvändigheten at Utdika och Upodla Kärr och Mossar i Finland* (Åbo: Frenckell, 1763). [in Swedish]

Kalm, Pehr (præses) and Wegelius, Johan (respondent), *Försök om Hushållningens Hinder och Hjelp i Kimi-Lappmark* (Åbo: Frenckell, 1758). [in Swedish]

Kasson, John F., *Civilizing the Machine: Technology and Republican Values in America, 1776–1900* (New York, 1976)

Kelly, Thomas, "Taranaki forest and forest farming," *New Zealand Country Journal* 1 (1877): 244.

Kern, Èduard È., "S Parižskoj vsemirnoj vystavki 1900 g. [Teil 1]," *Izvestiâ S.-Peterburgskogo Lesnogo Instituta* 7 (1901): 25–62. [in Russian]

Kern, Èduard È., "S Parižskoj vsemirnoj vystavki 1900 g. [Teil 2]," *Izvestiâ S.-Peterburgskogo Lesnogo Instituta* 8 (1902): 61–107. [in Russian]

Kirby, Jack Temple, *Poquosin* (Chapel Hill, NC: University of North Carolina Press, 1995), 147.

Kleinen, John, "Tropicality and topicality: Pierre Gourou and the genealogy of French colonial scholarship on rural Vietnam," *Singapore Journal of Tropical Geography* 26 (2005): 339–358.

Kline, Wendy, *Building a Better Race: Gender, Sexuality, and Eugenics from the Turn of the Century to the Baby Boom* (Berkeley: University of California Press, 2005).

Klingle, Matthew W., "Spaces of consumption in environmental history," *History and Theory* 42 (2003): 94–110.

Koerner, Lisbet, *Linnaeus: Nature and Nation* (Cambridge, MA: Harvard University Press, 1999).

Koshar, Rudy, " 'What ought to be seen:' Tourist's guidebooks and national identities in modern Germany and Europe," *Journal of Contemporary History* 33 (1998): 323–340.

Kraemer, Erich, *Land Settlement Techniques Abroad* (Washington, DC: Resettlement Administration, 1936).

Krämer, Christine, *Rebsorten in Württemberg. Herkunft, Einführung, Verbreitung und die Qualität der Weine vom Spätmittelalter bis ins 19. Jahrhundert* (Ostfildern: Thorbecke, 2006).

Krausmann, Fridolin, "Global human appropriation of net primary production doubled in the 20th century," *Proceedings of the National Academy of Sciences* 110 (2013): 10324–10329.

Krausmann, Fridolin, *Rekonstruktion der Entwicklung von Materialflüssen im Zuge der Industrialisierung: Veränderungen im sozioökonomischen Biomassenmetabolismus in Österreich 1830 bis 1998* (Stuttgart: Breuninger Foundation, 2001).

Kristjánsdóttir, Ragnheiður, "Communists and the national question in Scotland and Iceland, c. 1930 to c. 1940," *The Historical Journal* 45, no. 3: 605.

Kübler and Niethammer (ed.), *Papier aus Kriebstein* (Darmstadt, Heppenstedts Wirtschafts-Archiv, 1956), 57, 60.

Kuisma, Markku, *Kansan talous: Pellervo ja yhteisen yrittämisen idea 1899–1999* (Helsinki: Pellervo-seura, 1999). [in Finnish]

Kurtz, Christian, *Verbände der deutschen papiererzeugenden Industrie 1870–1933* (Berlin: Duncker & Humblot, 1966).

Lamberg, Juha-Antti, Ojala, Jari and Peltoniemi, Mirva (ed.), *The Evolution of Global Paper Industry 1800–2050: A Comparative Analysis* (Dordrecht: Springer, 2012).

Lamoreaux, Naomi R., Raff, Daniel M.G., Temin, Peter, "Beyond markets and hierarchies: Toward a new synthesis of American Business History," *The American Historical Review* 108, no. 2 (2003): 421–435.

LaMoreaux, Philip E. and Tanner, Judy T. (eds.), *Springs and Bottled Water of the World: Ancient History, Source, Occurrence, Quality and Use* (Berlin i.a.: Springer, 2001).

Landry, Donna, *The Invention of the Countryside. Hunting, Walking and Ecology in English Literature, 1671–1831* (Basingstocke i.a.: Palgrave, 2001).

Lappalainen, Eino, (ed.), *Global Peat Resources* (Jyväskylä: International Peat Society: 1996).

Latour, Bruno, *The Pasteurization of France* (Cambridge, MA: Harvard University Press, 1988).

Le Heron, Richard, "A political economy perspective on the expansion of New Zealand livestock farming, 1960–1984—Part I. Agricultural policy," *Journal of Rural Studies* 5 (1989): 17–32.

Le Heron, Richard, "A political economy perspective on the expansion of New Zealand livestock farming, Part II. Aggregate farmer responses—Evidence and policy implications 1960–1984," *Journal of Rural Studies* 5 (1989): 33–43.

Leach, William, *Land of Desire: Merchants, Power and the Rise of a New American Culture* (New York: Pantheon, 1993).

Leal, Claudia, "Usos del concepto raza en Colombia," in Claudia Mosquera, Agustín Laó-Montes and César Rodríguez (eds.), *Debates sobre ciudadanía y políticas raciales en las Américas negras* (Bogotá: Universidad Nacional, Universidad del Valle, 2010), 389–438.

Lears, Jackson, *Fables of Abundance: A Cultural History of Advertising in America* (New York: Basic Books, 1994).

LeGrand, Catherine, *Frontier Expansion and Peasant Protest in Colombia, 1850–1936* (Albuquerque: University of New Mexico Press, 1986).

Leighninger, Jr., Robert D., *Long-Range Public Investment: The Forgotten Legacy of the New Deal* (Columbia: University of South Carolina Press, 2007).

Leiningen, Wilhelm Graf zu, *Die Waldvegetation praealpiner bayerischen Moore, inbesondere der südlichen Chiemseemoore* (München: 1907).

Lie, Marit H., Torbjörn Josefsson, Ken Olaf Storaunet and Mikael Ohlson, "A refined view on the "Green lie": Forest structure and composition succeeding early twentieth century selective logging in South East Norway," *Scandinavian Journal of Forest Research* 27 (2012): 270–284.

Liljegren, Ronnie, "Pluddetorv, tramptorv och maskintorv: Om torvtäkt och torvanvändning I Sverige 1800–1950," in Leif Runefelt (ed.), *Svensk mosskultur: odling, torvanvändning och landskapets förändring 1750–2000* (Stockholm: Kungliga Skogs- och lantbruksakademien, 2008), 305–328. [in Swedish]

Lillehammer, Arnvid, "The Scottish-Norwegian timber trade in the Stavanger area in the sixteenth and seventeenth centuries," in Thomas Christopher Smout (ed.), *Scotland and Europe 1200–1850* (Edinburgh: John Donald Publishers, 1986), 97–111.

Livingstone, David, "Tropical climate and moral hygiene: The anatomy of a Victorian debate," *British Journal for the History of Science* 32 (1999): 93–110.

Lobkowitz, Ferdinand, (ed.), *Achter (VIII.) internationaler landwirtschaftlicher Kongreß, Wien 21.-25. Mai 1907*, Vol. 1 (Wien, 1907), 481.

Löfroth, Michael, *Våtmarkerna och deras betydelse*, Rapport 3824 (Solna: Naturvårdsverket, 1991). [in Swedish]

López, Alejandro, *Problemas colombianos* (París: Editorial París-América, 1927), 53–54.

López Jiménez, Manuel, "Algunos signos de degeneración colectiva en Colombia y en los países similares," in Luis López de Mesa (ed.), *Los problemas de la raza en Colombia* (Bogotá: El Espectador, 1920), 24.

Lotz, Christian, "Expanding the space for future resource management: Explorations of the timber frontier in Northern Europe and the rescaling of sustainability during the 19th century," *Environment and History* 21 (2015): 257–279.

Lübbren, Nina, *Rural Artist's Colonies in Europe 1870–1910* (Manchester University Press, 2001).

Lukkala, O.J., *Nälkävuosien suonkuivausten tuloksia* (Helsinki: Metsätieteellinen tutkimuslaitos, 1937). [in Finnish]

Lulka, David, "Grass or grain? Assessing the nature of the US bison industry," *Sociologia Ruralis* 46, no. 3 (2006): 173–191.

Machado, Adalberto, "La exportación de carne y el Packing House de Coveñas, 1918–1938" (BA thesis, La Corporación Tecnológica de Bolívar, 1989).

Maher, Neil M., *Nature's New Deal: The CCC and the Roots of the American Environmental Movement* (New York: Oxford University Press, 2008).

Majewski, John, *Modernizing a Slave Economy: The Economic Vision of the Confederate Nation* (Chapel Hill, NC: University of North Carolina Press, 2009), 54–59.

Małaczyński, Maryan, "Z wystawy paryskiej," *Sylwan* (1900): 356–359 (część I), and 392–394 (część II). [in Polish]

Mansvelt, Juliana, *Geographies of Consumption* (London: Sage, 2005).

Mansvelt, Juliana, "Geographies of consumption: Citizenship, space and practice," *Progress in Human Geography* 32 (2008): 105–117.

Mansvelt, Juliana, "Geographies of consumption: The unmanageable consumer?" *Progress in Human Geography* 33 (2009): 264–274.

Mansvelt, Juliana, "Geographies of consumption," *Progress in Human Geography* 34 (2010): 224–233.

Mantel, Kurt, *Holzmarktlehre: Ein Lehr- und Handbuch der Holzmarktökonomie und Holzwirtschaftspolitik* (Melsungen: Neumann-Neudamm, 1973), 153–157, 242–254.

Mariani, Alba, "La familia y las empresas de Samuel Fisher Lafone, 1805–1871," paper presented within the Asociación Uruguaya de Historia Económica, at the Sixth Jornadas de Investigación en Historia Económica, Montevideo (9–10 July 2009).

Martínez, R.A. et al., "Genetic variability in Colombian Creole cattle populations estimated by pedigree information," *Journal of Animal Science* 86 (2007): 545.

Marulanda Luis, "Intereses ganaderos," *El Agricultor Caucano* 3 (1935): 674–675.

Marx, Leo, *The Machine in the Garden: Technology and the Pastoral Ideal in America* (New York: Oxford University Press, 1964).

Marx, Leo, "Afterword: The machine in the garden," *Massachusetts Review* 40, no. 4 (1999): 483–496.

Maxwell, Herbert, "The forest resources of the United Kingdom," *Transactions of the Scottish Arboricultural Society*, XXII (1909): 1–7.

McAloon, Jim, "Resource frontiers, environment, and settler capitalism, 1769–1860," in Eric Pawson and Tom Brooking (eds.), *Environmental Histories of New Zealand* (Melbourne: Oxford University Press, 2002), 52–68.

McCann, Larry D. (ed.), *Heartland and Hinterland: A Geography of Canada* (Scarborough: Prentice Hall, 1987).

McClintock, Anne, *Imperial Leather: Race, Gender and Sexuality in the Colonial Conquest* (New York: Routledge, 1995).

McClure, Margaret, *The Wonder Country: Making New Zealand Tourism* (Auckland: Auckland University Press, 2004).

McCormick, Cyrus, *The Century of the Reaper* (Boston and New York: Houghton Mifflin Company, 1931), 4 and 16.

McCracken, Grant, "Culture and consumption. A theoretical account of the structure and movement of the cultural meaning of consumer goods," *Journal of Consumer Research* 13 (1986): 71–84.

McCracken, Grant, "The history of consumption: A literature review and consumer guide," *Journal of Consumer Policy* 10 (1987): 139–166.

McDonald, Michael J. and Muldowny, John, *TVA and the Dispossessed* (Knoxville: University of Tennessee Press, 1982).

McIntyre, Roberta, *Whose High Country? A History of the South Island High Country of New Zealand* (North Shore: Penguin, 2008).

McNeill, John R. and Winiwarter, Verena, "Soils, soil knowledge and environmental history," in John R. McNeill and Verena Winiwarter (eds.), *Soils and Societies: Perspectives from Environmental History*, (Isle of Harris: White Horse Press, 2006), 1–6.

Mead, W.R., "Renaissance of Iceland," *Economic Geography* 21, no. 2 (1945): 141.

Meikle, Jeffrey L., "Leo Marx's *The Machine in the Garden*," *Technology and Culture* 44, no. 1 (2003): 150.

Meisner Rosen, Christine, "The business-environment connection," *Environmental History* 10 (2005): 77–79.

Meisner Rosen, Christine and Sellers, Christopher C., "Business and the environment," in Regina Lee Blaszczyk and Philip B. Scranton (eds.), *Major Problems in American Business History: Documents and Essays* (Boston and New York: Houghton Mifflin, 2006), 28–35.

Mélard, Albert, "Insuffisance de la production des bois d'œuvre dans le monde," *Revue des eaux et forêts* 39 (1900): 402–408 and 417–432.

Mertz, Paul E., *New Deal Policy and Southern Rural Policy* (Baton Rouge: Louisiana State University Press, 1978).

Ministerio de Agricultura y Comercio, *Memoria del Ministro de Agricultura y Comercio al Congreso de 1918* (Bogotá: Imprenta Nacional, 1918), 173.

Ministerio de Agricultura y Comercio, *Memoria del Ministro de Agricultura y Comercio al Congreso de 1935* (Bogotá: Imprenta Nacional, 1935), 58–59.

Ministerio de Economía Nacional, *Informe del Ministro de la Economía Nacional presentado al Congreso de 1944* (Bogotá: Editorial Minerva, 1944), 78.

Ministerio de Industrias, *Memoria del Ministerio de Industrias al Congreso en las sesiones ordinarias de 1924*, Anexos (Bogotá: Imprenta Nacional, 1924), 23.

Ministerio de Industrias, *Memoria del Ministerio de Industrias al Congreso en las sesiones ordinarias de 1925* (Bogotá: Imprenta Nacional, 1925), 127–139.

Ministerio de Industrias, *Memoria del Ministerio de Industrias al Congreso en las sesiones ordinarias de 1927* (Bogotá: Imprenta Nacional, 1927), 99–101.

Ministerio de Industrias, *Memoria del Ministerio de Industrias al Congreso en las sesiones ordinarias de 1930* (Bogotá: Imprenta Nacional, 1930), 293–294.

Mitchel, Brian R., (ed.), *European Historical Statistics 1750–1975* (London/Basingstoke: Macmillan, 1975).

Mitchell, Bruce, "Politics, fish, and international resource management: The British-Icelandic Cod War," *The Geographical Review* 66, no. 2 (1976): 127–138.

Mitchell, Timothy, *Colonizing Egypt* (Berkeley, Los Angeles and London: University of California Press, 1991).

Mitchell, Timothy, *Rule of Experts: Egypt, Techno-politics, Modernity* (Berkeley, Los Angeles and London: University of California Press, 2003).

Moore, Jason W., "Amsterdam is standing on Norway," Part I: "The alchemy of capital, empire and nature in the diaspora of silver, 1545–1648," *Journal of Agrarian Change* 10, no. 2 (January 2010): 33–68.

Moore, Jason W., "Amsterdam is standing on Norway," Part II: "The global North Atlantic in the Ecological Revolution the long seventeenth century," *Journal of Agrarian Change* 10, no. 2 (April 2010): 188–227.

Müller, Susanne, *Die Welt des Baedeker. Eine Medienkulturgeschichte des Reiseführers 1830–1945* (Frankfurt am Main, New York: Campus, 2012).

Muñoz, Catalina, "Más allá del problema racial: el determinismo geográfico y las 'dolencias sociales'," in Catalina Muñoz (ed.), *Los problemas de la raza en Colombia* (Bogotá: Editorial Universidad del Rosaio, 2011), 11–58.

Muñoz, Laurentino, *La tragedia biológica del pueblo colombiano. Estudio de observación y de vulgarización*. (Editorial América: Cali, 1935), 14.

Mutz, Mathias, "Managing resources. Water and wood in the German pulp and paper industry (1870s-1930s)," *Jahrbuch für Wirtschaftsgeschichte* 50, no. 2 (2009): 45–68.

Mutz, Mathias, "Naturale Infrastrukturen im Unternehmen. Die Papierfabrik Kübler & Niethammer zwischen Umweltabhängigkeit und Umweltgestaltung," *Saeculum. Jahrbuch für Universalgeschichte* 58 (2007): 59–87.

Mutz, Mathias, "Nature's product? An environmental history of the German pulp and paper industry," in: Bernd Herrmann and Christine Dahlke (eds.), *Elements—Continents: Approaches to Determinants of Environmental History and Their Reifications* (Halle/Saale: Deutsche Akademie der Naturforscher Leopoldina; 2009), 259–264.

Nader, John, "The rise of an inventive profession: Learning effects in the Midwestern harvester industry, 1850–1890," *Journal of Economic History* 54 (1994): 397–408.

Nash, L., "The changing experience of nature: Historical encounters with a Northwest river," *The Journal of American History* 86, no. 4 (2000): 1600–1629.

Nash, Roderick, *Wilderness and the American Mind* (New Haven, CT: Yale University Press, 1982, first published 1967).

National Land-Use Planning Committee, *The Problems of "Submarginal" Areas, and Desirable Adjustments with Particular Reference to Public Acquisition of Land*, Publication 6 (Washington: Government Printing Office, 1933), 1.

Naylor, Robert T., "The rise and fall of the third commercial empire of the St. Lawrence," in Gary Teeple (ed.), *Capitalism and the National Question in Canada* (Toronto: University of Toronto Press, 1972), 1–41.

Naylor, Robert T., *The History of Canadian Business 1867–1914*, 2 vols. (Toronto: Lorimer, 1975).

Nicholson, F.A., *Note on Fisheries in Japan* (Madras: The Superintendent, Government Press, 1907), 40.

Nickel, Douglas, *Francis Frith in Egypt and Palestine: A Victorian Photographer Abroad* (Princeton, NJ: Princeton University Press, 2004).

Niethammer, Horst, "Papier: Rohstoffe und Arten einst und jetzt," *Abhandlungen und Berichte des Deutschen Museums* 22 (1954): 45–54.

Noble, David F., *America by Design: Science, Technology and the Rise of Corporate Capitalism* (New York: Knopf, 1977).

Nöllenburg, Wilhelm von, *Das Papier auf dem Weltmarkt: Statistische Zusammenstellung und geoökonomische Untersuchungen* (Leipzig: Neue Deutsche Papier-Zeitung, 1926), 193.

Nordenskiöld, Carl Fredrik, *Tal on nyttan af ofverflödig: vattens uttappande utur insjöar, kärr och måssar i Finland*; hållit för Kungl. Vetenskaps Academien, vid praesidii nedläggande den 20 augusti, år 1758 (Stockholm: Salvius, 1758). [in Swedish]

North, Michael, *"Material Delight and the Joy of Living:" Cultural Consumption in the Age of Enlightenment in Germany* (Aldershot i.a.: Ashgate, 2008).

North, Michael, "The great German banking houses and international merchants, sixteenth to nineteenth century," in Alice Teichova, Ginette Kurgan-van Hentenryk and Dieter Ziegler (eds.), *Banking, Trade and Industry: Europe, America and Asia from the Thirteenth to the Twentieth Century* (Cambridge: Cambridge University Press, 1997), 35–49.

Nuechterlein, Donald E., *Iceland, Reluctant Ally* (Ithaca, NY: Cornell University Press, 1961).

Nye, David E., *America as Second Creation: Technology and Narratives of New Beginnings* (Cambridge, MA: MIT Press, 2003).

Nye, David E., *American Technological Sublime* (Cambridge, MA: MIT Press, 1994).

Nye, David E., "Technologies of landscape," in David Nye (ed.), *Technologies of Landscape: From Reaping to Recycling* (Amherst, MA: University of Massachusetts Press, 1999), 3–17.

O'Brien, William, "Jim Crow NIMBYs: White resistance to proposed sites for state parks for African Americans," paper presented to the annual meeting of the American Society for Environmental History, 26 Feb 2009, Tallahassee, Fla.

Ochoa, Fidel, "Porqué se prohibió la importación de ganado cebú," *Boletín de Agricultura* 4 (1931): 535–540.

OECD (ed.), *Pollution by the Pulp and Paper Industry: Present Situation and Future Trends* (Paris: OECD, 1973).

Ogilvie, Sheilagh, "Consumption, social capital, and the "Industrious revolution" in early modern Germany," *Journal of Economic History* 70 (2010): 287–325.

Oreskes, Naomi, "Scaling up our vision," *ISIS* 105, no. 2 (2014): 384.

Ospina Pérez, Mariano, " 'El problema sanitario de Colombia es el primero dice el Dr. Mariano Ospina Pérez' (Bogota 23 ago 1934)," in Muñoz, *Tragedia Biológica*.

Osterhammel, Jürgen, *Die Verwandlung der Welt. Eine Geschichte des 19. Jahrhunderts* (Munich: C.H. Beck, 2009).

Osterhammel, Jürgen, *The transformation of the world. A global history of the nineteenth century* (Princeton, NJ: Princeton University Press, 2014) [First German edition 2009].

Östlund, Lars, "Logging the virgin forest. Northern Sweden in the early-nineteenth century," *Forest and Conservation History* 39 (1995): 160–171.

Osvald, Hugo, *Myrar och myrodling* (Uppsala: Landbrukshögskolan, 1937). [in Swedish]

Overton, Mark, Whittle, Jane, Dean, Darron and Hann, Andrew, *Production and Consumption in English Households 1600–1750* (London, New York: Routledge, 2004).

Ozanne, Robert, *A Century of Labor-Management Relations at McCormick and International Harvester* (Madison, WI: University of Wisconsin Press, 1967).

Ozanne, Robert, *Wages in Practice and Theory: McCormick and International Harvester 1860–1960* (Madison, WI: University of Wisconsin Press, 1968).

Palmén, Ilmari L., "Suonkuivaustyöt Suomessa XIX vuosisadalla: Historiallinen tutkimus," in *Suomen Suonviljelysyhdistyksen vuosikirja 1903* (Helsinki: Suomen Suonviljelysyhdistys, 1903). [in Finnish]

Palmer, Clare, "Taming the wild profusion of existing things? A study of Foucault, power, and human/animal relationships," *Environmental Ethics* 23, no. 4 (2001), 339–358.

Pawson, Eric, "Plants, mobilities and landscapes: Environmental histories of botanical exchange," *Geography Compass* 2 (2008): 1464–1477.

Pawson, Eric, "Creating public spaces for geography in New Zealand: Towards an assessment of the contributions of Kenneth Cumberland," *New Zealand Geographer* 67 (2011): 102–115.

Pawson, Eric and Brooking, Tom, (eds.), *Making a New Country* (Dunedin: Otago University Press, 2013).

Payne, William J. A., *An Introduction to Animal Husbandry in the Tropics* (Essex: Longman Scientific & Technical, 1990), 11–24.

Pearse, Albert W., *The World's Meat Future* (New York: E.P. Dutton, 1920).

Peden, Robert, " 'The exceeding joy of burning': Pastoralists and the Lucifer match: Burning the rangelands of the South Island of New Zealand in the nineteenth century, 1850 to 1890," *Agricultural History* 80 (2006): 17–34.

Peden, Robert, *Making Sheep Country: Mt Peel Station and the Transformation of the Tussock Lands* (Auckland: Auckland University Press, 2011).

Pedraza, Sandra, *En cuerpo y alma. Visiones del progreso y la felicidad* (Bogotá: Ediciones Uniandes, 1999).

Perren, Richard, *The Meat Trade in Britain, 1840–1914* (London: Routledge & Kegan Paul, 1978).

Pese, Claus, *Künstlerkolonien in Europa. Im Zeichen der Ebene und des Himmels* (Nürnberg: Germanisches Nationalmuseum, 2001).

Pettersson, Reidar, "Torvtäkt och torvanvändning under efterkrigstiden," in Leif Runefelt (ed.), *Svensk mosskultur: odling, torvanvändning och landskapets förändring 1750–2000* (Stockholm: Kungliga Skogs- och lantbruksakademien, 2008), 389–404. [in Swedish]

Pfeil, Wilhelm, *Grundsätze der Forstwirthschaft in Bezug auf die Nationalökonomie und die Staatsfinanzwissenschaft*, vol. 1 (Züllichau und Freistadt, 1822/1824), 137–147.

Pfister, Joel, "A garden in the machine: Reading a mid-nineteenth-century two-cylinder parlor stove as cultural text," *Technology and Society* 13, no. 3 (1991): 327–343.

Phillips, Sarah T., *This Land, This Nation: Conservation, Rural America and the New Deal* (New York: Cambridge University Press, 2007), 81–82.

Phimister, I.R., "Meat and monopolies: Beef cattle in Southern Rhodesia, 1890–1938," *The Journal of African History* 19 (1978): 391–414.

Pietarinen, Juhani, "The principal attitudes of humanity towards nature," in H. Odera Oruka (ed.), *Philosophy, Humanity, and Ecology: Philosophy of Nature and Environmental Ethics* (Nairobi: Proceedings of the World Conference of Philosophy, 1992), 290–294.

Pilcher, Jeffrey, *Que Vivan los Tamales!: Food and the Making of Mexican Identity* (Albuquerque: University of New Mexico Press, 1998), 77–97.

Platt, D.C.M., "Dependency in nineteenth-century Latin America: An historian objects," *Latin American Research Review* 15 (1980): 113–30.

Platt, D.C.M., *Latin America and British Trade, 1806–1914* (New York: Barnes and Noble, 1973).

Pohl-Valero, Stefan, "'La raza entra por la boca': Energy, diet, and eugenics in Colombia, 1890–1940," *Hispanic American Historical Review* 94 (2014): 455–486.

Posada-Carbó, Eduardo, *El caribe colombiano. Una historia regional, 1870–1950* (Bogotá: Banco de la República, Ancora Editores, 1998), 190.

Powell, Walter W. and Smith-Doerr, Laurel, "Networks and economic life," in Neil J. Smelser and Richard Swedberg (eds.), *The Handbook of Economic Sociology* (Princeton, NJ: Princeton University Press, 1994), 368–402.

Powell, Walter W., "Neither market nor hierarchy: Network forms of organization," *Research in Organizational Behavior* 12 (1990): 295–336.

Pratt, Mary Louise, *Imperial Eyes: Travel Writing and Transmigration* (London: Routledge, 1992), 109–140.

Prince, Hugh, "Art and agrarian change, 1710–1815," in Denis Cosgrove and Stephen Daniels (eds.), *The Iconography of Landscape* (Cambridge: Cambridge University Press: 1988), 98–118.

Pritchard, Sara P. and Zeller, Thomas, "The nature of industrialization," in Martin Reuss and Steven H. Cutcliffe (eds.), *The Illusory Boundary: Environment and Technology in History* (Charlottesville, VA: University of Virginia Press, 2010), 69–100, here 70.

Protschky, Susie, *Images of the Tropics: Environment and Visual Culture in Colonial Indonesia* (Leiden: kitlv Press, 2011).

Purcell, Carroll W., *The Machine in America: A Social History of Technology* (Baltimore: Johns Hopkins University Press, 1995).

Radcliffe, Sarah A., Watson, Elisabeth E., Simmons, Ian, Fernández-Armesto, Felipe, Sluyter, Andrew, "Environmentalist thinking and/in geography," *Progress in Human Geography* 34, no. 1 (2010): 98–116.

Radkau, Joachim, "Zur angeblichen Energiekrise im 18. Jahrhundert. Revisionistische Betrachtungen über die Holznot," *Vierteljahrschrift für Sozial- und Wirtschaftsgeschichte* 73 (1986): 1–37.

Radkau, Joachim, *Holz. Wie ein Naturstoff Geschichte schreibt* (München: Oekom-Verlag, 2007), 140–142.

Randall, Cortes G., *La industria ganadera en Colombia* (Washington, DC, 1953).

Reber, Vera Blinn, *British Mercantile Houses in Buenos Aires, 1810–1880* (Cambridge, MA: Harvard University Press, 1979).

Redclift, Michael, *Frontier: Histories of Civil Society and Nature.* (Cambridge, MA: MIT Press, 2006).

Reeves, William Pember, "The passing of the forest," in William F. Alexander and A.E. Currie (eds.), *A Treasury of New Zealand Verse* (Auckland: Whitcomb and Tombs, 1926), 58.

Reich, Justin, "Re-creating wilderness: Shaping narratives and landscapes in Shenandoah National Park," *Environmental History* 6, no. 1 (2001): 95–117.

Reinhold, Gerhard, *Die Papierholzversorgung* (Berlin: Carl Hofmann, 1927), 143.

Reinhold, Martin, "Forstwirtschaft und Papierindustrie," *Forstwissenschaftliches Zentralblatt* 54 (1932): 113–131.

Reischauer, Edwin O., *The United States and Japan* (Cambridge, MA: Harvard University Press, 1950), 241.

Reiter, Paul, "From Shakespeare to Defoe: Malaria in England in the Little Ice Age," *Emerging Infectious Diseases* 6, no. 1 (2000): 1–11.

Rejmánek, Marcel and Richardson, David M., "Eucalypts," in *Encyclopedia of Biological Invasions*, ed. Daniel Simberloff and Marcel Rejmánek (Berkeley: University of California Press, 2011), 203–209.

Rhein, Karin, "Vom Erkundungsauftrag über Künstlerkolonie und touristische Pfade zu den stillen Winkeln—Bayern in Zeichnungen," in Sigrid Sylfide Bertuleit (ed.), *Künstler sehen Bayern. Bayern lässt staunen* (Schweinfurt: Museum Georg Schäfer, 2013): 147–153.

Richards, John F., *The Unending Frontier: Environmental Histories of the Early Modern World* (Berkeley: University of California Press, 2006).

Rivas, Medardo, *Los trabajadores de tierra caliente* (Bogotá: Banco Popular, 1972).

Robertson, John Parish and Robertson, William Parish, *Letters on Paraguay: Comprising an Account of Four Years' Residence in That Republic under the Government of the Dictator Francia*, 3 vols. (London: John Murray, 1838–1839).

Robertson, John Parish and Robertson, William Parish, *Letters on South America: Comprising Travels on the Banks of the Paraná and Rio de la Plata*, 3 vols. (London: John Murray, 1843).

Robinson, Robb, *Trawling: The Rise and Fall of the British Trawl Fishery* (Exeter: University of Exeter Press, 1996), 105.

Roche, Michael, "Internationalisation as company and industry colonialisation: The frozen meat industry in New Zealand in the 1900s," *New Zealand Geographer* 49 (1993): 2–7.

Roche, Michael, *Land and Water: Water and Soil Conservation and Central Government in New Zealand, 1941–1988* (Wellington: Historical Branch, Dept. of Internal Affairs, 1994).

Roche, Michael, "Failure deconstructed: Histories and geographies of soldier settlement in New Zealand circa 1917–39," *New Zealand Geographer* 64 (2008): 46–56.

Rogin, L., *The Introduction of Farm Machinery in its Relation to the Productivity of Labor in the Agriculture of the United States During the Nineteenth Century* (New York: Johnson Reprint Company, 1931, reprinted 1966).

Rojas, Carlos Alberto, "Estado actual de la ganadería de Santander y sus perspectivas," B.S. thesis, Universidad Nacional de Colombia (1938), 16.

Rosenhain, C.M., *Holz-Cellulose in ihrer geschichtlichen Entwicklung: Fabrikation und bisherigen Verwendung* (Berlin: Polytechnische Buchhandlung, 1878), 9.

Rose-Redwood, Ruben, Alderman, Derek and Azaryahu, Maoz, "Geographies of topnymic inscription: New directions in critical place-name studies," *Progress in Human Geography* 34, no. 4 (2010): 453–470.

Rubner, Konrad, "Steigerung der Papierholzproduktion Deutschlands durch waldbauliche Maßnahmen," *Wochenblatt für Papierfabrikation* 69, no. 42 (1931): 1–10.

Rudel, Carl Adolf Alwin, "Zur Disputation über die Surrogate in der Papierfabrikation," *Central-Blatt für die deutsche Papier-Fabrikation* 17 (1866): 89–91, 97–99.

Runefelt, Leif, "Svensk mosskultur som överhetsprojekt före 1886," in Leif Runefelt (ed.), *Svensk mosskultur: odling, torvanvändning och landskapets förändring 1750–2000* (Stockholm: Kungliga Skogs- och lantbruksakademien, 2008a), 27–52. [in Swedish]

Runefelt, Leif, "Svenska Mosskulturföreningen 1886–1939," in Leif Runefelt (ed.), *Svensk mosskultur: odling, torvanvändning och landskapets förändring 1750–2000* (Stockholm: Kungliga Skogs- och lantbruksakademien, 2008b), 53–96. [in Swedish]

Runefelt, Leif, "Torvbubblan 1900–1925," in Leif Runefelt (ed.), *Svensk mosskultur: odling, torvanvändning och landskapets förändring 1750–2000* (Stockholm: Kungliga Skogs- och lantbruksakademien, 2008c), 329–358. [in Swedish]

Ruuskanen, Esa, *Suosta voimaa ja lämpöä: Turve Suomen energiapolitiikassa 1940–2010* [Power and Heat from Peat: Peat in Finnish energy policy] with English summaries (Jyväskylä: WS Bookwell Oy, 2010). [in Finnish]

Sabel, Charles F., Zeitlin, Jonathan, "Historical alternatives to mass production: Politics, markets and technology in nineteenth century industrialization," *Past and Present* 108 (1985): 133–176.

Sanders, James O., "History and development of Zebu cattle in the United States," *Journal of Animal Science* 50 (1980): 1193.

Savage, Victor R., "Tropicality imagined and experienced," *Singapore Journal of Tropical Geography* 25 (2004): 26–31.

Schaefer, Franz, *Die wirtschaftliche Bedeutung der technischen Entwicklung in der Papierfabrikation* (Leipzig: Klinkhardt, 1909), 117–151.

Schimel, D., Redman, C., Dearing, J., Graumlich, L., Leemans, R., Crumley, C., Hibbard, K., Steffen W., and Costanza, R., "Evolution of the human-environment relationship," *The Encyclopedia of Earth* (May 2, 2007).

Schlich, William, *Schlich's Manual of Forestry, Vol. 1: The Utility of Forests and Fundamental Principles of Sylviculture* (London: Bradbury, Agnew & Co., 1889), 62.

Schlich, William, "The outlook of the world's timber supply," *Transactions of the Scottish Arboricultural Society* XVI (1901): 355–383.

Schlich, William, "Über die Unzulänglichkeit der Nutzholzerzeugung der Erde," *Forstwissenschaftliches Centralblatt* 23 (1901): 289–297.

Schmidt, Frieder, "Tilghman, Mitscherlich und der Fall des Reichspatents 4179," *IPH Congress Book* 9 (1992): 26–32.

Schmoll, Friedemann, *Erinnerung an die Natur. Die Geschichte des Naturschutzes im deutschen Kaiserreich* (Frankfurt am Main, New York: Campus, 2004).

Schneider, Margarete and Schneider Wolfgang, (eds.), *Justus von Liebig: Briefe an Vieweg* (Braunschweig, Friedrich Vieweg & Sohn, 1986), 288–289.

Schrage, Dominik, *Die Verfügbarkeit der Dinge. Eine historische Soziologie des Konsums* (Frankfurt am Main, New York: Campus, 2009).

Schrage, Dominik, "The availability of things: A short genealogy of consumption," *Krisis. Journal of contemporary philosophy* 1 (2012): 5–19.

Schultze, Julius, *Die Papierfabrikation im Königreich Sachsen unter besonderer Berücksichtigung ihrer Beziehungen zu den Holzschleifereien* (Tübingen: Kloere, 1912), 97.

Schuster, Erhard,"Der Einfluß der wirtschaftlichen Entwicklung des aufstrebenden Kapitalismus auf Holznutzung und Baumartenwahl in der Forstwirtschaft, dargestellt vor allem am Beispiel Sachsens," *Archiv für Forstwesen* 10 (1961): 1208–1227.

Schwalbe, Carl Gustav, "Die chemischen Arbeiten der Papierfabrikation während der letzten 50 Jahre," in Verein deutscher Papierfabrikanten (ed.), *Festschrift zum 50jährigen Jubiläum des Vereines: Der Verein deutscher Papierfabrikanten* (Berlin: Eigenverlag, 1922), 211–216.

Sejersted, Francis, "Veien mot øst,"in Sievert Langholm and Francis Sejersted (eds.), *Vandringer* (Oslo: Aschehoug, 1980), 163–204. [in Norwegian]

Seymour, Susanne, "Historical geographies of landscape," in Brian Graham and Catherine Nash (eds.), *Modern Historical Geographies* (Harlow: Pearson Education, 2000): 193–217.

Seymour, Susanne, Daniels, Stephen and Watkins, C., "Estate and empire: Sir George Cornewall's management of Moccas, Herefordshire and La Taste, Grenada, 1771–1819," *Journal of Historical Geography* 24, no. 3 (1988): 313–351.

Shannon, Fred, *The Farmers' Last Frontier: Agriculture 1860–1897* (New York, 1945).

Shimada, Bell M., "Japanese tuna-mothership operations in the Western Equatorial Pacific Ocean," *Commercial Fisheries Review* June (1951): 2.

Simmonds, Peter Lund, *A Dictionary of Trade Products, Commercial, Manufacturing, and Technical Terms With a Definition of the Moneys, Weights, and Measures of All Countries, Reduced to the British Standard* (new edition, rev. and enlarged) (London: Warne and Routledge, 1863).

Simmonds, Peter Lund, *Waste Products and Undeveloped Substances: A Synopsis of Progress Made in Their Economic Utilisation During the Last Quarter of a Century at Home and Abroad* (London: R. Hardwicke, 1873).

Simmonds, Peter Lund, "Past, present and future sources of the timber supplies of Great Britain," *Journal of the Society of Arts* 19 (1884): 102–121.

Simmons, Ian G., *An Environmental History of Great Britain. From 10,000 Years Ago to the Present* (Edinburgh: Edinburgh University Press, 2001), 153.

Simola, E.F., *Suomen uutisviljelystavoista* (Helsinki: Asutushallitus, 1921). [in Finnish]

Sims, Peter, "Networks and the British community of Uruguay, 1830–1875: Outline and case studies," paper prepared for the Department of Economic History, London School of Economics and Political Science (October 2010).

Sjöberg, Gösta H., "Våtmarkerna i människans tjänst," in Rune Engström, Sigfried Leander and Birgitta von Malmborg (eds.), *Myrmarker: En bok om bruket av våtmarkerna förr och nu* (Stockholm: Riksförbundet för hembygdsvård, 1976), 118. [in Swedish]

Sjögren, Hans, "Welfare capitalism: The Swedish economy, 1850–2005," in Susanna Fellman, Martin Jes Iversen, Hans Sjögren and Lars Thue (eds.), *Creating Nordic Capitalism: The Business History of a Competitive Periphery* (Basingstoke: Palgrave Macmillan, 2008), 22–74.

Sokołowski, Stanisław, "Miśdzynarodowy kongres rolniczy w Wiedniu 1907," *Sylwan* 25 (1907): 219f and 269–275. [in Polish]

Spencer, Stephanie and Bedford, Francis, *Landscape Photography and Nineteenth-century British Culture: The Artist as Entrepreneur* (Farnham i.a.: Ashgate, 2011).

Staudt, Richard, "Die Standortwahl der deutschen Papierindustrie in theoretischer und historischer Untersuchung" (PhD diss., Köln, 1930), 29.

Stearns, Peter N., "Stages of consumerism. Recent work on the issues of periodization," *Journal of Modern History* 69 (1997): 102–117.

Stearns, Peter N., *Consumerism in World History. The Global Transformation of Desire* (London, New York: Routledge, 2001).

Stegemann, Gustav Wilhelm, *Die Papierherstellung der Vereinigten Bautzener Papierfabriken, Bautzen* (Leipzig: Übersee-Post, 1934), 45–48.

Stein, Stanley J. and Stein, Barbara H., "D.C.M. Platt: The anatomy of 'autonomy'," *Latin American Research Review* 15 (1980): 131–146.

Stenius, Jacob, *Kort underrättelse om kiärr och mossar samt deras nyttiande, efter flere åhrs giorde försök* (Stockholm: Merckell, 1749). [in Swedish]

Stepan, Nancy Leys, *"The Hour of Eugenics": Race, Gender, and Nation in Latin America, 1890–1916* (Ithaca, NY: Cornell University Press, 1991).

Stepan, Nancy Leys, *Picturing Tropical Nature* (Ithaca, NY: Cornell University Press, 2001).

Stewart, W. Downie, "Land tenure and land monopoly in New Zealand," *Journal of Political Economy*, 17 (1909): 82–91.

Stobbs, T.H. and Thompson, P.A.C., "Milk production from tropical pastures," in *Ruminant Nutrition: Selected articles from the World Animal Review* (Rome: FAO, 1978), accessed February 3, 2015, http://www.fao.org/docrep/004/X6512E/X6512E04.htm

Stoll, Steven, *Larding the Lean Earth: Soil and Society in Nineteenth Century America* (New York: Hill and Wang, 2002), 178–183.

Stone, Russell, *Makers of Fortune: A Colonial Business Community and Its Fall* (Auckland: Auckland University Press, 1974).

Storaunet, Ken Olaf, Rolstad, Jørund and Groven, Rune, "Reconstructing 100–150 years of logging history in coastal spruce forest (Picea abies) with special conservation values in central Norway," *Scandinavian Journal of Forest Research* 15 (2000): 591–604.

Swartz Cowan, Ruth, *A Social History of American Technology* (New York: Oxford University Press, 1977).

Tanttu, Antti, *Tutkimuksia ojitettujen soiden metsittymisestä* (Helsinki: Suomen Keisarillisen Aleksanterin Yliopisto, 1915). [in Finnish]

Taussig, Michael, *Shamanism, Colonialism, and the Wild Man: A Study in Terror and Healing*, (Chicago: University of Chicago Press, 1987), 287.

Taylor, Norman, "Land deterioration in the heavier rainfall districts of New Zealand," *New Zealand Journal of Science and Technology* 11 (1938): 657–681.

Tello, Enric and Ramos Ostos, Joan, "Water consumption in Barcelona and its regional environmental imprint: A long term history (1717–2008)," *Regional Environmental Change* 12 (2012): 347–361.

The Japan Times and Mail, *Japan's Fisheries Industry 1939* (1939), 21.

Thielemann, Max, *Die Eisverhältnisse der Elbe und ihrer Nebenflüsse* (Halle/Saale: C.A. Kaemmerer & Co., 1907).

Thom, David, *Heritage: Parks for the People*, (Auckland: Lansdowne Press, 1987).

Thor, Jon, *British Trawlers in Icelandic Waters: History of British Steam Trawling off Iceland, 1889–1916* (Reykjavik: Fjolvi Publishers, 1992), 15.

Thrower, Norman, *Original Survey and Land Subdivision* (Chicago: Monograph Series of the Association of American Geographers, 1966).

Thünen, Johann Heinrich von, *Von Thünen's Isolated State*, translated by Carla M. Wartenberg, edited by Peter Hall (New York: Pergamon Press, 1966) first published 1826.

Tiernan, John, "Mrs Gaskell—Liverpool, Wirral & the Holland family connection," meeting reports of the Liverpool History Society (talk given on 20 June 2010).

Tietjen, Aug., "El ganado zebú en Colombia," *Revista Nacional de Agricultura* 33 (1939): 336–337.

Tirkkonen, O.O.J., "Suomen metsäojitus 1900-luvun alkupuoliskolla," with English summary, *Silva Fennica* (1952): 72. [in Finnish]

Towner, John, *An Historical Geography of Recreation and Tourism in the Western World 1540–1940* (Chichester i.a.: Wiley, 1996), 53–95.

Trentmann, Frank, "Beyond consumerism: New historical perspectives on consumption," *Journal of Contemporary History* 39 (2004): 373–401.

Trentmann, Frank, "Consumption and globalization in history," *Journal of Consumer Culture* 9 (2009): 187–220.

Trentmann, Frank, "Introduction," in Frank Trentmann (ed.), *The Oxford Handbook of the History of Consumption* (Oxford: Oxford University Press, 2012), 1–19.

Tschudin, Peter. F., *Grundzüge der Papiergeschichte*, 2nd edition (Stuttgart: Hiersemann, 2007), 166–195.

Tsing, Anna L., *Friction: An Ethnography of Global Connection* (Princeton, NJ: Princeton University Press, 2011).

Tuan, Yi-Fu, *Topophilia: A Study of Environmental Perception, Attitudes and Values* (Englewood Cliffs, NJ: Prentice-Hall, 1974).

Tuan, Yi-Fu, "Language and the making of place: A narrative-descriptive approach," *Annals of the Association of American Geographers* 81, no. 4 (1991): 684–696.

Tugwell, Rexford G., "The resettlement idea," *Agricultural History* 33, no. 4 (1959): 159–164.

U.S. Department of Agriculture, Resettlement Administration, *Report of the Administrator of the Resettlement Administration, 1937* (Washington, DC: U.S. Department of Agriculture, 1937), 9–10.

Uekötter, Frank, *Umweltgeschichte im 19. und 20. Jahrhundert* (München: Oldenbourg Verlag, 2007), 44–46.

Unwin, Tim, *Wine and the Vine: An Historical Geography of Viticulture and the Wine Trade* (London, New York: Routledge, 1991), 278–283.

urgewald e.V. (ed.), *Update zum Alternativen Waldschadensbericht 2010* (Sassenberg: urgewald e.V., 2012). Download at https://urgewald.org/sites/default/files/update_wsb_2010.pdf (15.12.2014).

Urry, John, *Consuming Places*, 2nd edition (London, New York: Routledge, 2002).

Urry, John, *The Tourist Gaze*, 2nd edition (London i.a.: Sage, 2002).

Van Ausdal, Shawn, "Pasture, power, and profit: An environmental history of cattle ranching in Colombia, 1850–1950," *Geoforum* 40 (2009): 707–719.

Van Ausdal, Shawn, "Productivity gains and the limits of tropical ranching in Colombia, 1850–1950," *Agricultural History* 86 (2012): 1–32.

Vance, Rupert B., "What of submarginal areas in regional planning?" *Social Forces* 12, no. 3 (1933): 315–329.

Varela, Raúl, "Memorándum sobre el Departamento del Atlántico," *Boletín de Agricultura* 3 (1930): 630.

Veblen, Thorstein, *The Theory of the Leisure Class. An Economic Study of Institutions* (New York: Macmillan, 1899).

Velasco, Eugelio, "Desconcierto ganadero," *Revista Agrícola y Ganadera* 3 (1939): 14–17.

Verein Deutscher Papierfabriken (ed.), *Papier-Kompass 2014* (Bonn: VDP, 2014). Download at http://www.vdp-online.de/de/publikationen/angebot.html (15.12.2014).

Villegas, Alvaro, "Nación, intelectuales de elite y representaciones de degeneración y regeneración, Colombia 1909–1937," *Iberoamericana* 7 (2007): 7–24.

Wackernagel, Mathis and Rees, William, *Unser ökologischer Fussabdruck. Wie der Mensch Einfluss auf die Umwelt nimmt* (Basel i.a.: Birkhäuser, 1997) [Updated version of: Our ecological footprint; reducing human impact on the earth, 1996].

Walvin, James, *Fruits of Empire. Exotic Produce and British Taste, 1660–1860* (Basingstoke i.a.: Macmillan, 1997).

Warren, Sarah T. and Zabawa, Robert E., "The origins of the Tuskegee National Forest: Nineteenth-and twentieth-century resettlement and land development programs in the Black Belt region of Alabama," *Agricultural History* 72, no. 2 (1998): 487–508.

Waterson, Duncan, "The Matamata Estate, 1904–1959: Land transfers and subdivision in the Waikato," *New Zealand Journal of History* 3 (1969): 32–51.

Watkins, Mel, "A staple theory of economic growth," in W.T. Easterbrook and M. Watkins (eds.), *Approaches to Canadian Economic History* (Toronto: McClelland and Stewart, 1967), 49–60.

Watkins, Mel, "The staple theory revisited," *Journal of Canadian Studies* 12, no. 5 (1977): 83–95.

Watkins, Mel, "The Innis tradition in Canadian political economy," *Canadian Journal of Political Science and Social Theory* 6 (1–2) (1982): 12–34.

Weaver, John C., *The Great Land Rush and the Making of the Modern World 1650–1900* (Montreal, McGill: Queens University Press, 2003), 81.

Weigert, Hans W., "Iceland, Greenland, and the United States." *Foreign Affairs* 23 (1) (1944): 113.

Weightman, Gavin, *The Frozen Water Trade: How Ice From New England Kept the World Cool* (London: HarperCollins, 2003).

Whelan, David A. and O'Keeffe, Tadgh, "The house of Ussher: Histories and heritages of improvement. Conspicious consumption and eviction on an early nineteenth-century Irish estate," *International Journal of Historical Archaeology* 18 (2014): 700–725.

Whitbeck, R.H., *Economic Geography of South America* (New York: McGraw-Hill, 1926), 230.

White, Richard, *The Organic Machine: The Remaking of the Columbia River* (New York: Hill and Wang, 1995).

White, Richard, *Railroaded: The Transcontinentals and the Making of Modern America* (New York: W.W. Norton and Company, 2011).

Wilcox, Robert, "Zebu's elbows: Cattle breeding and the environment in central Brazil, 1890–1960," in Christian Brannstrom (ed.), *Territories, Commodities and Knowledges: Latin American Environmental Histories in the Nineteenth and Twentieth Centuries* (London: Institute for the Study of the Americas, 2004), 218–246.

Williams, Michael, *Deforesting the Earth: From Prehistory to Global Crisis* (Chicago: University of Chicago Press, 2003), 384.

Winder, Gordon M., "Before the corporation and mass production? The licensing regime in the manufacture of North American harvesting machinery, 1830–1910," *Annals of the Association of American Geographers* 85/3 (1995): 521–552.

Winder, Gordon M., "Building trust and managing business over distance: A geography of reaper manufacturer D.S. Morgan's correspondence, 1867," *Economic Geography* 77, no. 2 (2001): 95–121.

Winder, Gordon M., "Following America into the second industrial revolution: New rules of competition and Ontario's farm machinery industry, 1850–1930," *The Canadian Geographer/Le Géographe canadien* 46, no. 4 (2002): 292–309.

Winder, Gordon M., "Webs of enterprise 1850–1914: Applying a broad definition of FDI," *Annals of the Association of American Geographers* 96, no. 4 (2006): 788–806.

Winder, Gordon M., "A trans-national machine on the world stage: Representing McCormick's reaper through world fairs, 1851–1902," *Journal of Historical Geography* XXXIII (2007): 352–376.

Winder, Gordon M., "Grassland revolutions: Disaggregating a national story," *New Zealand Geographer* 65 (2009): 187–200.

Winder, Gordon M., *The American Reaper: Harvesting Networks and Technology, 1830–1910* (Farnham, Surrey and Burlington, VT: Ashgate Publishing, 2012).

Winn, Peter, *El imperio informal británico en el Uruguay en el siglo XIX* (Montevideo: Ediciones de la Banda Oriental, 1975).

Witt, Ulrich, "Learning to consume—A theory of wants and the growth of demand," *Journal of Evolutionary Economics* 11 (2001): 23–36.

Wobst, Alfred, *Forstgeschichte Sachsens 1919–1945* (Hannover: Schaper, 1967), 10.

Woeikof, Alexandre Ivanovitch, [Александр Иванович Воейков]: "De l'influence de l'homme sur la terre," *Annales de Géographie* 10 (1901): 97–114.

Wynn, Graeme, '"Deplorably dark and demoralized lumberers?" Rhetoric and reality in early nineteenth-century New Brunswick,' *Journal of Forest History* 24, no. 4 (1980): 168–187.

Young, Terence, "False, cheap and degraded: When history, economy, and environment collided at Cades Cove, Great Smoky Mountains National Park," *Journal of Historical Geography* 32, no. 1 (2006): 169–189.

Żabko-Potopowicz, Antoni, "Wpływ zachodnioeuropejskiego piśmiennictwa i idei ekonomicznych na rozwój wczesnokapitalistycznego gospodarstwa leśnego w Królestwie Polskim," *Studia z Dziejów Gospodarstwa Wiejskiego* 8 (1966): 311–320. [in Polish]

Zapata, Antonio, "El ganado de raza cebú," *Boletín de Agricultura* 4 (1931): 125–128.

Zelinsky, Wilbur, "The imprint of central authority," in Michael P. Conzen (ed.), *The Making of the American Landscape* (Boston: Unwin Hyman, 1990), 311–334.

Zschimmer, "Eine neue Holzverwendung," *Tharander Forstliches Jahrbuch* 25(1875): 25–28.

Zschimmer, "Holzstoff- und Holzcellulosefabrikation in Beziehung auf Ausnutzung und Verwerthung der Hölzer," *Tharander Forstliches Jahrbuch* 40 (1890): 239–259.

Zschimmer, "Mittheilungen über die Fabrikation von Cellulose," *Tharander Forstliches Jahrbuch* 31 (1881): 104–107.

Index

For Product Safety Concerns and Information please contact our EU
representative GPSR@taylorandfrancis.com
Taylor & Francis Verlag GmbH, Kaufingerstraße 24, 80331 München, Germany

www.ingramcontent.com/pod-product-compliance
Ingram Content Group UK Ltd.
Pitfield, Milton Keynes, MK11 3LW, UK
UKHW020937180425
457613UK00019B/437